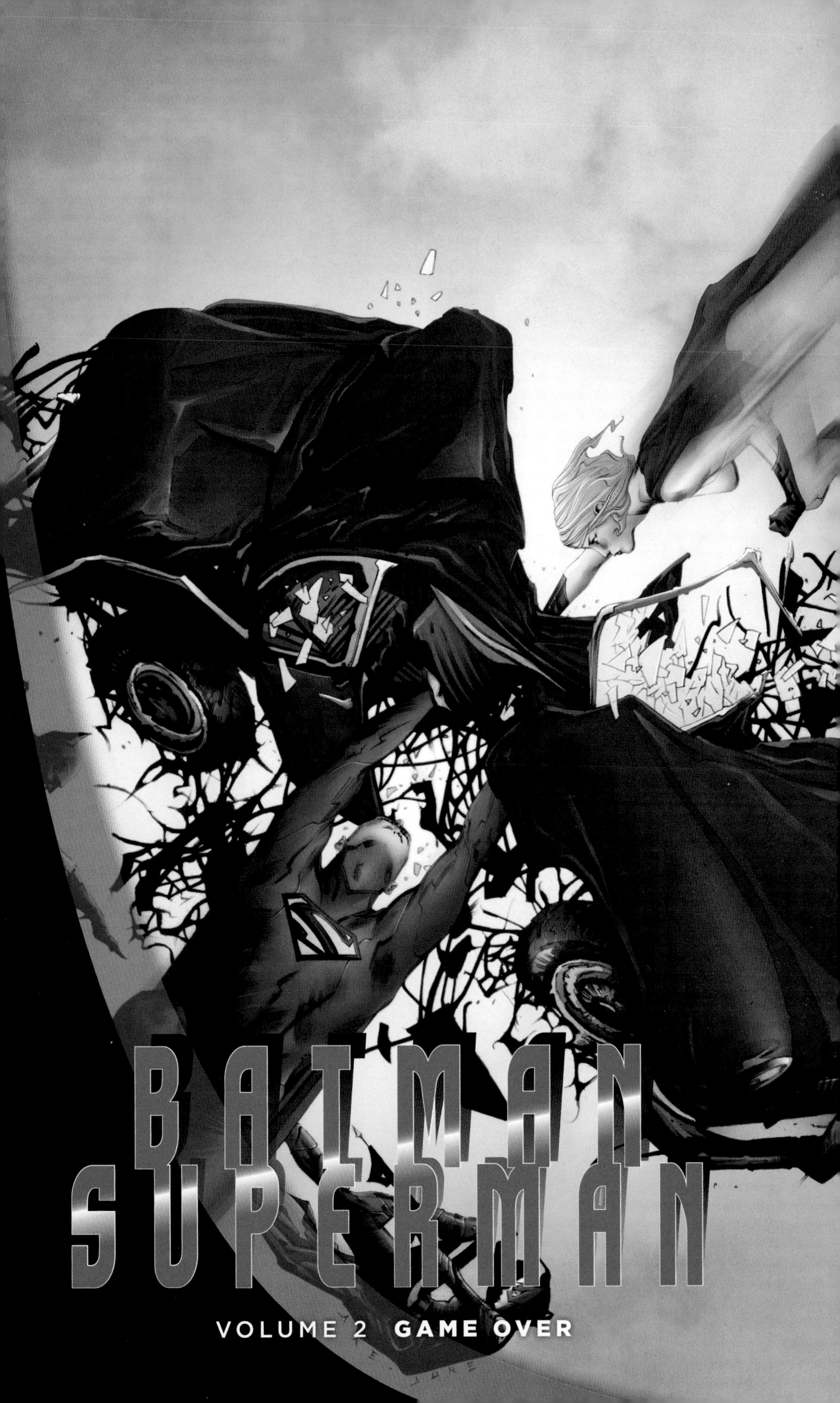

BATMAN SUPERMAN

VOLUME 2 GAME OVER

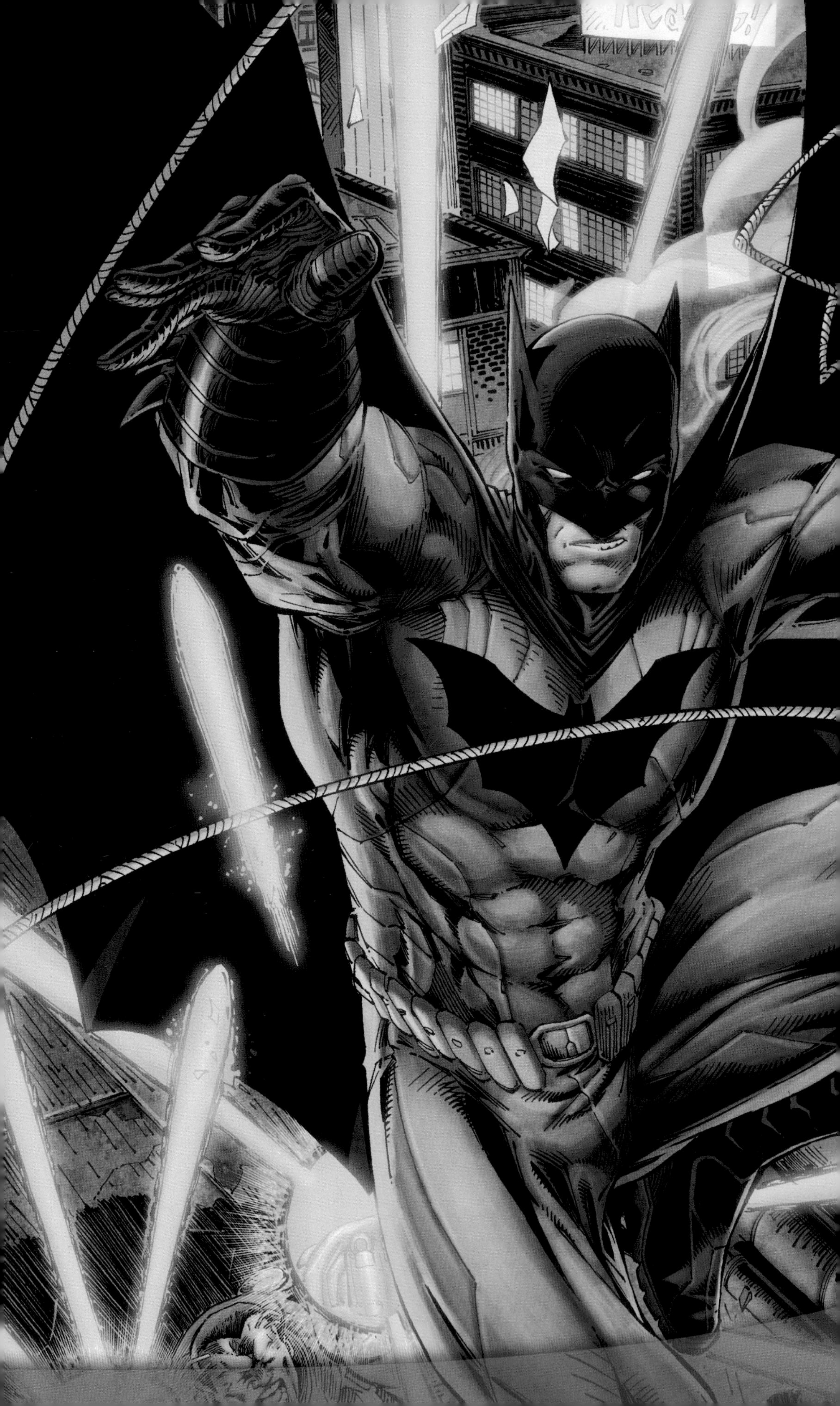

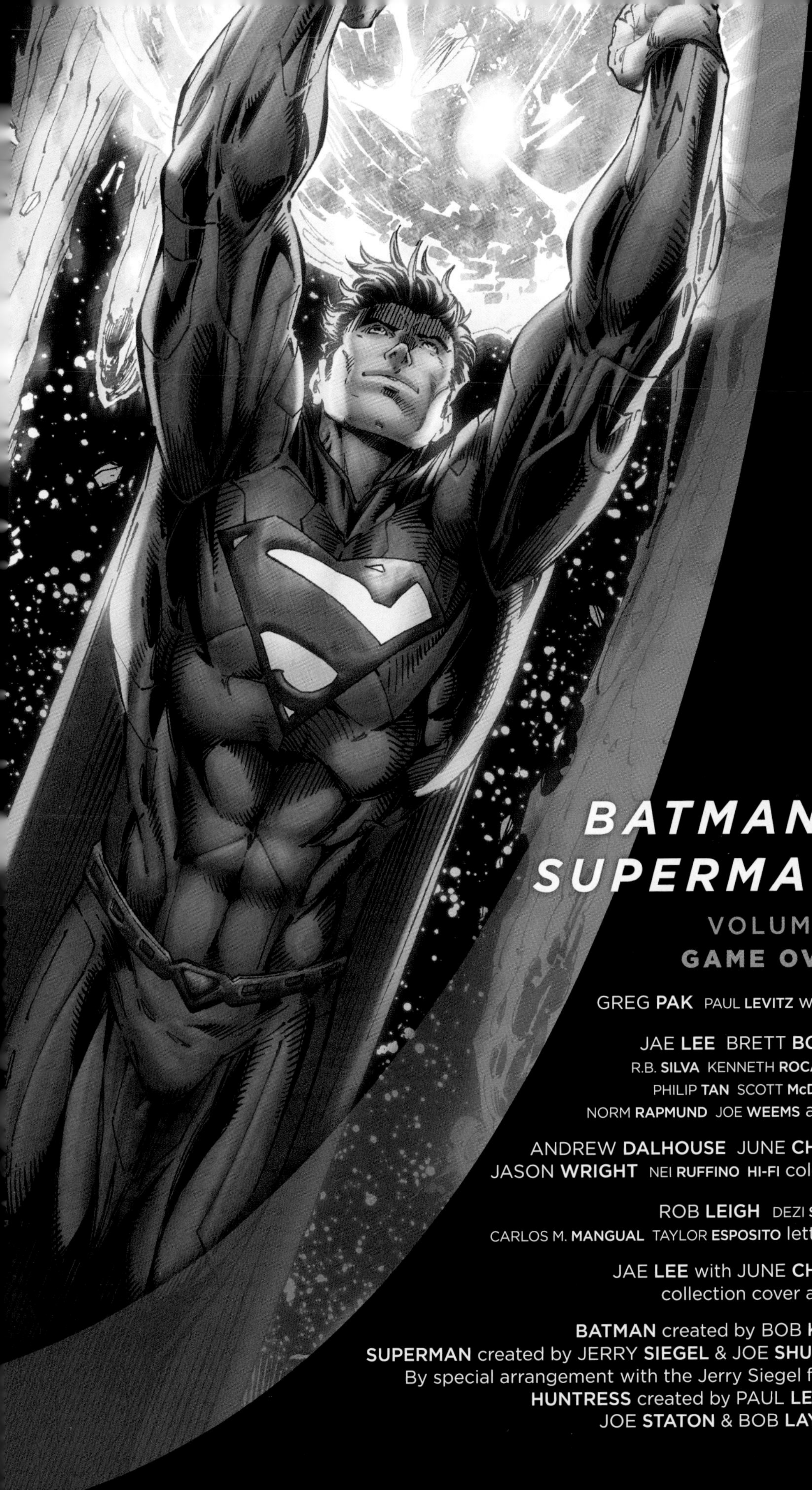

BATMAN/ SUPERMAN

VOLUME 2
GAME OVER

GREG **PAK** PAUL **LEVITZ** writers

JAE **LEE** BRETT **BOOTH**
R.B. **SILVA** KENNETH **ROCAFORT**
PHILIP **TAN** SCOTT **McDANIEL**
NORM **RAPMUND** JOE **WEEMS** artists

ANDREW **DALHOUSE** JUNE **CHUNG**
JASON **WRIGHT** NEI **RUFFINO** **HI-FI** colorists

ROB **LEIGH** DEZI **SIENTY**
CARLOS M. **MANGUAL** TAYLOR **ESPOSITO** letterers

JAE **LEE** with JUNE **CHUNG**
collection cover artists

BATMAN created by BOB **KANE**
SUPERMAN created by JERRY **SIEGEL** & JOE **SHUSTER**
By special arrangement with the Jerry Siegel family
HUNTRESS created by PAUL **LEVITZ**,
JOE **STATON** & BOB **LAYTON**

EDDIE BERGANZA MIKE COTTON Editors – Original Series RICKEY PURDIN Associate Editor – Original Series
ANTHONY MARQUES Assistant Editor – Original Series ROBIN WILDMAN Editor ROBBIN BROSTERMAN Design Director – Books
ROBBIE BIEDERMAN Publication Design

BOB HARAS Senior VP – Editor-in-Chief, DC Comics

DIANE NELSON President DAN DIDIO and JIM LEE Co-Publishers GEOFF JOHNS Chief Creative Officer
AMIT DESAI Senior VP – Marketing and Franchise Management
AMY GENKINS Senior VP – Business and Legal Affairs NAIRI GARDINER Senior VP – Finance
JEFF BOISON VP – Publishing Planning MARK CHIARELLO VP – Art Direction and Design
JOHN CUNNINGHAM VP – Marketing TERRI CUNNINGHAM VP – Editorial Administration
LARRY GANEM VP – Talent Relations and Services ALISON GILL Senior VP – Manufacturing and Operations
HANK KANALZ Senior VP – Vertigo and Integrated Publishing JAY KOGAN VP – Business and Legal Affairs, Publishing
JACK MAHAN VP – Business Affairs, Talent NICK NAPOLITANO VP – Manufacturing Administration SUE POHJA VP – Book Sales
FRED RUIZ VP – Manufacturing Operations COURTNEY SIMMONS Senior VP – Publicity BOB WAYNE Senior VP – Sales

BATMAN/SUPERMAN VOLUME 2: GAME OVER

DC Comics, 1700 Broadway, New York, NY 10019
A Warner Bros. Entertainment Company.
Printed by RR Donnelley, Salem, VA, USA. 10/10/14. First Printing.

HC ISBN: 978-1-4012-4935-9
SC ISBN: 978-1-4012-4934-2

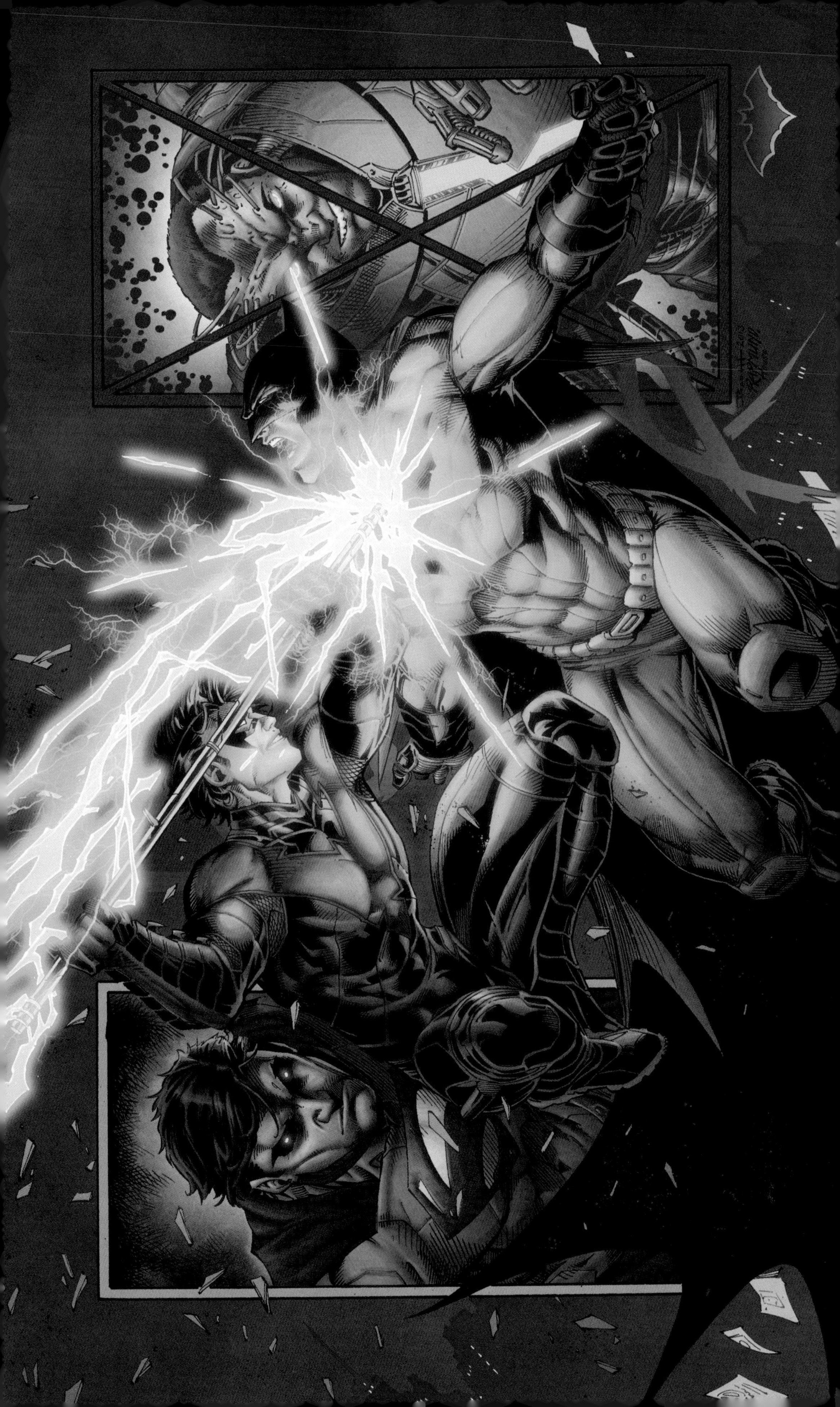

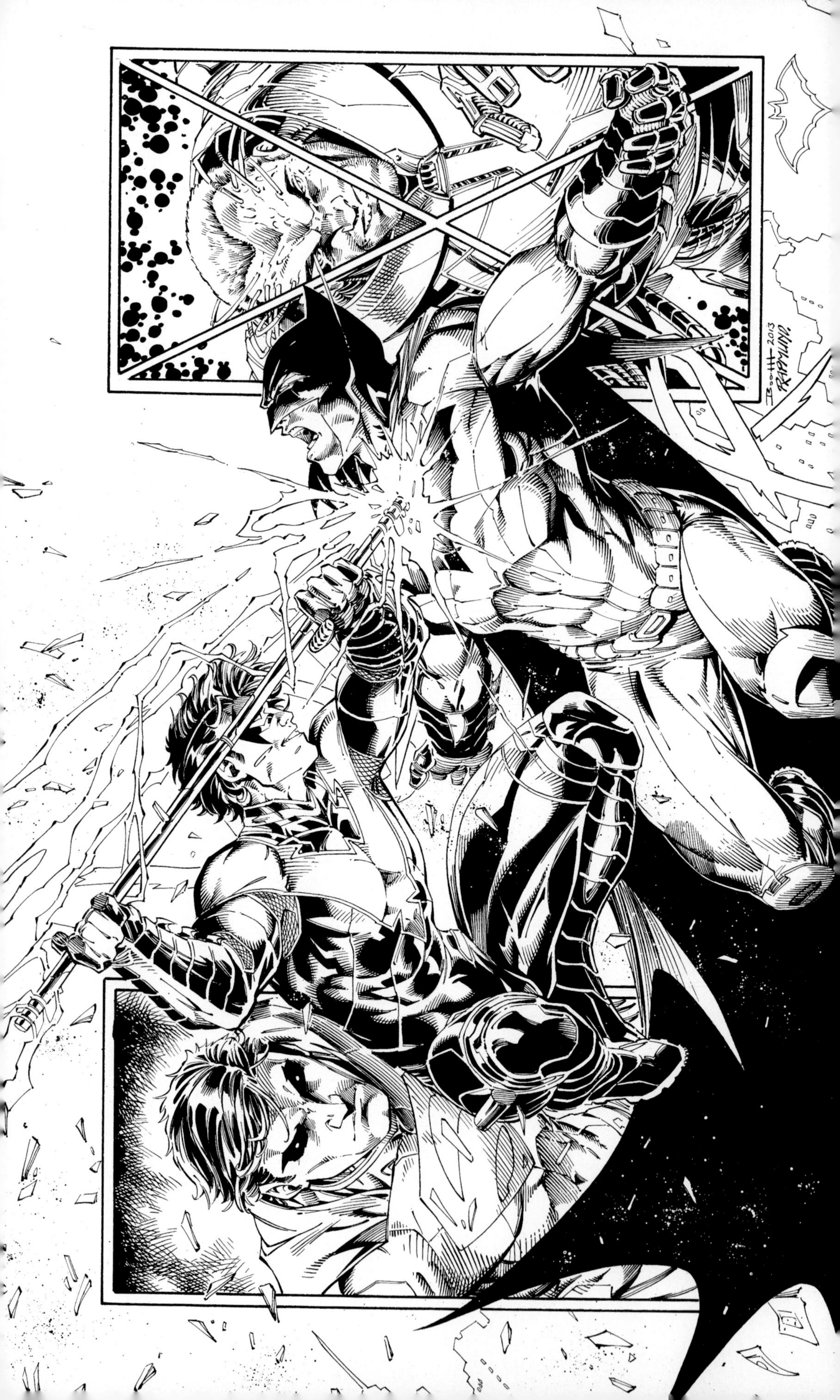

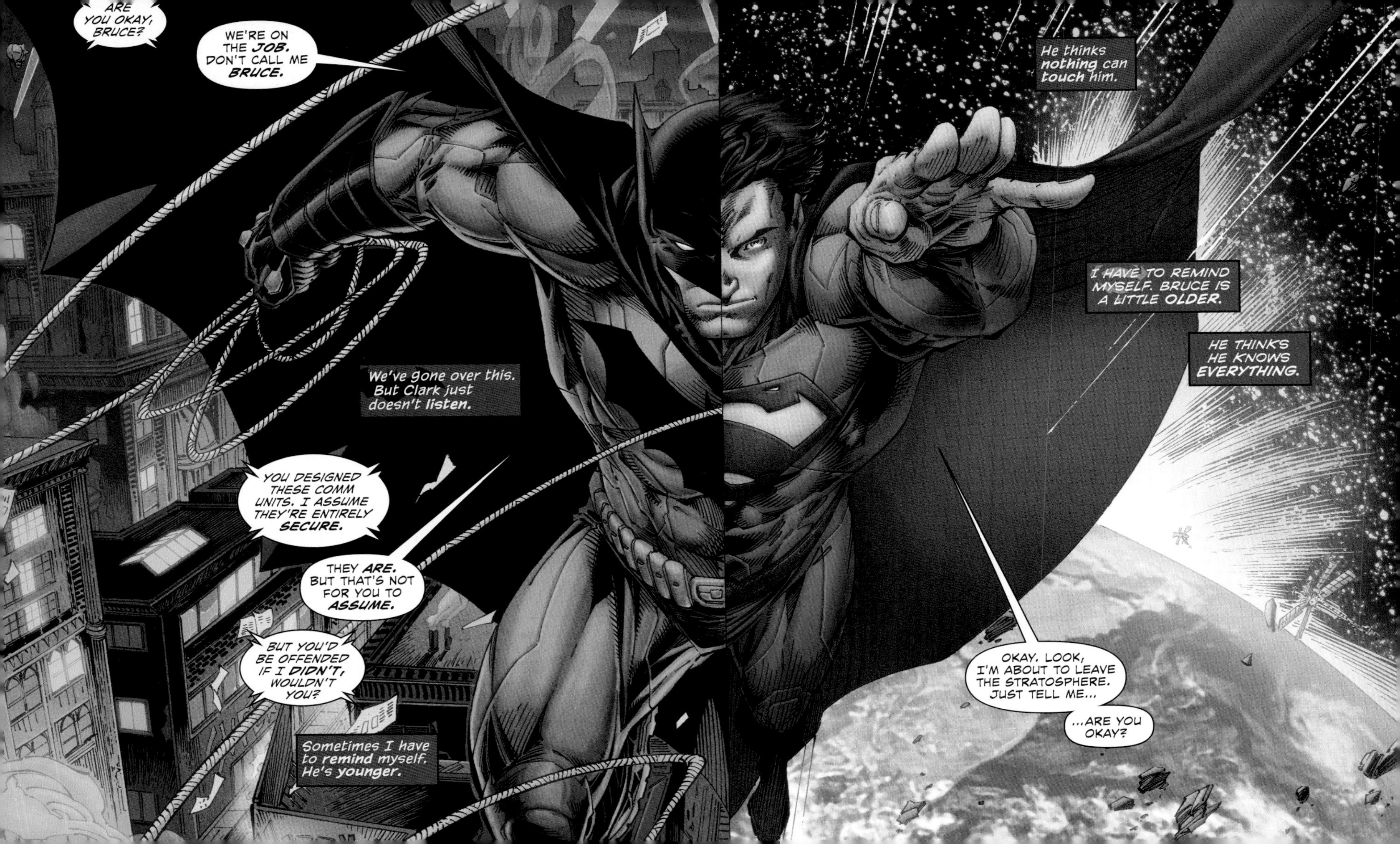

ARE YOU OKAY, BRUCE?
WE'RE ON THE JOB. DON'T CALL ME BRUCE.
We've gone over this. But Clark just doesn't listen.
YOU DESIGNED THESE COMM UNITS. I ASSUME THEY'RE ENTIRELY SECURE.
THEY ARE. BUT THAT'S NOT FOR YOU TO ASSUME.
BUT YOU'D BE OFFENDED IF I DIDN'T, WOULDN'T YOU?
Sometimes I have to remind myself. He's younger.
He thinks nothing can touch him.
I HAVE TO REMIND MYSELF. BRUCE IS A LITTLE OLDER.
HE THINKS HE KNOWS EVERYTHING.
OKAY. LOOK, I'M ABOUT TO LEAVE THE STRATOSPHERE. JUST TELL ME...
...ARE YOU OKAY?

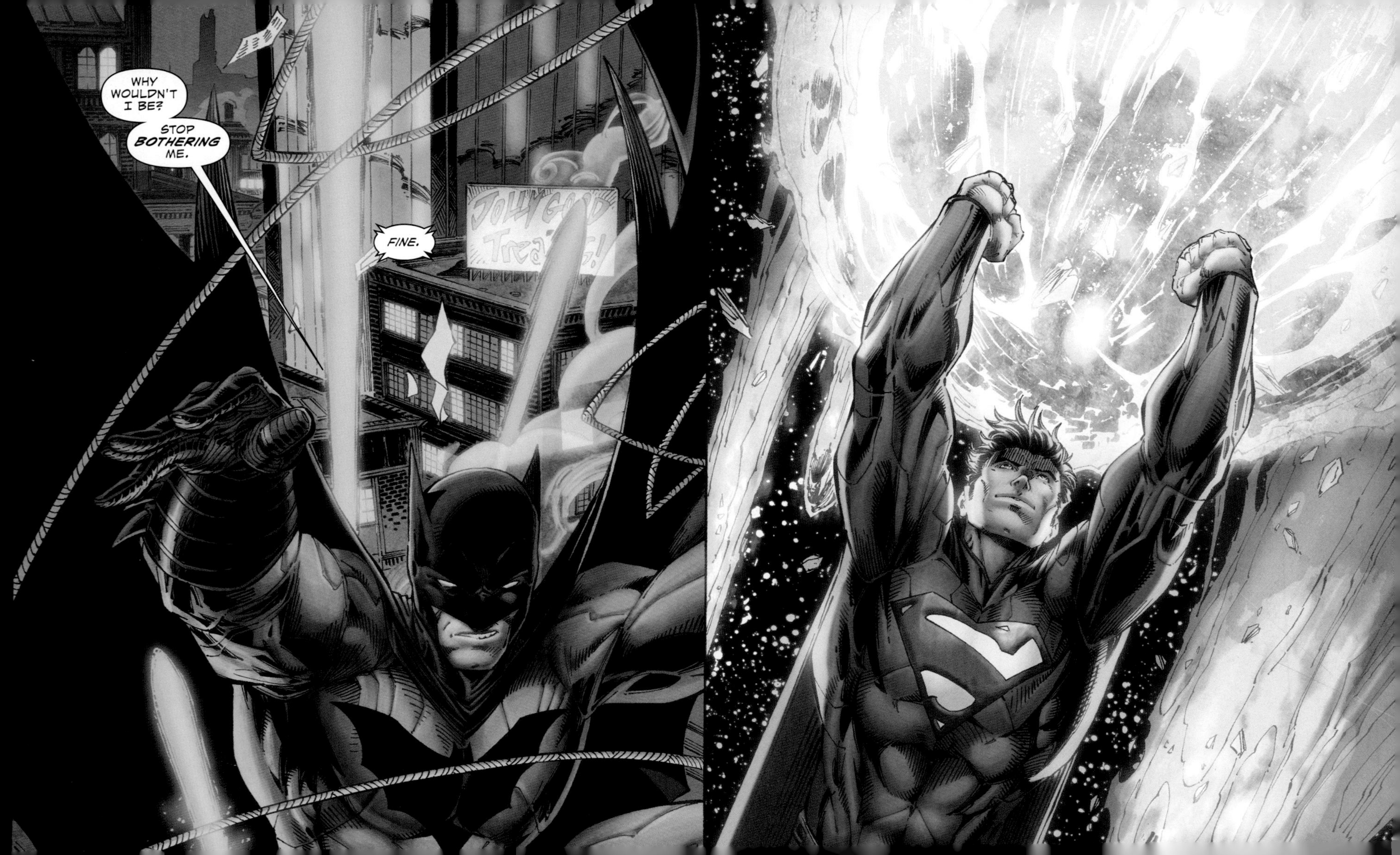
WHY WOULDN'T I BE?
STOP *BOTHERING* ME.
FINE.

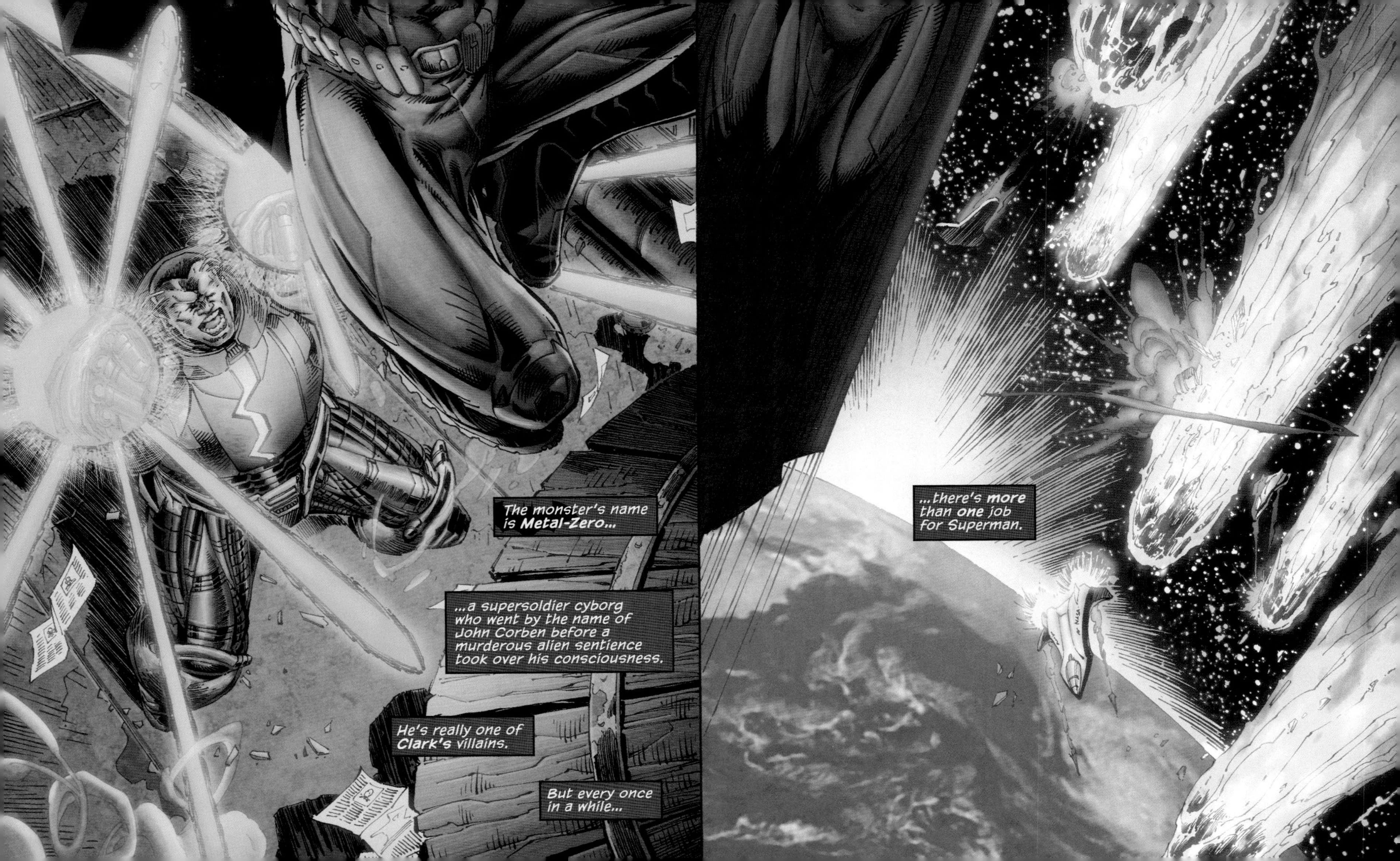
The monster's name is **Metal-Zero...**
...a supersoldier cyborg who went by the name of John Corben before a murderous alien sentience took over his consciousness.
He's really one of **Clark's** villains.
But every once in a while...
...there's **more** than **one** job for Superman.

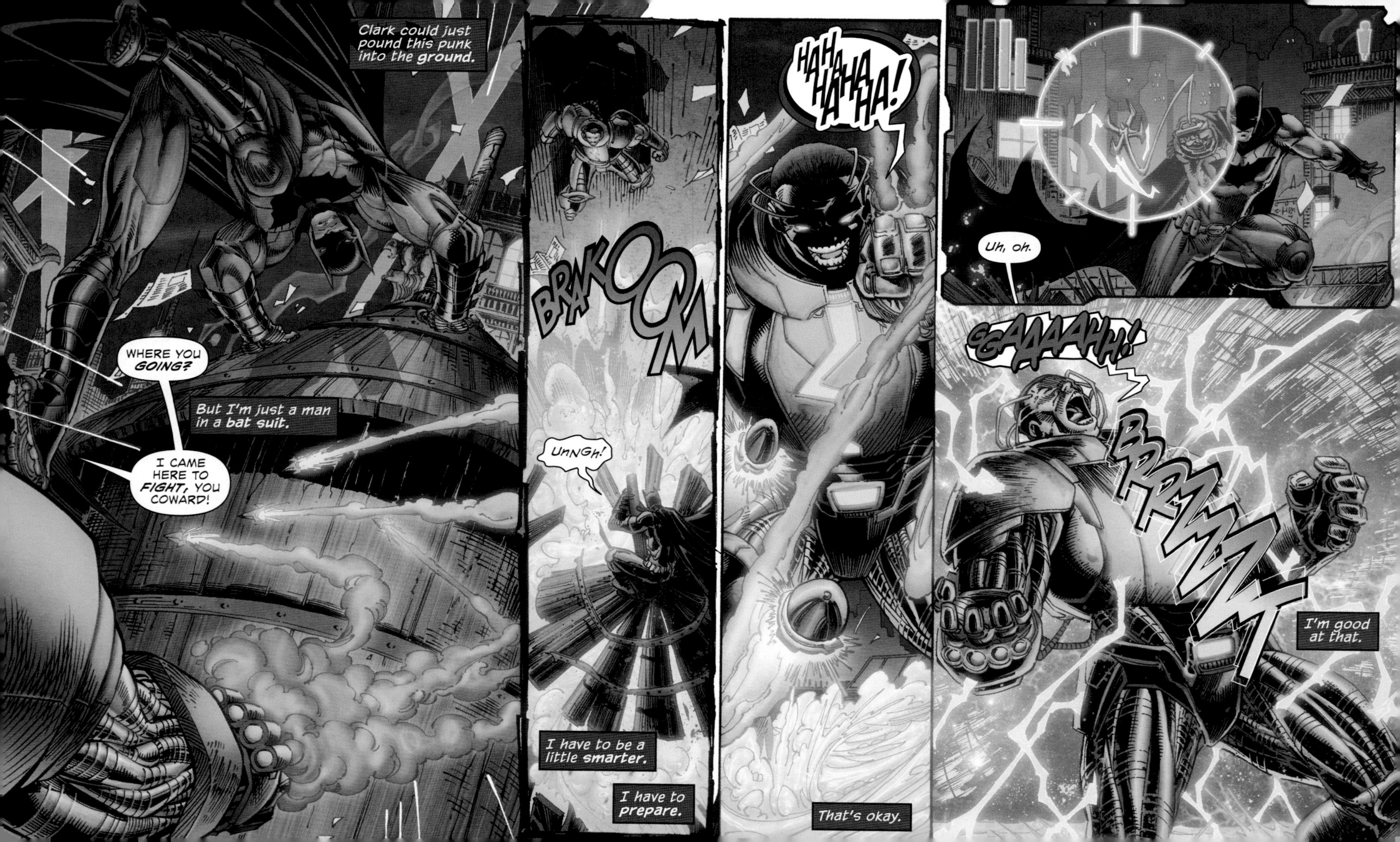
Clark could just pound this punk into the ground.
WHERE YOU GOING?
But I'm just a man in a bat suit.
I CAME HERE TO FIGHT, YOU COWARD!
BRAKOOOM
UnNGh!
I have to be a little smarter.
I have to prepare.
HAHAHAHAHAHA!
That's okay.
Uh, oh.
GGAAAAHH!
BRRZZZZT
I'm good at that.

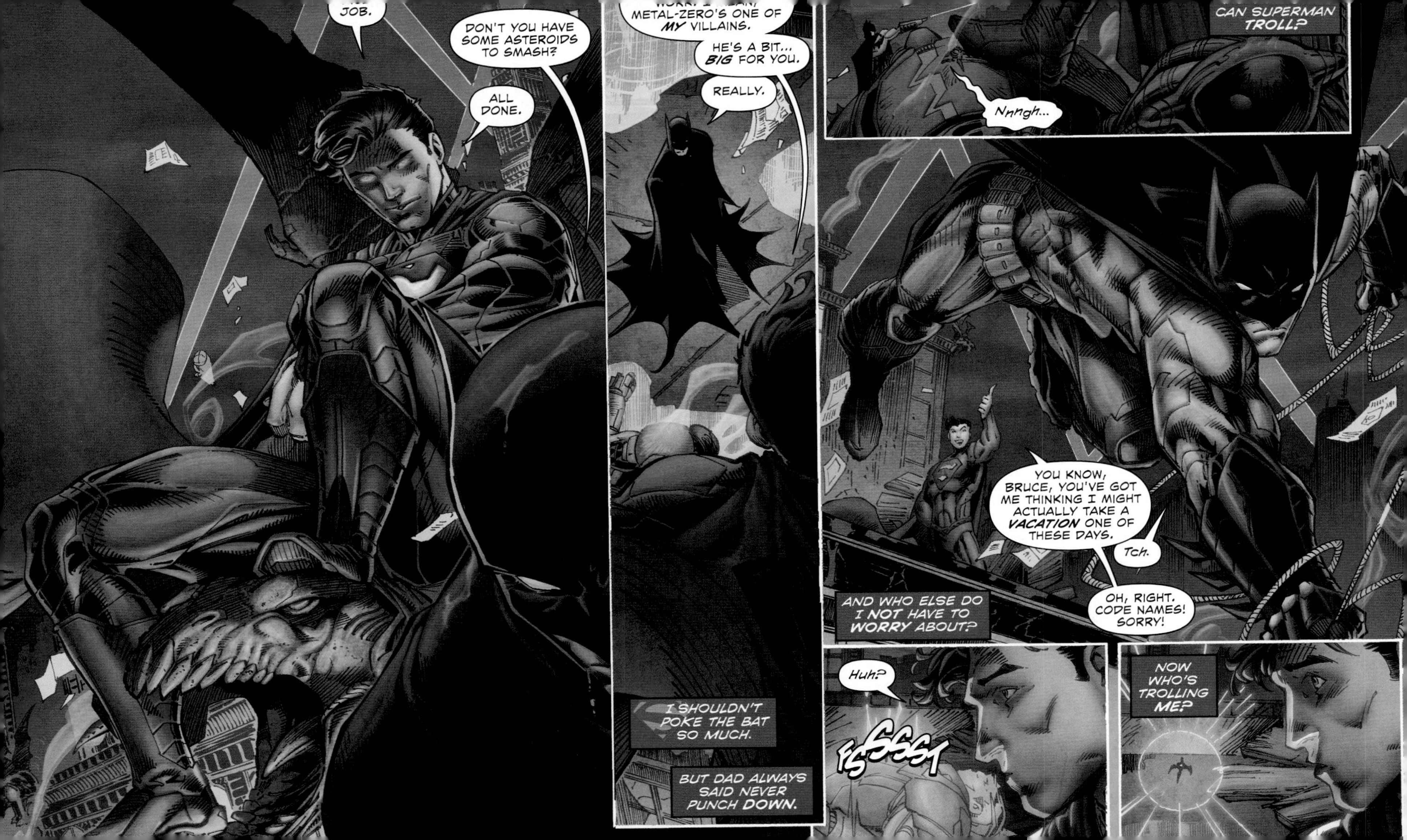

JOB.
DON'T YOU HAVE SOME ASTEROIDS TO SMASH?
ALL DONE.
METAL-ZERO'S ONE OF MY VILLAINS.
HE'S A BIT... BIG FOR YOU.
REALLY.
I SHOULDN'T POKE THE BAT SO MUCH.
BUT DAD ALWAYS SAID NEVER PUNCH DOWN.
CAN SUPERMAN TROLL?
Nnngh...
YOU KNOW, BRUCE, YOU'VE GOT ME THINKING I MIGHT ACTUALLY TAKE A VACATION ONE OF THESE DAYS.
Tch.
OH, RIGHT. CODE NAMES! SORRY!
AND WHO ELSE DO I NOT HAVE TO WORRY ABOUT?
Huh?
FSSSST
NOW WHO'S TROLLING ME?

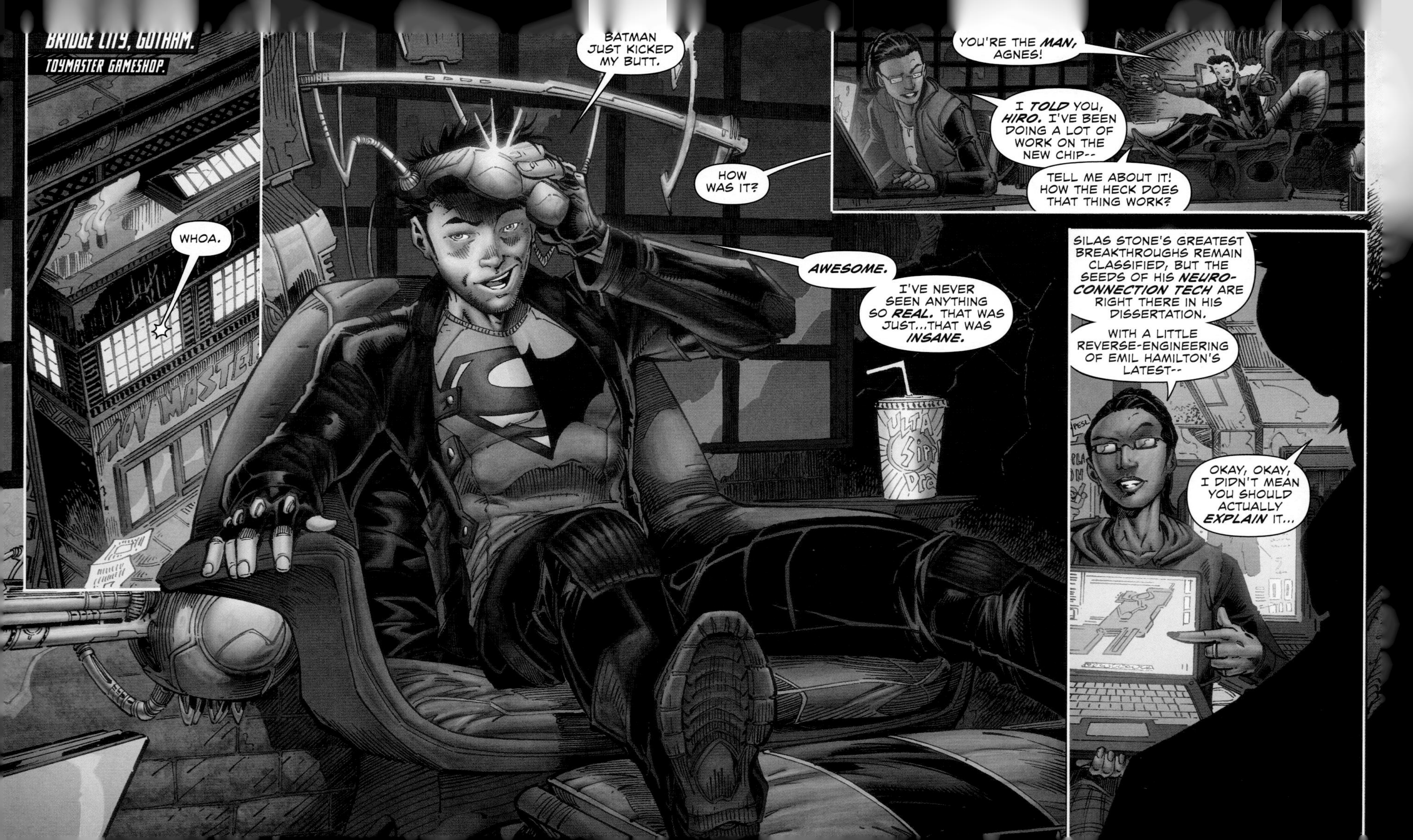
BRIDGE CITY, GOTHAM.
TOYMASTER GAMESHOP.
WHOA.
BATMAN JUST KICKED MY BUTT.
HOW WAS IT?
AWESOME.
I'VE NEVER SEEN ANYTHING SO REAL. THAT WAS JUST...THAT WAS INSANE.
YOU'RE THE MAN, AGNES!
I TOLD YOU, HIRO. I'VE BEEN DOING A LOT OF WORK ON THE NEW CHIP--
TELL ME ABOUT IT! HOW THE HECK DOES THAT THING WORK?
SILAS STONE'S GREATEST BREAKTHROUGHS REMAIN CLASSIFIED, BUT THE SEEDS OF HIS NEURO-CONNECTION TECH ARE RIGHT THERE IN HIS DISSERTATION.
WITH A LITTLE REVERSE-ENGINEERING OF EMIL HAMILTON'S LATEST--
OKAY, OKAY, I DIDN'T MEAN YOU SHOULD ACTUALLY EXPLAIN IT...

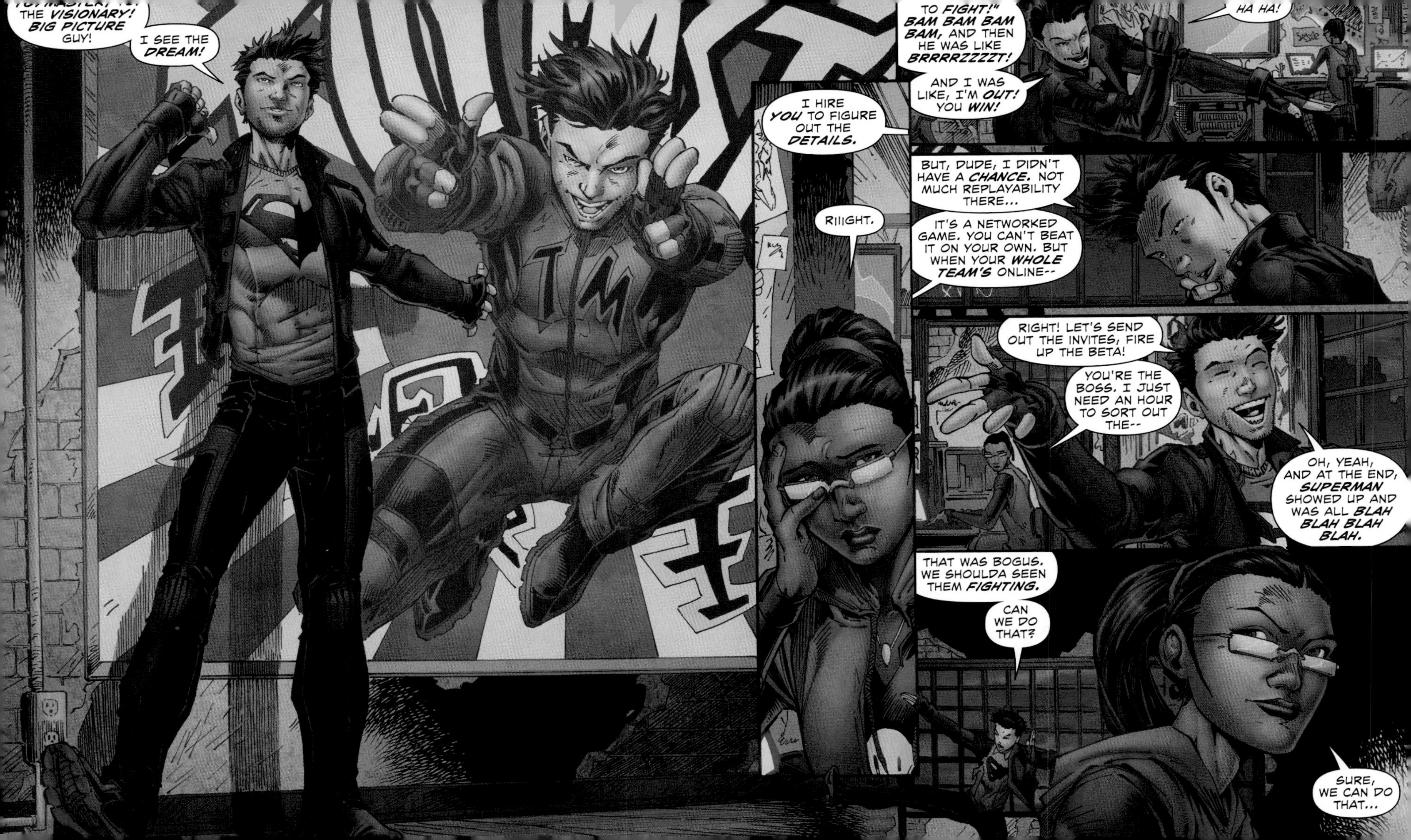
THE VISIONARY! BIG PICTURE GUY!
I SEE THE DREAM!
I HIRE YOU TO FIGURE OUT THE DETAILS.
RIIIGHT.
TO FIGHT!" BAM BAM BAM BAM, AND THEN HE WAS LIKE BRRRRZZZZT!
AND I WAS LIKE, I'M OUT! YOU WIN!
HA HA!
BUT, DUDE, I DIDN'T HAVE A CHANCE. NOT MUCH REPLAYABILITY THERE...
IT'S A NETWORKED GAME. YOU CAN'T BEAT IT ON YOUR OWN. BUT WHEN YOUR WHOLE TEAM'S ONLINE--
RIGHT! LET'S SEND OUT THE INVITES, FIRE UP THE BETA!
YOU'RE THE BOSS. I JUST NEED AN HOUR TO SORT OUT THE--
OH, YEAH, AND AT THE END, SUPERMAN SHOWED UP AND WAS ALL BLAH BLAH BLAH BLAH.
THAT WAS BOGUS. WE SHOULDA SEEN THEM FIGHTING.
CAN WE DO THAT?
SURE, WE CAN DO THAT...

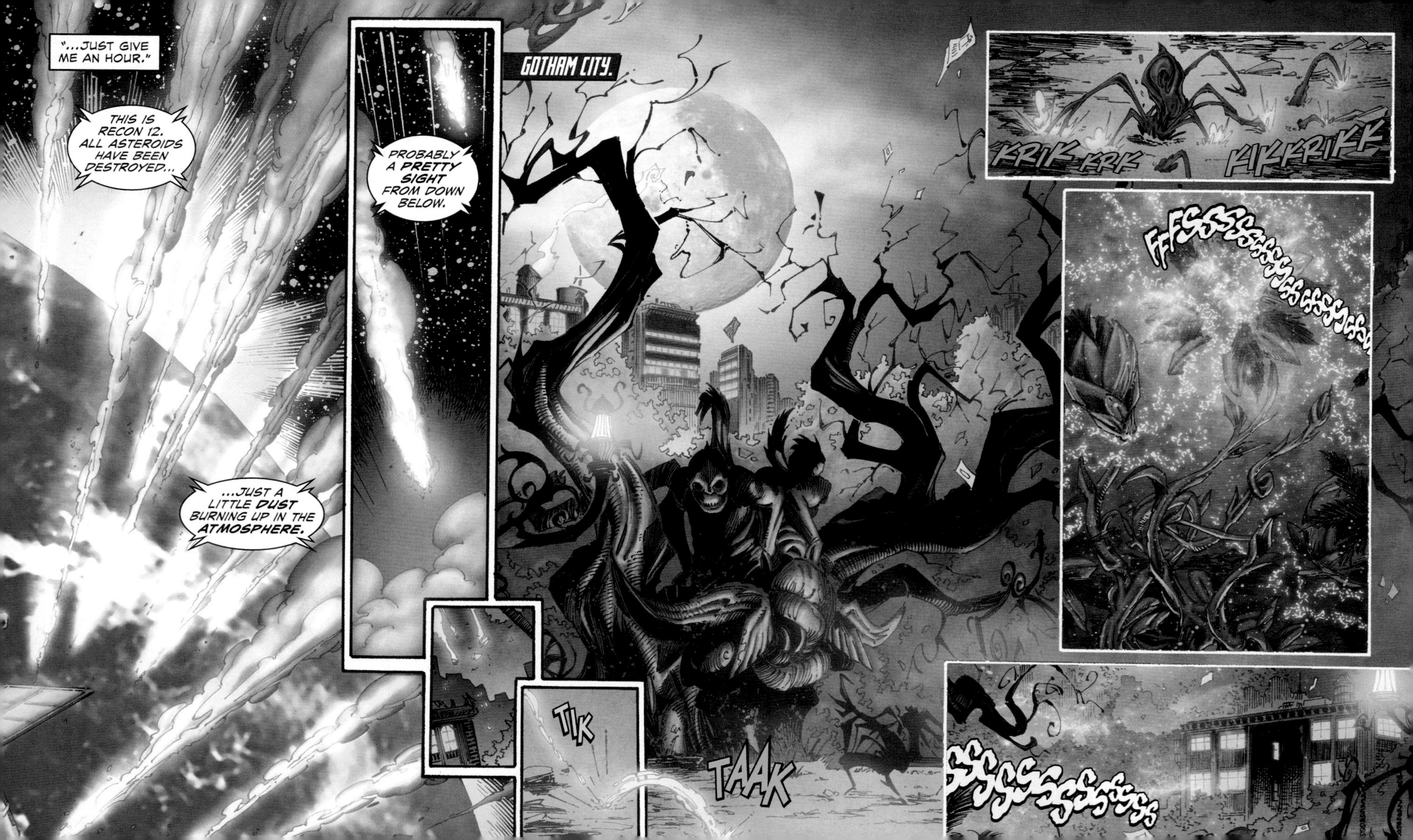
"...JUST GIVE ME AN HOUR."
THIS IS RECON 12. ALL ASTEROIDS HAVE BEEN DESTROYED...
...JUST A LITTLE DUST BURNING UP IN THE ATMOSPHERE.
PROBABLY A PRETTY SIGHT FROM DOWN BELOW.
GOTHAM CITY.
TIK
TAAK
KRIK KRIK
KIKKRIKK
FFFSSSSSSSSSSSSSSSSSSS
SSSSSSSSSSSSS

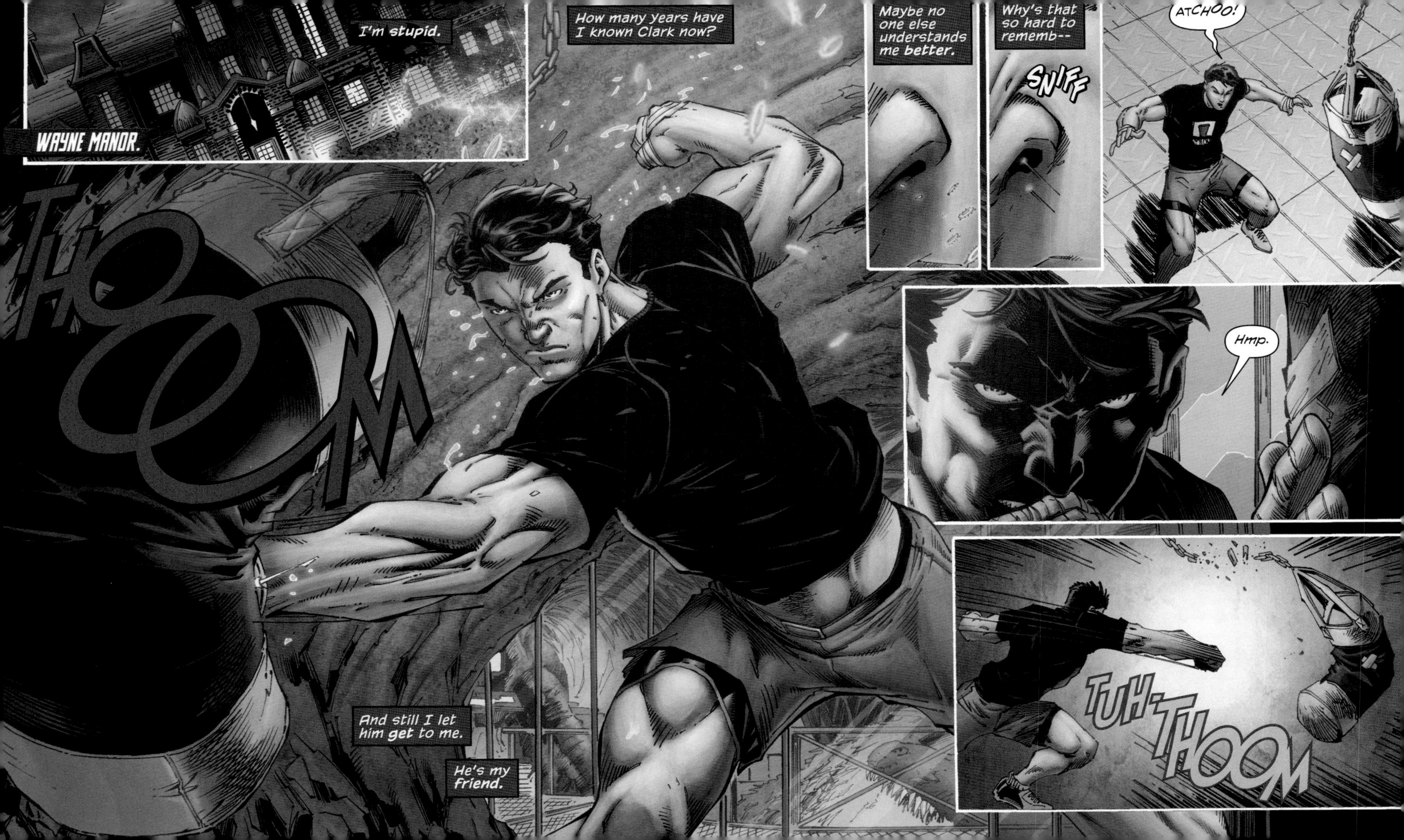
WAYNE MANOR.
I'm stupid.
How many years have I known Clark now?
THOOM
And still I let him get to me.
He's my friend.
Maybe no one else understands me better.
Why's that so hard to rememb--
SNIFF
ATCHOO!
Hmp.
TUH-THOOM

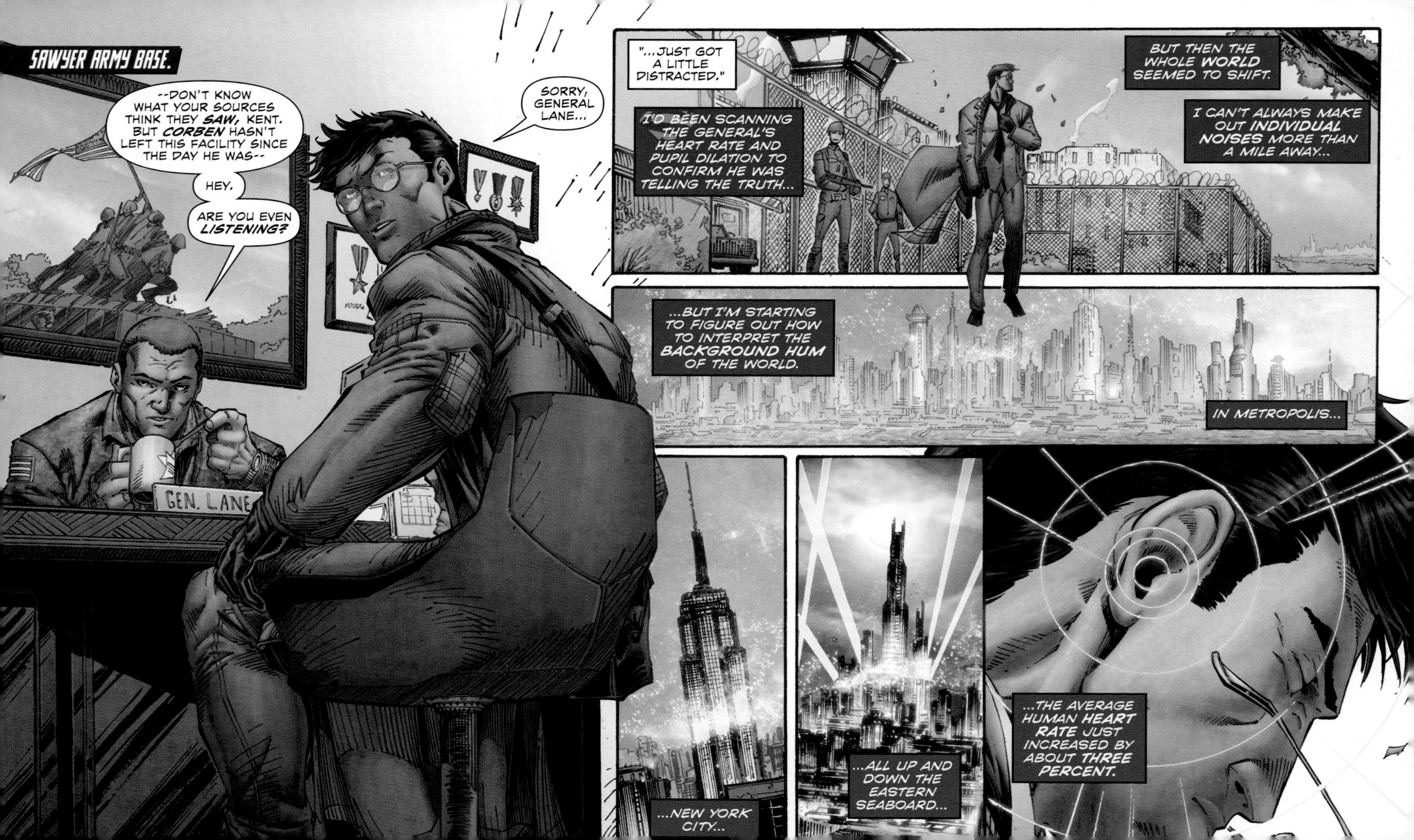
SAWYER ARMY BASE.
--DON'T KNOW WHAT YOUR SOURCES THINK THEY **SAW,** KENT. BUT **CORBEN** HASN'T LEFT THIS FACILITY SINCE THE DAY HE WAS--
HEY.
ARE YOU EVEN **LISTENING?**
SORRY, GENERAL LANE...
GEN. LANE
"...JUST GOT A LITTLE DISTRACTED."
I'D BEEN SCANNING THE GENERAL'S HEART RATE AND PUPIL DILATION TO CONFIRM HE WAS TELLING THE TRUTH...
BUT THEN THE WHOLE **WORLD** SEEMED TO SHIFT.
I CAN'T ALWAYS MAKE OUT **INDIVIDUAL NOISES** MORE THAN A MILE AWAY...
...BUT I'M STARTING TO FIGURE OUT HOW TO INTERPRET THE **BACKGROUND HUM** OF THE WORLD.
IN METROPOLIS...
...NEW YORK CITY...
...ALL UP AND DOWN THE EASTERN SEABOARD...
...THE AVERAGE HUMAN **HEART RATE** JUST INCREASED BY ABOUT **THREE PERCENT.**

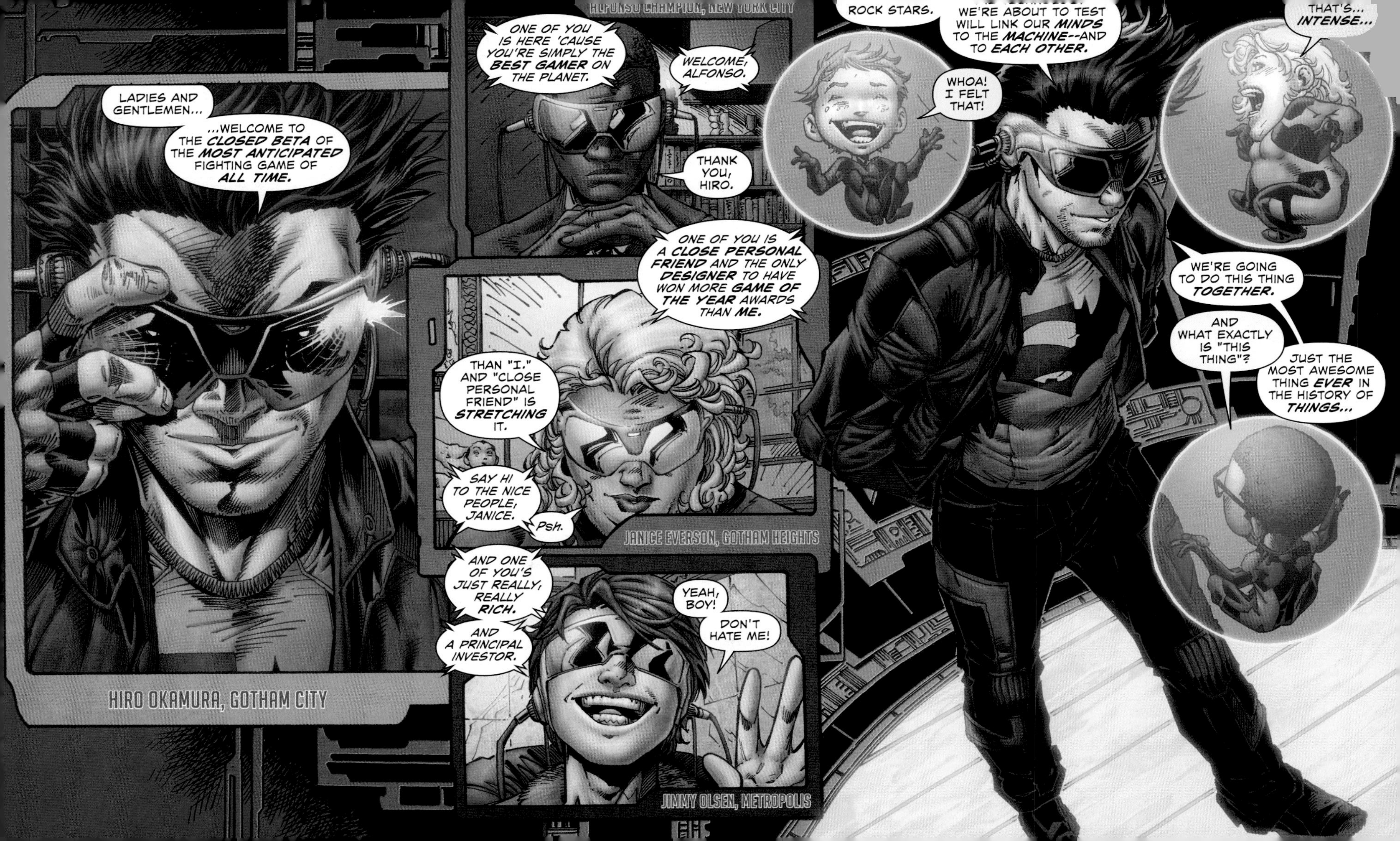

LADIES AND GENTLEMEN...
...WELCOME TO THE CLOSED BETA OF THE MOST ANTICIPATED FIGHTING GAME OF ALL TIME.
HIRO OKAMURA, GOTHAM CITY
ALFONSO CHAMPION, NEW YORK CITY
ONE OF YOU IS HERE 'CAUSE YOU'RE SIMPLY THE BEST GAMER ON THE PLANET.
WELCOME, ALFONSO.
THANK YOU, HIRO.
ONE OF YOU IS A CLOSE PERSONAL FRIEND AND THE ONLY DESIGNER TO HAVE WON MORE GAME OF THE YEAR AWARDS THAN ME.
THAN "I." AND "CLOSE PERSONAL FRIEND" IS STRETCHING IT.
SAY HI TO THE NICE PEOPLE, JANICE.
Psh.
JANICE EVERSON, GOTHAM HEIGHTS
AND ONE OF YOU'S JUST REALLY, REALLY RICH.
AND A PRINCIPAL INVESTOR.
YEAH, BOY!
DON'T HATE ME!
JIMMY OLSEN, METROPOLIS
ROCK STARS.
WE'RE ABOUT TO TEST WILL LINK OUR MINDS TO THE MACHINE--AND TO EACH OTHER.
WHOA! I FELT THAT!
THAT'S... INTENSE...
WE'RE GOING TO DO THIS THING TOGETHER.
AND WHAT EXACTLY IS "THIS THING"?
JUST THE MOST AWESOME THING EVER IN THE HISTORY OF THINGS...

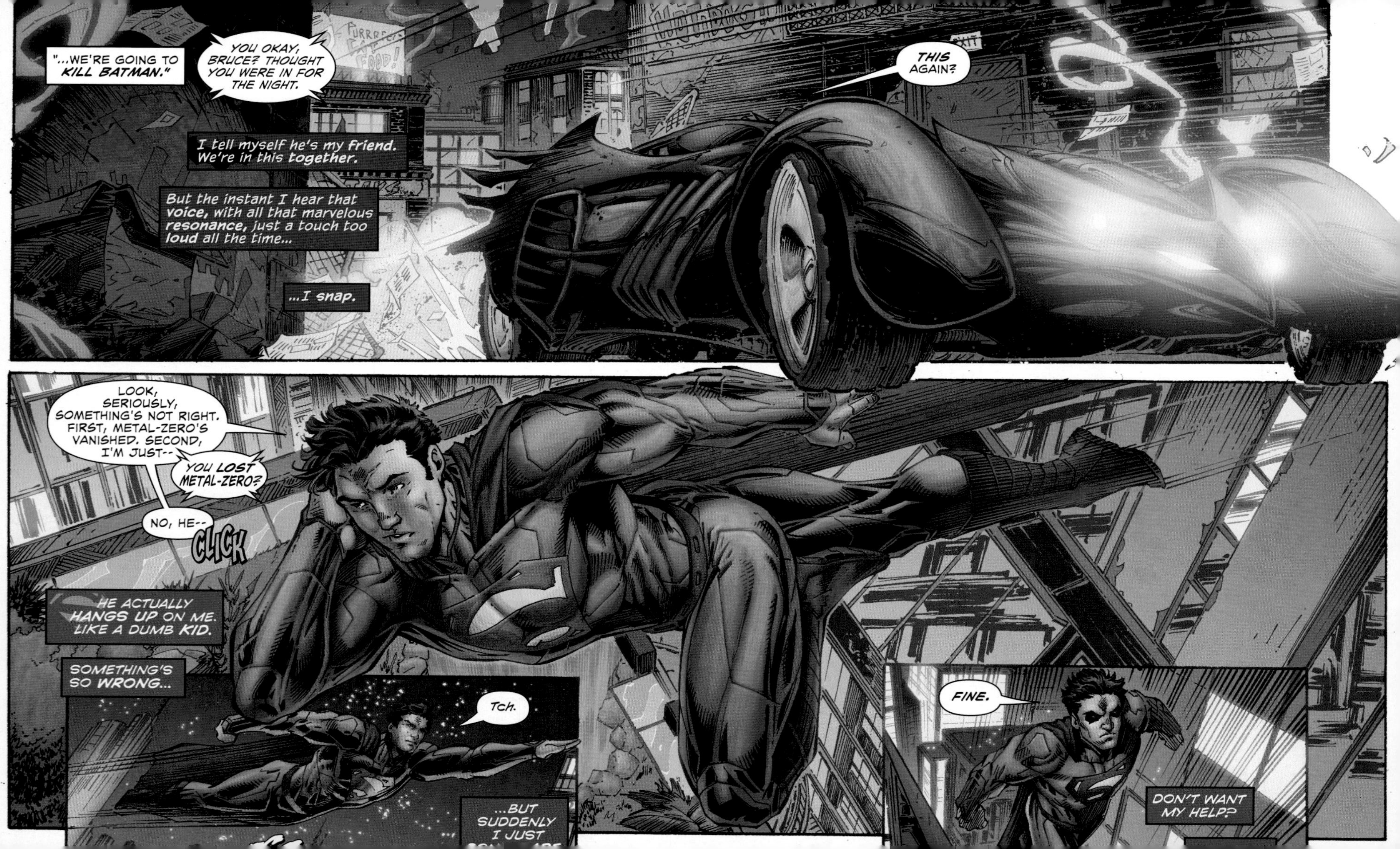

"...WE'RE GOING TO KILL BATMAN."
YOU OKAY, BRUCE? THOUGHT YOU WERE IN FOR THE NIGHT.
THIS AGAIN?
I tell myself he's my friend. We're in this together.
But the instant I hear that voice, with all that marvelous resonance, just a touch too loud all the time...
...I snap.
LOOK, SERIOUSLY, SOMETHING'S NOT RIGHT. FIRST, METAL-ZERO'S VANISHED. SECOND, I'M JUST--
YOU LOST METAL-ZERO?
NO, HE--
CLICK
HE ACTUALLY HANGS UP ON ME. LIKE A DUMB KID.
SOMETHING'S SO WRONG...
Tch.
...BUT SUDDENLY I JUST
FINE.
DON'T WANT MY HELP?

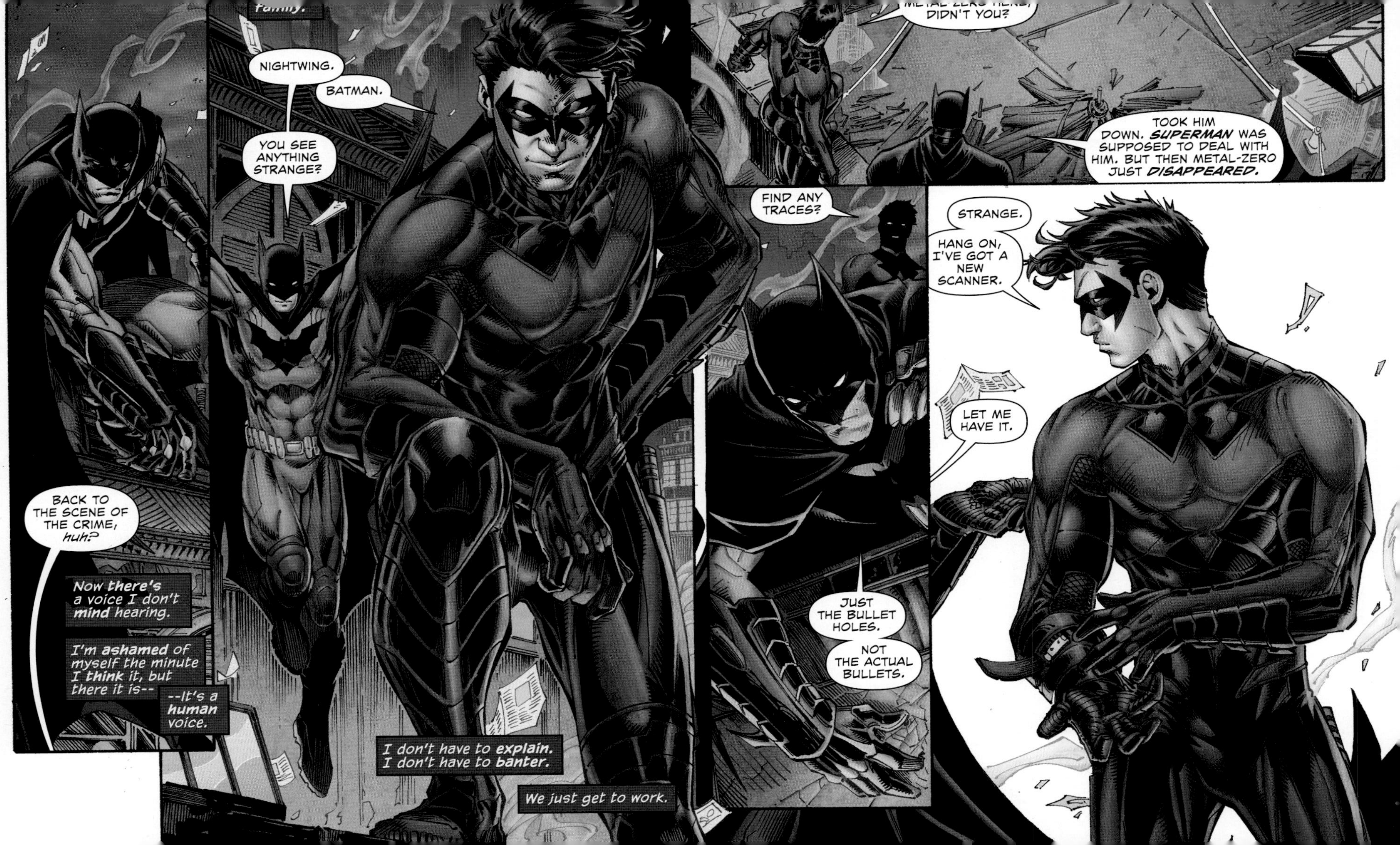

BACK TO THE SCENE OF THE CRIME, *huh?*
Now ***there's*** *a voice I don't* ***mind*** *hearing.*
I'm ***ashamed*** *of myself the minute I* ***think*** *it, but there it is--*
--It's a ***human*** *voice.*
NIGHTWING.
BATMAN.
YOU SEE ANYTHING STRANGE?
I don't have to ***explain.*** *I don't have to* ***banter.***
We just get to work.
DIDN'T YOU?
TOOK HIM DOWN. ***SUPERMAN*** WAS SUPPOSED TO DEAL WITH HIM. BUT THEN METAL-ZERO JUST ***DISAPPEARED.***
FIND ANY TRACES?
JUST THE BULLET HOLES.
NOT THE ACTUAL BULLETS.
STRANGE.
HANG ON, I'VE GOT A NEW SCANNER.
LET ME HAVE IT.

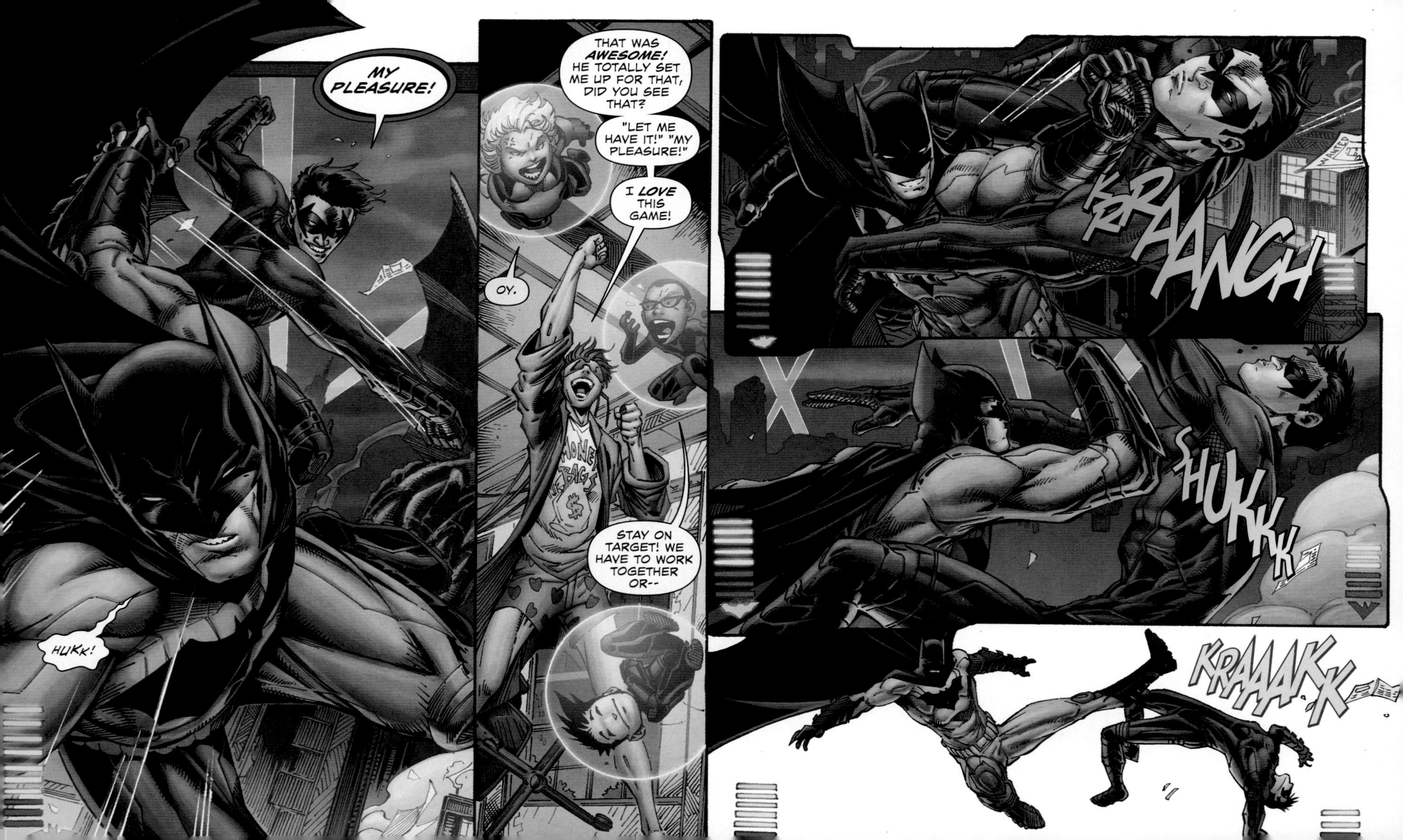
MY PLEASURE!
HUKK!
THAT WAS AWESOME! HE TOTALLY SET ME UP FOR THAT, DID YOU SEE THAT?
"LET ME HAVE IT!" "MY PLEASURE!"
OY.
I LOVE THIS GAME!
STAY ON TARGET! WE HAVE TO WORK TOGETHER OR--
KRRAANCH
SHUKKK
KRAAAKK

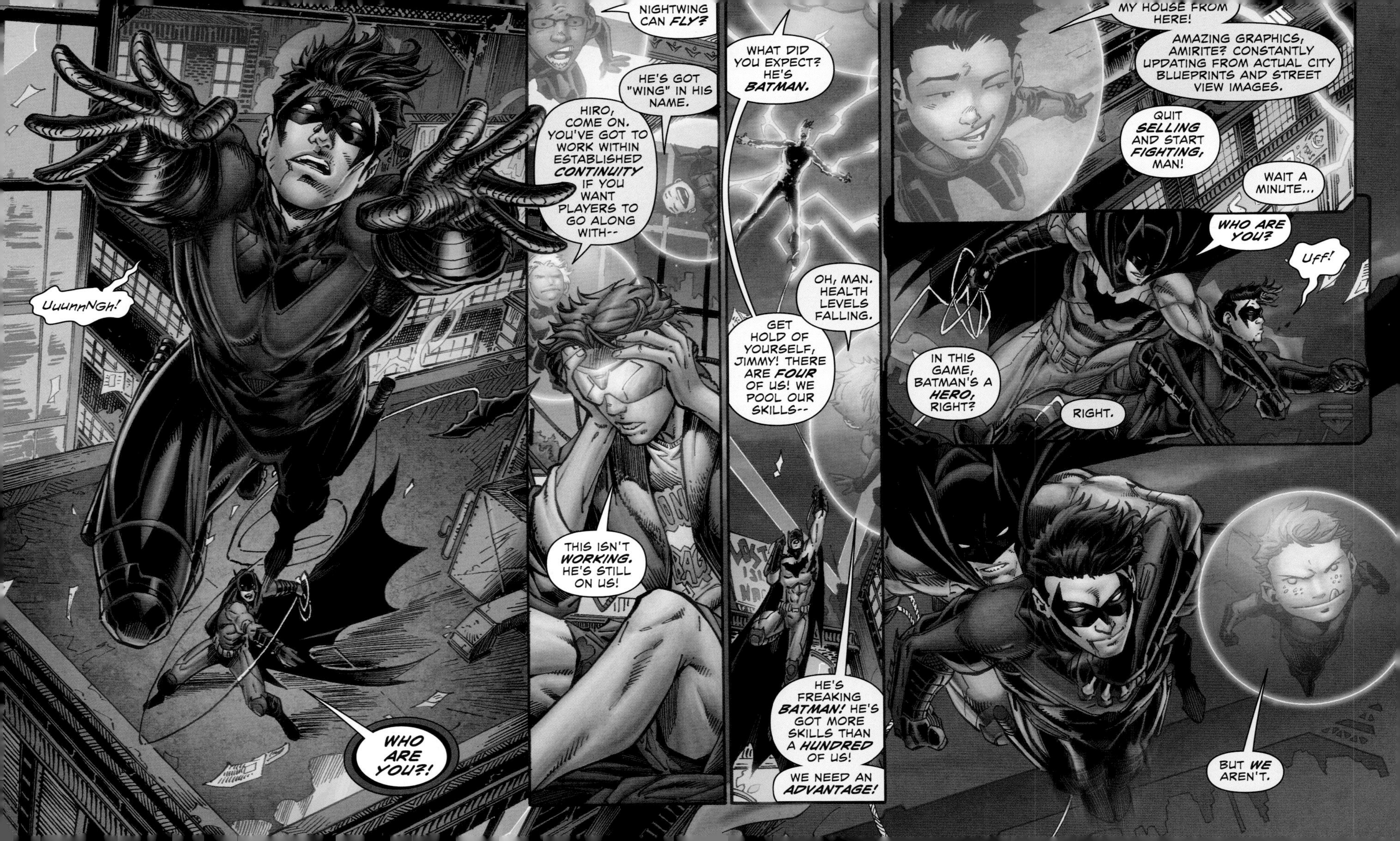
UuunnNGh!
WHO ARE YOU?!
NIGHTWING CAN FLY?
HE'S GOT "WING" IN HIS NAME.
HIRO, COME ON. YOU'VE GOT TO WORK WITHIN ESTABLISHED CONTINUITY IF YOU WANT PLAYERS TO GO ALONG WITH--
THIS ISN'T WORKING. HE'S STILL ON US!
WHAT DID YOU EXPECT? HE'S BATMAN.
OH, MAN. HEALTH LEVELS FALLING.
GET HOLD OF YOURSELF, JIMMY! THERE ARE FOUR OF US! WE POOL OUR SKILLS--
HE'S FREAKING BATMAN! HE'S GOT MORE SKILLS THAN A HUNDRED OF US!
WE NEED AN ADVANTAGE!
MY HOUSE FROM HERE!
AMAZING GRAPHICS, AMIRITE? CONSTANTLY UPDATING FROM ACTUAL CITY BLUEPRINTS AND STREET VIEW IMAGES.
QUIT SELLING AND START FIGHTING, MAN!
WAIT A MINUTE...
WHO ARE YOU?
Uff!
IN THIS GAME, BATMAN'S A HERO, RIGHT?
RIGHT.
BUT WE AREN'T.

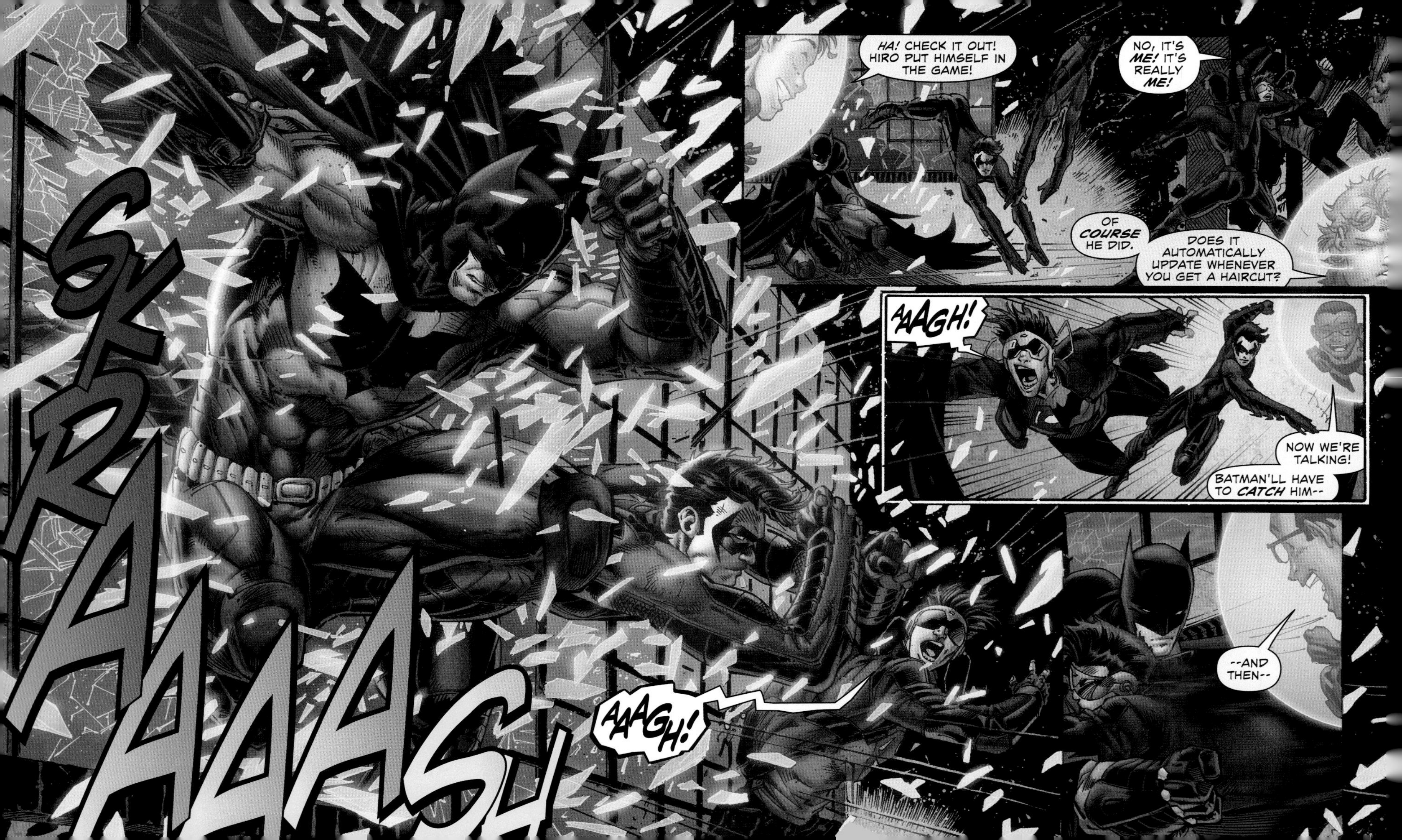
HA! CHECK IT OUT! HIRO PUT HIMSELF IN THE GAME!
NO, IT'S ME! IT'S REALLY ME!
OF COURSE HE DID.
DOES IT AUTOMATICALLY UPDATE WHENEVER YOU GET A HAIRCUT?
AAAGH!
NOW WE'RE TALKING!
BATMAN'LL HAVE TO CATCH HIM--
--AND THEN--
SKRAAAASH
AAAGH!

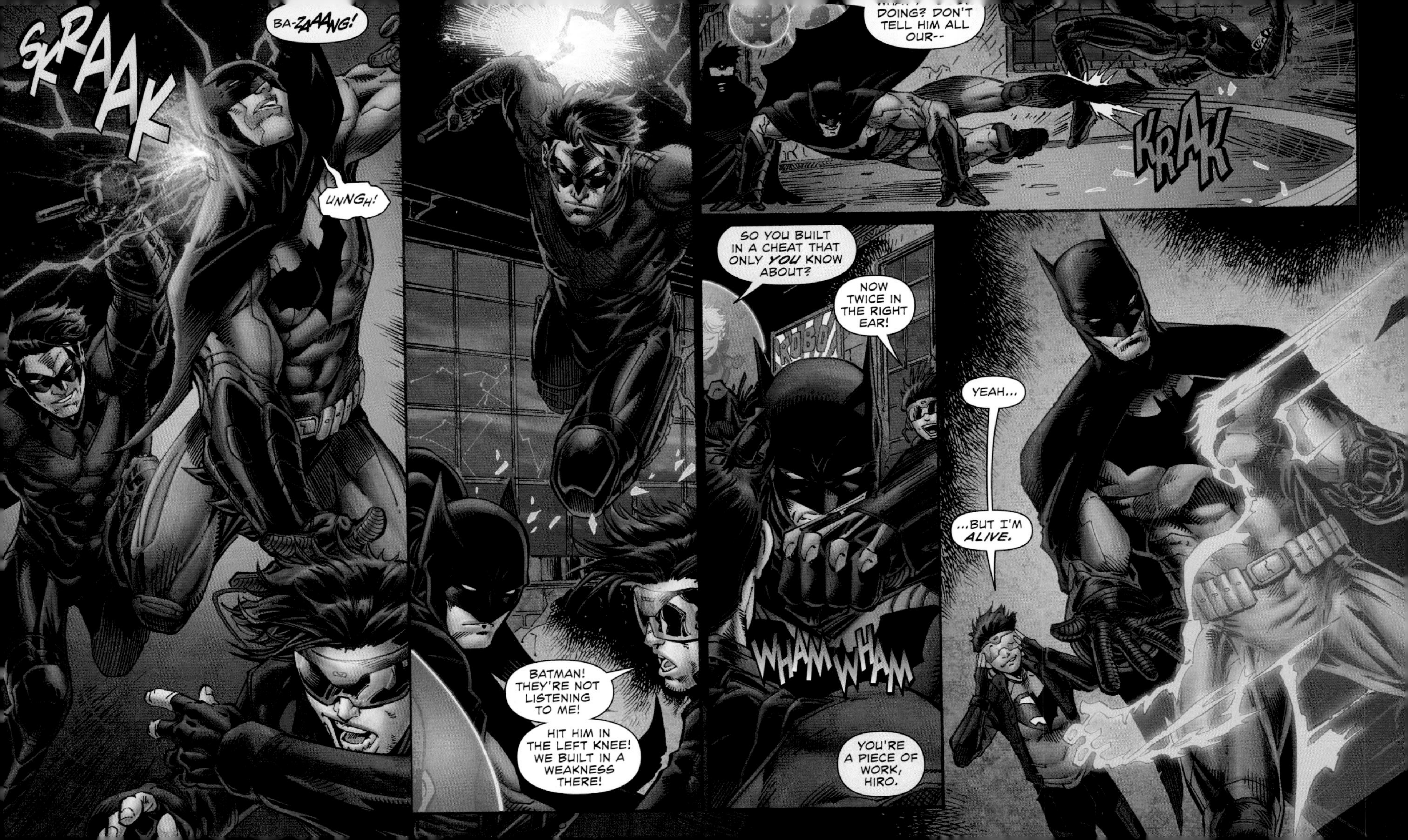
SKRAAK
BA-ZAAANG!
UNNGH!
DOING? DON'T TELL HIM ALL OUR--
KRAK
BATMAN! THEY'RE NOT LISTENING TO ME!
HIT HIM IN THE LEFT KNEE! WE BUILT IN A WEAKNESS THERE!
SO YOU BUILT IN A CHEAT THAT ONLY YOU KNOW ABOUT?
NOW TWICE IN THE RIGHT EAR!
WHAM WHAM
YOU'RE A PIECE OF WORK, HIRO.
YEAH...
...BUT I'M ALIVE.

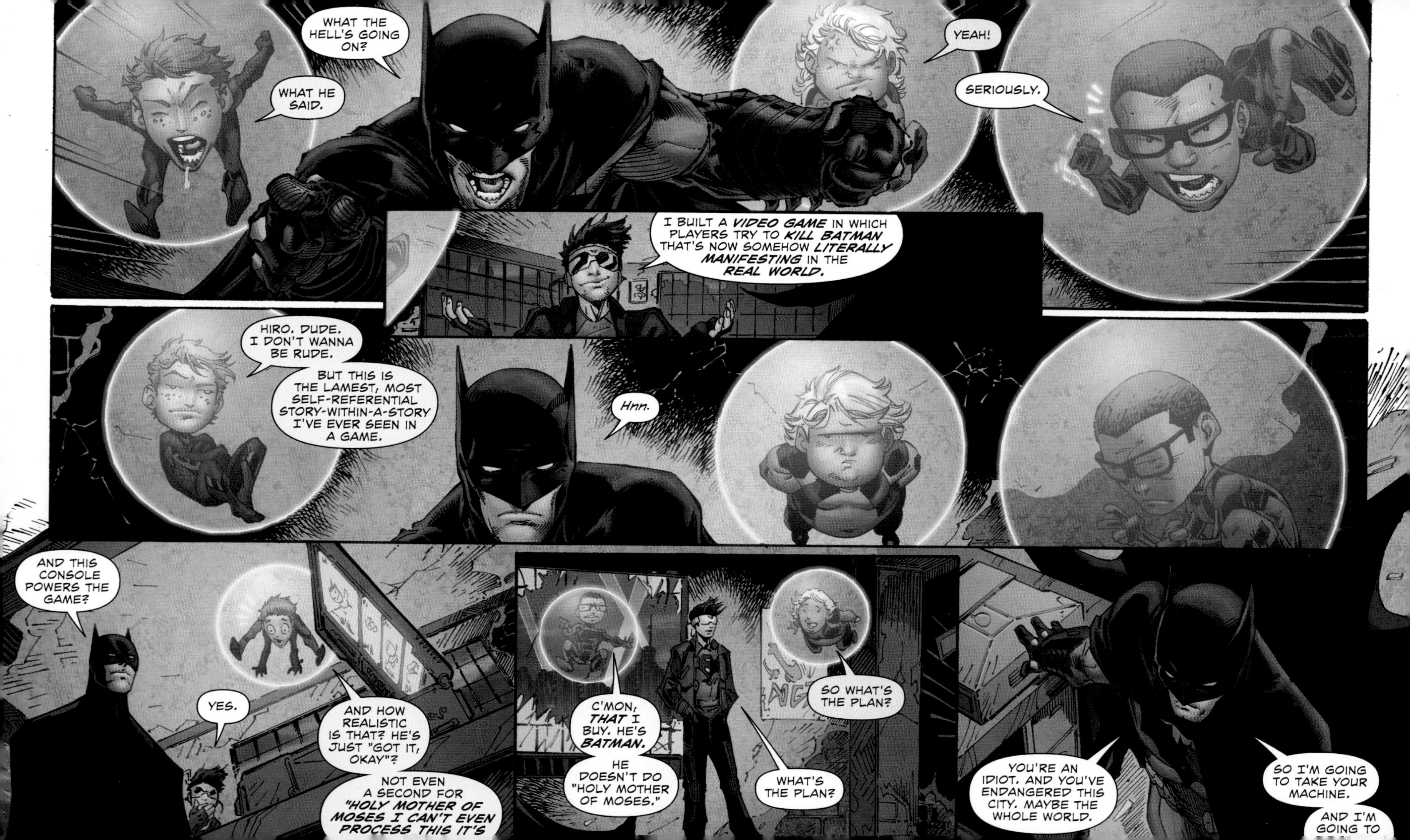

WHAT THE HELL'S GOING ON?
WHAT HE SAID.
YEAH!
SERIOUSLY.
I BUILT A *VIDEO GAME* IN WHICH PLAYERS TRY TO *KILL BATMAN* THAT'S NOW SOMEHOW *LITERALLY MANIFESTING* IN THE *REAL WORLD*.
HIRO. DUDE. I DON'T WANNA BE RUDE.
BUT THIS IS THE LAMEST, MOST SELF-REFERENTIAL STORY-WITHIN-A-STORY I'VE EVER SEEN IN A GAME.
Hnn.
AND THIS CONSOLE POWERS THE GAME?
YES.
AND HOW REALISTIC IS THAT? HE'S JUST "GOT IT, OKAY"?
NOT EVEN A SECOND FOR *"HOLY MOTHER OF MOSES I CAN'T EVEN PROCESS THIS IT'S*
C'MON, *THAT* I BUY. HE'S *BATMAN.*
HE DOESN'T DO "HOLY MOTHER OF MOSES."
SO WHAT'S THE PLAN?
WHAT'S THE PLAN?
YOU'RE AN IDIOT. AND YOU'VE ENDANGERED THIS CITY. MAYBE THE WHOLE WORLD.
SO I'M GOING TO TAKE YOUR MACHINE.
AND I'M GOING TO

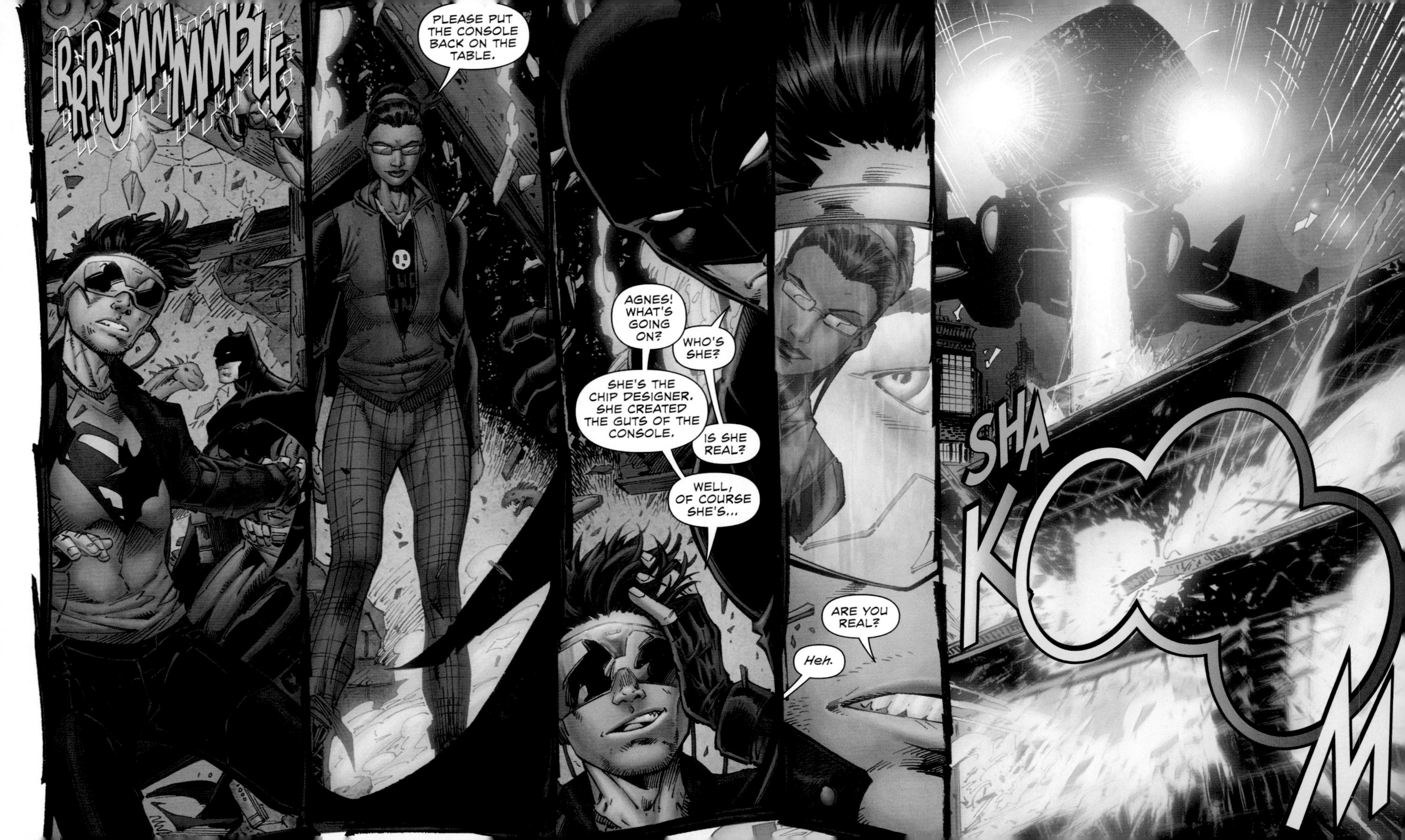
RRRUMMMMBLE
PLEASE PUT THE CONSOLE BACK ON THE TABLE.
AGNES! WHAT'S GOING ON?
WHO'S SHE?
SHE'S THE CHIP DESIGNER. SHE CREATED THE GUTS OF THE CONSOLE.
IS SHE REAL?
WELL, OF COURSE SHE'S...
ARE YOU REAL?
Heh.
SHA KOOM

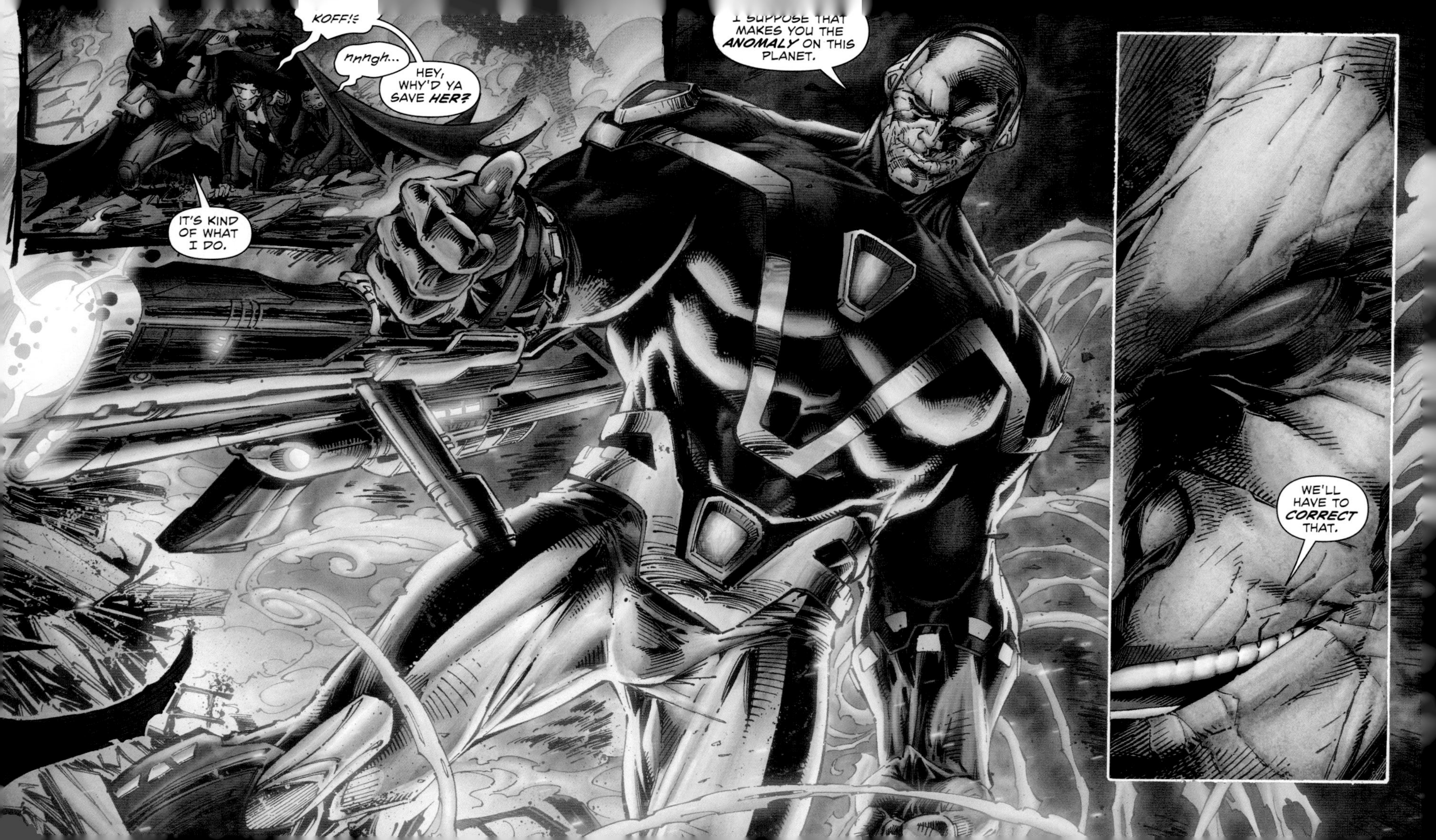
KOFF!$
nnngh...
HEY, WHY'D YA SAVE *HER?*
IT'S KIND OF WHAT I DO.
I SUPPOSE THAT MAKES YOU THE *ANOMALY* ON THIS PLANET.
WE'LL HAVE TO *CORRECT* THAT.

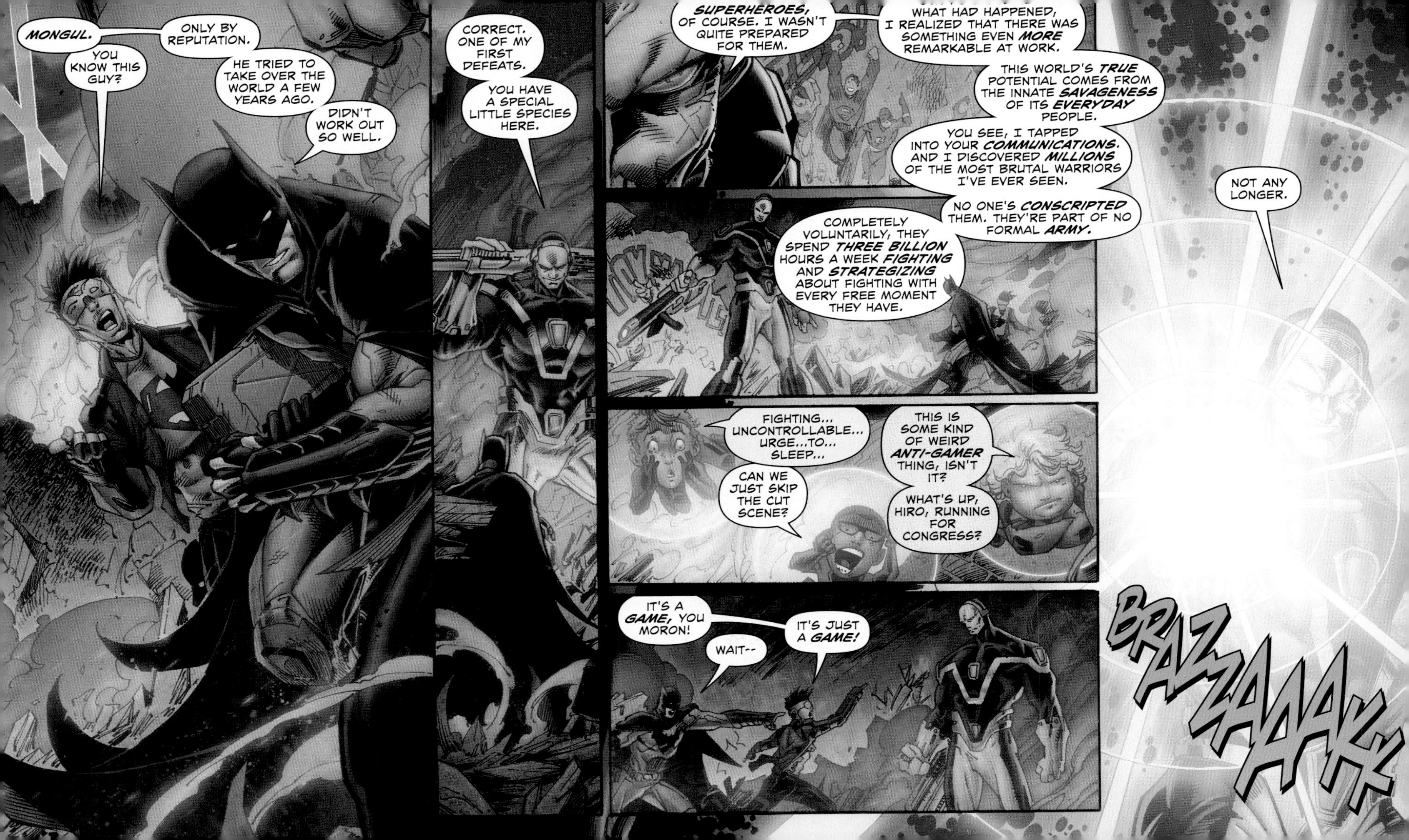
MONGUL.
YOU KNOW THIS GUY?
ONLY BY REPUTATION.
HE TRIED TO TAKE OVER THE WORLD A FEW YEARS AGO.
DIDN'T WORK OUT SO WELL.
CORRECT. ONE OF MY FIRST DEFEATS.
YOU HAVE A SPECIAL LITTLE SPECIES HERE.
SUPERHEROES, OF COURSE. I WASN'T QUITE PREPARED FOR THEM.
WHAT HAD HAPPENED, I REALIZED THAT THERE WAS SOMETHING EVEN MORE REMARKABLE AT WORK.
THIS WORLD'S TRUE POTENTIAL COMES FROM THE INNATE SAVAGENESS OF ITS EVERYDAY PEOPLE.
YOU SEE, I TAPPED INTO YOUR COMMUNICATIONS. AND I DISCOVERED MILLIONS OF THE MOST BRUTAL WARRIORS I'VE EVER SEEN.
NO ONE'S CONSCRIPTED THEM. THEY'RE PART OF NO FORMAL ARMY.
COMPLETELY VOLUNTARILY, THEY SPEND THREE BILLION HOURS A WEEK FIGHTING AND STRATEGIZING ABOUT FIGHTING WITH EVERY FREE MOMENT THEY HAVE.
FIGHTING... UNCONTROLLABLE... URGE...TO... SLEEP...
CAN WE JUST SKIP THE CUT SCENE?
THIS IS SOME KIND OF WEIRD ANTI-GAMER THING, ISN'T IT?
WHAT'S UP, HIRO, RUNNING FOR CONGRESS?
IT'S A GAME, YOU MORON!
WAIT--
IT'S JUST A GAME!
NOT ANY LONGER.
BRAZZAAAKK

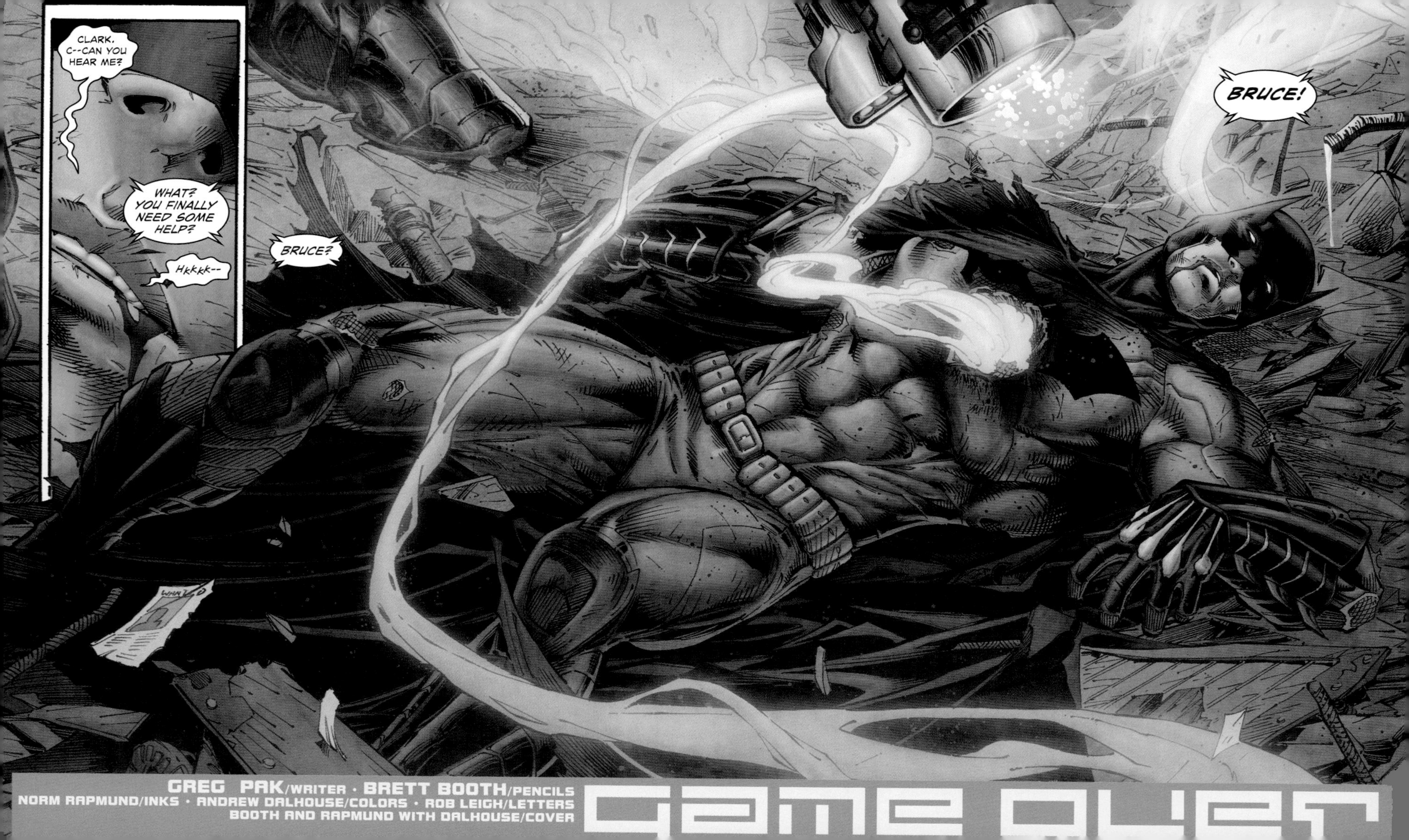
CLARK. C--CAN YOU HEAR ME?
WHAT? YOU FINALLY NEED SOME HELP?
Hkkkk--
BRUCE?
BRUCE!
GREG PAK/WRITER · BRETT BOOTH/PENCILS
NORM RAPMUND/INKS · ANDREW DALHOUSE/COLORS · ROB LEIGH/LETTERS
BOOTH AND RAPMUND WITH DALHOUSE/COVER
GAME OVER

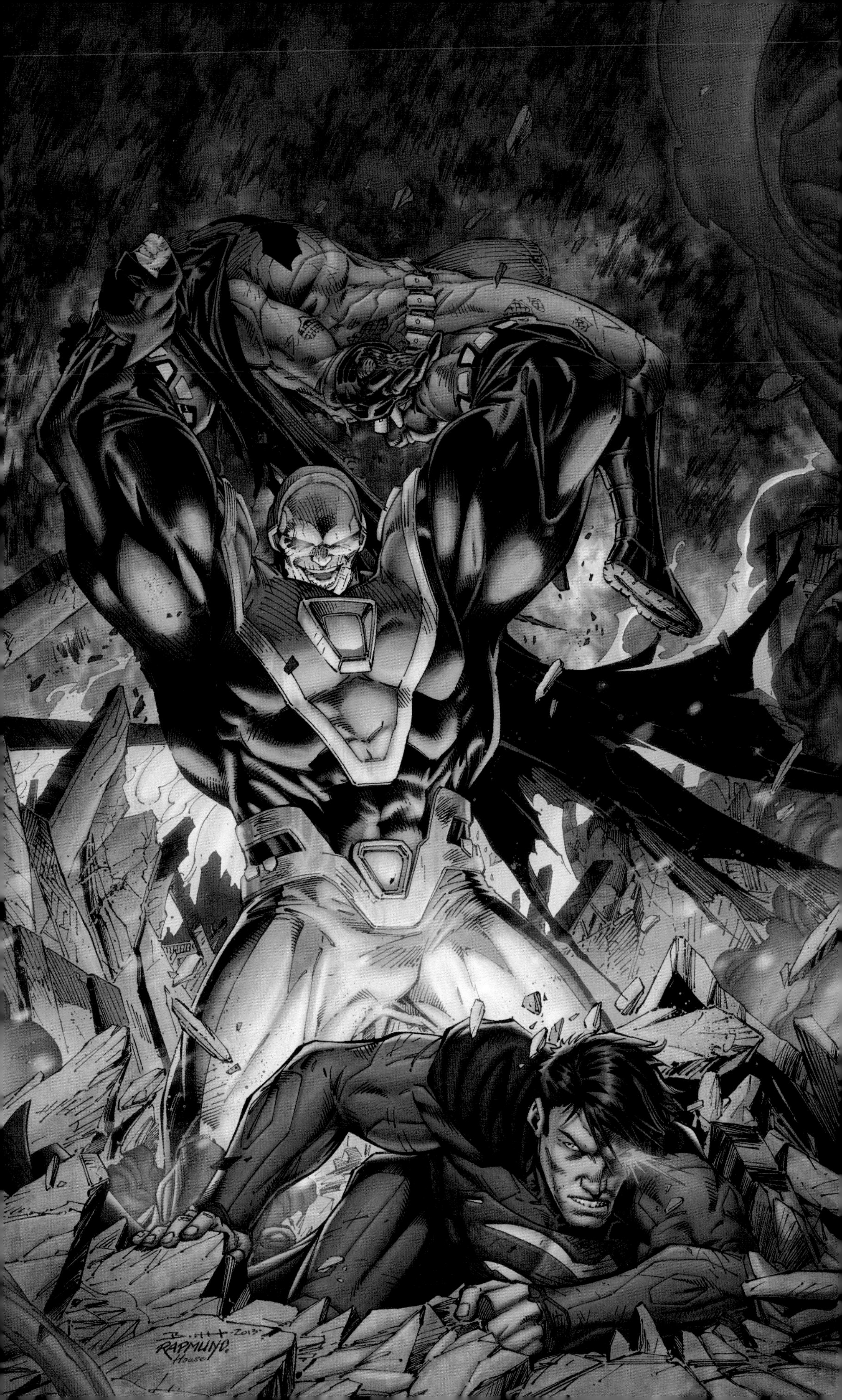

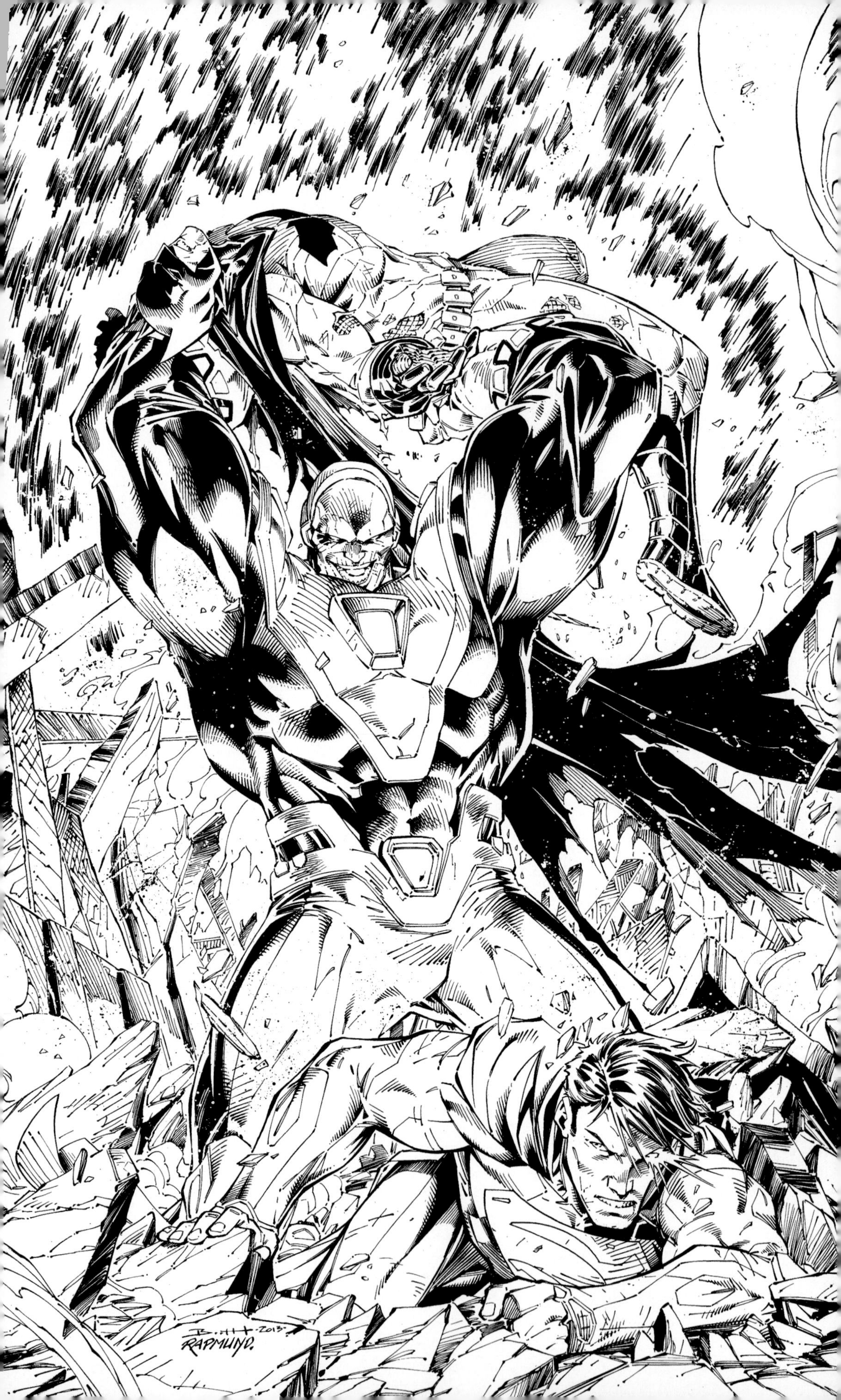
B. HH -2013-
RAPMUND.

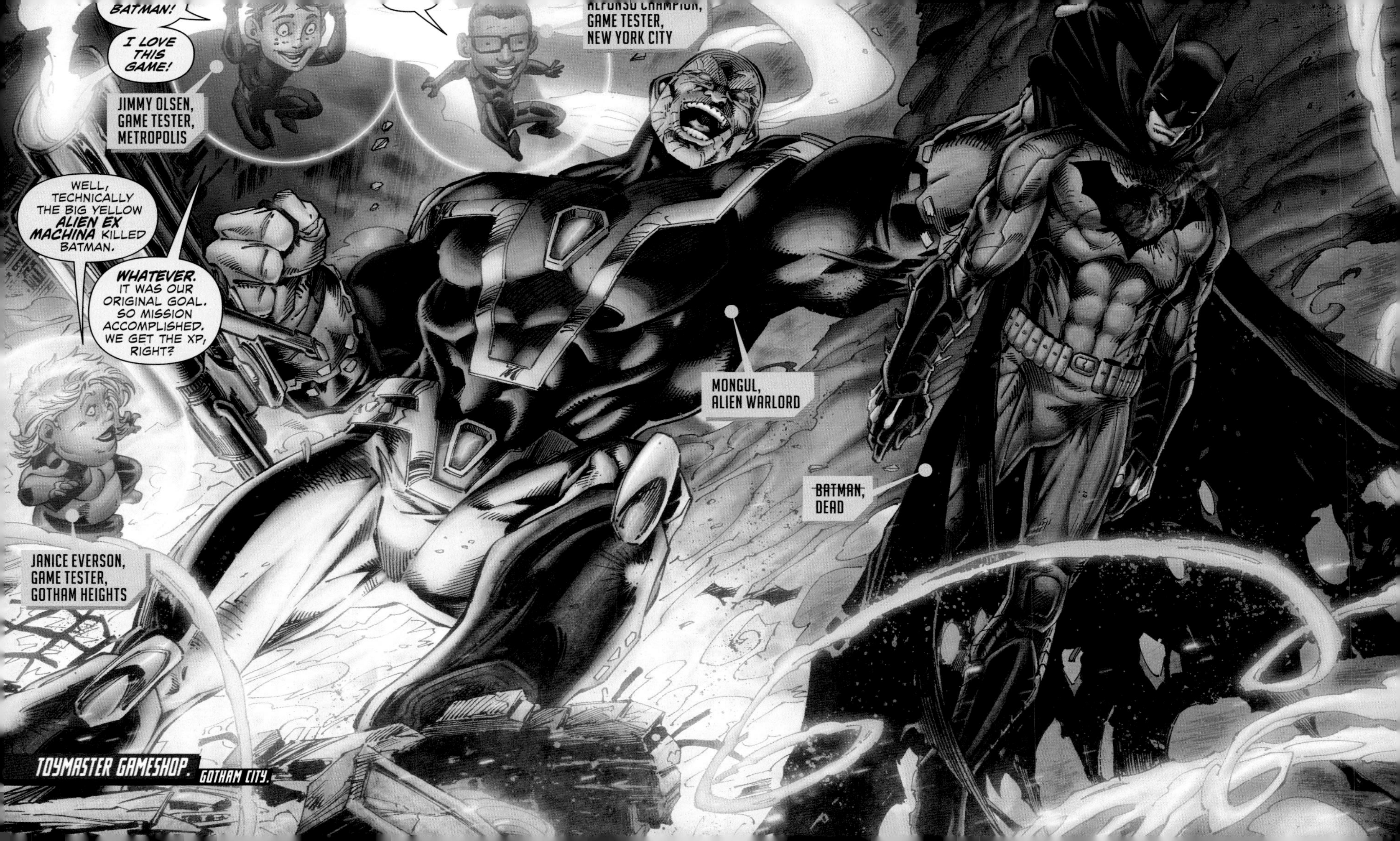
BATMAN!
I LOVE THIS GAME!
JIMMY OLSEN, GAME TESTER, METROPOLIS
GAME TESTER, NEW YORK CITY
WELL, TECHNICALLY THE BIG YELLOW ALIEN EX MACHINA KILLED BATMAN.
WHATEVER. IT WAS OUR ORIGINAL GOAL. SO MISSION ACCOMPLISHED. WE GET THE XP, RIGHT?
JANICE EVERSON, GAME TESTER, GOTHAM HEIGHTS
MONGUL, ALIEN WARLORD
~~BATMAN~~, DEAD
TOYMASTER GAMESHOP. GOTHAM CITY.

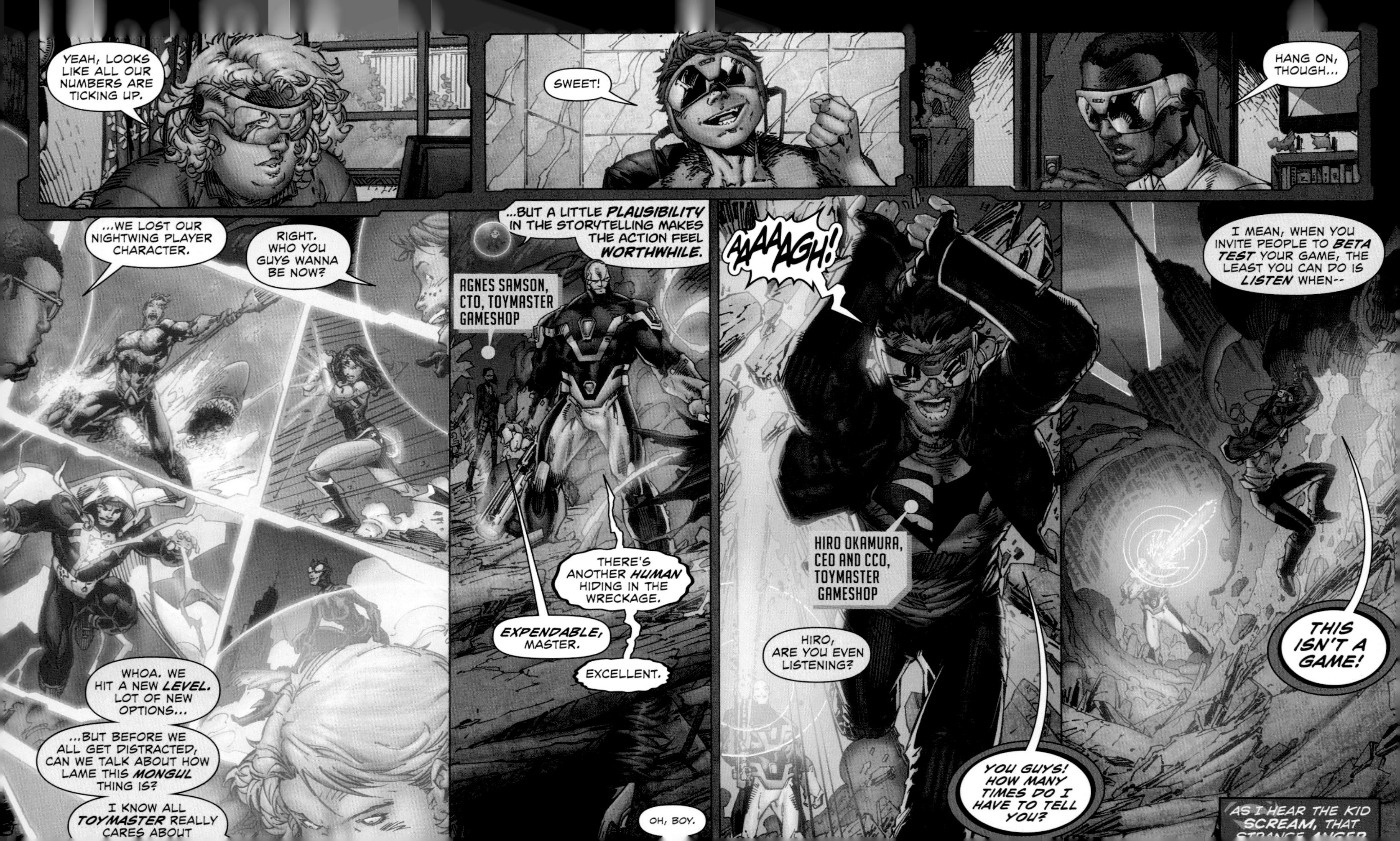
YEAH, LOOKS LIKE ALL OUR NUMBERS ARE TICKING UP.
SWEET!
HANG ON, THOUGH...
...WE LOST OUR NIGHTWING PLAYER CHARACTER.
RIGHT. WHO YOU GUYS WANNA BE NOW?
WHOA. WE HIT A NEW LEVEL. LOT OF NEW OPTIONS...
...BUT BEFORE WE ALL GET DISTRACTED, CAN WE TALK ABOUT HOW LAME THIS MONGUL THING IS?
I KNOW ALL TOYMASTER REALLY CARES ABOUT
...BUT A LITTLE PLAUSIBILITY IN THE STORYTELLING MAKES THE ACTION FEEL WORTHWHILE.
AGNES SAMSON, CTO, TOYMASTER GAMESHOP
THERE'S ANOTHER HUMAN HIDING IN THE WRECKAGE.
EXPENDABLE, MASTER.
EXCELLENT.
OH, BOY.
AAAAAGH!
HIRO OKAMURA, CEO AND CCO, TOYMASTER GAMESHOP
HIRO, ARE YOU EVEN LISTENING?
YOU GUYS! HOW MANY TIMES DO I HAVE TO TELL YOU?
I MEAN, WHEN YOU INVITE PEOPLE TO BETA TEST YOUR GAME, THE LEAST YOU CAN DO IS LISTEN WHEN--
THIS ISN'T A GAME!
AS I HEAR THE KID SCREAM, THAT

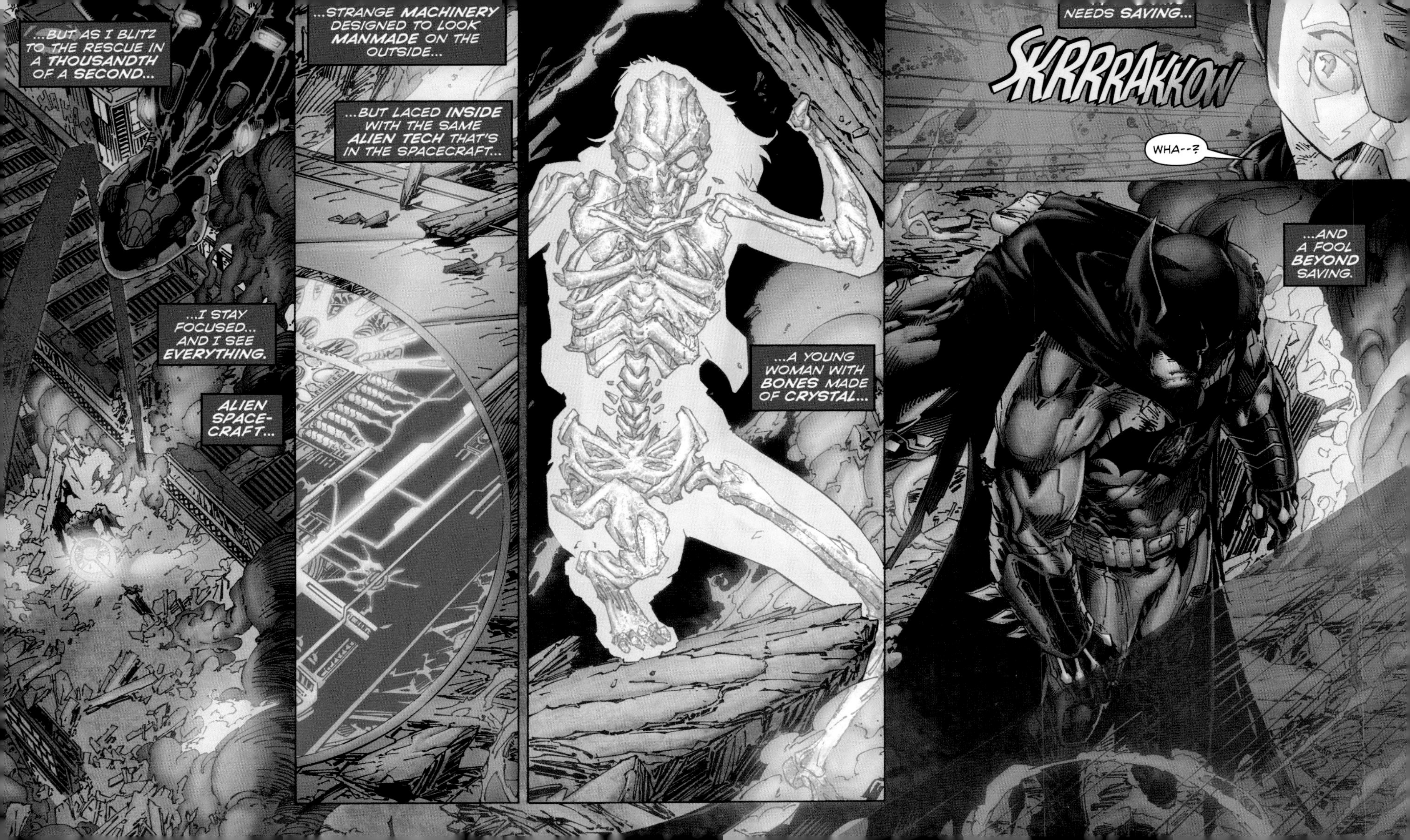
...BUT AS I BLITZ TO THE RESCUE IN A THOUSANDTH OF A SECOND...
...I STAY FOCUSED... AND I SEE EVERYTHING.
ALIEN SPACE-CRAFT...
...STRANGE MACHINERY DESIGNED TO LOOK MANMADE ON THE OUTSIDE...
...BUT LACED INSIDE WITH THE SAME ALIEN TECH THAT'S IN THE SPACECRAFT...
...A YOUNG WOMAN WITH BONES MADE OF CRYSTAL...
NEEDS SAVING...
SKRRRAKKOW
WHA--?
...AND A FOOL BEYOND SAVING.

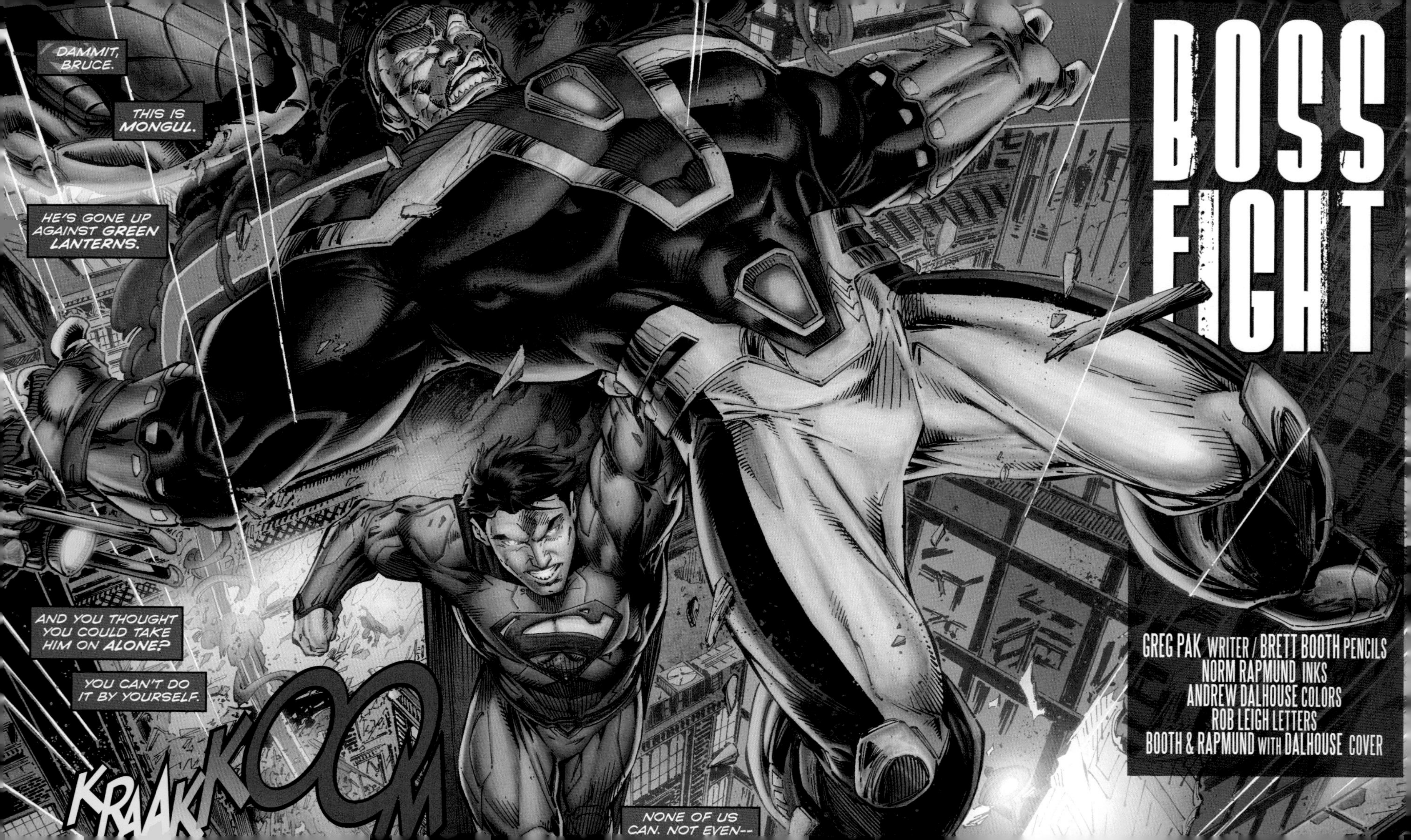

BOSS FIGHT
GREG PAK WRITER / BRETT BOOTH PENCILS
NORM RAPMUND INKS
ANDREW DALHOUSE COLORS
ROB LEIGH LETTERS
BOOTH & RAPMUND WITH DALHOUSE COVER
DAMMIT, BRUCE.
THIS IS MONGUL.
HE'S GONE UP AGAINST GREEN LANTERNS.
AND YOU THOUGHT YOU COULD TAKE HIM ON ALONE?
YOU CAN'T DO IT BY YOURSELF.
KRAAKKOOM
NONE OF US CAN. NOT EVEN--

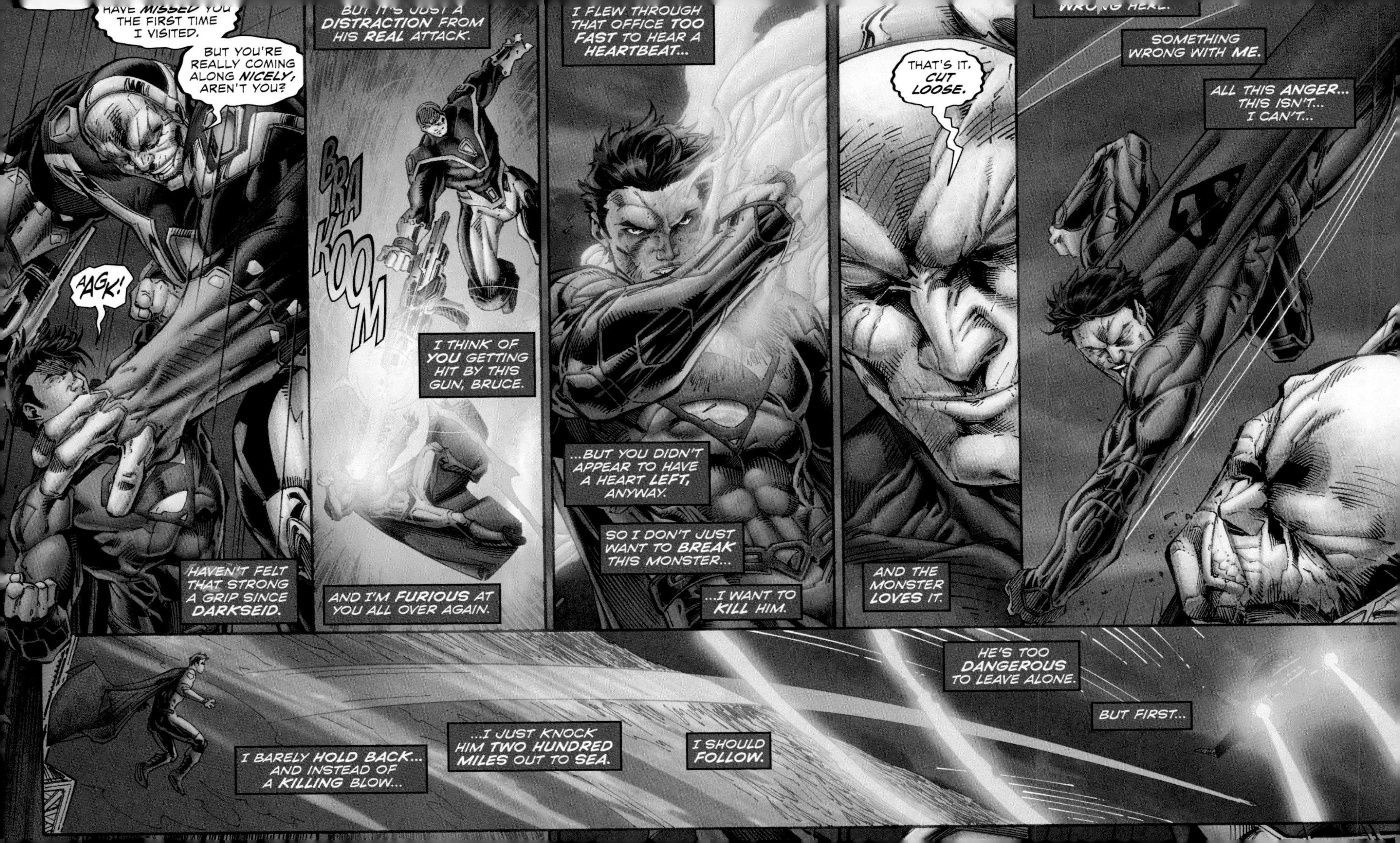

HAVE MISSED YOU THE FIRST TIME I VISITED.
BUT YOU'RE REALLY COMING ALONG NICELY, AREN'T YOU?
AAGK!
HAVEN'T FELT THAT STRONG A GRIP SINCE DARKSEID.
BUT IT'S JUST A DISTRACTION FROM HIS REAL ATTACK.
BRAKOOM
I THINK OF YOU GETTING HIT BY THIS GUN, BRUCE.
AND I'M FURIOUS AT YOU ALL OVER AGAIN.
I FLEW THROUGH THAT OFFICE TOO FAST TO HEAR A HEARTBEAT...
...BUT YOU DIDN'T APPEAR TO HAVE A HEART LEFT, ANYWAY.
SO I DON'T JUST WANT TO BREAK THIS MONSTER...
...I WANT TO KILL HIM.
THAT'S IT. CUT LOOSE.
AND THE MONSTER LOVES IT.
SOMETHING WRONG WITH ME.
ALL THIS ANGER... THIS ISN'T... I CAN'T...
I BARELY HOLD BACK... AND INSTEAD OF A KILLING BLOW...
...I JUST KNOCK HIM TWO HUNDRED MILES OUT TO SEA.
I SHOULD FOLLOW.
HE'S TOO DANGEROUS TO LEAVE ALONE.
BUT FIRST...

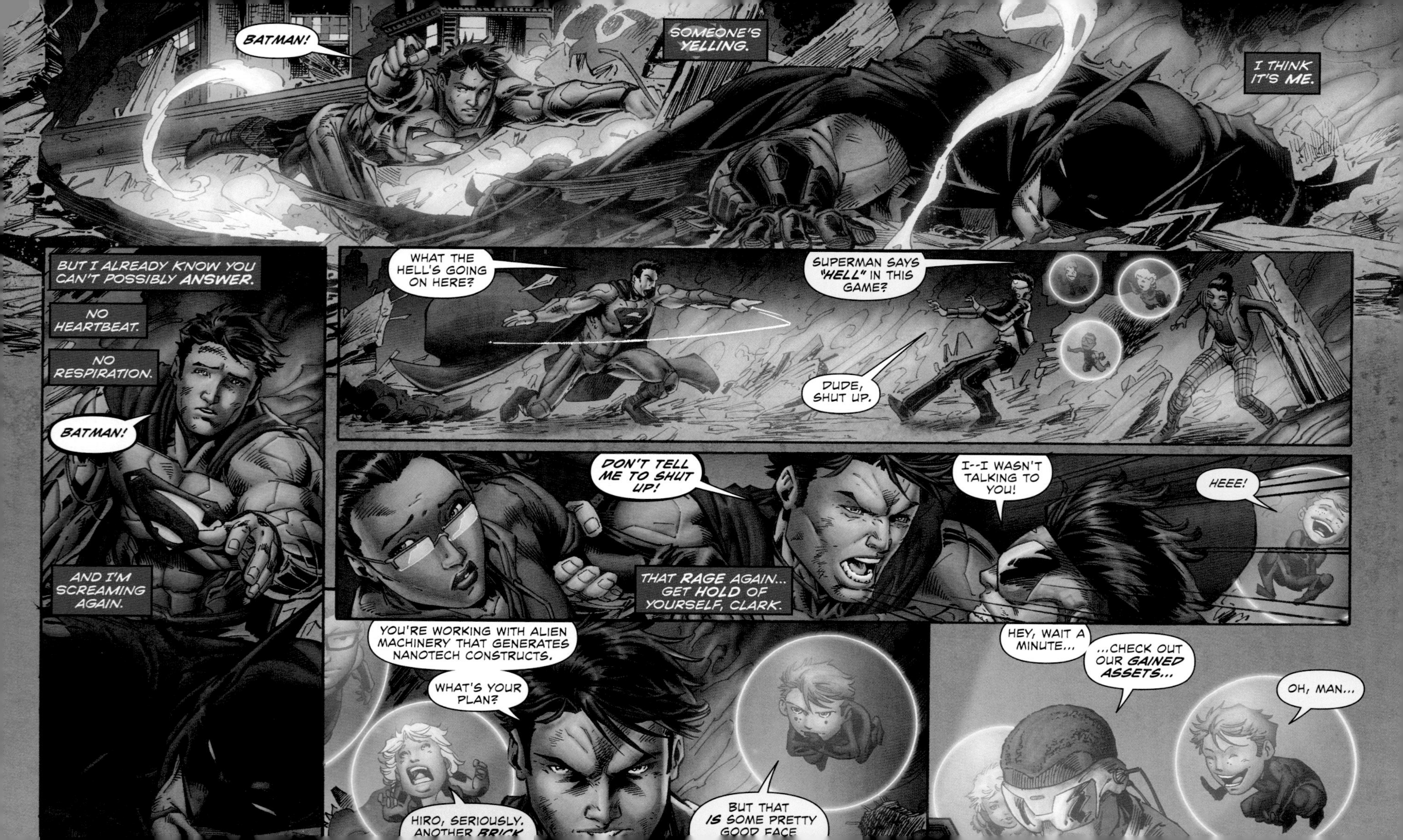
BATMAN!
SOMEONE'S YELLING.
I THINK IT'S ME.
BUT I ALREADY KNOW YOU CAN'T POSSIBLY ANSWER.
NO HEARTBEAT.
NO RESPIRATION.
BATMAN!
AND I'M SCREAMING AGAIN.
WHAT THE HELL'S GOING ON HERE?
SUPERMAN SAYS "HELL" IN THIS GAME?
DUDE, SHUT UP.
DON'T TELL ME TO SHUT UP!
THAT RAGE AGAIN... GET HOLD OF YOURSELF, CLARK.
I--I WASN'T TALKING TO YOU!
HEEE!
YOU'RE WORKING WITH ALIEN MACHINERY THAT GENERATES NANOTECH CONSTRUCTS.
WHAT'S YOUR PLAN?
HIRO, SERIOUSLY. ANOTHER BRICK
BUT THAT IS SOME PRETTY GOOD FACE
HEY, WAIT A MINUTE...
...CHECK OUT OUR GAINED ASSETS...
OH, MAN...

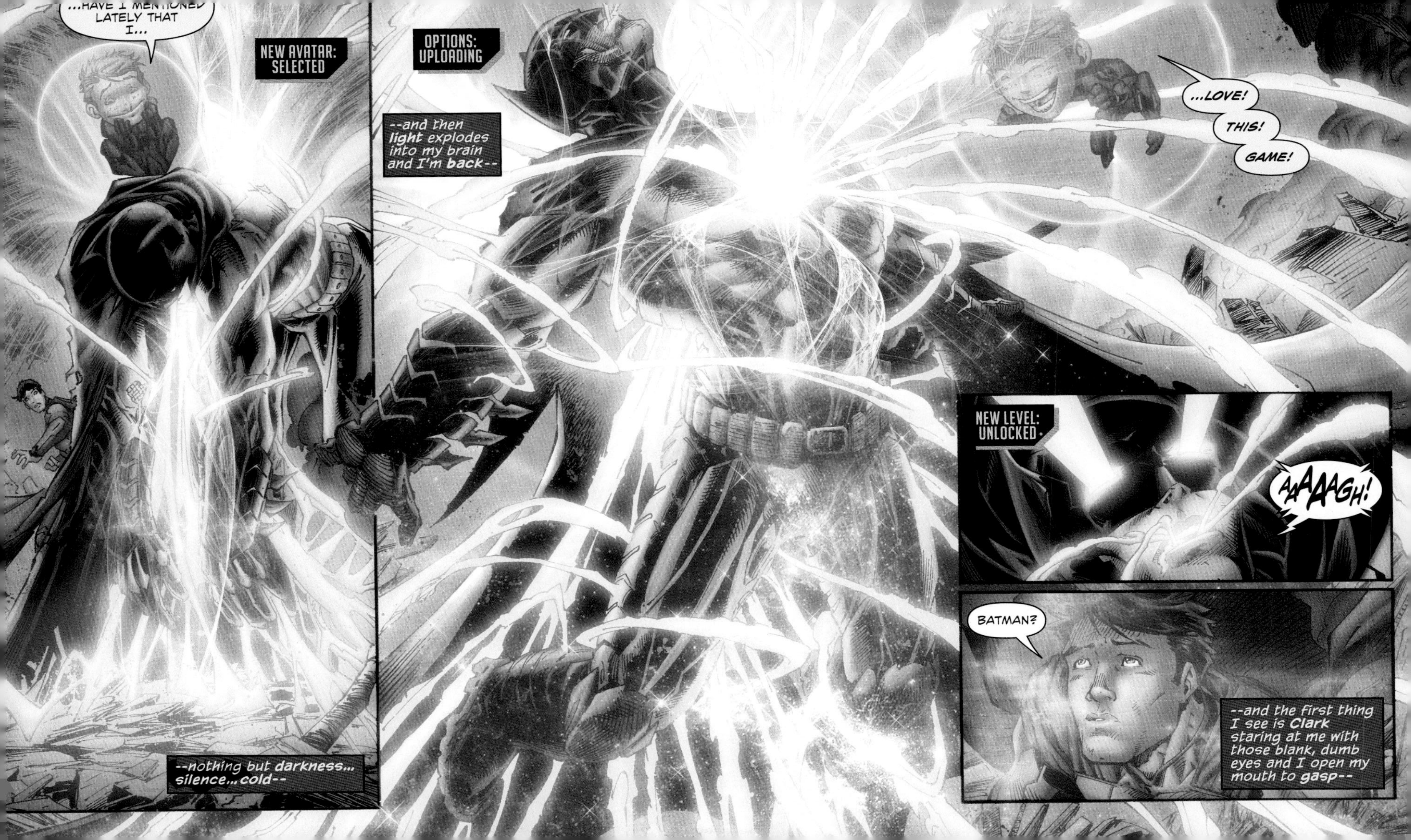
...HAVE I MENTIONED LATELY THAT I...
NEW AVATAR: SELECTED
--nothing but darkness... silence... cold--
OPTIONS: UPLOADING
--and then light explodes into my brain and I'm back--
...LOVE!
THIS!
GAME!
NEW LEVEL: UNLOCKED.
AAAAAGH!
BATMAN?
--and the first thing I see is Clark staring at me with those blank, dumb eyes and I open my mouth to gasp--

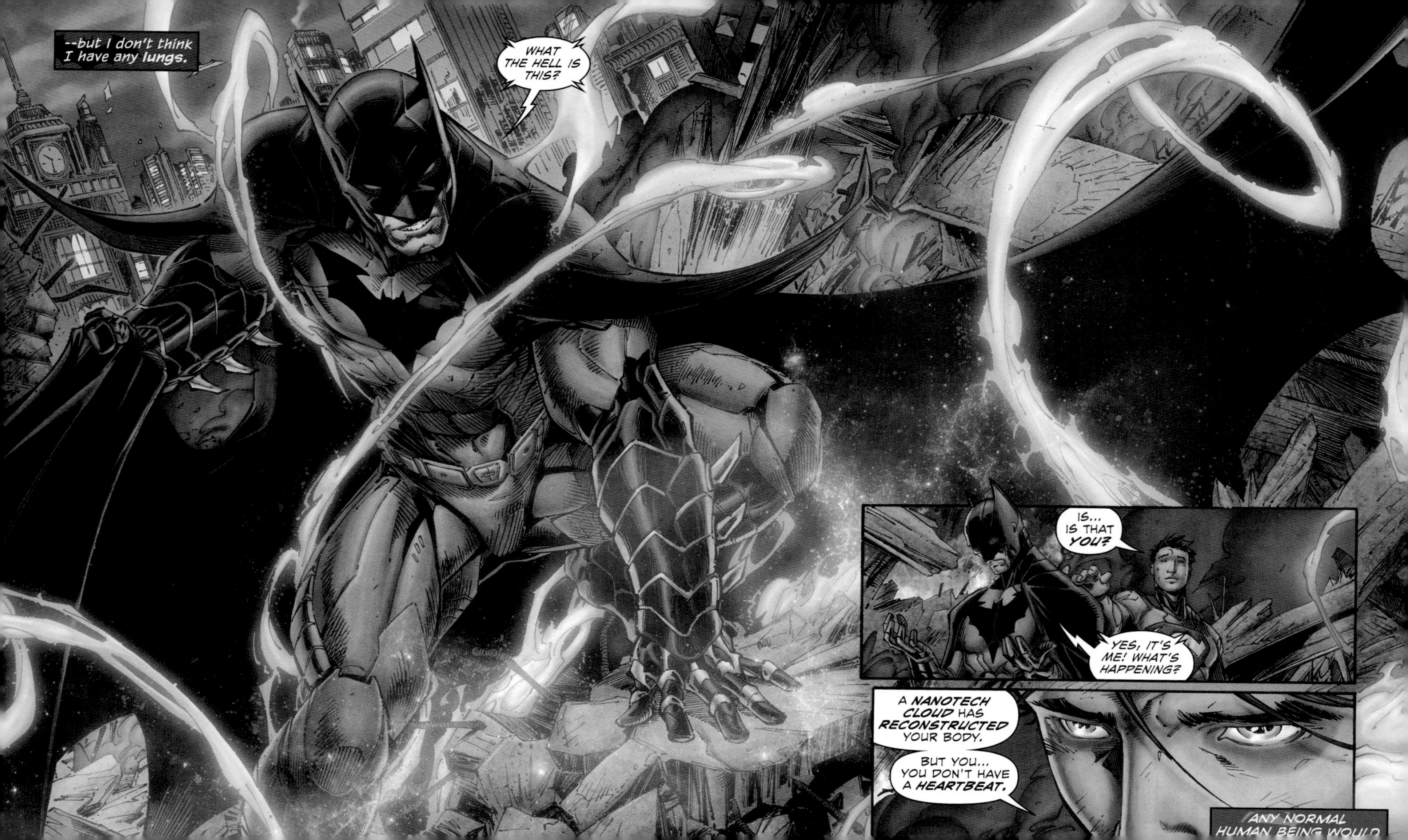
--but I don't think I have any **lungs.**
WHAT THE HELL IS THIS?
IS... IS THAT ***YOU?***
YES, IT'S ME! WHAT'S HAPPENING?
A ***NANOTECH CLOUD*** HAS ***RECONSTRUCTED*** YOUR BODY.
BUT YOU... YOU DON'T HAVE A ***HEARTBEAT.***
ANY NORMAL HUMAN BEING WOULD

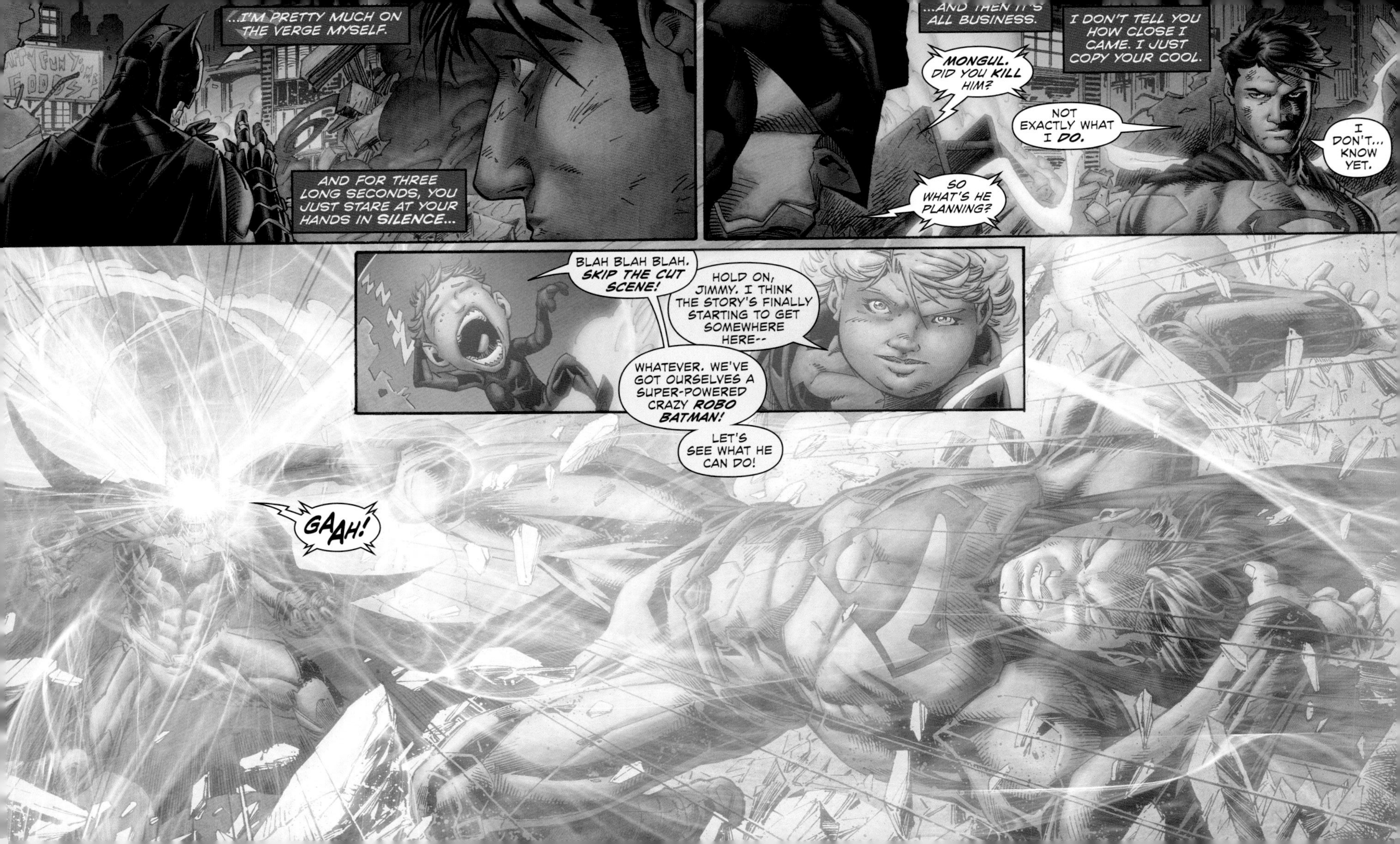
...I'M PRETTY MUCH ON THE VERGE MYSELF.
AND FOR THREE LONG SECONDS, YOU JUST STARE AT YOUR HANDS IN SILENCE...
...AND THEN IT'S ALL BUSINESS.
I DON'T TELL YOU HOW CLOSE I CAME. I JUST COPY YOUR COOL.
MONGUL. DID YOU KILL HIM?
NOT EXACTLY WHAT I DO.
SO WHAT'S HE PLANNING?
I DON'T... KNOW YET.
BLAH BLAH BLAH. SKIP THE CUT SCENE!
HOLD ON, JIMMY. I THINK THE STORY'S FINALLY STARTING TO GET SOMEWHERE HERE--
WHATEVER. WE'VE GOT OURSELVES A SUPER-POWERED CRAZY ROBO BATMAN!
LET'S SEE WHAT HE CAN DO!
GAAH!

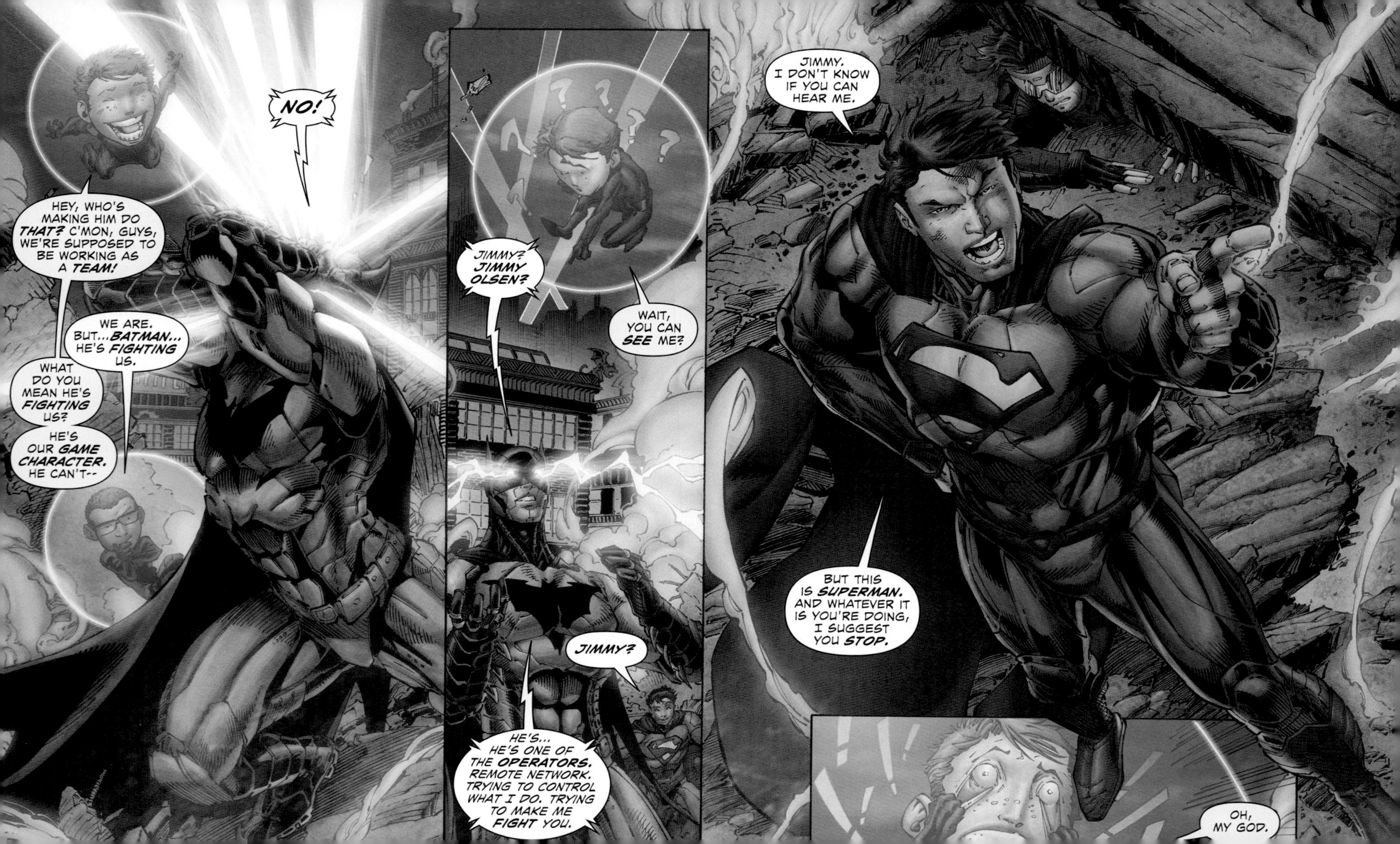
HEY, WHO'S MAKING HIM DO THAT? C'MON, GUYS, WE'RE SUPPOSED TO BE WORKING AS A TEAM!
NO!
WE ARE. BUT...BATMAN... HE'S FIGHTING US.
WHAT DO YOU MEAN HE'S FIGHTING US?
HE'S OUR GAME CHARACTER. HE CAN'T--
JIMMY? JIMMY OLSEN?
WAIT, YOU CAN SEE ME?
JIMMY?
HE'S... HE'S ONE OF THE OPERATORS. REMOTE NETWORK. TRYING TO CONTROL WHAT I DO. TRYING TO MAKE ME FIGHT YOU.
JIMMY. I DON'T KNOW IF YOU CAN HEAR ME.
BUT THIS IS SUPERMAN. AND WHATEVER IT IS YOU'RE DOING, I SUGGEST YOU STOP.
OH, MY GOD.

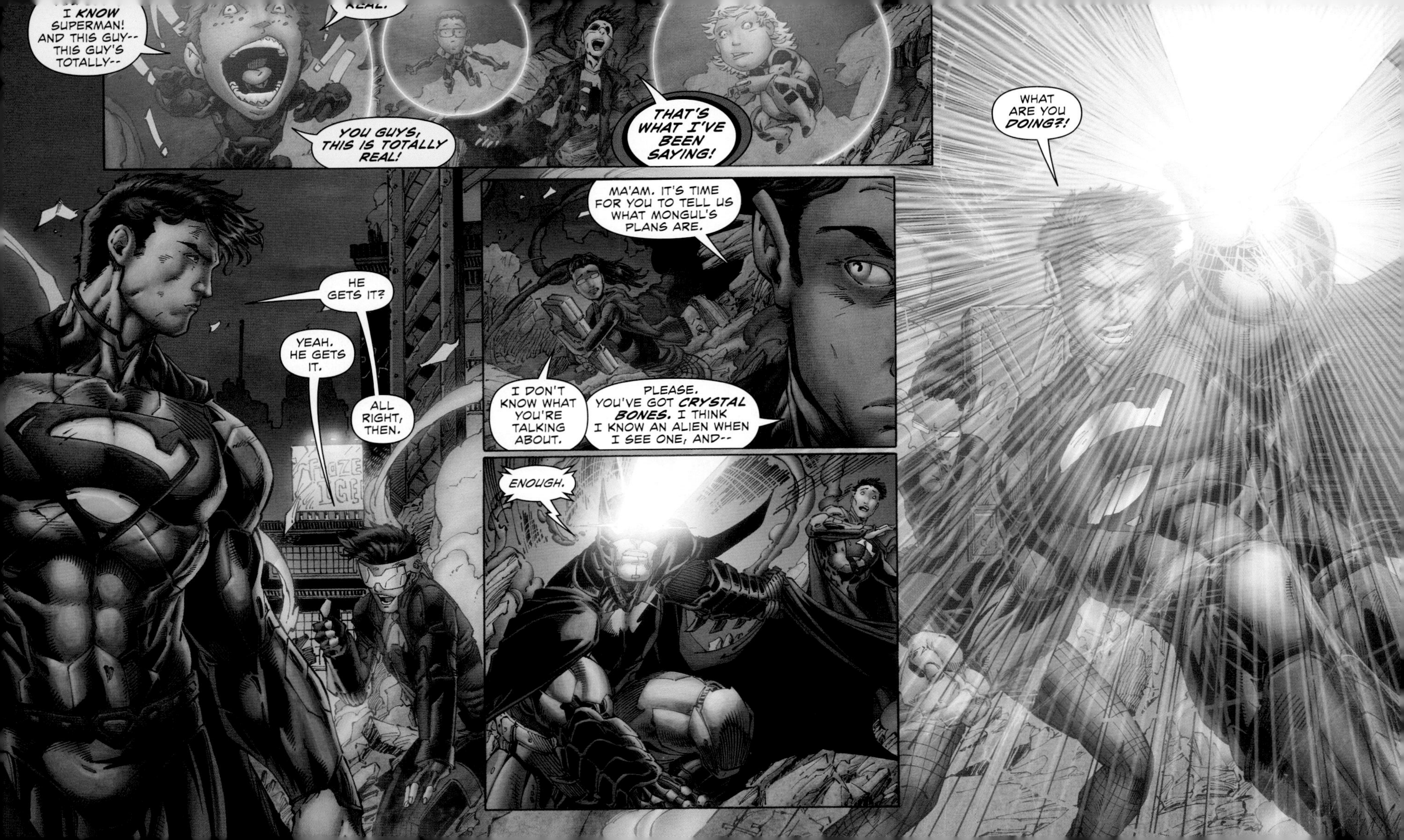
I KNOW SUPERMAN! AND THIS GUY-- THIS GUY'S TOTALLY--
YOU GUYS, THIS IS TOTALLY REAL!
THAT'S WHAT I'VE BEEN SAYING!
HE GETS IT?
YEAH. HE GETS IT.
ALL RIGHT, THEN.
MA'AM. IT'S TIME FOR YOU TO TELL US WHAT MONGUL'S PLANS ARE.
I DON'T KNOW WHAT YOU'RE TALKING ABOUT.
PLEASE. YOU'VE GOT CRYSTAL BONES. I THINK I KNOW AN ALIEN WHEN I SEE ONE, AND--
ENOUGH.
WHAT ARE YOU DOING?!

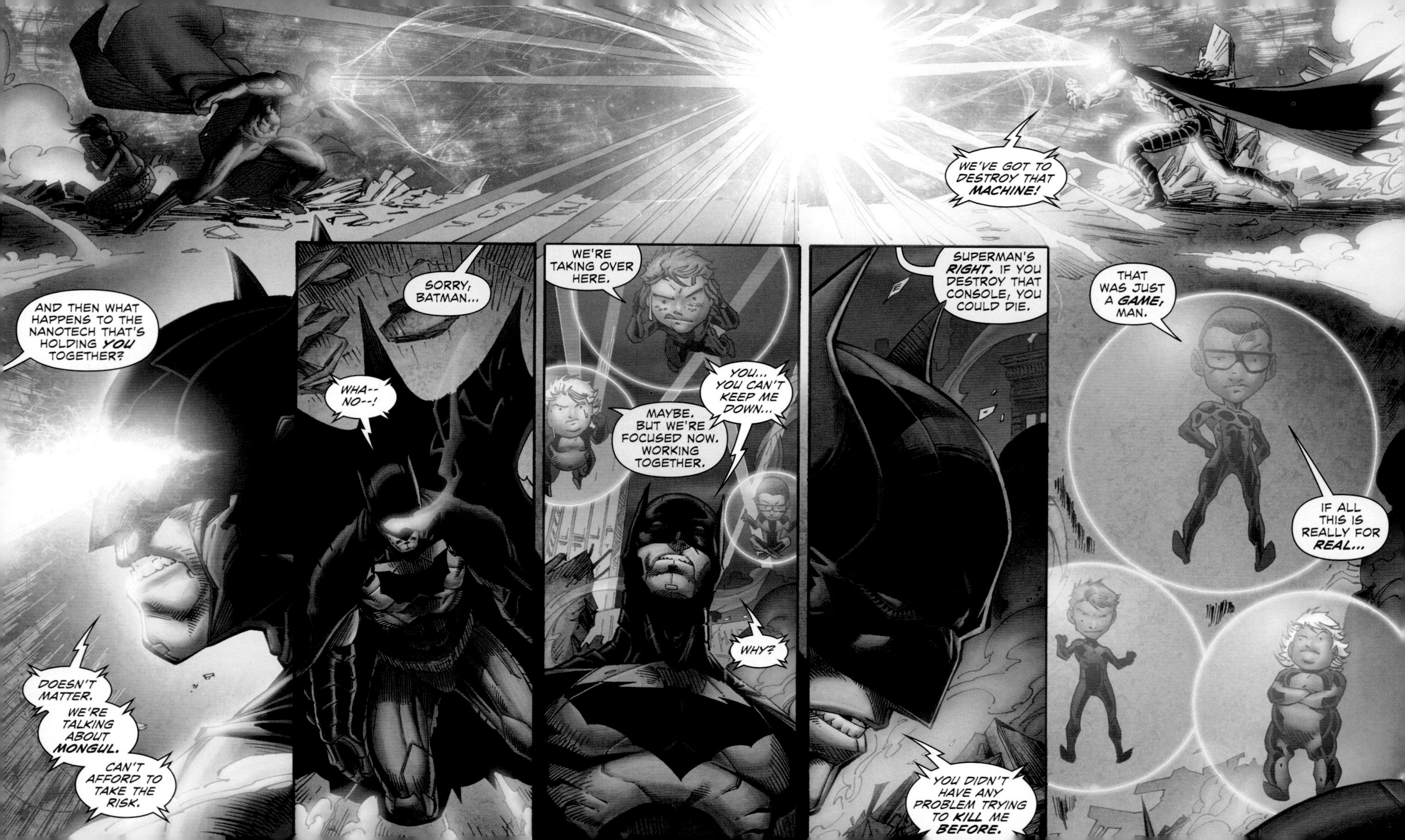
WE'VE GOT TO DESTROY THAT **MACHINE!**
AND THEN WHAT HAPPENS TO THE NANOTECH THAT'S HOLDING **YOU** TOGETHER?
DOESN'T MATTER.
WE'RE TALKING ABOUT **MONGUL.**
CAN'T AFFORD TO TAKE THE RISK.
SORRY, BATMAN...
WHA-- NO--!
WE'RE TAKING OVER HERE.
YOU... YOU CAN'T KEEP ME DOWN...
MAYBE. BUT WE'RE FOCUSED NOW. WORKING TOGETHER.
WHY?
SUPERMAN'S **RIGHT.** IF YOU DESTROY THAT CONSOLE, YOU COULD DIE.
YOU DIDN'T HAVE ANY PROBLEM TRYING TO **KILL** ME **BEFORE.**
THAT WAS JUST A **GAME,** MAN.
IF ALL THIS IS REALLY FOR **REAL...**

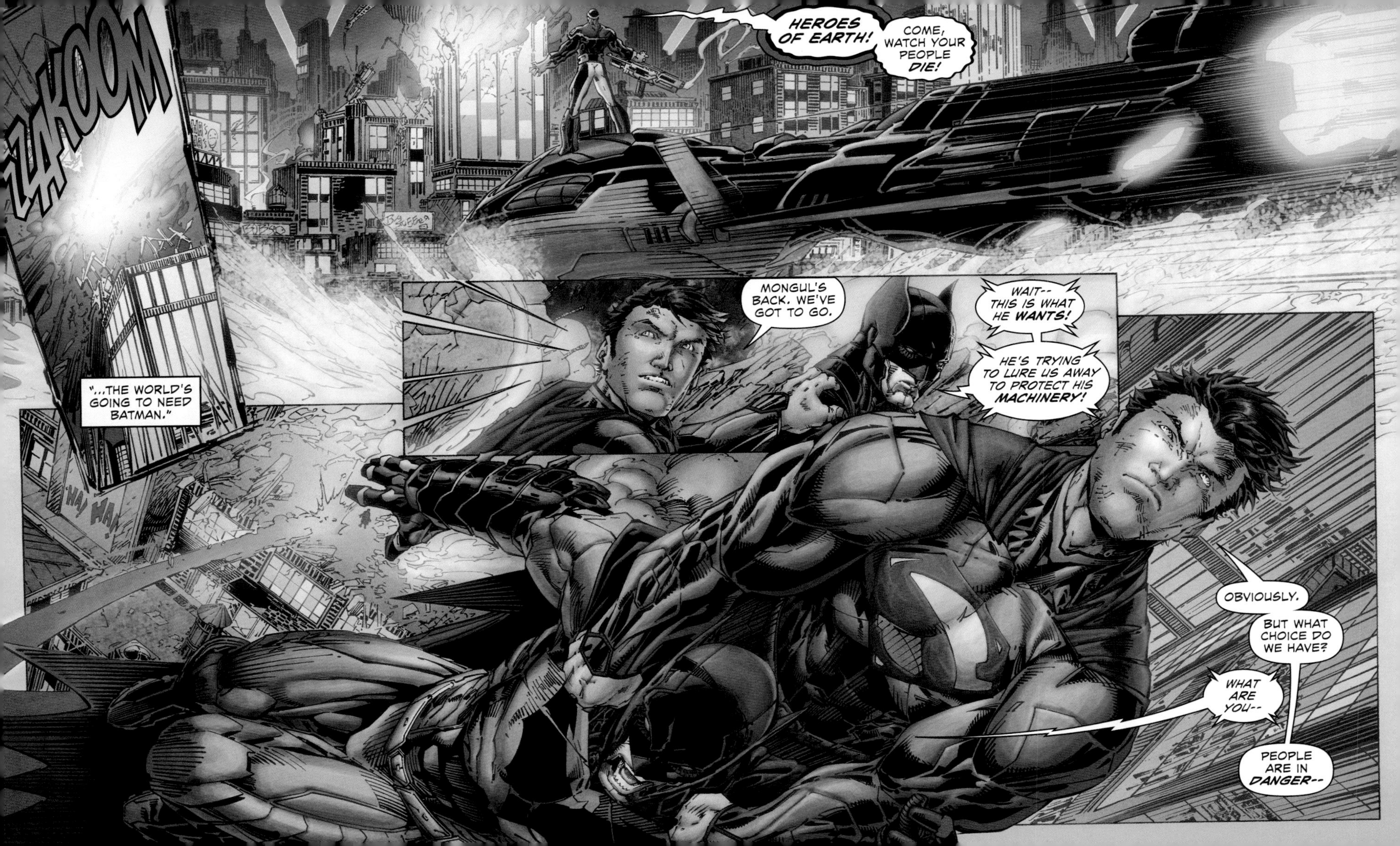
ZZAKOOM
HEROES OF EARTH!
COME, WATCH YOUR PEOPLE DIE!
"...THE WORLD'S GOING TO NEED BATMAN."
MONGUL'S BACK. WE'VE GOT TO GO.
WAIT-- THIS IS WHAT HE WANTS!
HE'S TRYING TO LURE US AWAY TO PROTECT HIS MACHINERY!
OBVIOUSLY.
BUT WHAT CHOICE DO WE HAVE?
WHAT ARE YOU--
PEOPLE ARE IN DANGER--

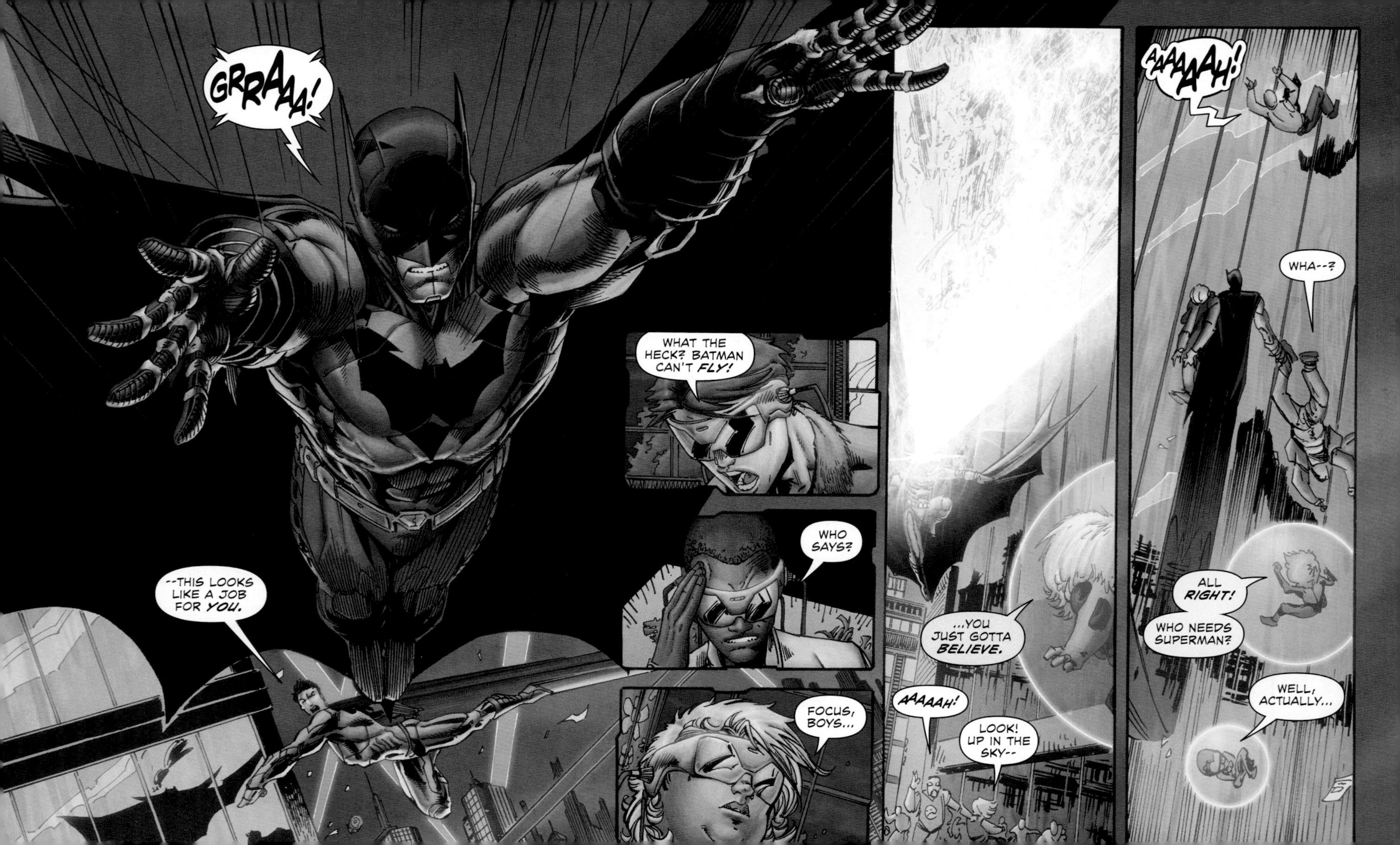
GRRAAAA!
--THIS LOOKS LIKE A JOB FOR *YOU.*
WHAT THE HECK? BATMAN CAN'T *FLY!*
WHO SAYS?
FOCUS, BOYS...
...YOU JUST GOTTA *BELIEVE.*
AAAAAH!
LOOK! UP IN THE SKY--
AAAAAAH!
WHA--?
ALL *RIGHT!*
WHO NEEDS SUPERMAN?
WELL, ACTUALLY...

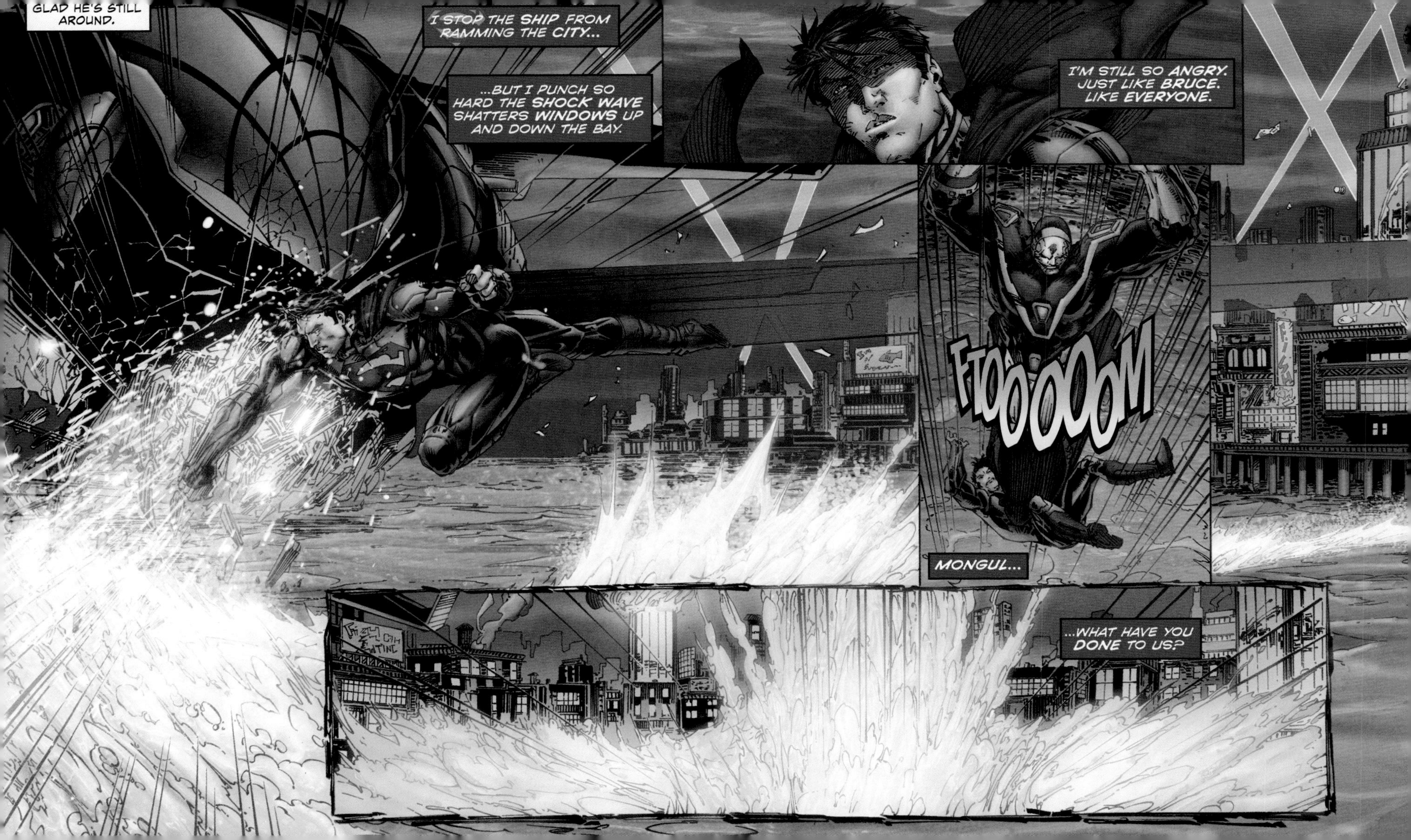
GLAD HE'S STILL AROUND.
I STOP THE SHIP FROM RAMMING THE CITY...
...BUT I PUNCH SO HARD THE SHOCK WAVE SHATTERS WINDOWS UP AND DOWN THE BAY.
I'M STILL SO ANGRY. JUST LIKE BRUCE. LIKE EVERYONE.
FTOOOOOM
MONGUL...
...WHAT HAVE YOU DONE TO US?

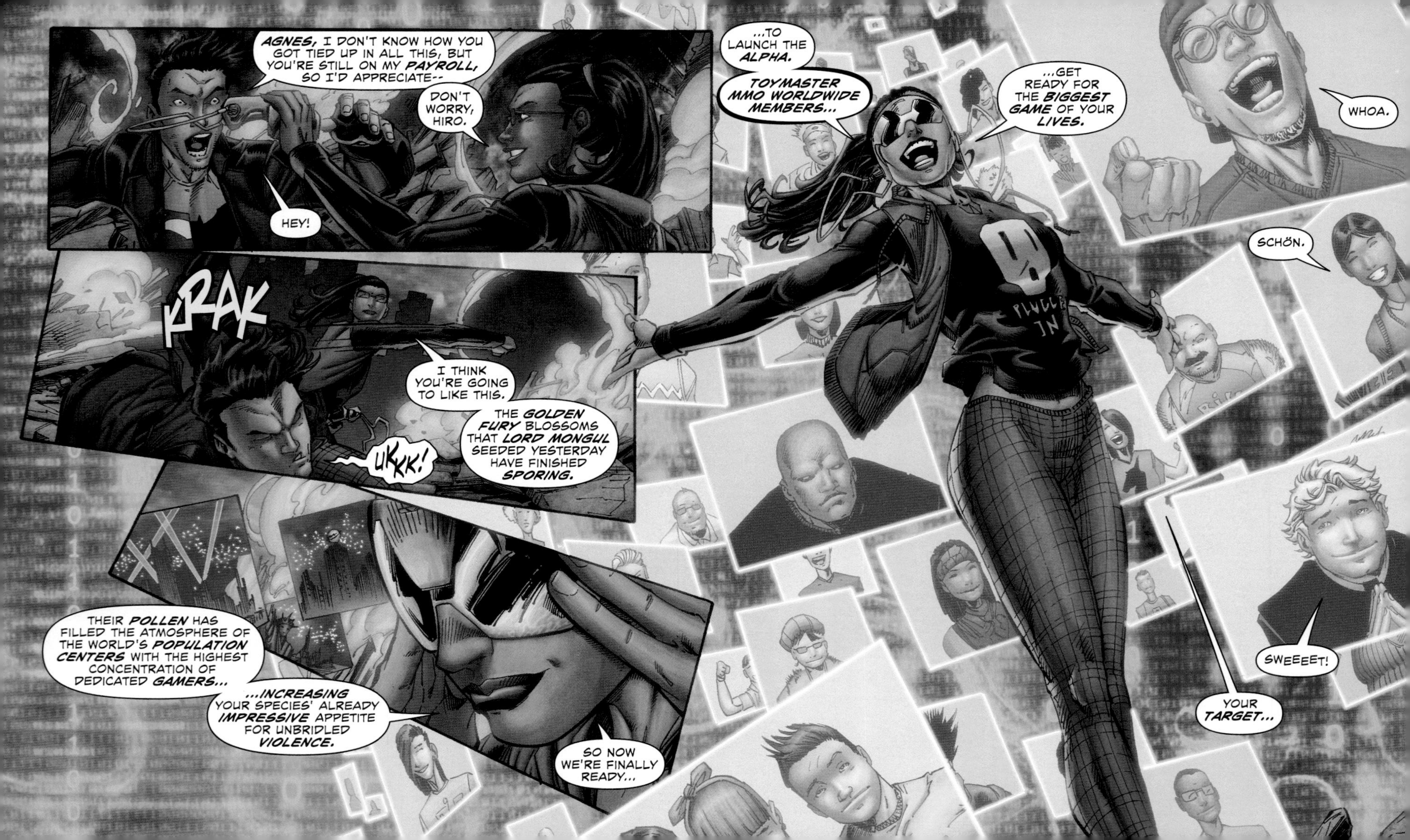

AGNES, I DON'T KNOW HOW YOU GOT TIED UP IN ALL THIS, BUT YOU'RE STILL ON MY PAYROLL, SO I'D APPRECIATE--
DON'T WORRY, HIRO.
HEY!
KRAK
I THINK YOU'RE GOING TO LIKE THIS.
THE GOLDEN FURY BLOSSOMS THAT LORD MONGUL SEEDED YESTERDAY HAVE FINISHED SPORING.
UKKK!
THEIR POLLEN HAS FILLED THE ATMOSPHERE OF THE WORLD'S POPULATION CENTERS WITH THE HIGHEST CONCENTRATION OF DEDICATED GAMERS...
...INCREASING YOUR SPECIES' ALREADY IMPRESSIVE APPETITE FOR UNBRIDLED VIOLENCE.
SO NOW WE'RE FINALLY READY...
...TO LAUNCH THE ALPHA.
TOYMASTER MMO WORLDWIDE MEMBERS...
...GET READY FOR THE BIGGEST GAME OF YOUR LIVES.
WHOA.
SCHÖN.
SWEEEET!
YOUR TARGET...

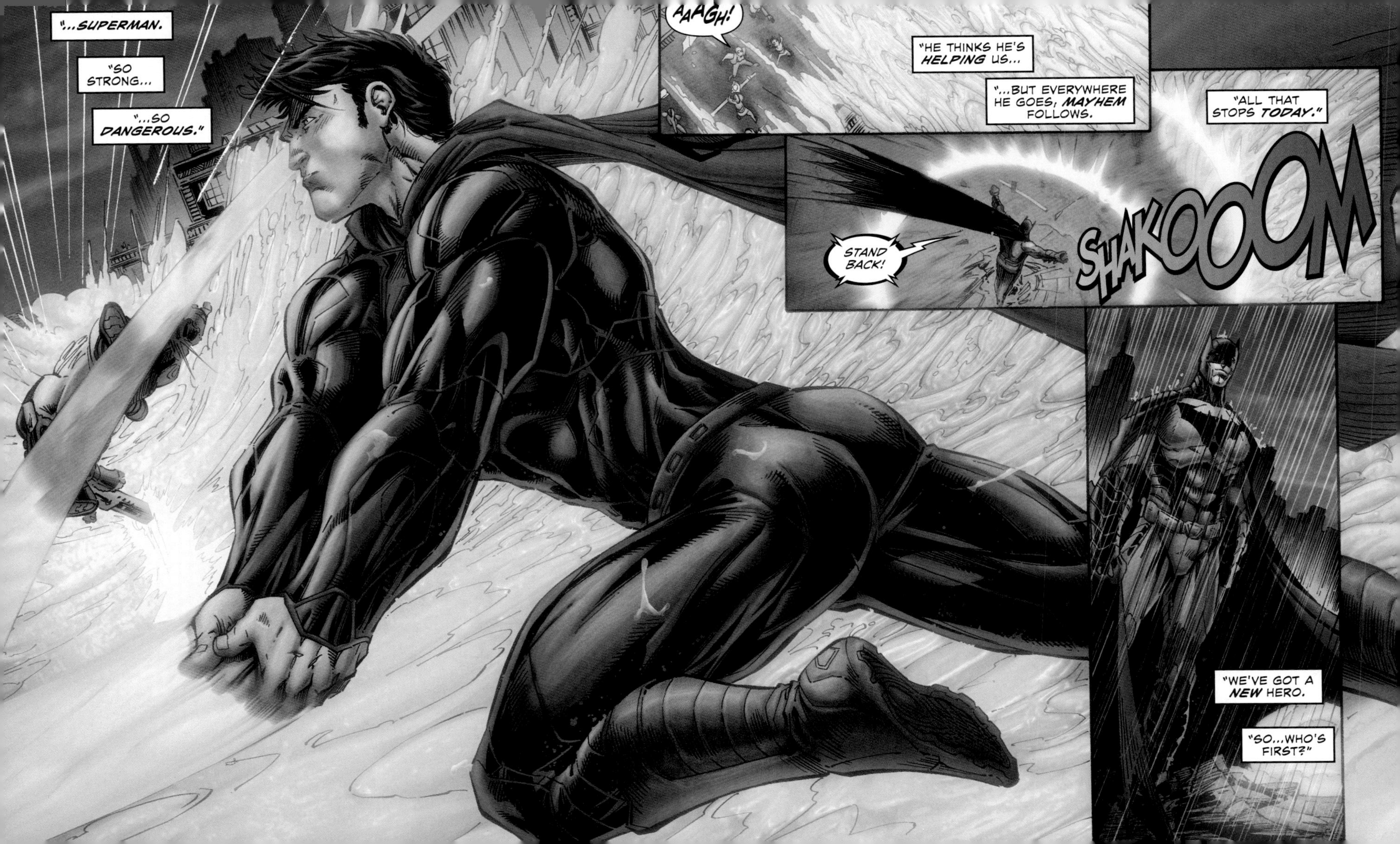
"...SUPERMAN.
"SO STRONG...
"...SO DANGEROUS."
AAAGH!
"HE THINKS HE'S HELPING US...
"...BUT EVERYWHERE HE GOES, MAYHEM FOLLOWS.
"ALL THAT STOPS TODAY."
STAND BACK!
SHAKOOOM
"WE'VE GOT A NEW HERO.
"SO...WHO'S FIRST?"

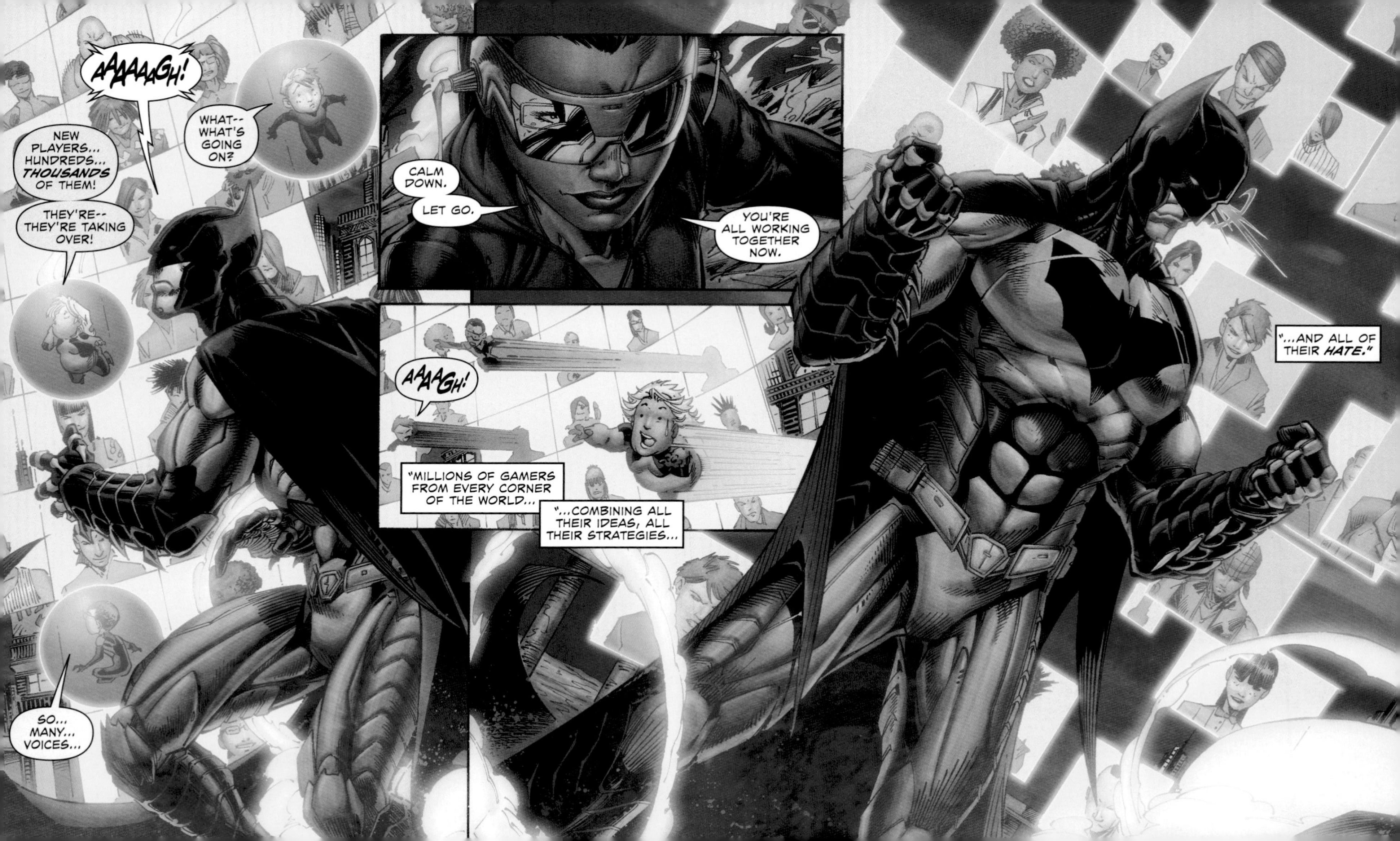
AAAAAAGH!
NEW PLAYERS... HUNDREDS... *THOUSANDS* OF THEM!
WHAT-- WHAT'S GOING ON?
THEY'RE-- THEY'RE TAKING OVER!
SO... MANY... VOICES...
CALM DOWN.
LET GO.
YOU'RE ALL WORKING TOGETHER NOW.
AAAAGH!
"MILLIONS OF GAMERS FROM EVERY CORNER OF THE WORLD...
"...COMBINING ALL THEIR IDEAS, ALL THEIR STRATEGIES...
"...AND ALL OF THEIR *HATE.*"

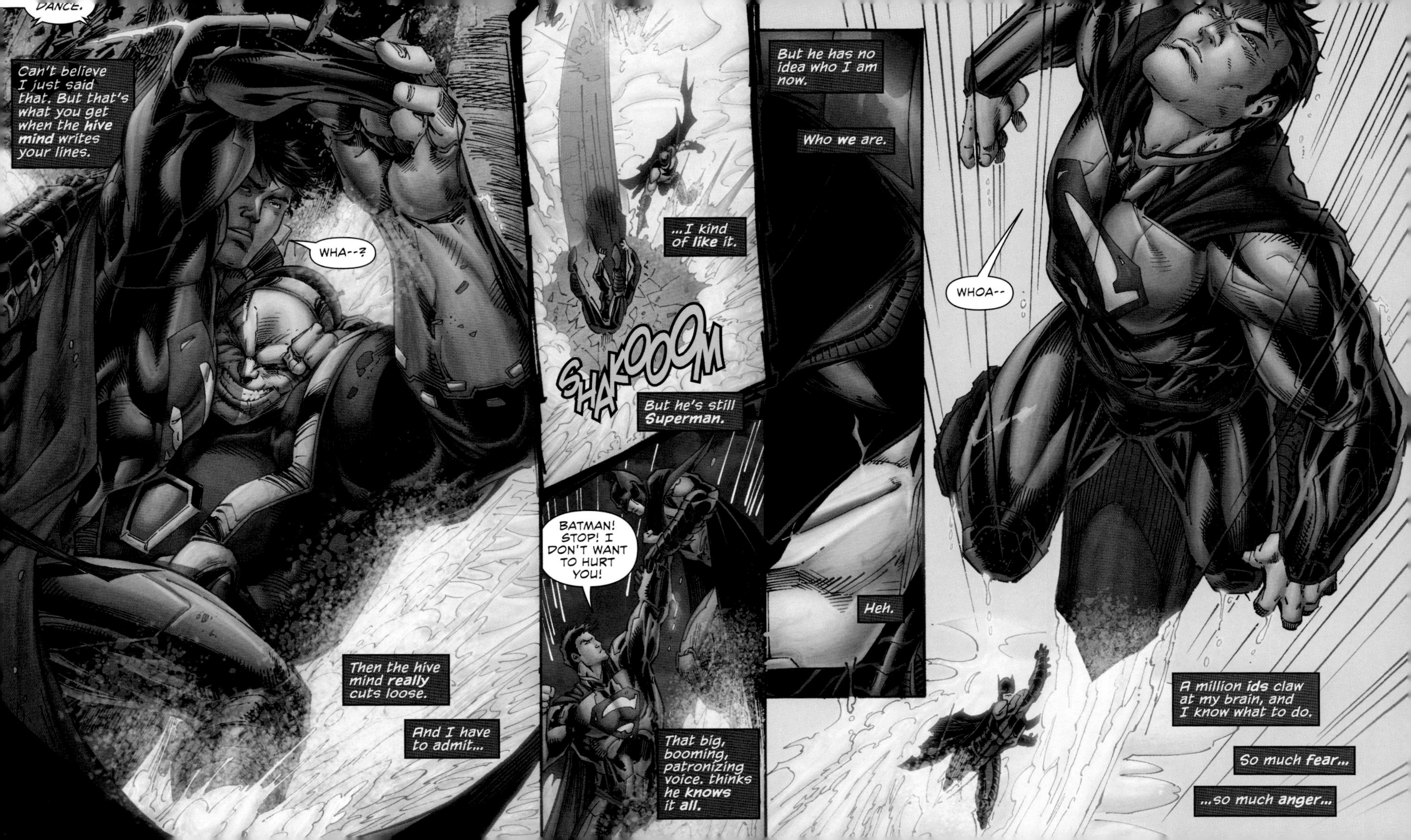
DANCE.
Can't believe I just said that. But that's what you get when the **hive mind** writes your lines.
WHA--?
Then the hive mind **really** cuts loose.
And I have to admit...
...I kind of **like** it.
SHAKOOOM
But he's still **Superman**.
BATMAN! STOP! I DON'T WANT TO HURT YOU!
That big, booming, patronizing voice. thinks he **knows** it **all**.
But he has no idea who I am now.
Who **we** are.
Heh.
WHOA--
A million **ids** claw at my brain, and I know what to do.
So much **fear**...
...so much **anger**...

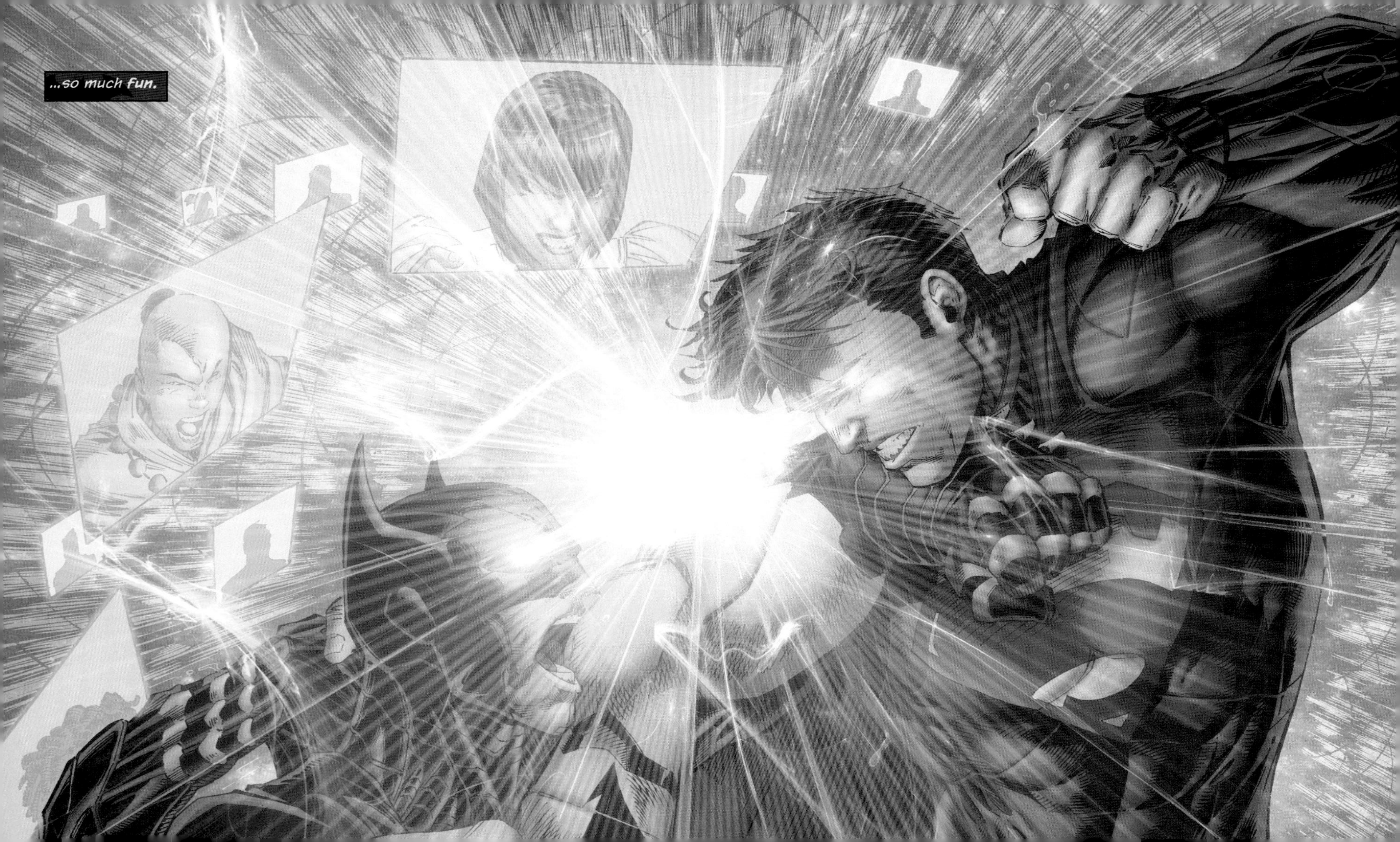
...so much fun.

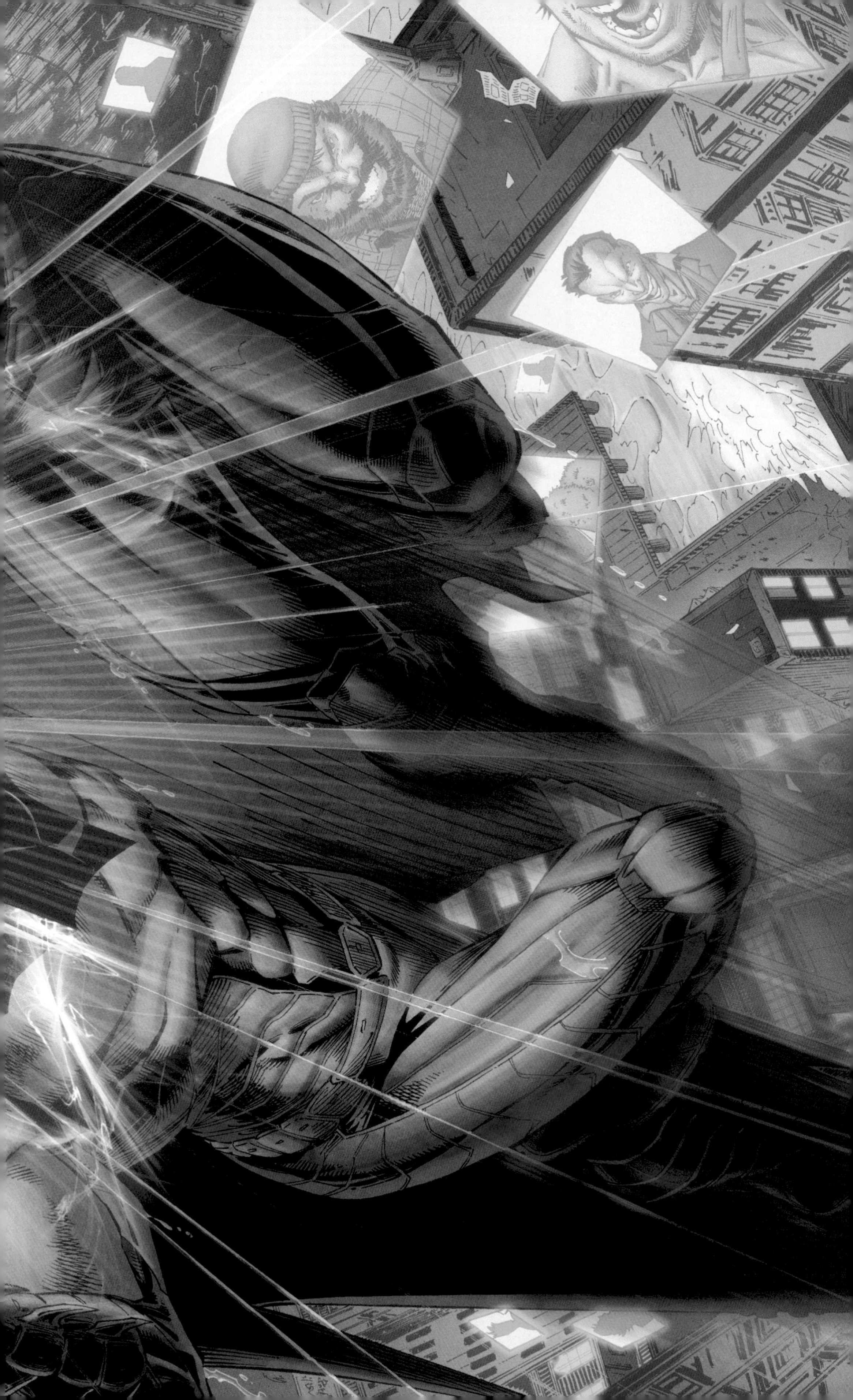

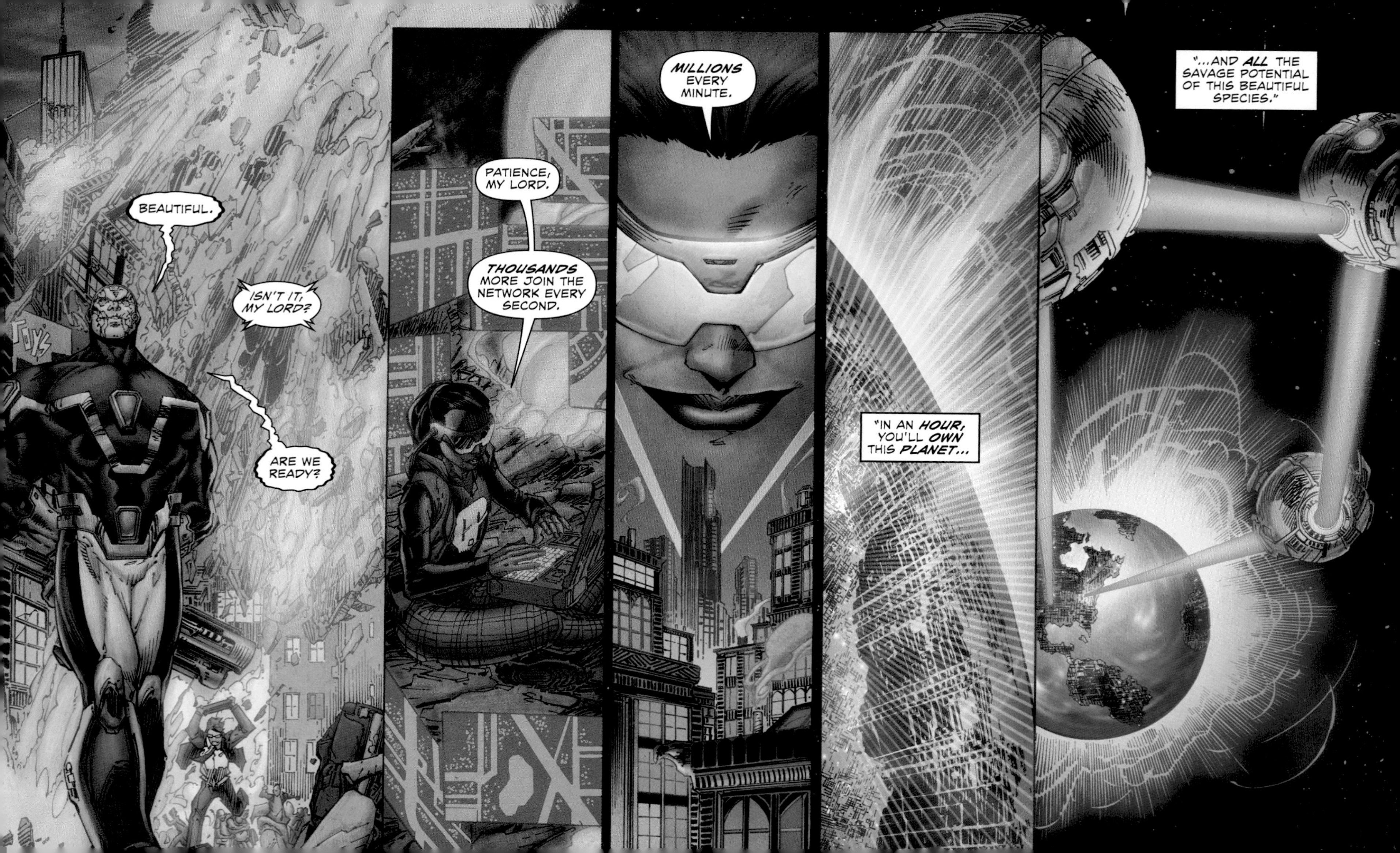

ARE WE READY?
ISN'T IT, MY LORD?
BEAUTIFUL.
PATIENCE, MY LORD.
THOUSANDS MORE JOIN THE NETWORK EVERY SECOND.
MILLIONS EVERY MINUTE.
"IN AN HOUR, YOU'LL OWN THIS PLANET...
"...AND ALL THE SAVAGE POTENTIAL OF THIS BEAUTIFUL SPECIES."

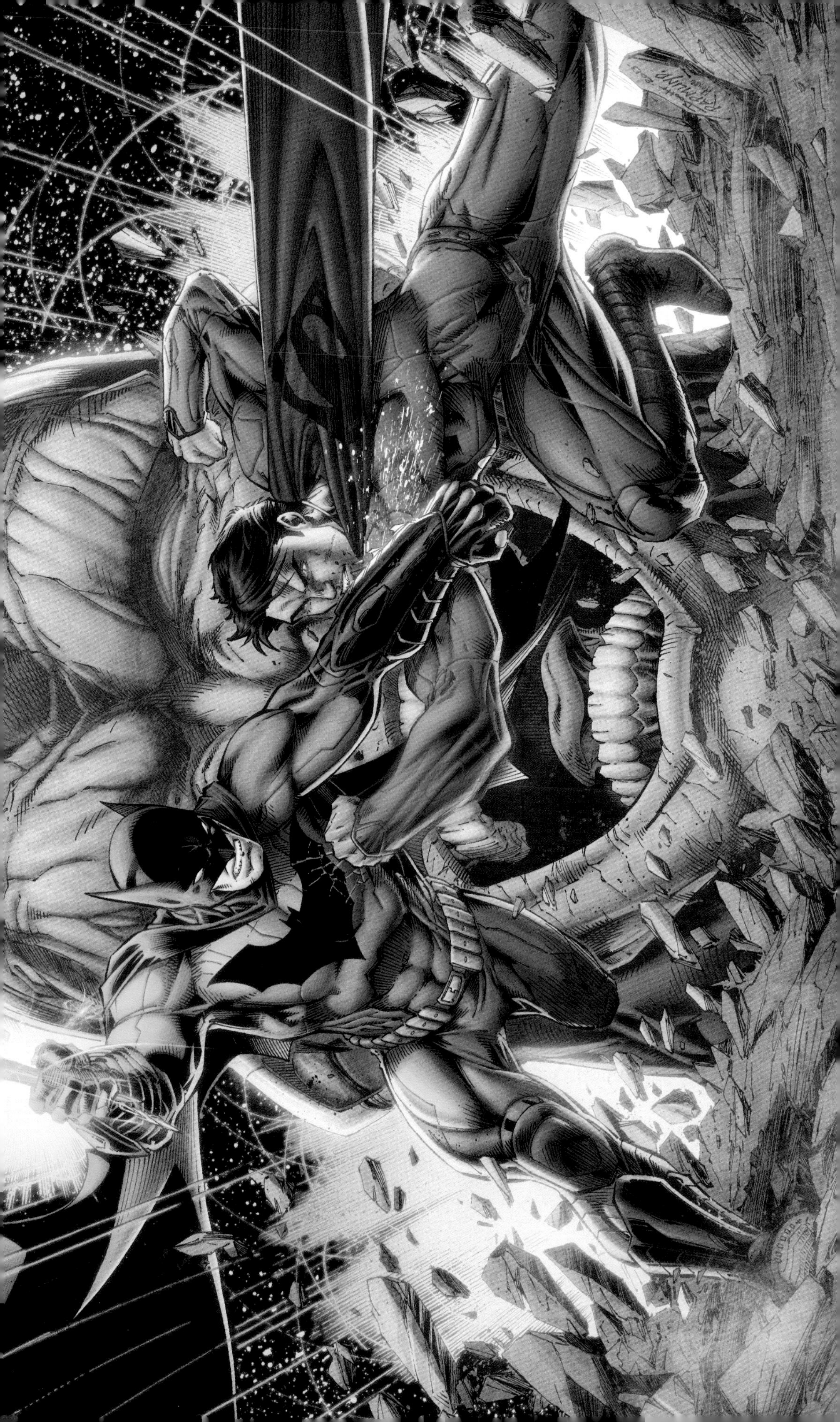

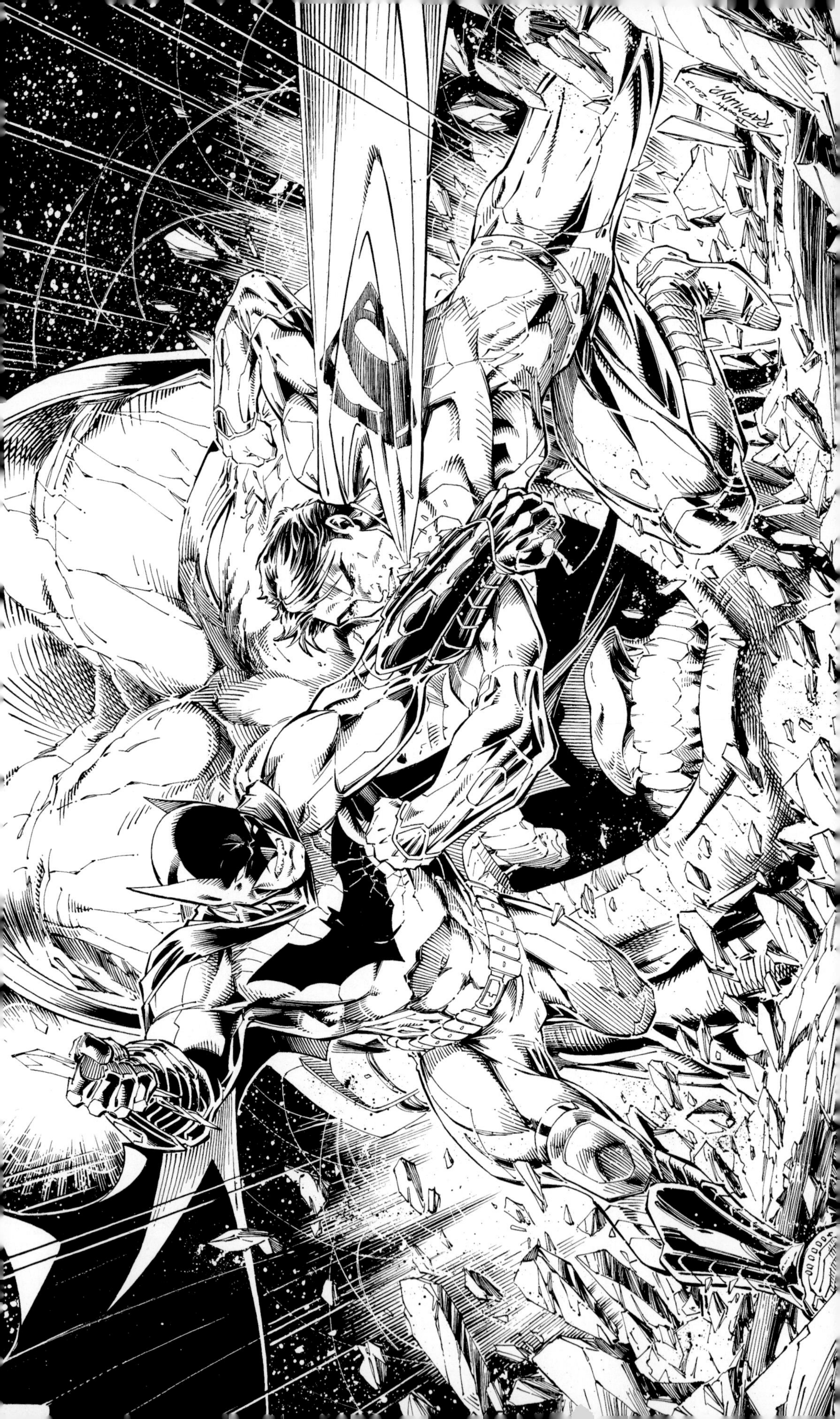

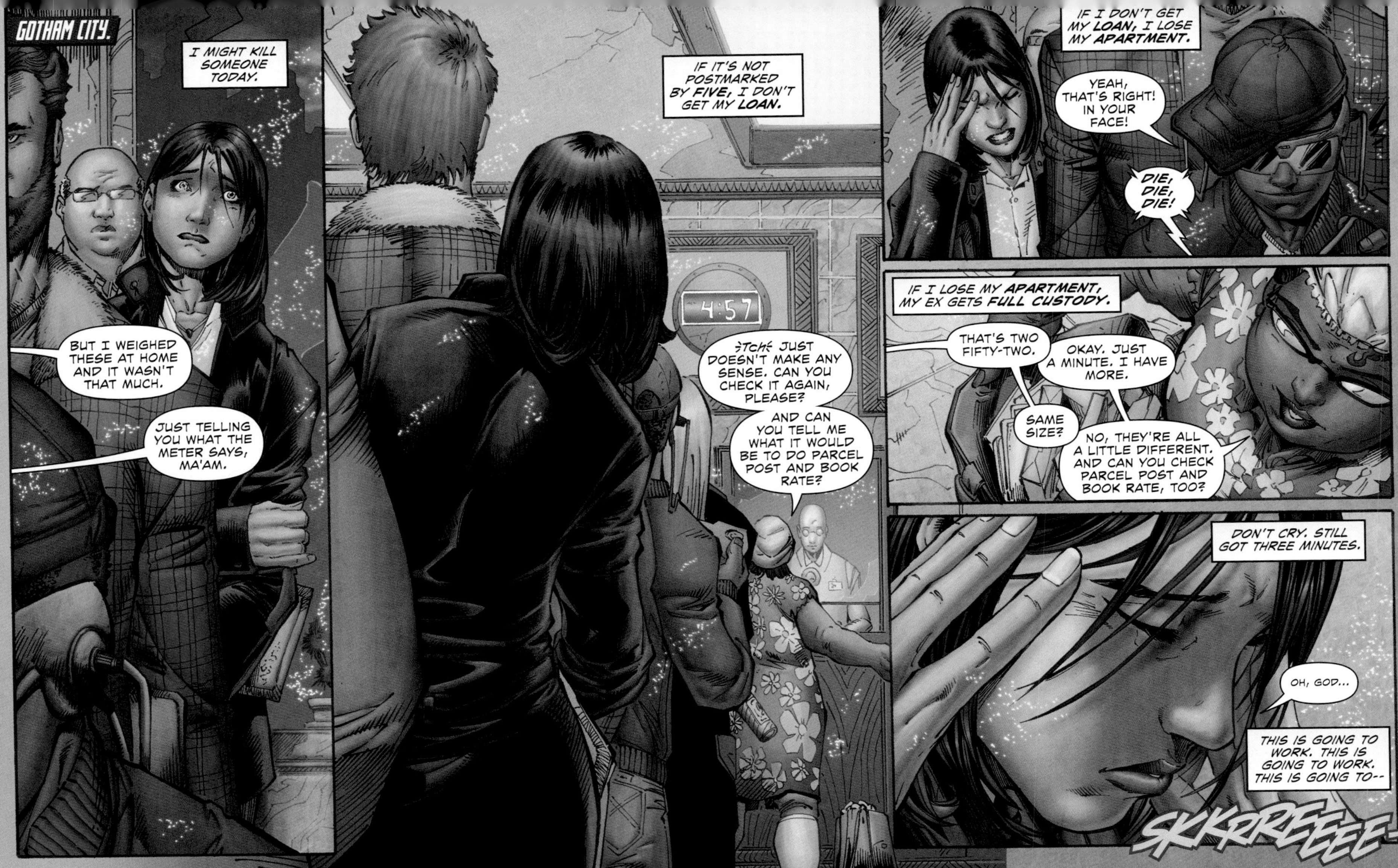
GOTHAM CITY.
I MIGHT KILL SOMEONE TODAY.
BUT I WEIGHED THESE AT HOME AND IT WASN'T THAT MUCH.
JUST TELLING YOU WHAT THE METER SAYS, MA'AM.
IF IT'S NOT POSTMARKED BY FIVE, I DON'T GET MY LOAN.
4:57
TCH JUST DOESN'T MAKE ANY SENSE. CAN YOU CHECK IT AGAIN, PLEASE?
AND CAN YOU TELL ME WHAT IT WOULD BE TO DO PARCEL POST AND BOOK RATE?
IF I DON'T GET MY LOAN, I LOSE MY APARTMENT.
YEAH, THAT'S RIGHT! IN YOUR FACE!
DIE, DIE, DIE!
IF I LOSE MY APARTMENT, MY EX GETS FULL CUSTODY.
THAT'S TWO FIFTY-TWO.
OKAY. JUST A MINUTE. I HAVE MORE.
SAME SIZE?
NO, THEY'RE ALL A LITTLE DIFFERENT. AND CAN YOU CHECK PARCEL POST AND BOOK RATE, TOO?
DON'T CRY. STILL GOT THREE MINUTES.
OH, GOD...
THIS IS GOING TO WORK. THIS IS GOING TO WORK. THIS IS GOING TO--
SKKRREEEEE--

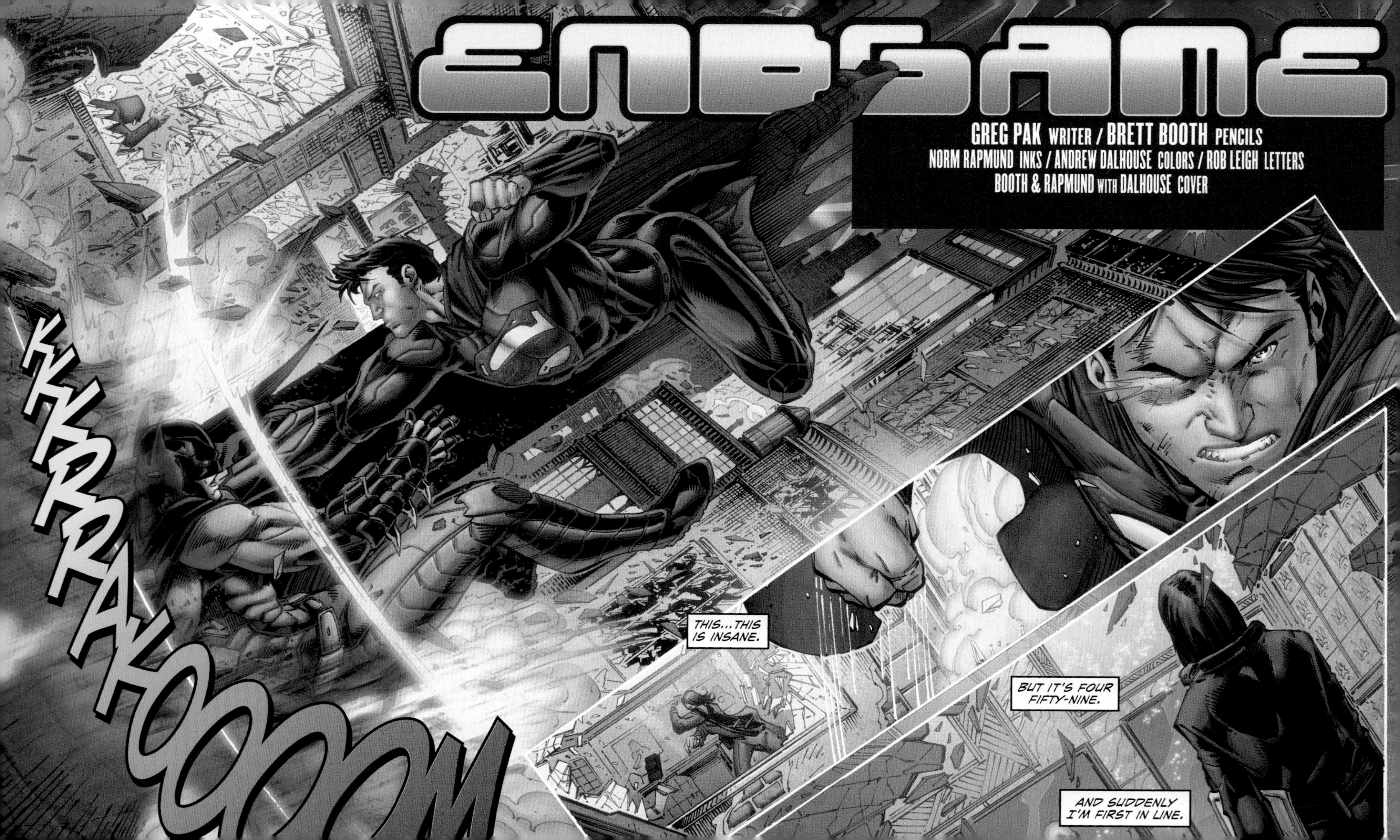
ENDGAME
GREG PAK WRITER / BRETT BOOTH PENCILS
NORM RAPMUND INKS / ANDREW DALHOUSE COLORS / ROB LEIGH LETTERS
BOOTH & RAPMUND WITH DALHOUSE COVER
KKKRRAKOOOOM
THIS...THIS IS INSANE.
BUT IT'S FOUR FIFTY-NINE.
AND SUDDENLY I'M FIRST IN LINE.

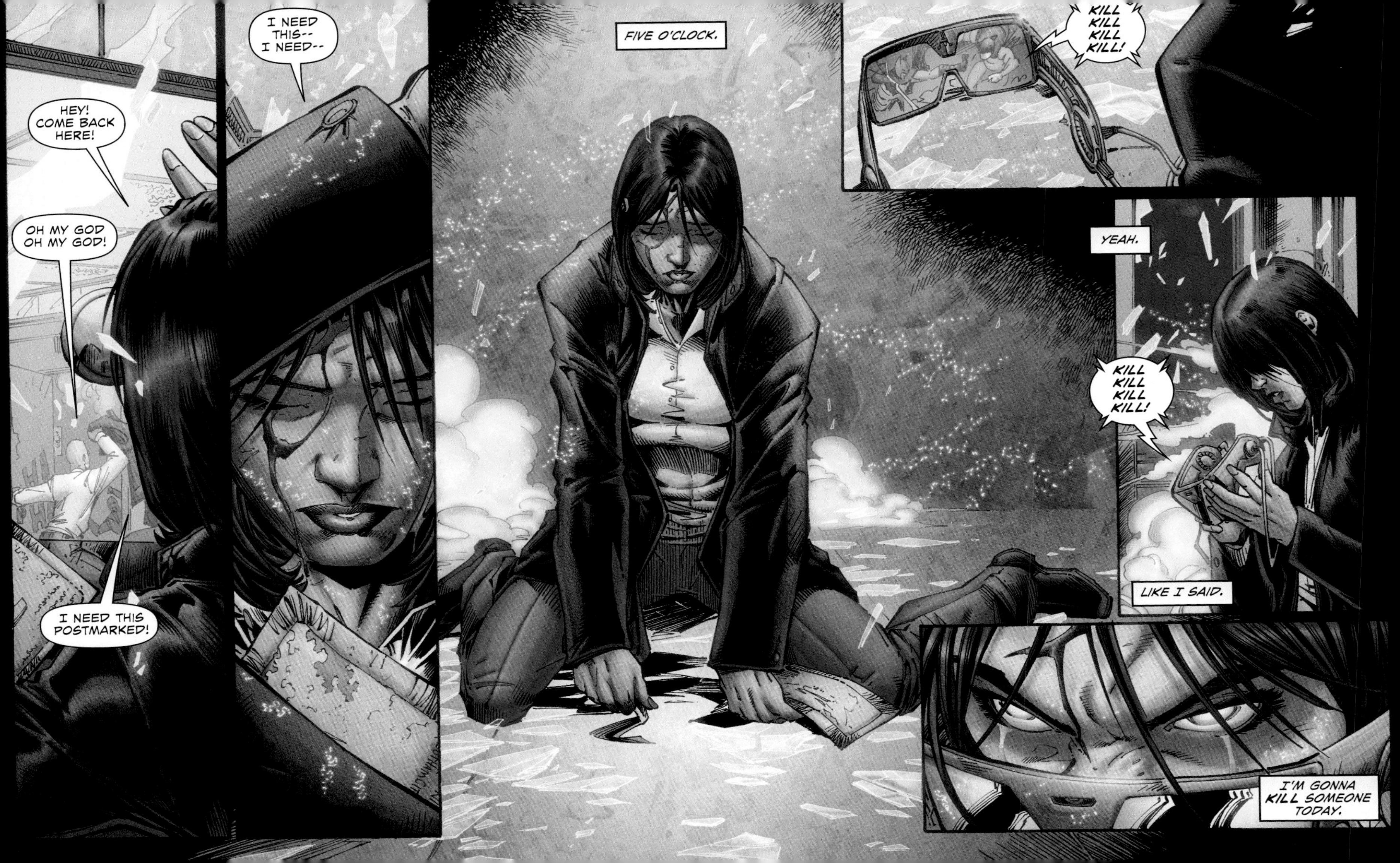
HEY! COME BACK HERE!
OH MY GOD OH MY GOD!
I NEED THIS POSTMARKED!
I NEED THIS-- I NEED--
FIVE O'CLOCK.
KILL KILL KILL KILL!
YEAH.
KILL KILL KILL KILL!
LIKE I SAID.
I'M GONNA **KILL** SOMEONE TODAY.

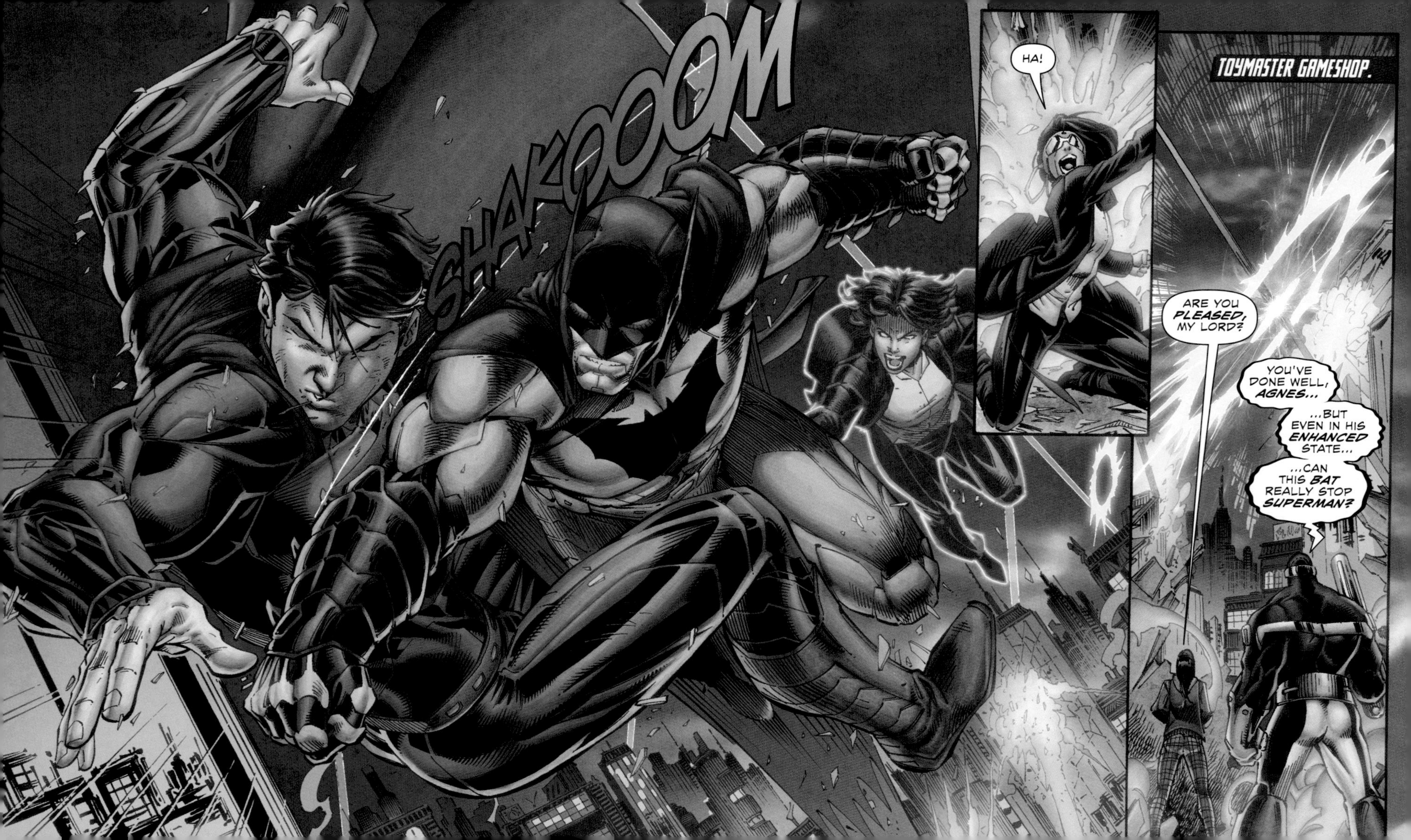
SHAKOOOM
HA!
TOYMASTER GAMESHOP.
ARE YOU PLEASED, MY LORD?
YOU'VE DONE WELL, AGNES...
...BUT EVEN IN HIS ENHANCED STATE...
...CAN THIS BAT REALLY STOP SUPERMAN?

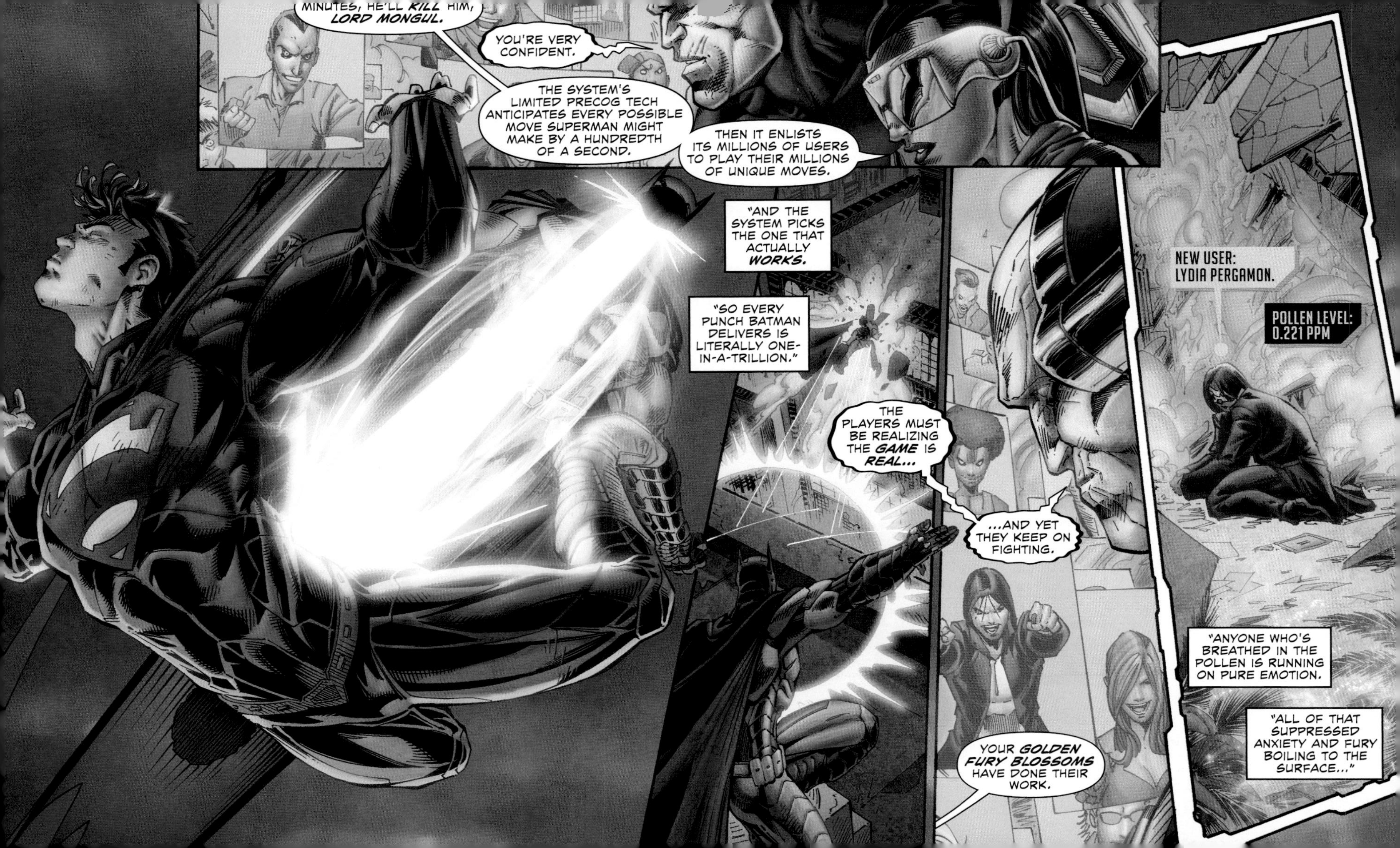
MINUTES, HE'LL KILL HIM, LORD MONGUL.
YOU'RE VERY CONFIDENT.
THE SYSTEM'S LIMITED PRECOG TECH ANTICIPATES EVERY POSSIBLE MOVE SUPERMAN MIGHT MAKE BY A HUNDREDTH OF A SECOND.
THEN IT ENLISTS ITS MILLIONS OF USERS TO PLAY THEIR MILLIONS OF UNIQUE MOVES.
"AND THE SYSTEM PICKS THE ONE THAT ACTUALLY WORKS.
"SO EVERY PUNCH BATMAN DELIVERS IS LITERALLY ONE-IN-A-TRILLION."
THE PLAYERS MUST BE REALIZING THE GAME IS REAL...
...AND YET THEY KEEP ON FIGHTING.
YOUR GOLDEN FURY BLOSSOMS HAVE DONE THEIR WORK.
NEW USER: LYDIA PERGAMON.
POLLEN LEVEL: 0.221 PPM
"ANYONE WHO'S BREATHED IN THE POLLEN IS RUNNING ON PURE EMOTION.
"ALL OF THAT SUPPRESSED ANXIETY AND FURY BOILING TO THE SURFACE..."

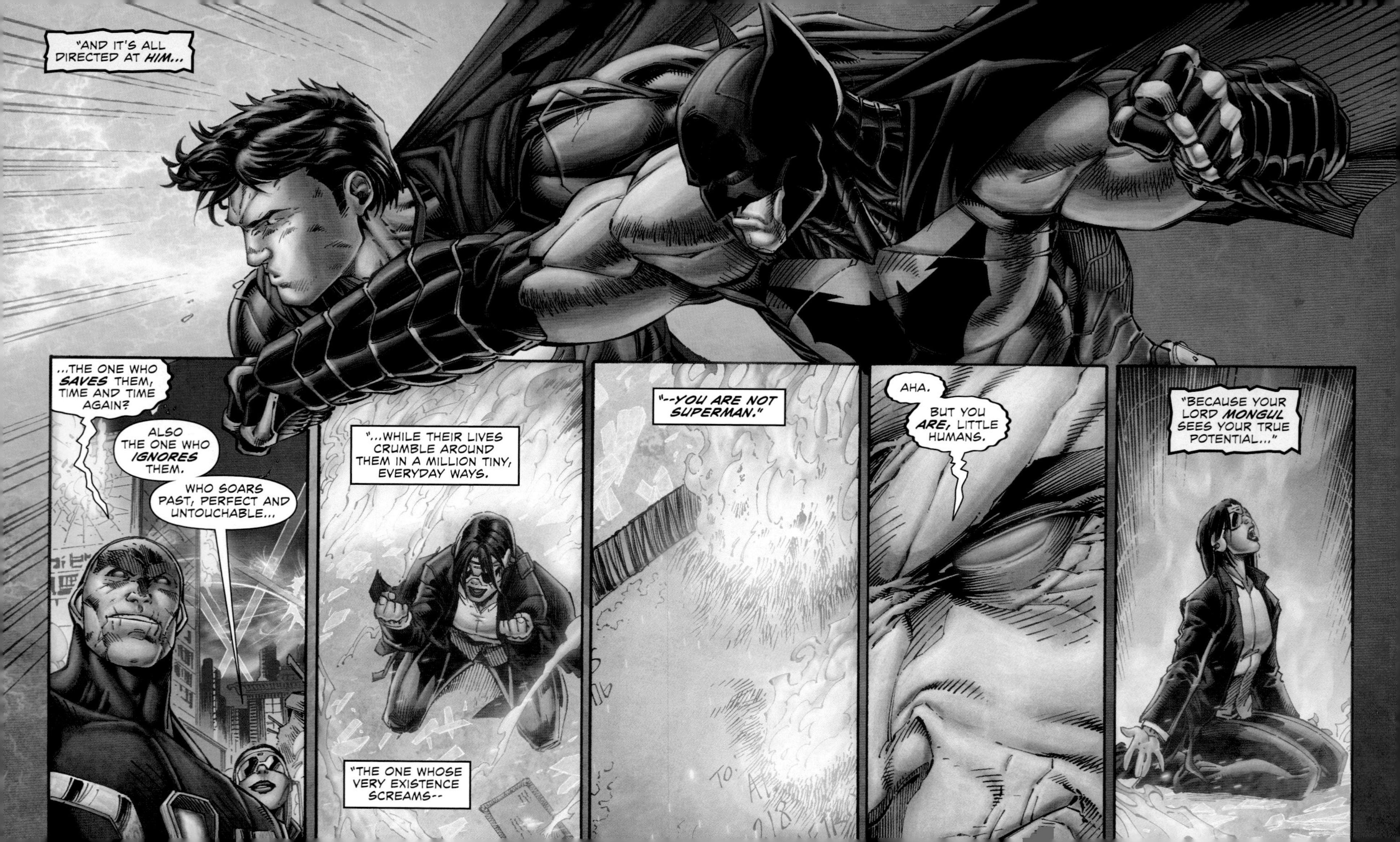
"AND IT'S ALL DIRECTED AT *HIM*...
...THE ONE WHO *SAVES* THEM, TIME AND TIME AGAIN?
ALSO THE ONE WHO *IGNORES* THEM.
WHO SOARS PAST, PERFECT AND UNTOUCHABLE...
"...WHILE THEIR LIVES CRUMBLE AROUND THEM IN A MILLION TINY, EVERYDAY WAYS.
"THE ONE WHOSE VERY EXISTENCE SCREAMS--
"*--YOU ARE NOT SUPERMAN.*"
AHA.
BUT YOU *ARE,* LITTLE HUMANS.
"BECAUSE YOUR LORD *MONGUL* SEES YOUR TRUE POTENTIAL..."

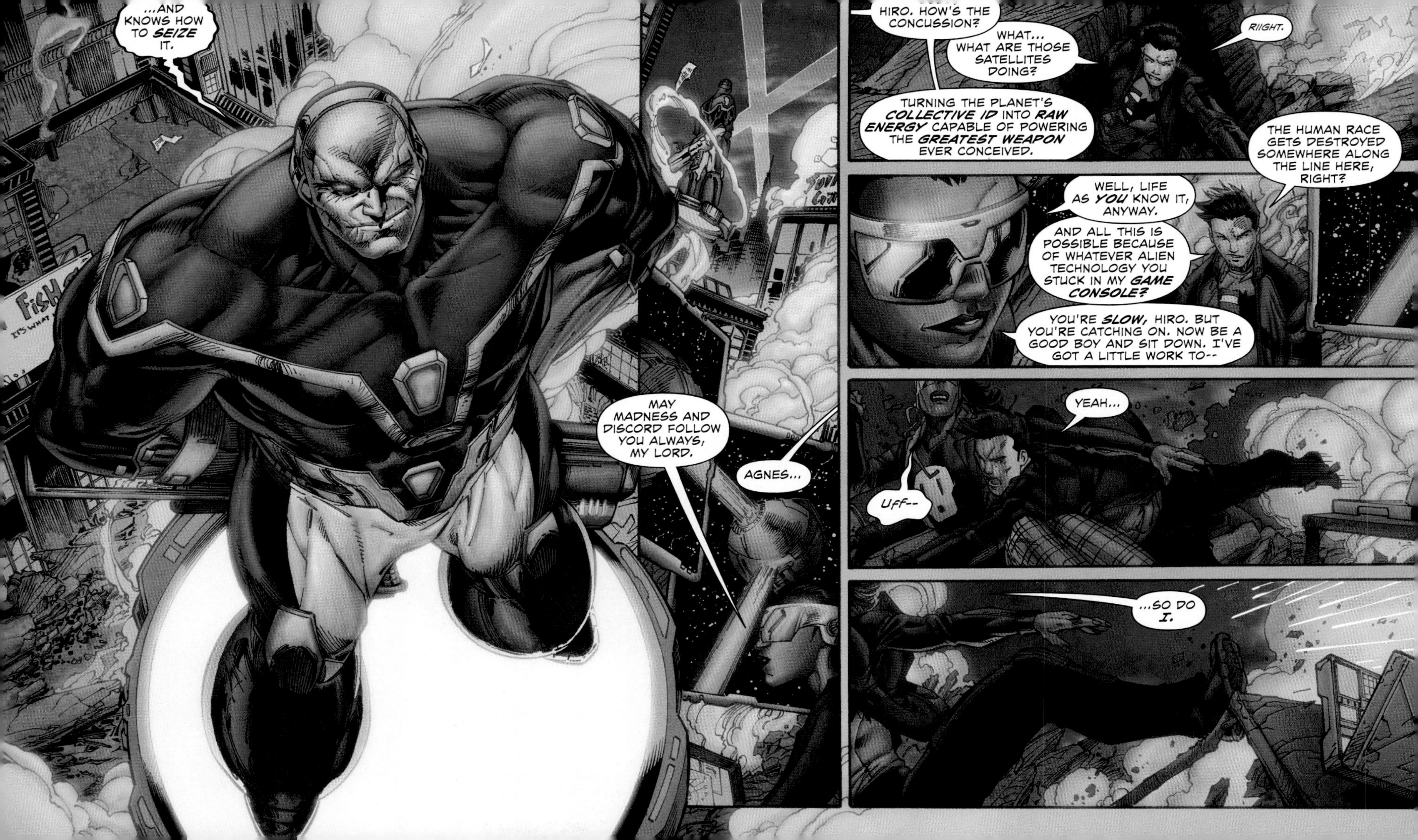
...AND KNOWS HOW TO *SEIZE* IT.
MAY MADNESS AND DISCORD FOLLOW YOU ALWAYS, MY LORD.
AGNES...
HIRO. HOW'S THE CONCUSSION?
WHAT... WHAT ARE THOSE SATELLITES DOING?
RIIGHT.
TURNING THE PLANET'S ***COLLECTIVE ID*** INTO ***RAW ENERGY*** CAPABLE OF POWERING THE ***GREATEST WEAPON*** EVER CONCEIVED.
THE HUMAN RACE GETS DESTROYED SOMEWHERE ALONG THE LINE HERE, RIGHT?
WELL, LIFE AS ***YOU*** KNOW IT, ANYWAY.
AND ALL THIS IS POSSIBLE BECAUSE OF WHATEVER ALIEN TECHNOLOGY YOU STUCK IN MY ***GAME CONSOLE?***
YOU'RE ***SLOW,*** HIRO. BUT YOU'RE CATCHING ON. NOW BE A GOOD BOY AND SIT DOWN. I'VE GOT A LITTLE WORK TO--
YEAH...
UFF--
...SO DO ***I.***

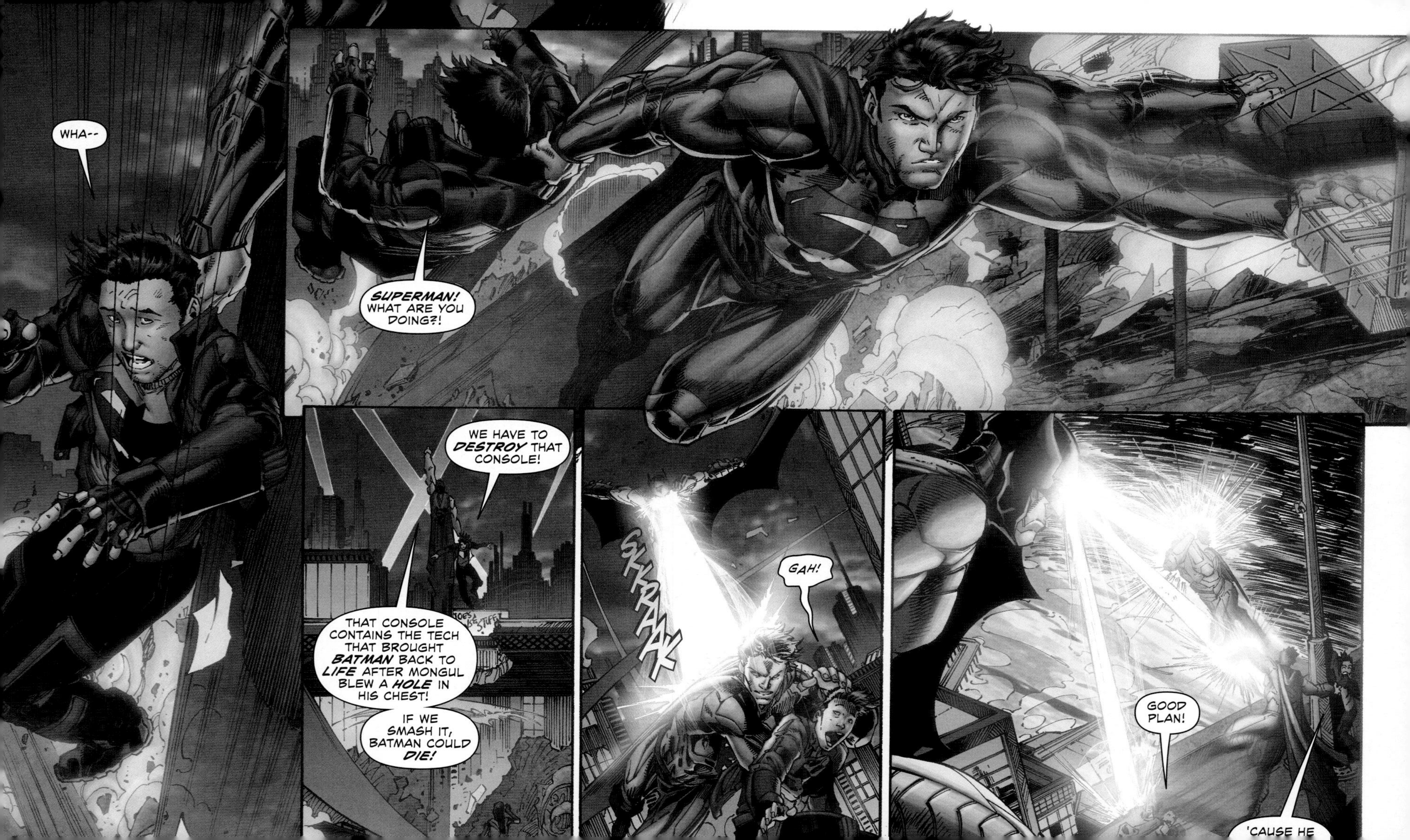
WHA--
SUPERMAN! WHAT ARE YOU DOING?!
WE HAVE TO DESTROY THAT CONSOLE!
THAT CONSOLE CONTAINS THE TECH THAT BROUGHT BATMAN BACK TO LIFE AFTER MONGUL BLEW A HOLE IN HIS CHEST!
IF WE SMASH IT, BATMAN COULD DIE!
SKKRAAK
GAH!
GOOD PLAN!
'CAUSE HE

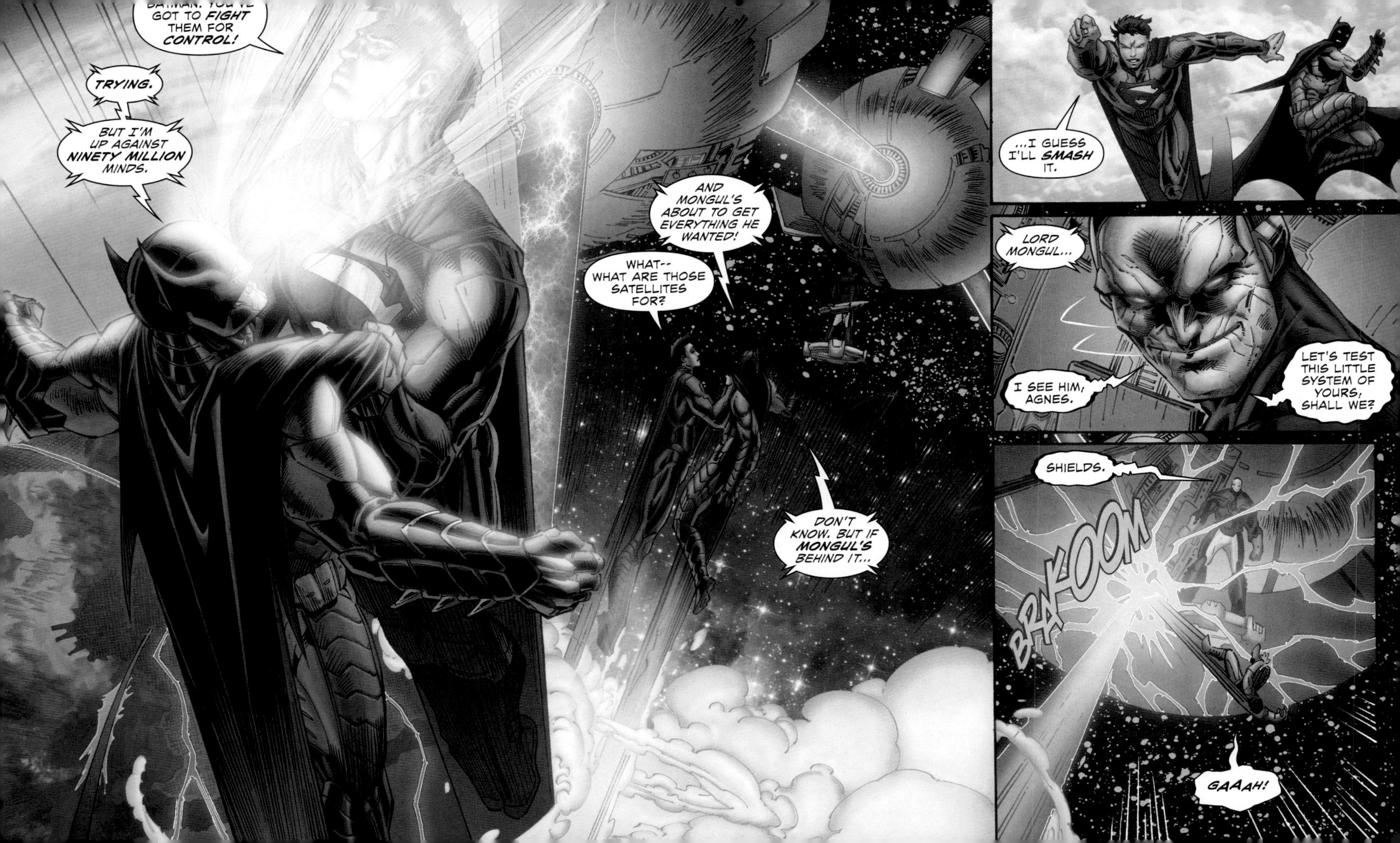

GOT TO FIGHT THEM FOR CONTROL!
TRYING.
BUT I'M UP AGAINST NINETY MILLION MINDS.
AND MONGUL'S ABOUT TO GET EVERYTHING HE WANTED!
WHAT-- WHAT ARE THOSE SATELLITES FOR?
DON'T KNOW. BUT IF MONGUL'S BEHIND IT...
...I GUESS I'LL SMASH IT.
LORD MONGUL...
I SEE HIM, AGNES.
LET'S TEST THIS LITTLE SYSTEM OF YOURS, SHALL WE?
SHIELDS.
BRAKOOM
GAAAH!

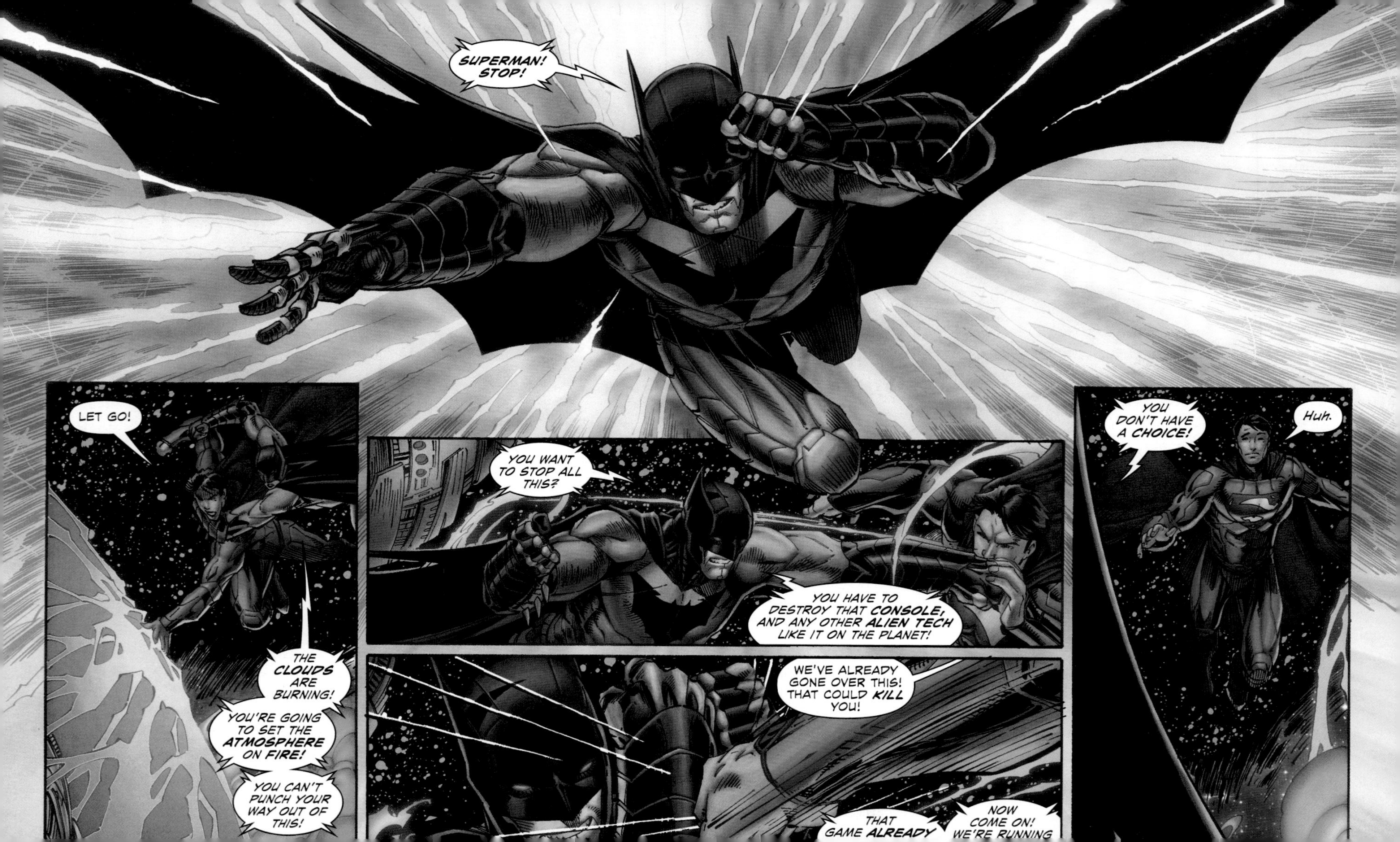
SUPERMAN! STOP!
LET GO!
THE CLOUDS ARE BURNING!
YOU'RE GOING TO SET THE ATMOSPHERE ON FIRE!
YOU CAN'T PUNCH YOUR WAY OUT OF THIS!
YOU WANT TO STOP ALL THIS?
YOU HAVE TO DESTROY THAT CONSOLE, AND ANY OTHER ALIEN TECH LIKE IT ON THE PLANET!
WE'VE ALREADY GONE OVER THIS! THAT COULD KILL YOU!
NOW COME ON! WE'RE RUNNING
THAT GAME ALREADY
Huh.
YOU DON'T HAVE A CHOICE!

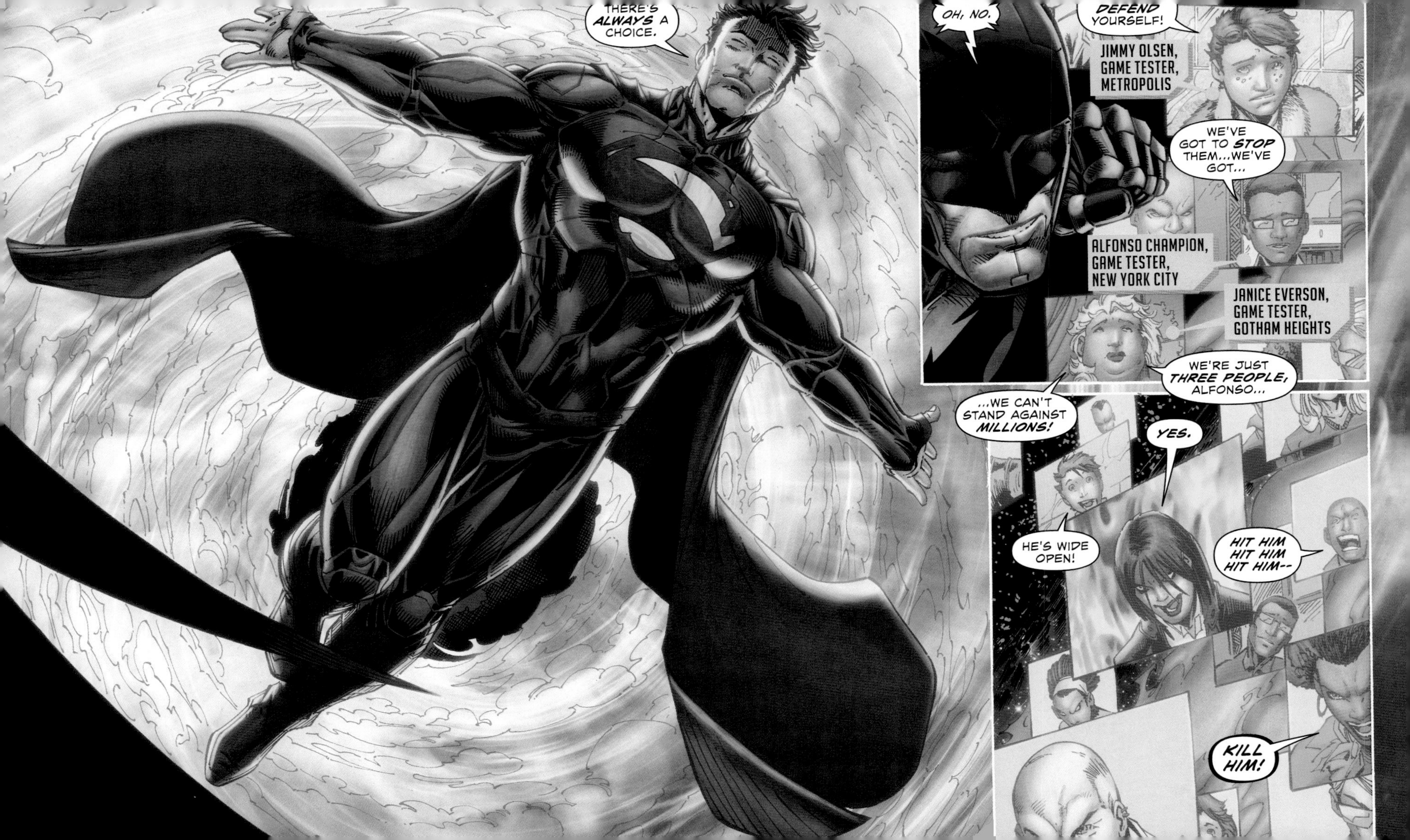

THERE'S ALWAYS A CHOICE.
OH, NO.
DEFEND YOURSELF!
JIMMY OLSEN, GAME TESTER, METROPOLIS
WE'VE GOT TO STOP THEM...WE'VE GOT...
ALFONSO CHAMPION, GAME TESTER, NEW YORK CITY
JANICE EVERSON, GAME TESTER, GOTHAM HEIGHTS
WE'RE JUST THREE PEOPLE, ALFONSO...
...WE CAN'T STAND AGAINST MILLIONS!
YES.
HE'S WIDE OPEN!
HIT HIM HIT HIM HIT HIM--
KILL HIM!

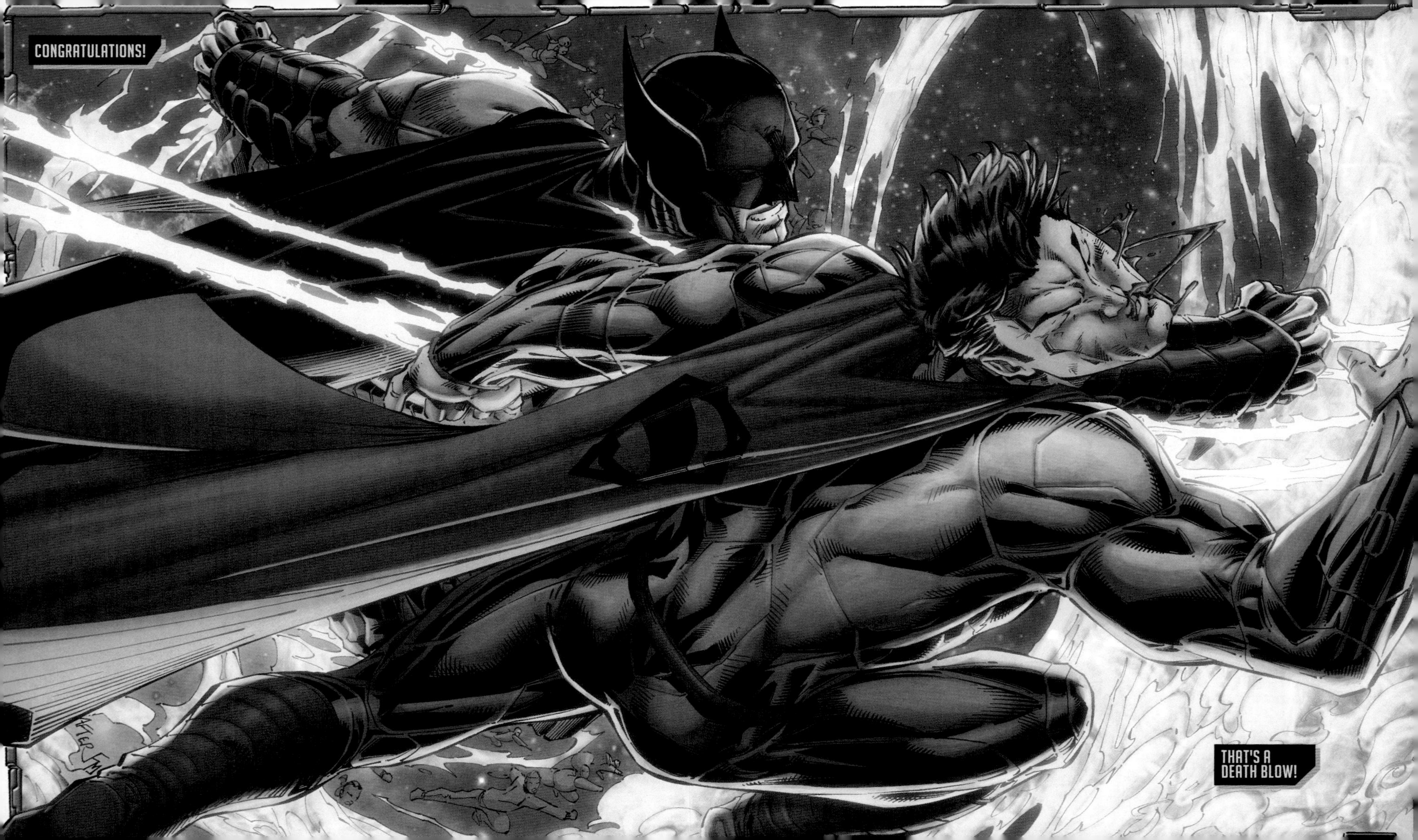
CONGRATULATIONS!
THAT'S A DEATH BLOW!

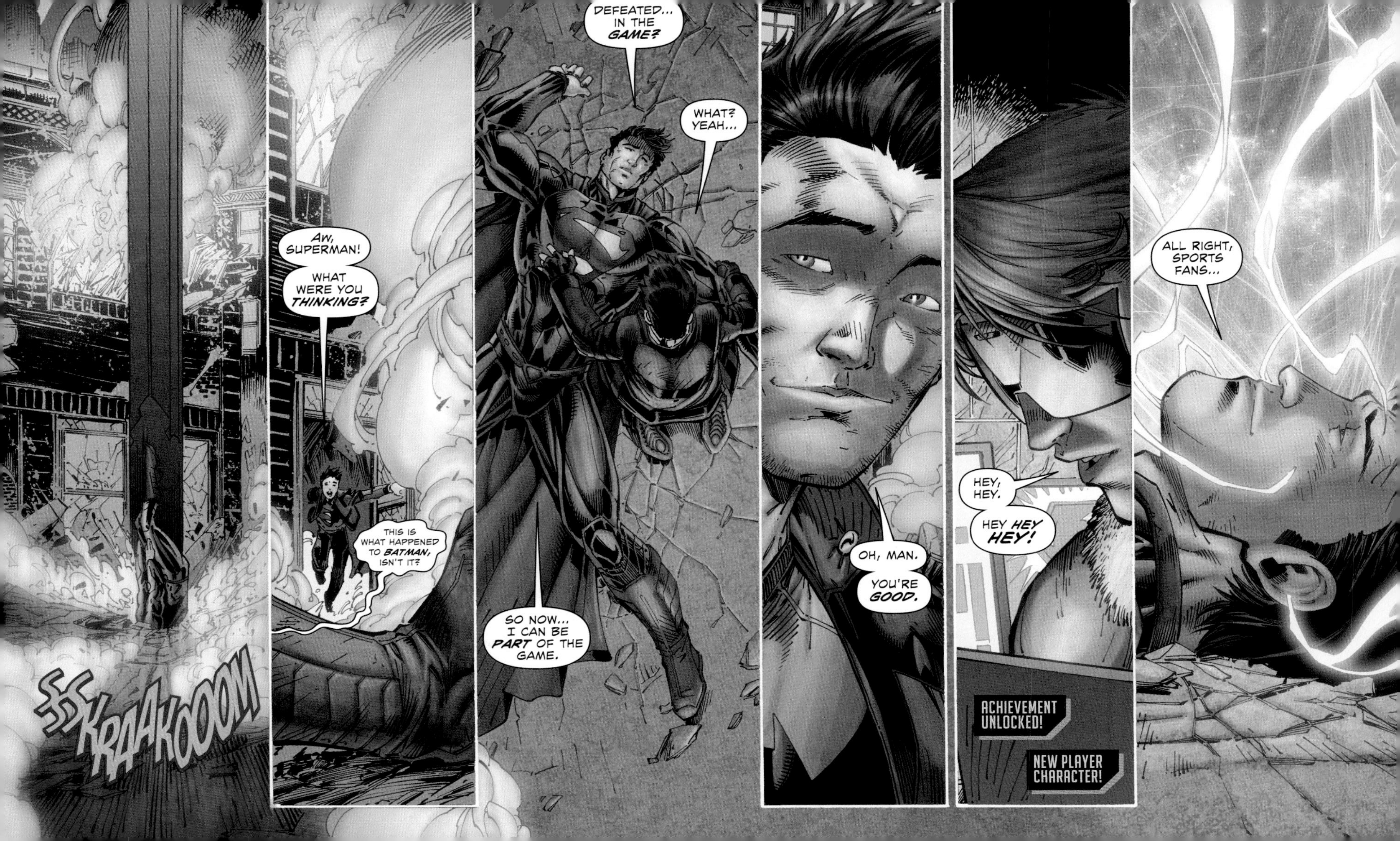
SSKRAAKOOOM
AW, SUPERMAN!
WHAT WERE YOU THINKING?
THIS IS WHAT HAPPENED TO BATMAN, ISN'T IT?
DEFEATED... IN THE GAME?
WHAT? YEAH...
SO NOW... I CAN BE PART OF THE GAME.
OH, MAN.
YOU'RE GOOD.
HEY, HEY.
HEY HEY HEY!
ACHIEVEMENT UNLOCKED!
NEW PLAYER CHARACTER!
ALL RIGHT, SPORTS FANS...

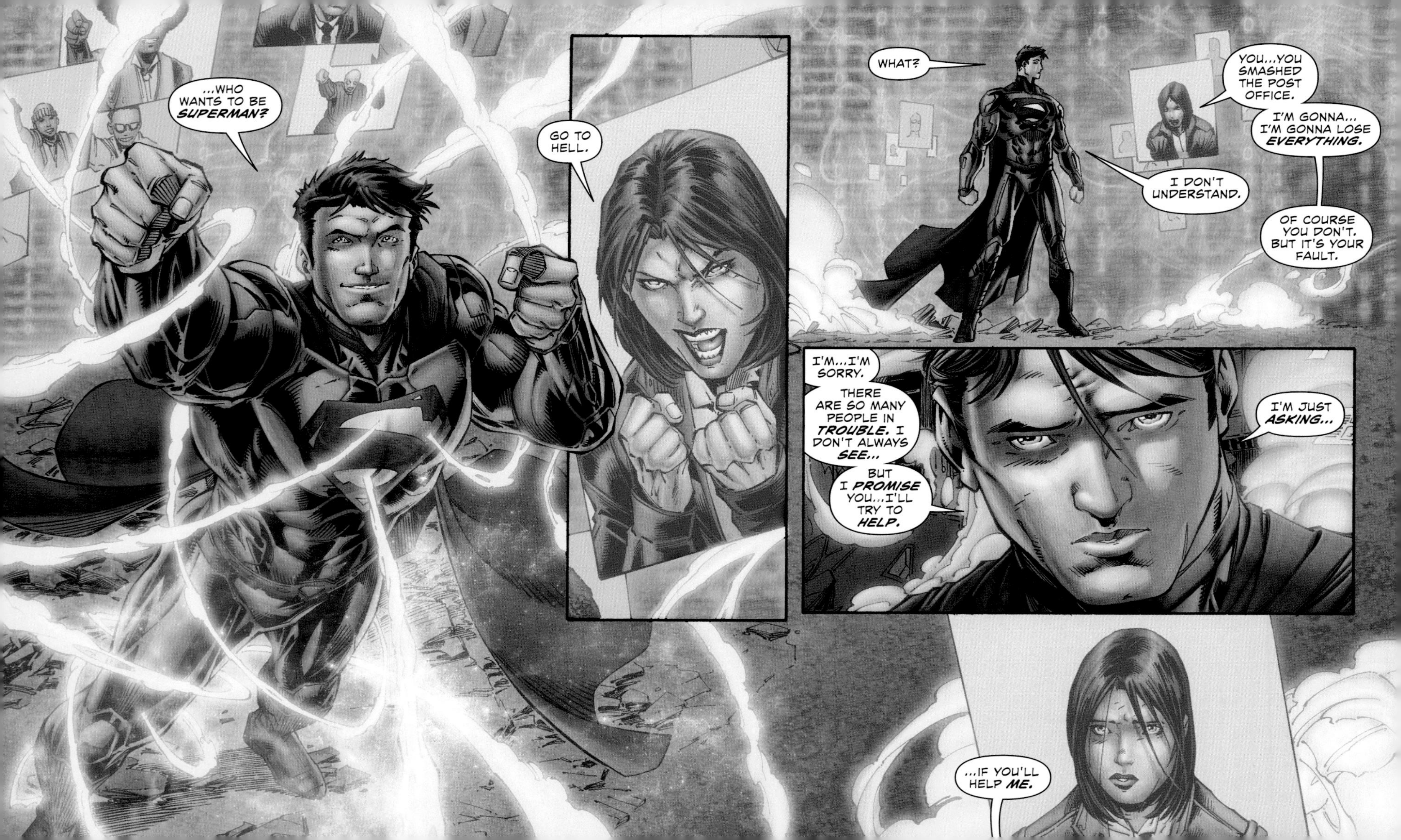
...WHO WANTS TO BE *SUPERMAN?*
GO TO HELL.
WHAT?
YOU...YOU SMASHED THE POST OFFICE.
I'M GONNA... I'M GONNA LOSE *EVERYTHING.*
I DON'T UNDERSTAND.
OF COURSE YOU DON'T. BUT IT'S YOUR FAULT.
I'M...I'M SORRY.
THERE ARE SO MANY PEOPLE IN *TROUBLE.* I DON'T ALWAYS *SEE...*
BUT I *PROMISE* YOU...I'LL TRY TO *HELP.*
I'M JUST *ASKING...*
...IF YOU'LL HELP *ME.*

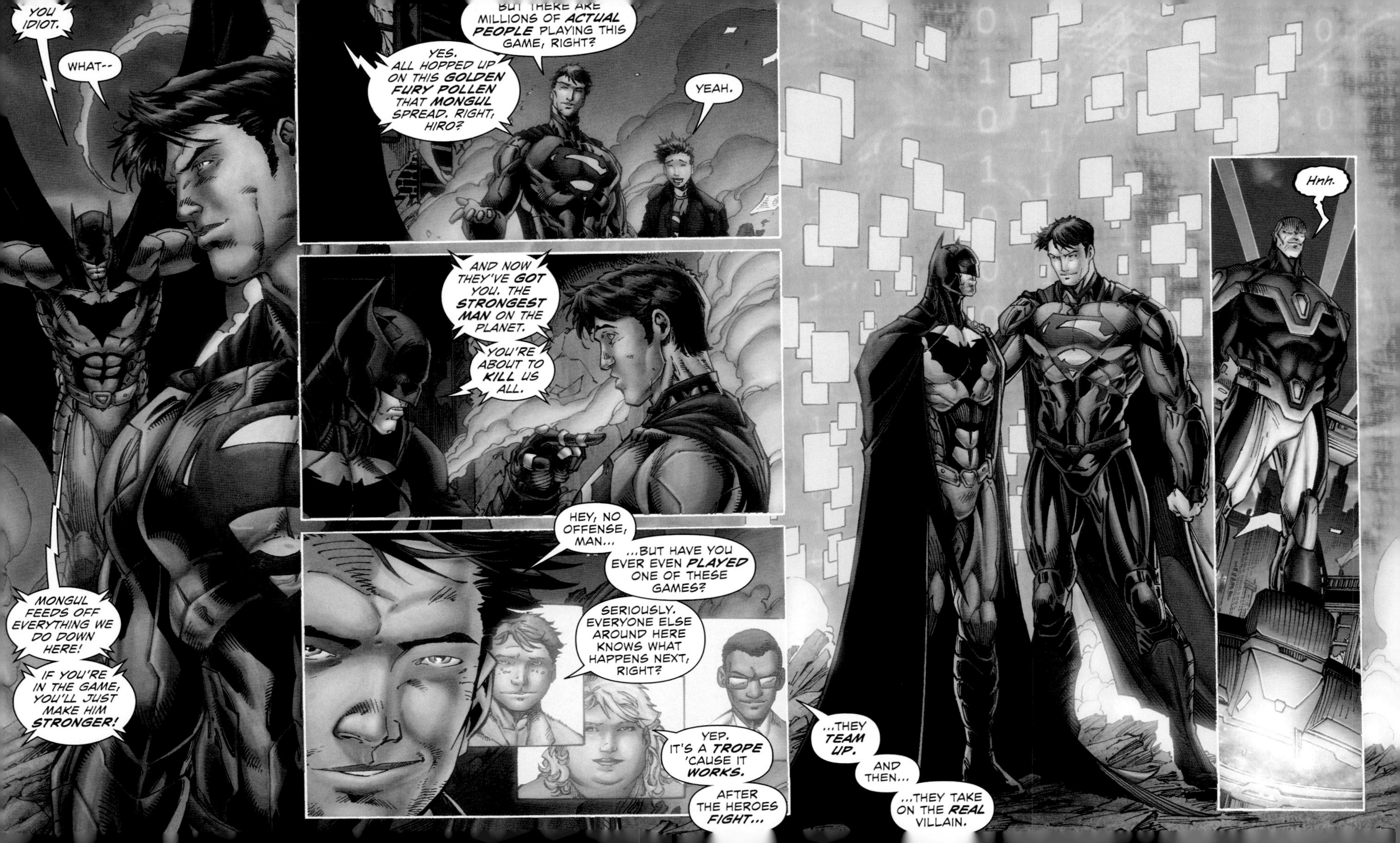
YOU IDIOT.
WHAT--
MONGUL FEEDS OFF EVERYTHING WE DO DOWN HERE!
IF YOU'RE IN THE GAME, YOU'LL JUST MAKE HIM STRONGER!
BUT THERE ARE MILLIONS OF ACTUAL PEOPLE PLAYING THIS GAME, RIGHT?
YES. ALL HOPPED UP ON THIS GOLDEN FURY POLLEN THAT MONGUL SPREAD. RIGHT, HIRO?
YEAH.
AND NOW THEY'VE GOT YOU. THE STRONGEST MAN ON THE PLANET.
YOU'RE ABOUT TO KILL US ALL.
HEY, NO OFFENSE, MAN...
...BUT HAVE YOU EVER EVEN PLAYED ONE OF THESE GAMES?
SERIOUSLY. EVERYONE ELSE AROUND HERE KNOWS WHAT HAPPENS NEXT, RIGHT?
YEP. IT'S A TROPE 'CAUSE IT WORKS.
AFTER THE HEROES FIGHT...
...THEY TEAM UP.
AND THEN...
...THEY TAKE ON THE REAL VILLAIN.
Hnh.

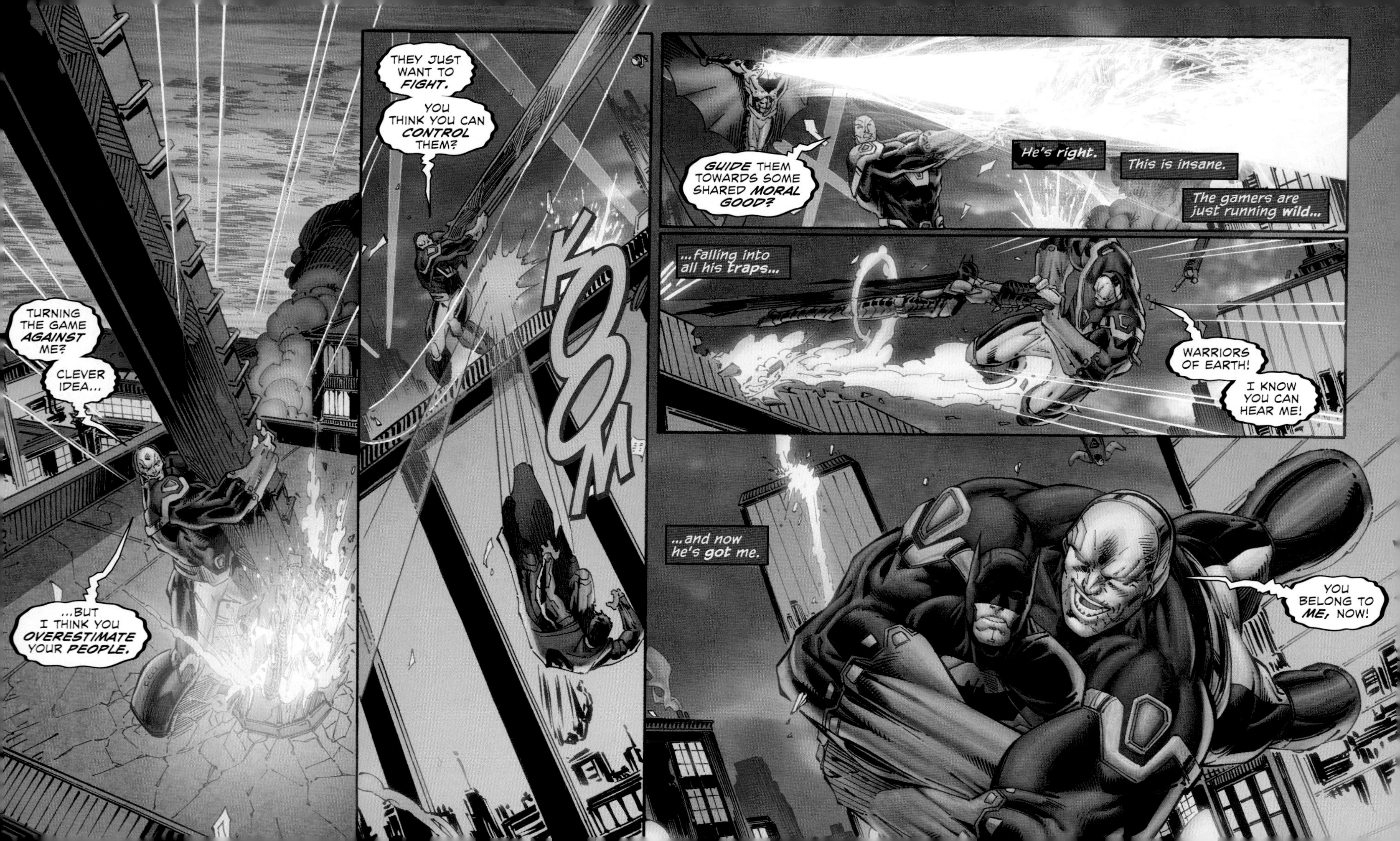

TURNING THE GAME AGAINST ME?
CLEVER IDEA...
...BUT I THINK YOU OVERESTIMATE YOUR PEOPLE.
THEY JUST WANT TO FIGHT.
YOU THINK YOU CAN CONTROL THEM?
KOOM
GUIDE THEM TOWARDS SOME SHARED MORAL GOOD?
He's right.
This is insane.
The gamers are just running wild...
...falling into all his traps...
WARRIORS OF EARTH!
I KNOW YOU CAN HEAR ME!
...and now he's got me.
YOU BELONG TO ME, NOW!

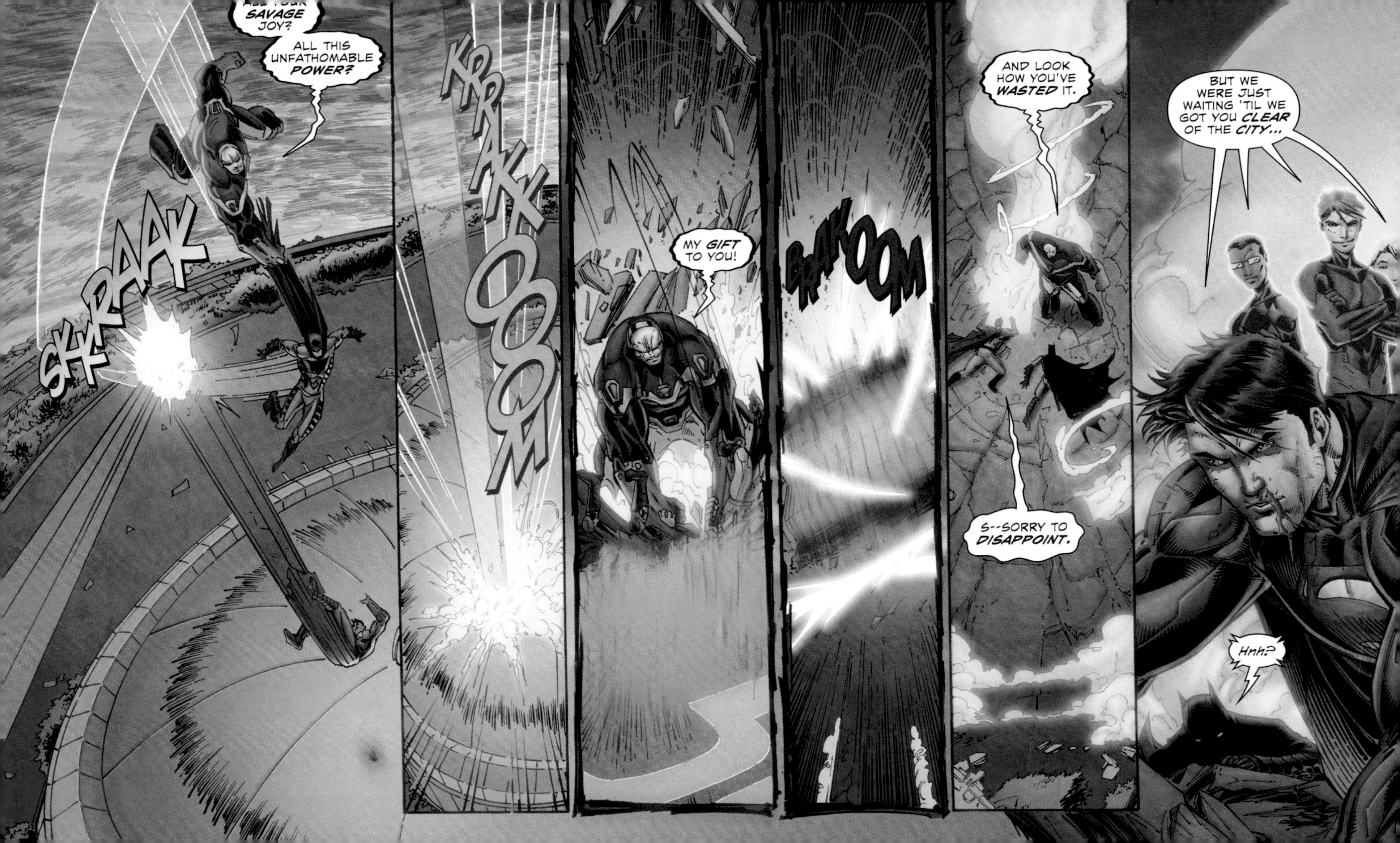
SAVAGE JOY?
ALL THIS UNFATHOMABLE POWER?
SKRAAK
KRRAKKOOOM
MY GIFT TO YOU!
BRAKOOM
AND LOOK HOW YOU'VE WASTED IT.
S--SORRY TO DISAPPOINT.
BUT WE WERE JUST WAITING 'TIL WE GOT YOU CLEAR OF THE CITY...
Hnh?

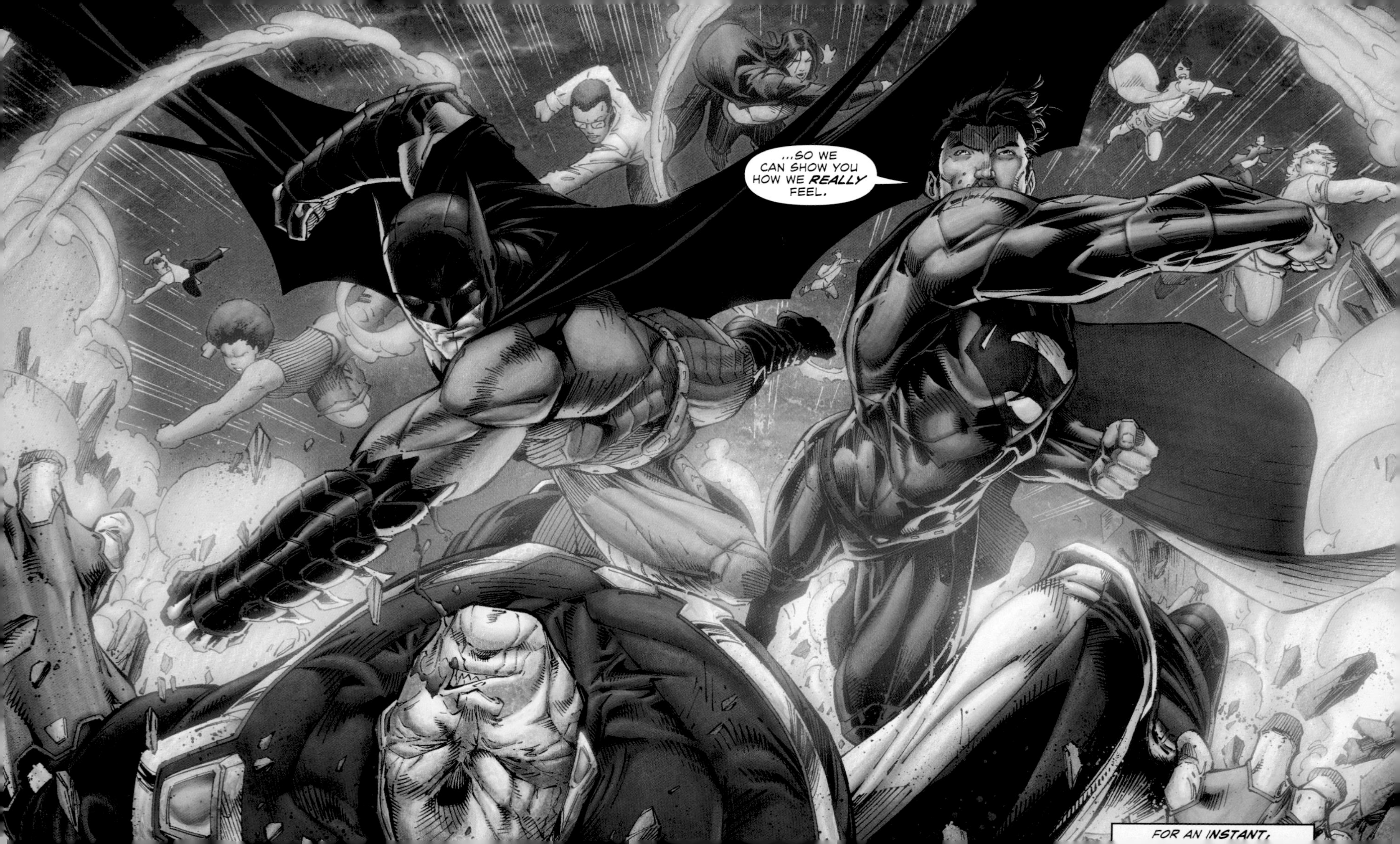
...SO WE CAN SHOW YOU HOW WE *REALLY* FEEL.
FOR AN *INSTANT*,

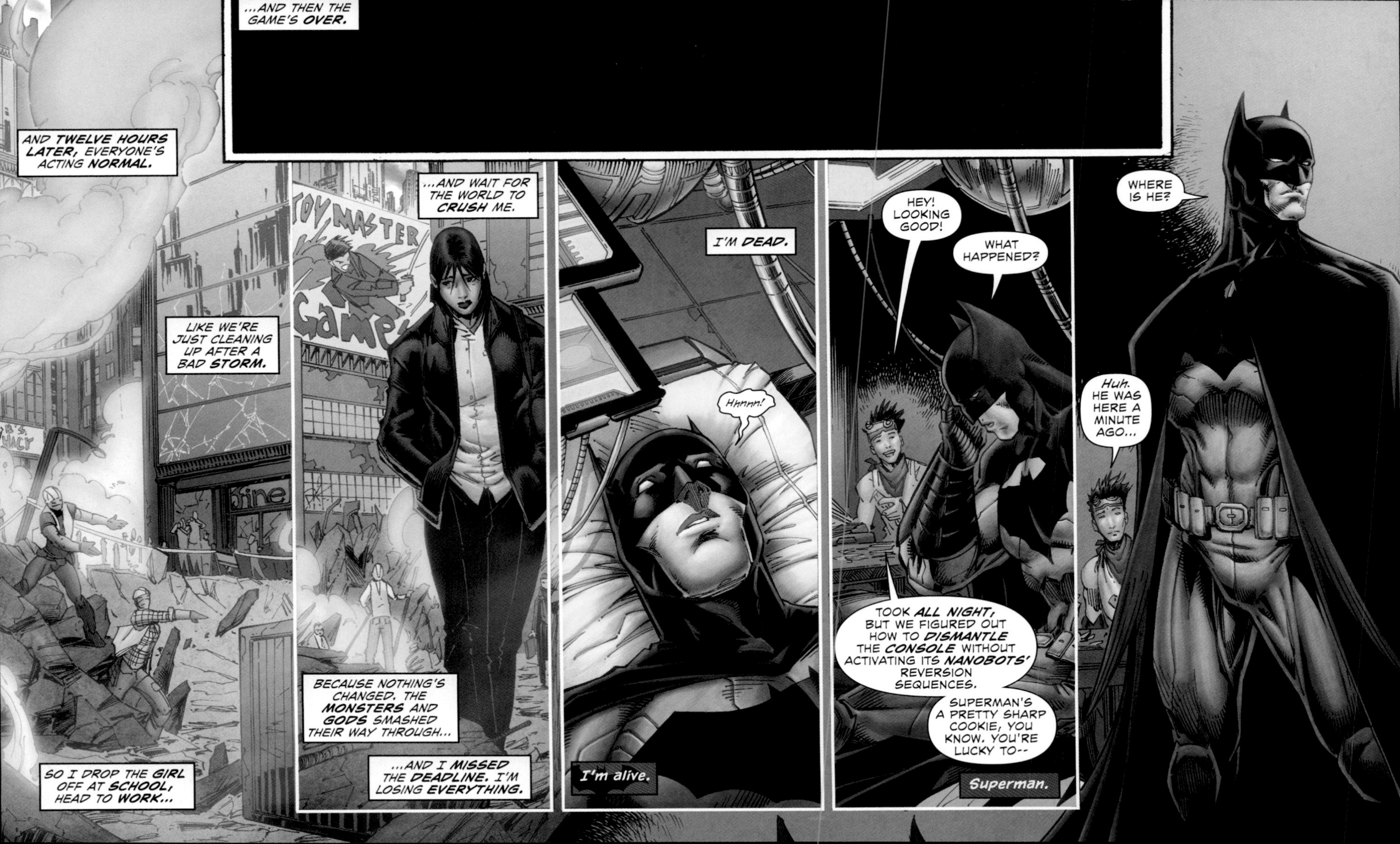
...AND THEN THE GAME'S OVER.
AND TWELVE HOURS LATER, EVERYONE'S ACTING NORMAL.
LIKE WE'RE JUST CLEANING UP AFTER A BAD STORM.
SO I DROP THE GIRL OFF AT SCHOOL, HEAD TO WORK...
TOYMASTER GAMES
...AND WAIT FOR THE WORLD TO CRUSH ME.
BECAUSE NOTHING'S CHANGED. THE MONSTERS AND GODS SMASHED THEIR WAY THROUGH...
...AND I MISSED THE DEADLINE. I'M LOSING EVERYTHING.
I'M DEAD.
Hhnnn!
I'm alive.
HEY! LOOKING GOOD!
WHAT HAPPENED?
TOOK ALL NIGHT, BUT WE FIGURED OUT HOW TO DISMANTLE THE CONSOLE WITHOUT ACTIVATING ITS NANOBOTS' REVERSION SEQUENCES.
SUPERMAN'S A PRETTY SHARP COOKIE, YOU KNOW. YOU'RE LUCKY TO--
Superman.
WHERE IS HE?
Huh. HE WAS HERE A MINUTE AGO...

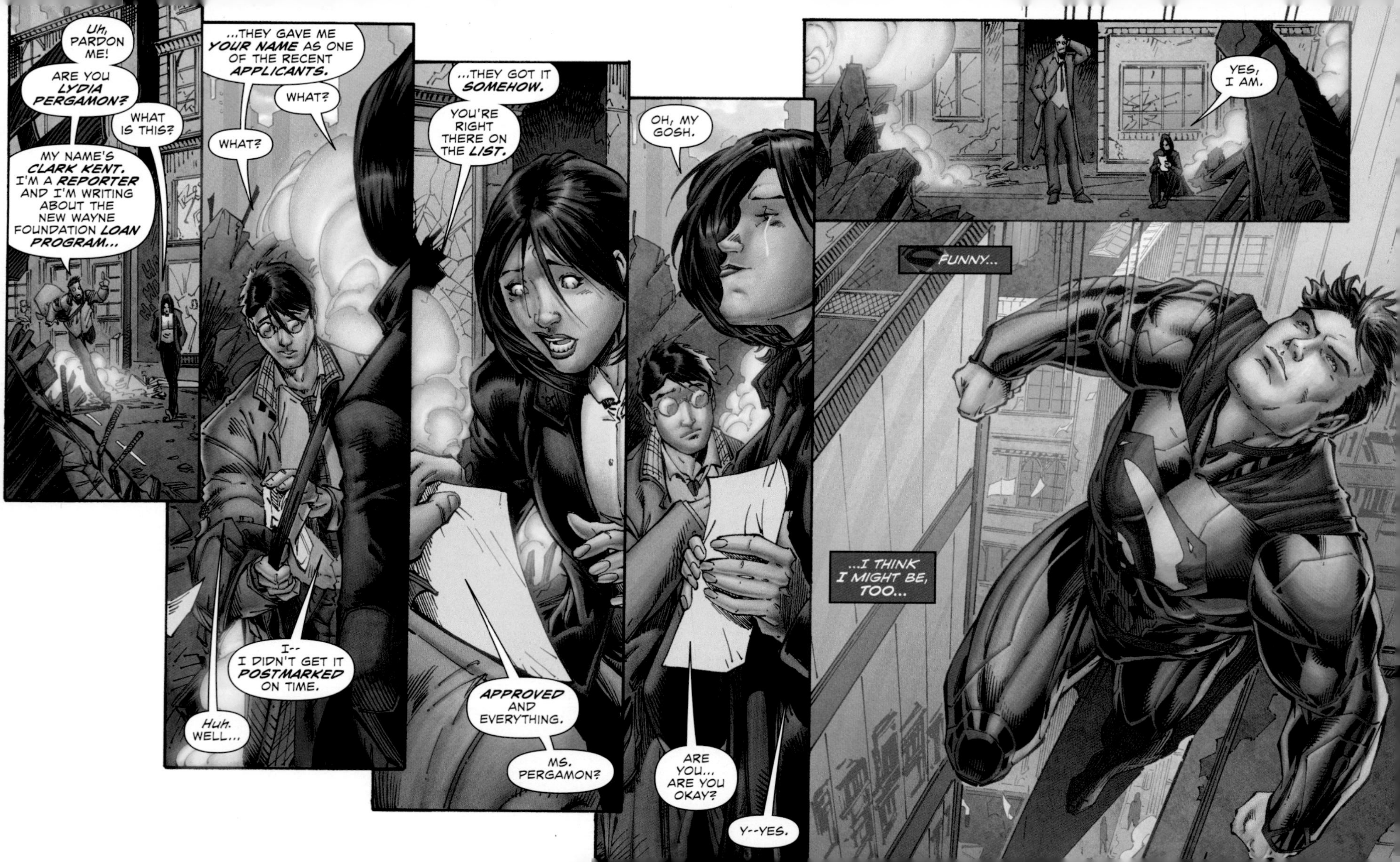

UH, PARDON ME!
ARE YOU LYDIA PERGAMON?
WHAT IS THIS?
MY NAME'S CLARK KENT. I'M A REPORTER AND I'M WRITING ABOUT THE NEW WAYNE FOUNDATION LOAN PROGRAM...
...THEY GAVE ME YOUR NAME AS ONE OF THE RECENT APPLICANTS.
WHAT?
WHAT?
I-- I DIDN'T GET IT POSTMARKED ON TIME.
HUH. WELL...
...THEY GOT IT SOMEHOW.
YOU'RE RIGHT THERE ON THE LIST.
APPROVED AND EVERYTHING.
MS. PERGAMON?
OH, MY GOSH.
ARE YOU... ARE YOU OKAY?
Y--YES.
YES, I AM.
FUNNY...
...I THINK I MIGHT BE, TOO...

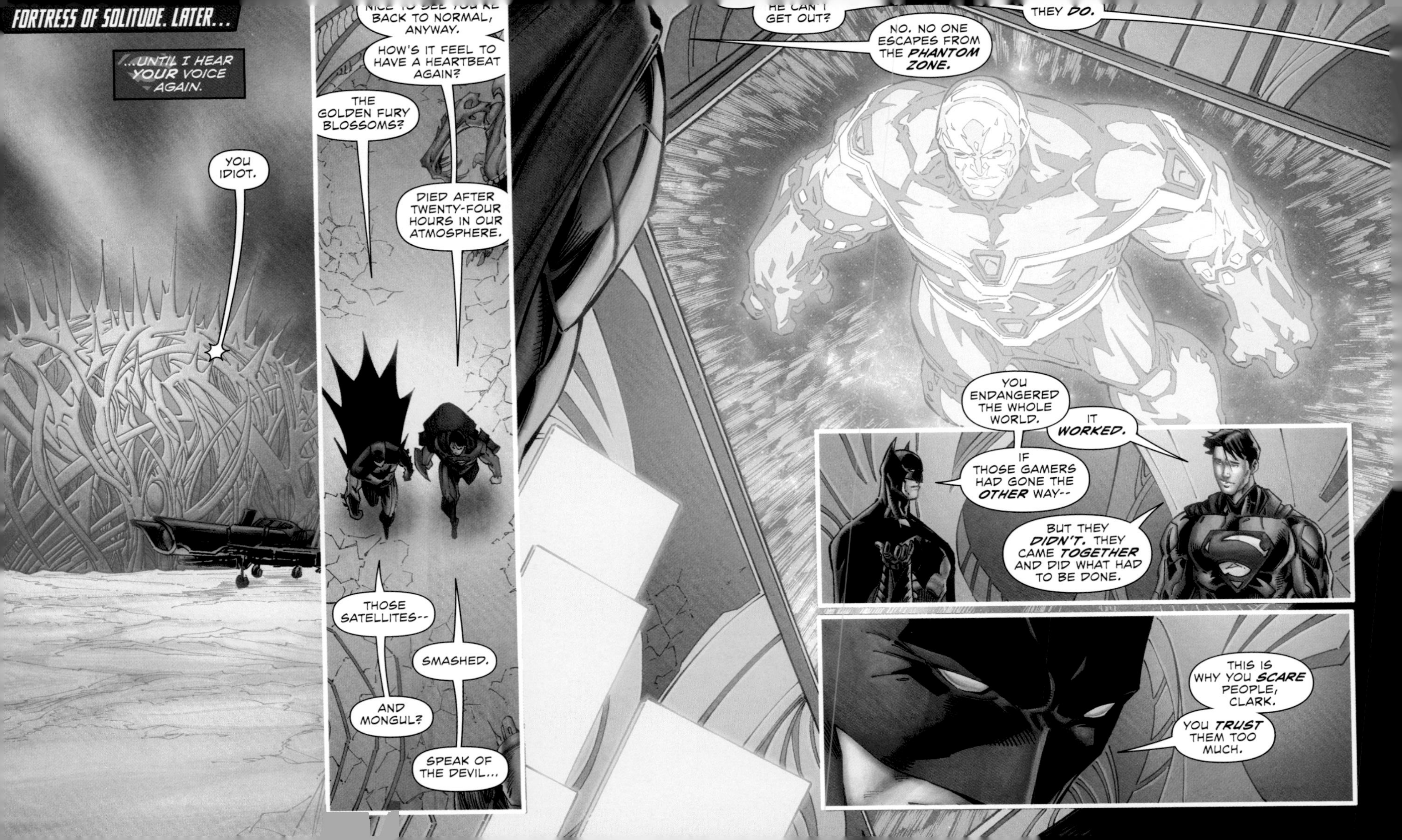
FORTRESS OF SOLITUDE. LATER...
...UNTIL I HEAR YOUR VOICE AGAIN.
YOU IDIOT.
BACK TO NORMAL, ANYWAY.
HOW'S IT FEEL TO HAVE A HEARTBEAT AGAIN?
THE GOLDEN FURY BLOSSOMS?
DIED AFTER TWENTY-FOUR HOURS IN OUR ATMOSPHERE.
THOSE SATELLITES--
SMASHED.
AND MONGUL?
SPEAK OF THE DEVIL...
GET OUT?
NO. NO ONE ESCAPES FROM THE PHANTOM ZONE.
THEY DO.
YOU ENDANGERED THE WHOLE WORLD.
IT WORKED.
IF THOSE GAMERS HAD GONE THE OTHER WAY--
BUT THEY DIDN'T. THEY CAME TOGETHER AND DID WHAT HAD TO BE DONE.
THIS IS WHY YOU SCARE PEOPLE, CLARK.
YOU TRUST THEM TOO MUCH.

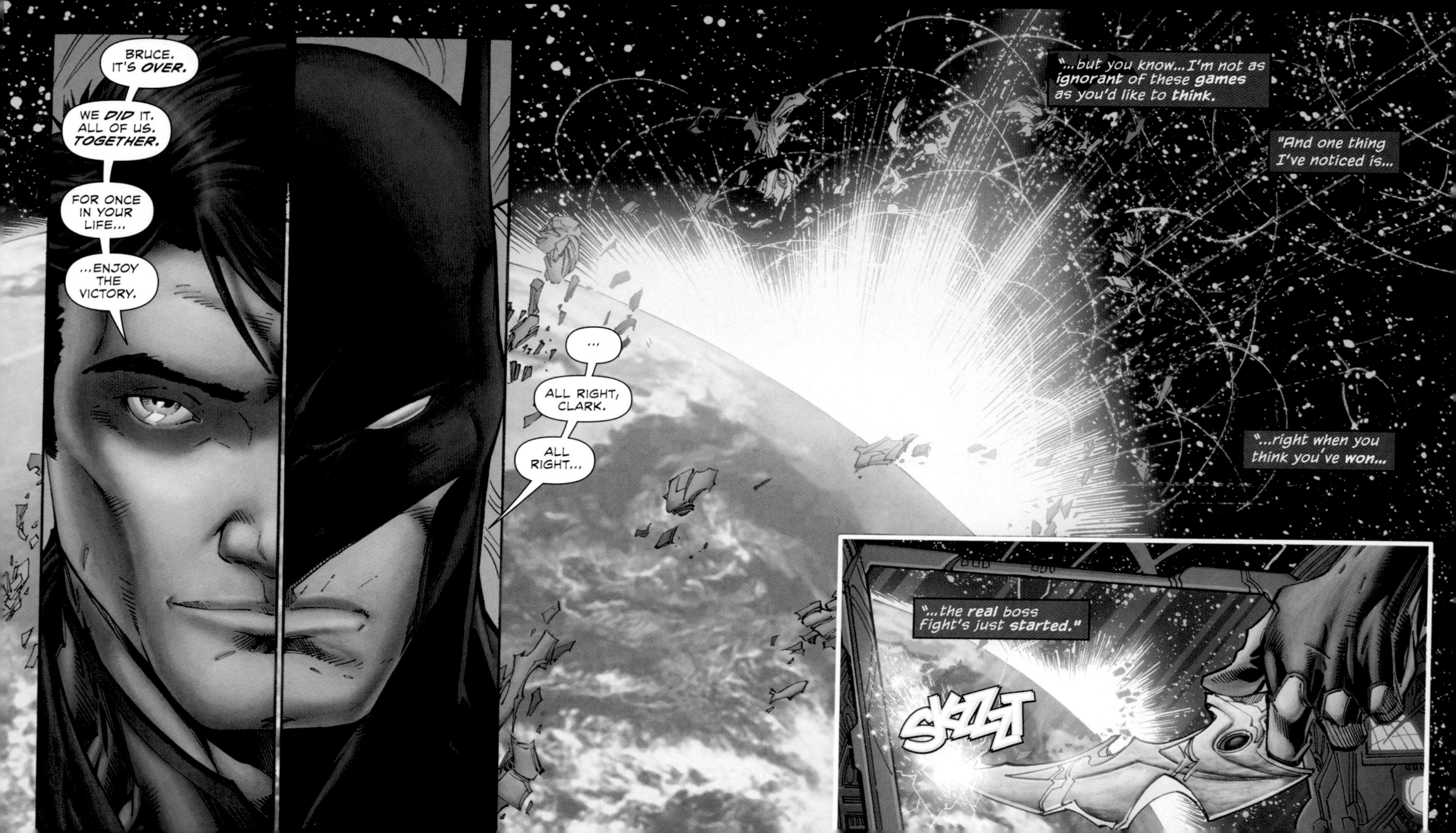

BRUCE. IT'S *OVER.*
WE *DID* IT. ALL OF US. *TOGETHER.*
FOR ONCE IN YOUR LIFE...
...ENJOY THE VICTORY.
...
ALL RIGHT, CLARK.
ALL RIGHT...
"...but you know...I'm not as **ignorant** of these **games** as you'd like to **think.**
"And one thing I've noticed is...
"...right when you think you've **won**...
"...the **real** boss fight's just **started.**"
SKZZT

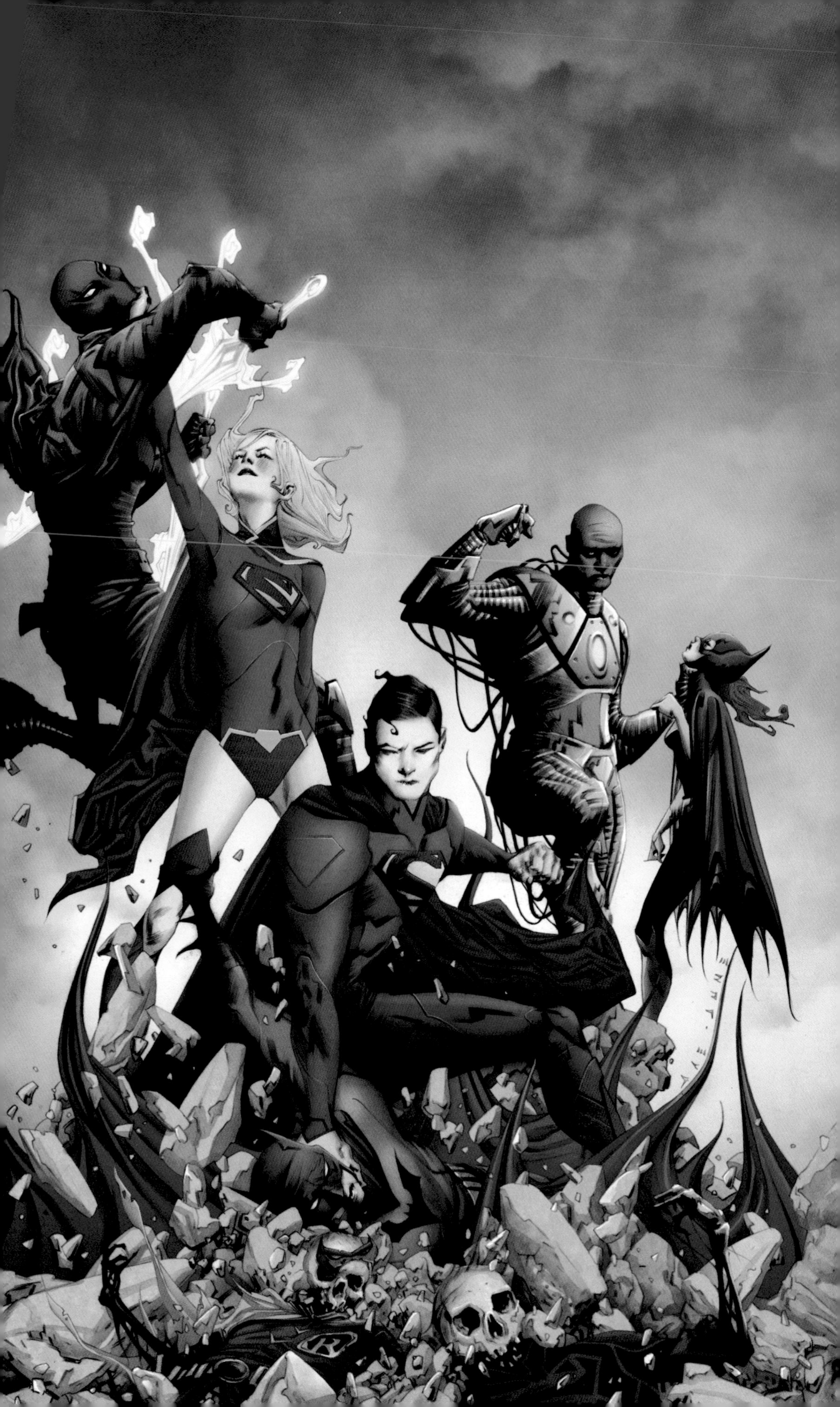

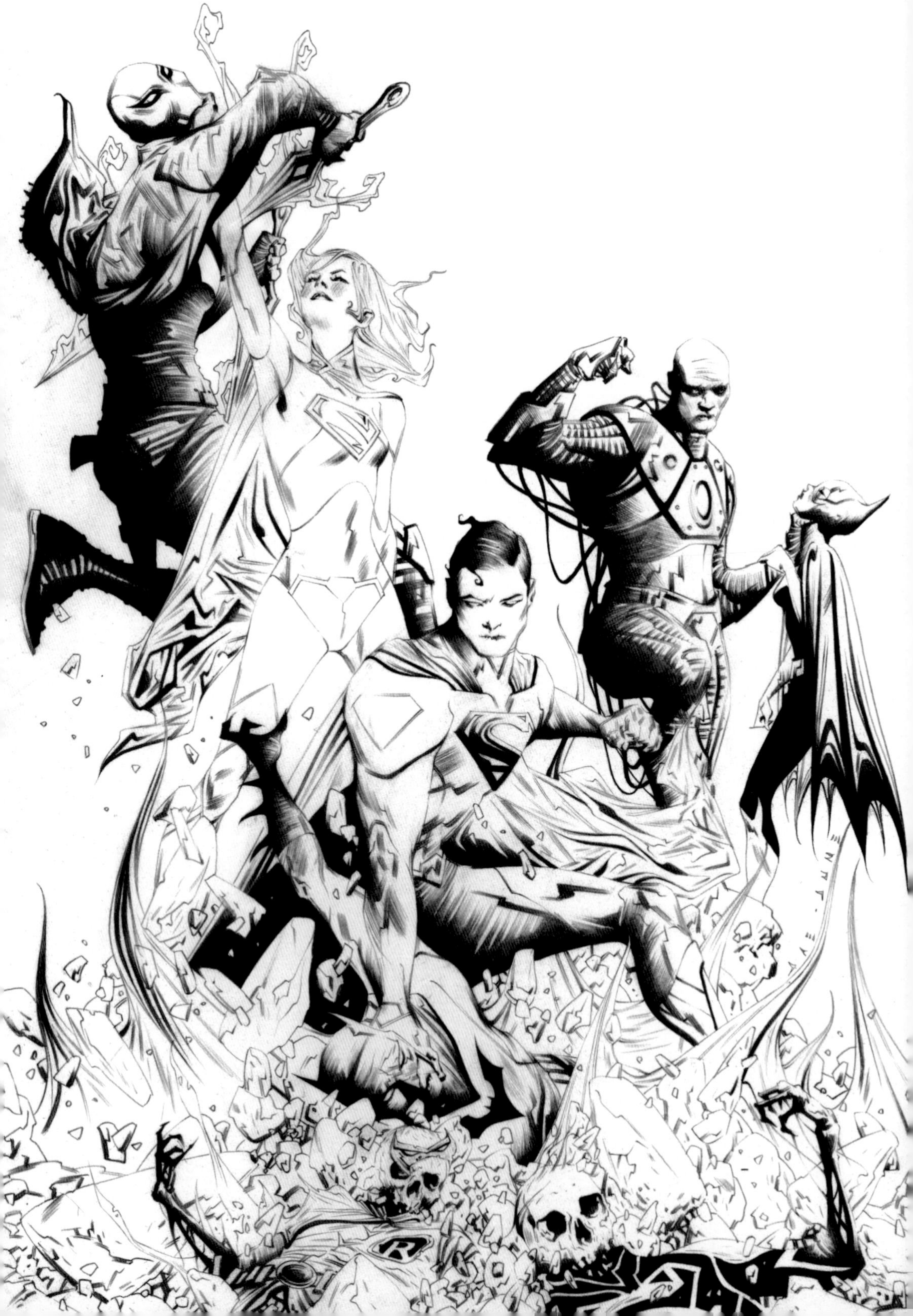

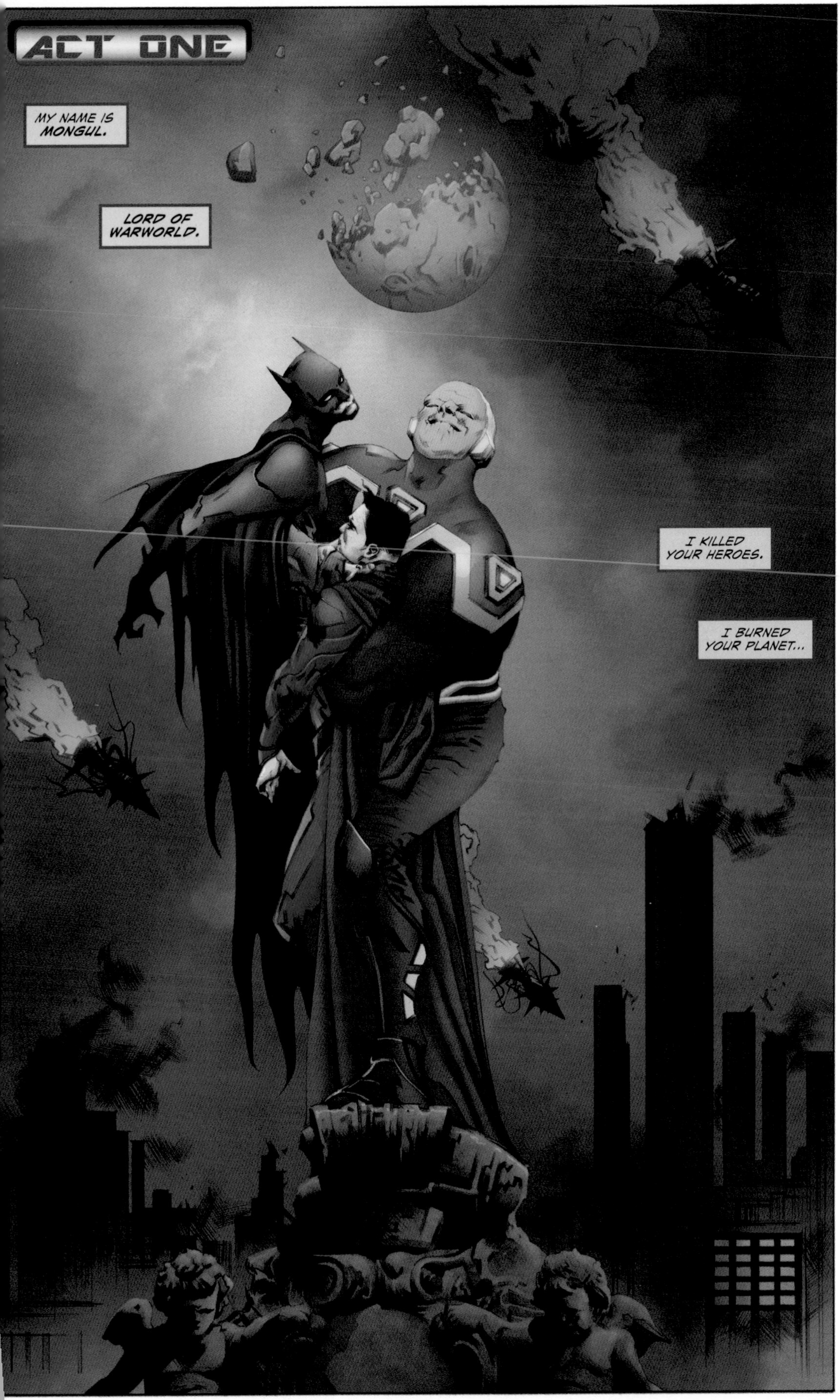
ACT ONE
MY NAME IS MONGUL.
LORD OF WARWORLD.
I KILLED YOUR HEROES.
I BURNED YOUR PLANET...

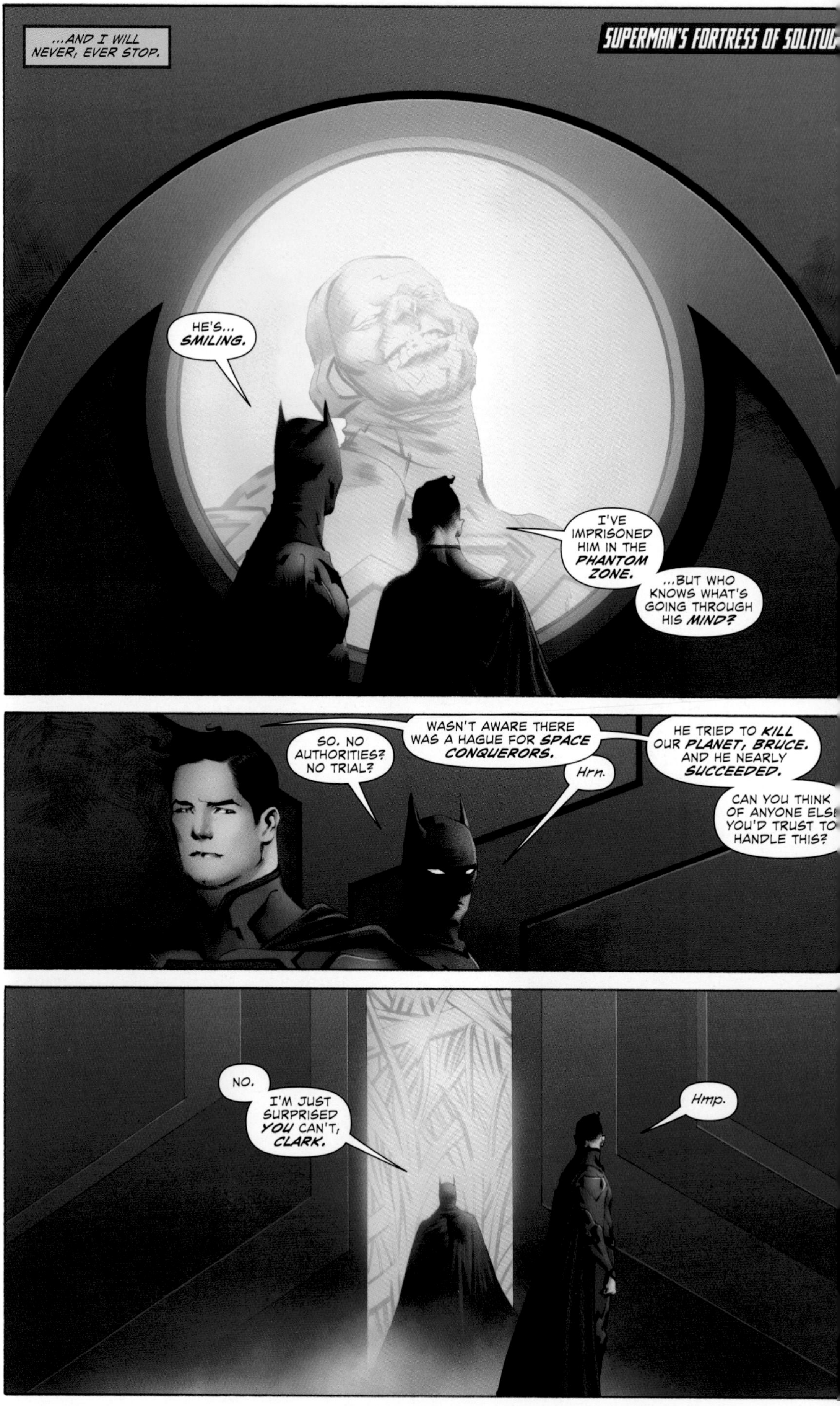
...AND I WILL NEVER, EVER STOP.
SUPERMAN'S FORTRESS OF SOLITUD
HE'S... SMILING.
I'VE IMPRISONED HIM IN THE PHANTOM ZONE.
...BUT WHO KNOWS WHAT'S GOING THROUGH HIS MIND?
SO. NO AUTHORITIES? NO TRIAL?
WASN'T AWARE THERE WAS A HAGUE FOR SPACE CONQUERORS.
Hrn.
HE TRIED TO KILL OUR PLANET, BRUCE. AND HE NEARLY SUCCEEDED.
CAN YOU THINK OF ANYONE ELSE YOU'D TRUST TO HANDLE THIS?
NO.
I'M JUST SURPRISED YOU CAN'T, CLARK.
Hmp.

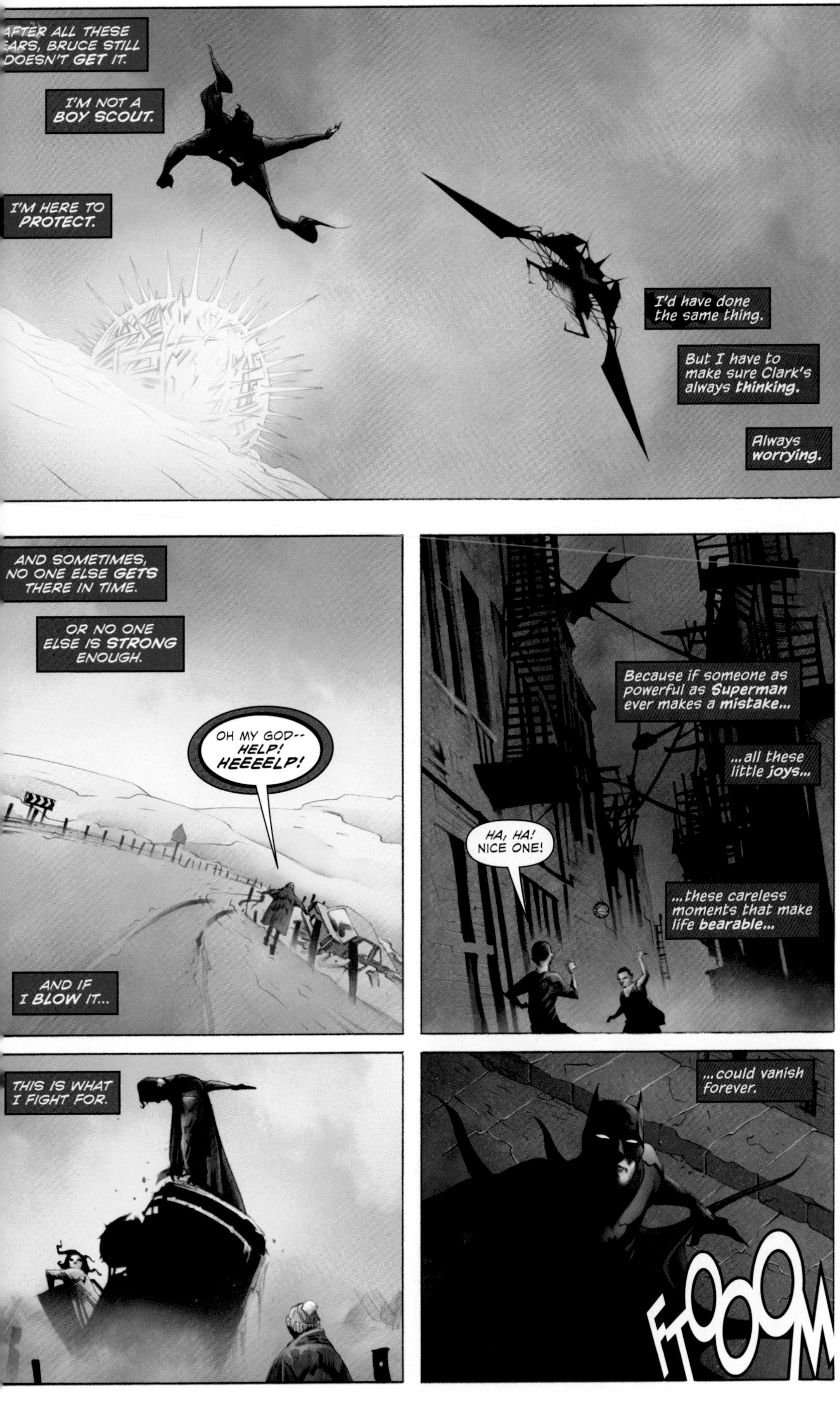
AFTER ALL THESE YEARS, BRUCE STILL DOESN'T GET IT.
I'M NOT A BOY SCOUT.
I'M HERE TO PROTECT.
I'd have done the same thing.
But I have to make sure Clark's always thinking.
Always worrying.
AND SOMETIMES, NO ONE ELSE GETS THERE IN TIME.
OR NO ONE ELSE IS STRONG ENOUGH.
OH MY GOD-- HELP! HEEEELP!
AND IF I BLOW IT...
Because if someone as powerful as Superman ever makes a mistake...
...all these little joys...
HA, HA! NICE ONE!
...these careless moments that make life bearable...
THIS IS WHAT I FIGHT FOR.
...could vanish forever.
FTOOOM

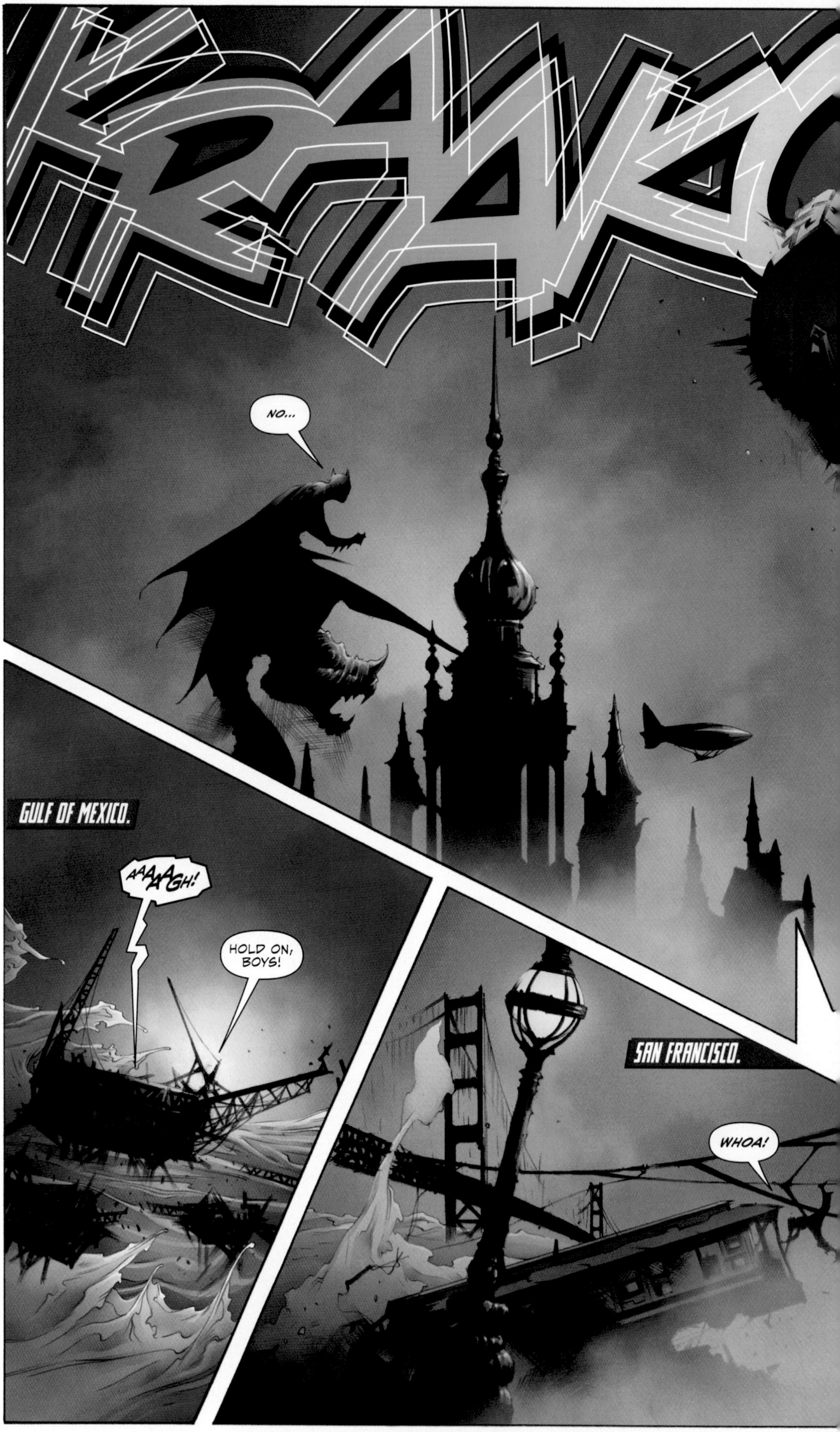
KRAKAKA
NO...
GULF OF MEXICO.
AAAAAGH!
HOLD ON, BOYS!
SAN FRANCISCO.
WHOA!

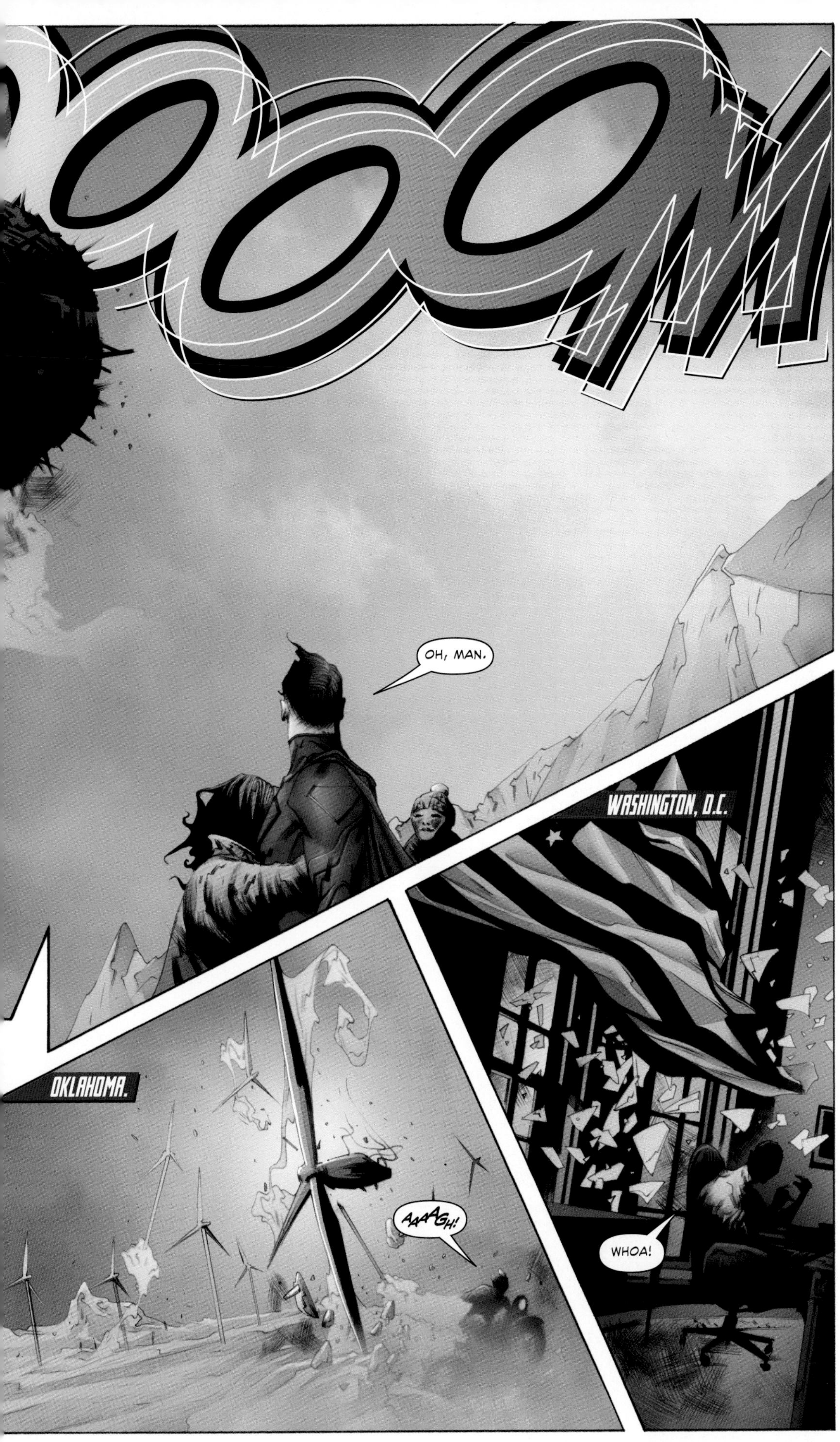
OOOM
OH, MAN.
WASHINGTON, D.C.
OKLAHOMA.
AAAAGH!
WHOA!

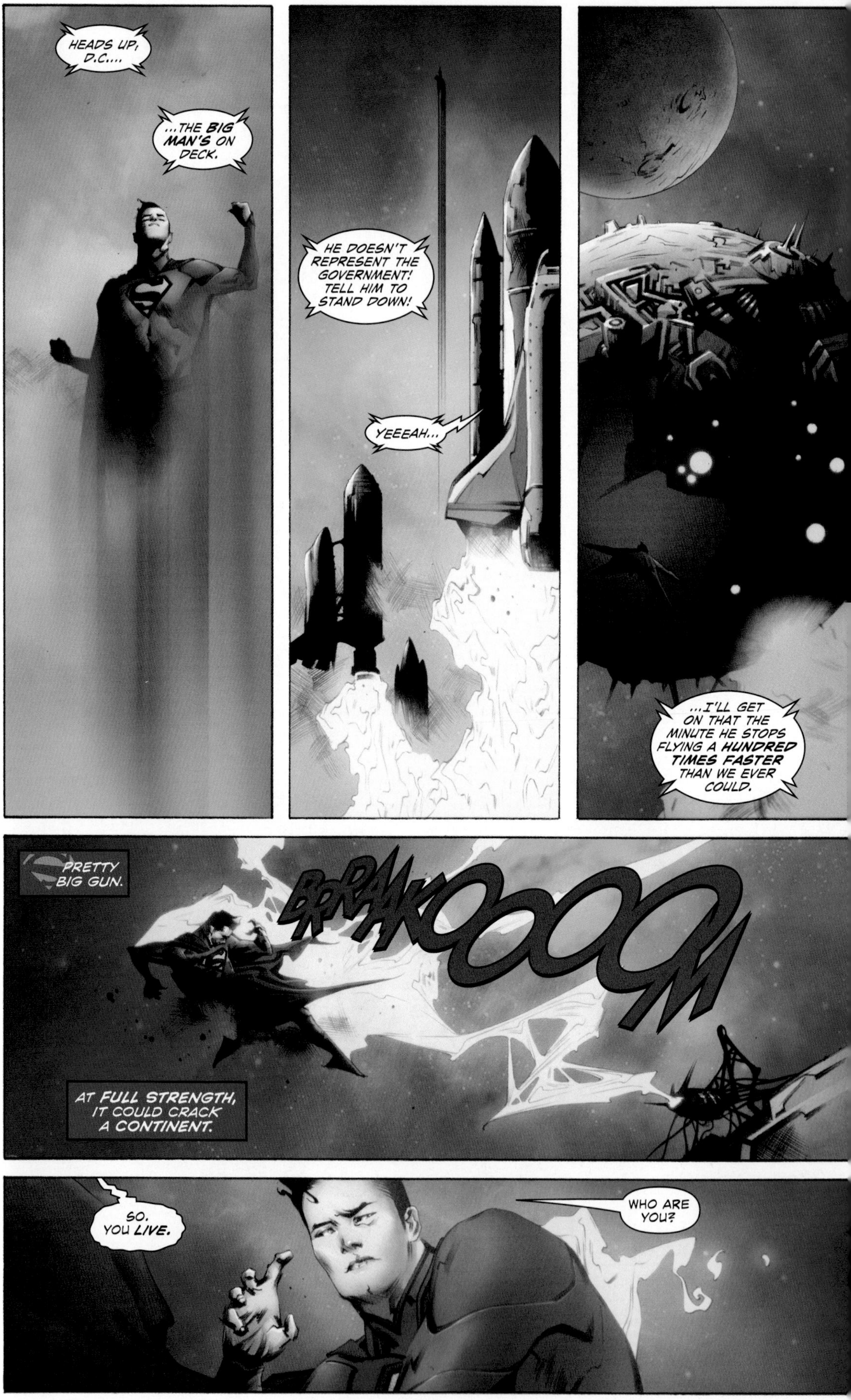
HEADS UP, D.C....
...THE BIG MAN'S ON DECK.
HE DOESN'T REPRESENT THE GOVERNMENT! TELL HIM TO STAND DOWN!
YEEEAH...
...I'LL GET ON THAT THE MINUTE HE STOPS FLYING A HUNDRED TIMES FASTER THAN WE EVER COULD.
PRETTY BIG GUN.
BRRAKOOOOM
AT FULL STRENGTH, IT COULD CRACK A CONTINENT.
SO. YOU LIVE.
WHO ARE YOU?

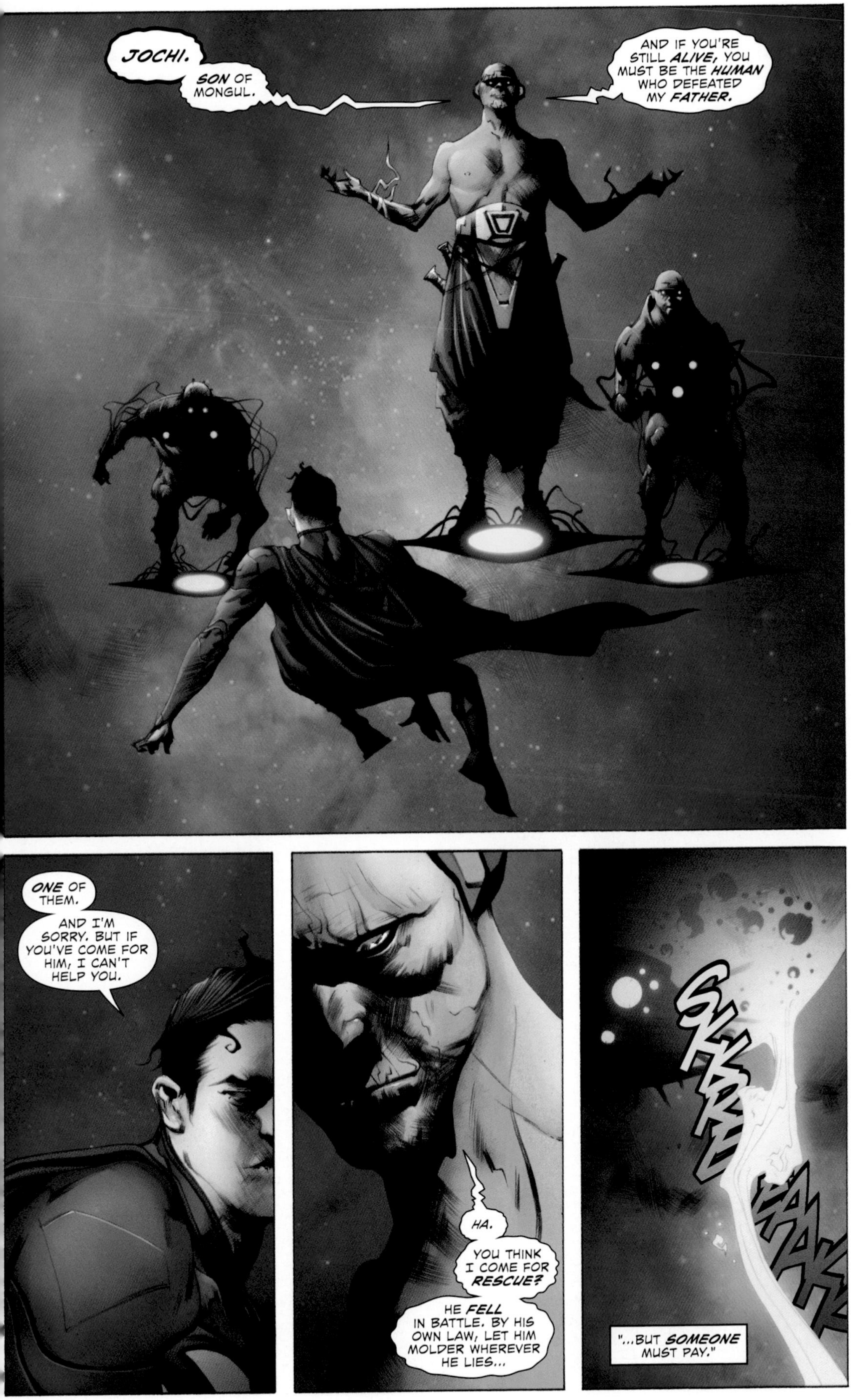
JOCHI.
SON OF MONGUL.
AND IF YOU'RE STILL ALIVE, YOU MUST BE THE HUMAN WHO DEFEATED MY FATHER.
ONE OF THEM.
AND I'M SORRY. BUT IF YOU'VE COME FOR HIM, I CAN'T HELP YOU.
HA.
YOU THINK I COME FOR RESCUE?
HE FELL IN BATTLE. BY HIS OWN LAW, LET HIM MOLDER WHEREVER HE LIES...
"...BUT SOMEONE MUST PAY."

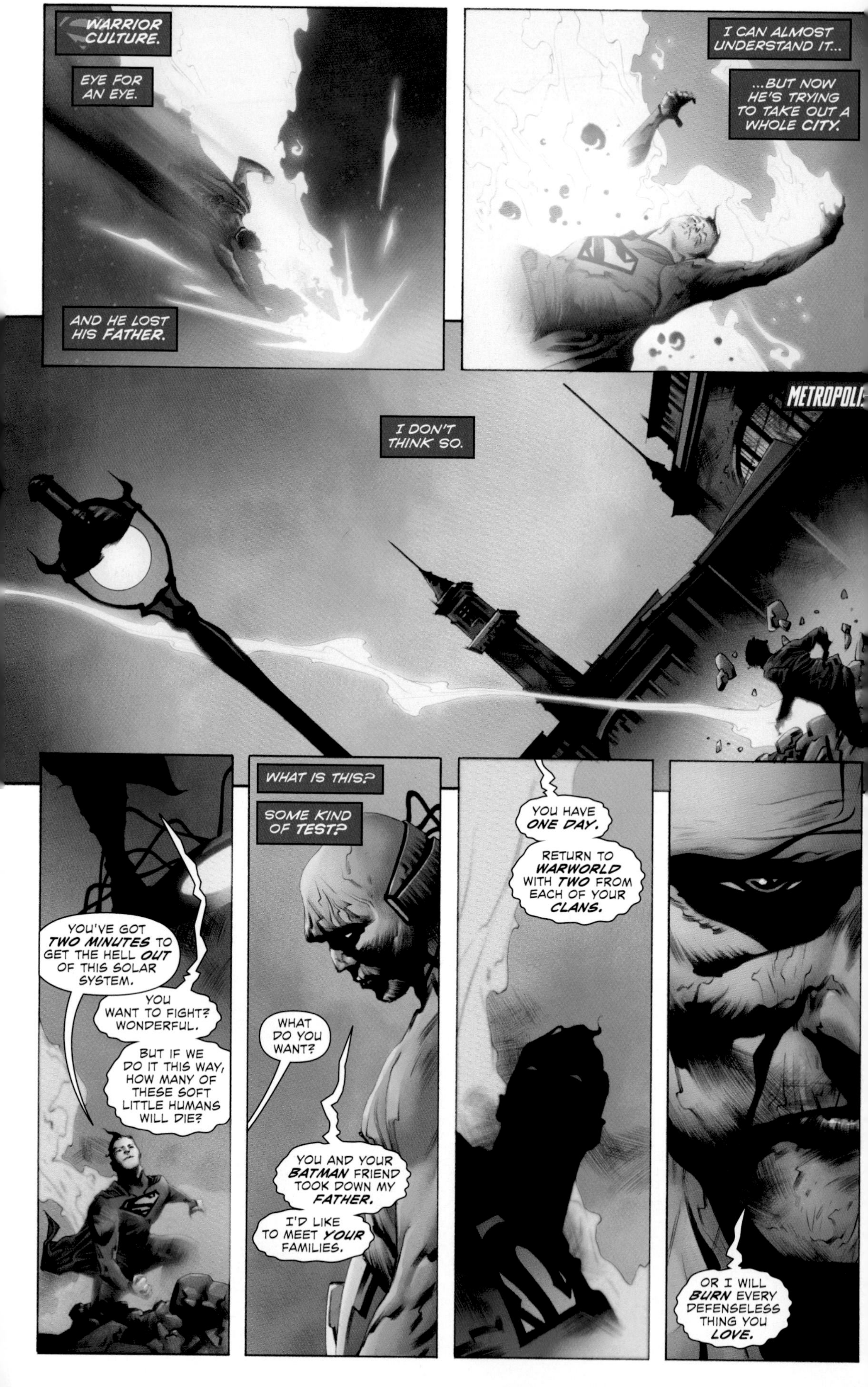

WARRIOR CULTURE.
EYE FOR AN EYE.
AND HE LOST HIS FATHER.
I CAN ALMOST UNDERSTAND IT...
...BUT NOW HE'S TRYING TO TAKE OUT A WHOLE CITY.
METROPOLI
I DON'T THINK SO.
YOU'VE GOT TWO MINUTES TO GET THE HELL OUT OF THIS SOLAR SYSTEM.
YOU WANT TO FIGHT? WONDERFUL.
BUT IF WE DO IT THIS WAY, HOW MANY OF THESE SOFT LITTLE HUMANS WILL DIE?
WHAT IS THIS?
SOME KIND OF TEST?
WHAT DO YOU WANT?
YOU AND YOUR BATMAN FRIEND TOOK DOWN MY FATHER.
I'D LIKE TO MEET YOUR FAMILIES.
YOU HAVE ONE DAY.
RETURN TO WARWORLD WITH TWO FROM EACH OF YOUR CLANS.
OR I WILL BURN EVERY DEFENSELESS THING YOU LOVE.

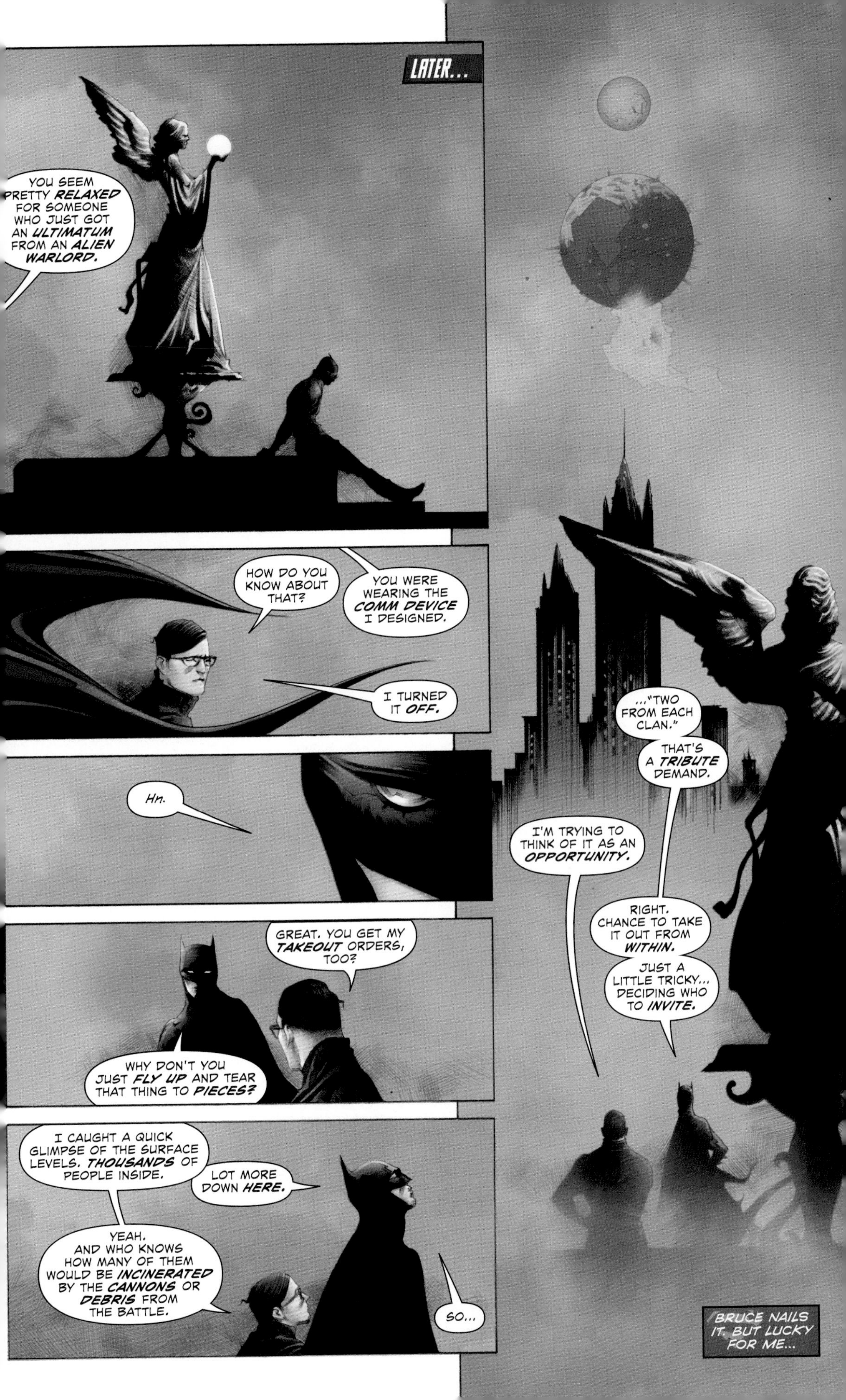
LATER...
YOU SEEM PRETTY RELAXED FOR SOMEONE WHO JUST GOT AN ULTIMATUM FROM AN ALIEN WARLORD.
HOW DO YOU KNOW ABOUT THAT?
YOU WERE WEARING THE COMM DEVICE I DESIGNED.
I TURNED IT OFF.
Hn.
GREAT. YOU GET MY TAKEOUT ORDERS, TOO?
WHY DON'T YOU JUST FLY UP AND TEAR THAT THING TO PIECES?
I CAUGHT A QUICK GLIMPSE OF THE SURFACE LEVELS. THOUSANDS OF PEOPLE INSIDE.
LOT MORE DOWN HERE.
YEAH. AND WHO KNOWS HOW MANY OF THEM WOULD BE INCINERATED BY THE CANNONS OR DEBRIS FROM THE BATTLE.
SO...
..."TWO FROM EACH CLAN."
THAT'S A TRIBUTE DEMAND.
I'M TRYING TO THINK OF IT AS AN OPPORTUNITY.
RIGHT. CHANCE TO TAKE IT OUT FROM WITHIN.
JUST A LITTLE TRICKY... DECIDING WHO TO INVITE.
BRUCE NAILS IT, BUT LUCKY FOR ME...

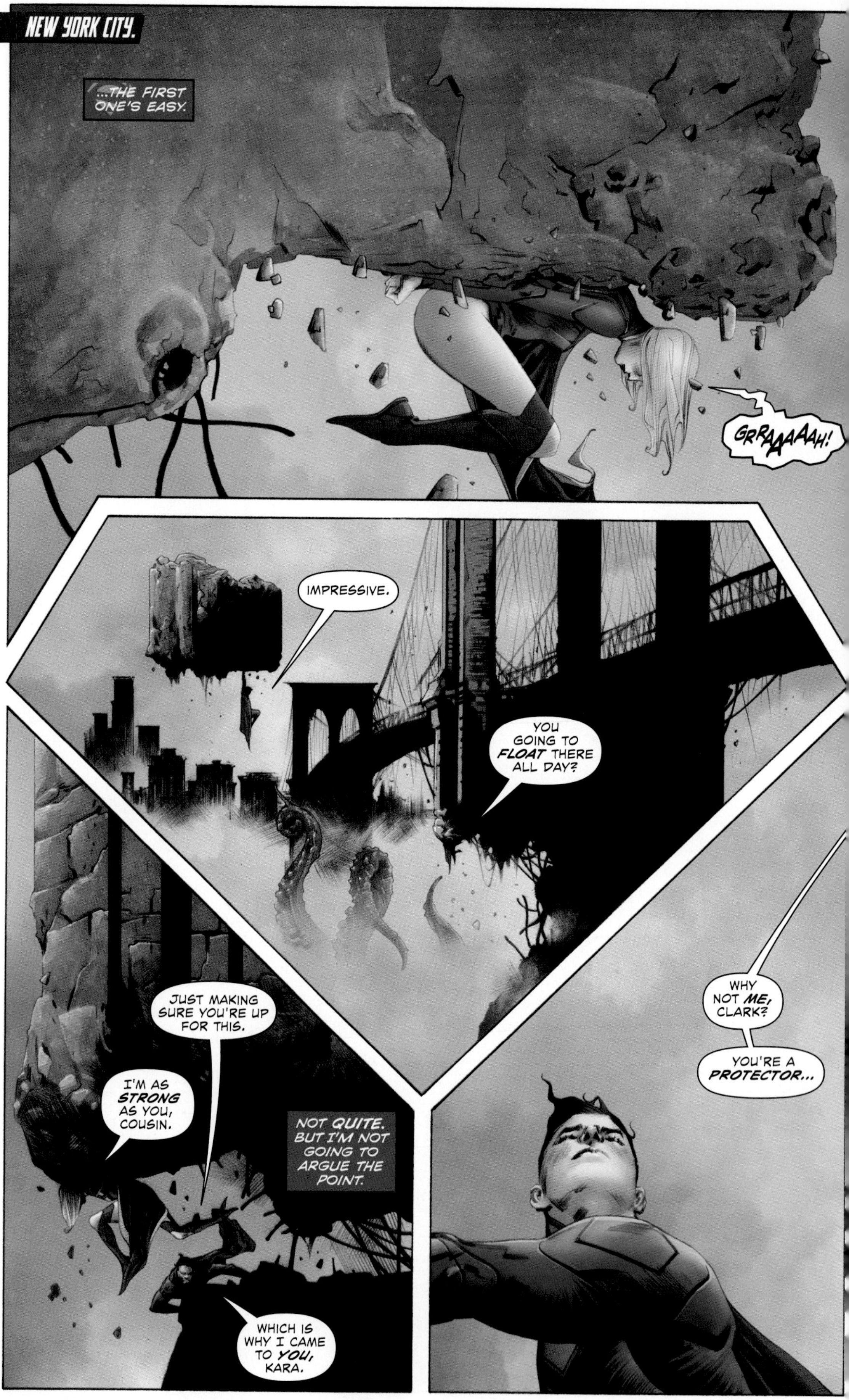
NEW YORK CITY.
...THE FIRST ONE'S EASY.
GRRAAAAAH!
IMPRESSIVE.
YOU GOING TO FLOAT THERE ALL DAY?
JUST MAKING SURE YOU'RE UP FOR THIS.
I'M AS STRONG AS YOU, COUSIN.
NOT QUITE. BUT I'M NOT GOING TO ARGUE THE POINT.
WHICH IS WHY I CAME TO YOU, KARA.
WHY NOT ME, CLARK?
YOU'RE A PROTECTOR...

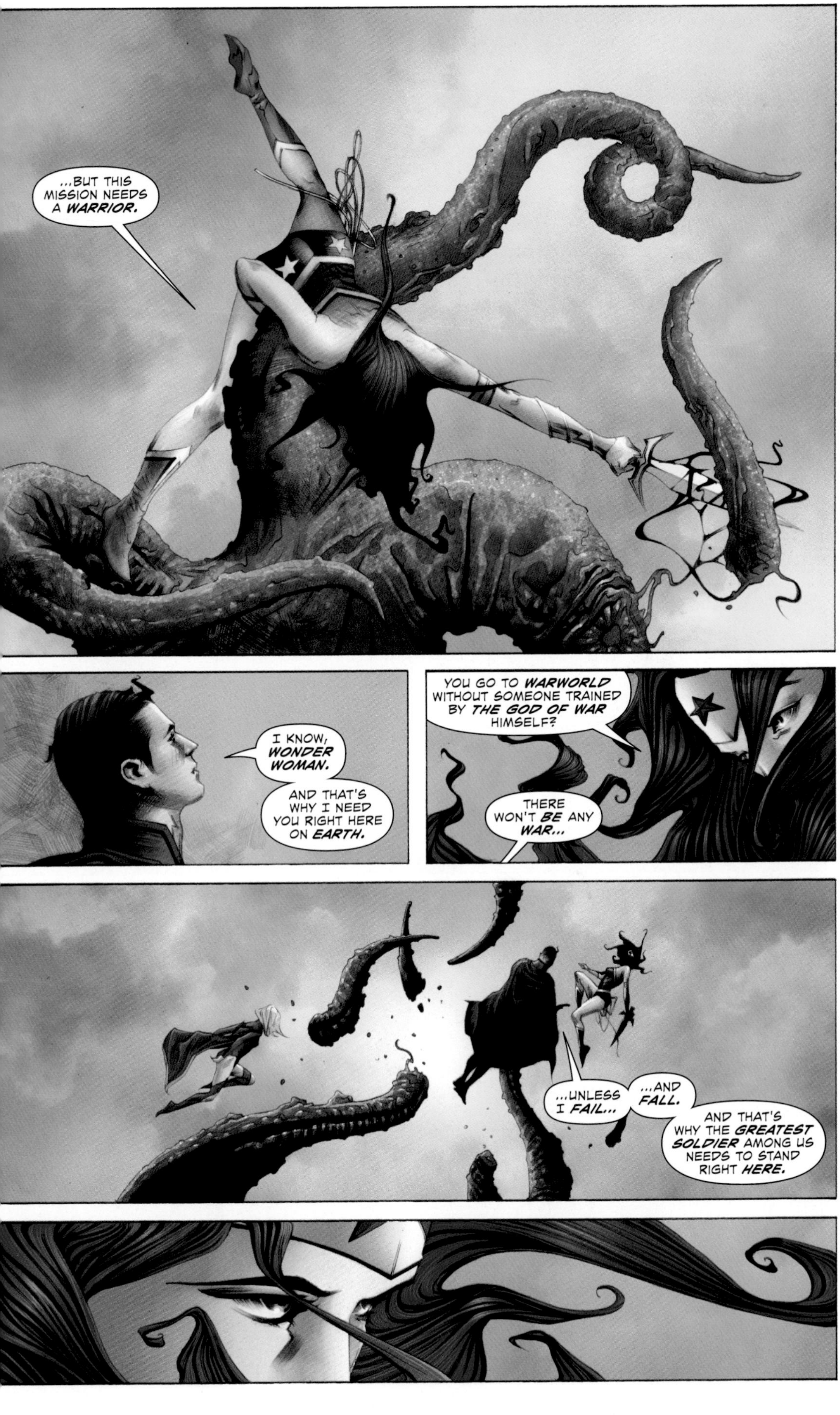
...BUT THIS MISSION NEEDS A WARRIOR.
I KNOW, WONDER WOMAN.
AND THAT'S WHY I NEED YOU RIGHT HERE ON EARTH.
YOU GO TO WARWORLD WITHOUT SOMEONE TRAINED BY THE GOD OF WAR HIMSELF?
THERE WON'T BE ANY WAR...
...UNLESS I FAIL...
...AND FALL.
AND THAT'S WHY THE GREATEST SOLDIER AMONG US NEEDS TO STAND RIGHT HERE.

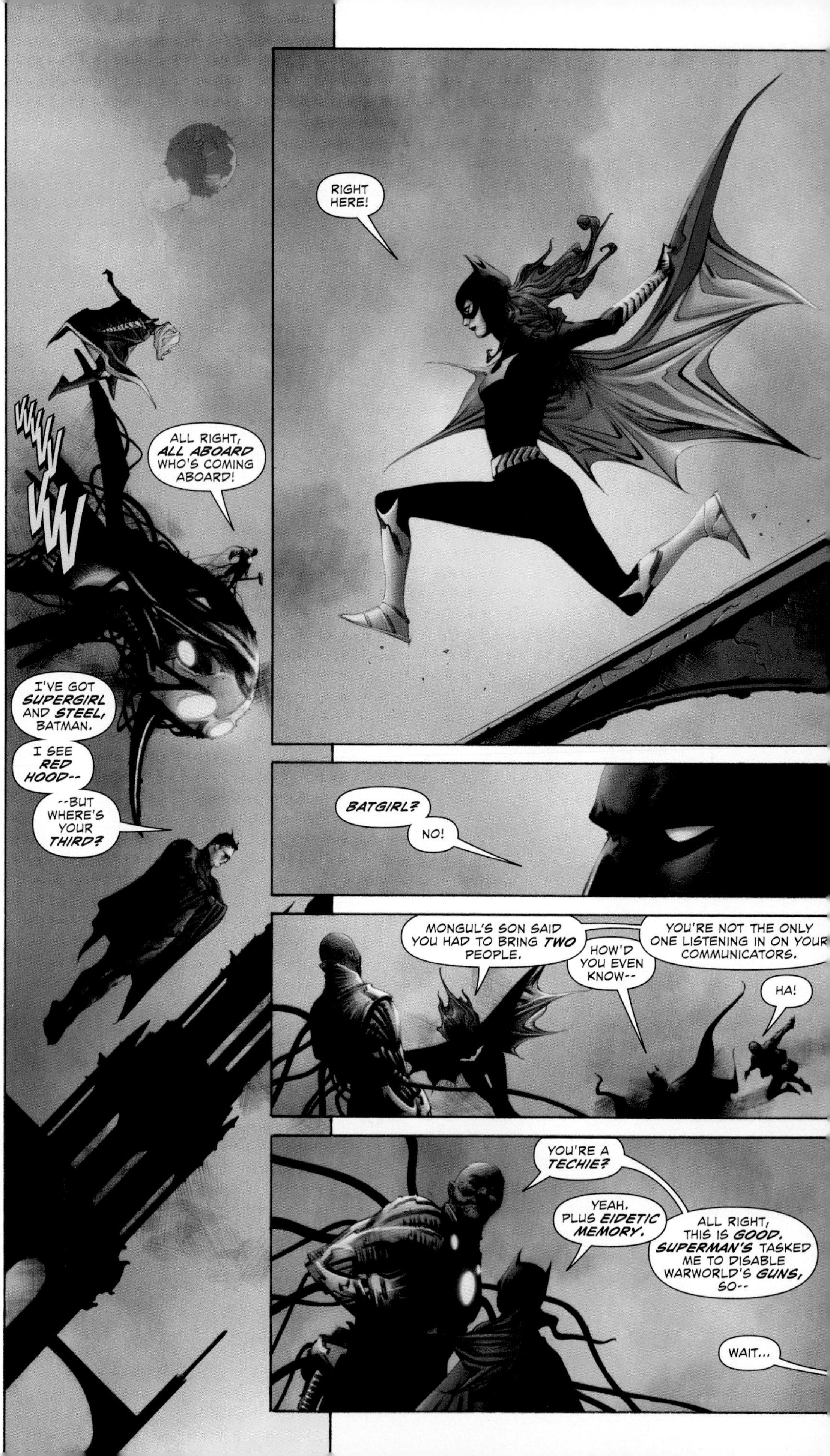
WWWWWW
ALL RIGHT, ALL ABOARD WHO'S COMING ABOARD!
I'VE GOT SUPERGIRL AND STEEL, BATMAN.
I SEE RED HOOD--
--BUT WHERE'S YOUR THIRD?
RIGHT HERE!
BATGIRL?
NO!
MONGUL'S SON SAID YOU HAD TO BRING TWO PEOPLE.
HOW'D YOU EVEN KNOW--
YOU'RE NOT THE ONLY ONE LISTENING IN ON YOUR COMMUNICATORS.
HA!
YOU'RE A TECHIE?
YEAH. PLUS EIDETIC MEMORY.
ALL RIGHT, THIS IS GOOD. SUPERMAN'S TASKED ME TO DISABLE WARWORLD'S GUNS, SO--
WAIT...

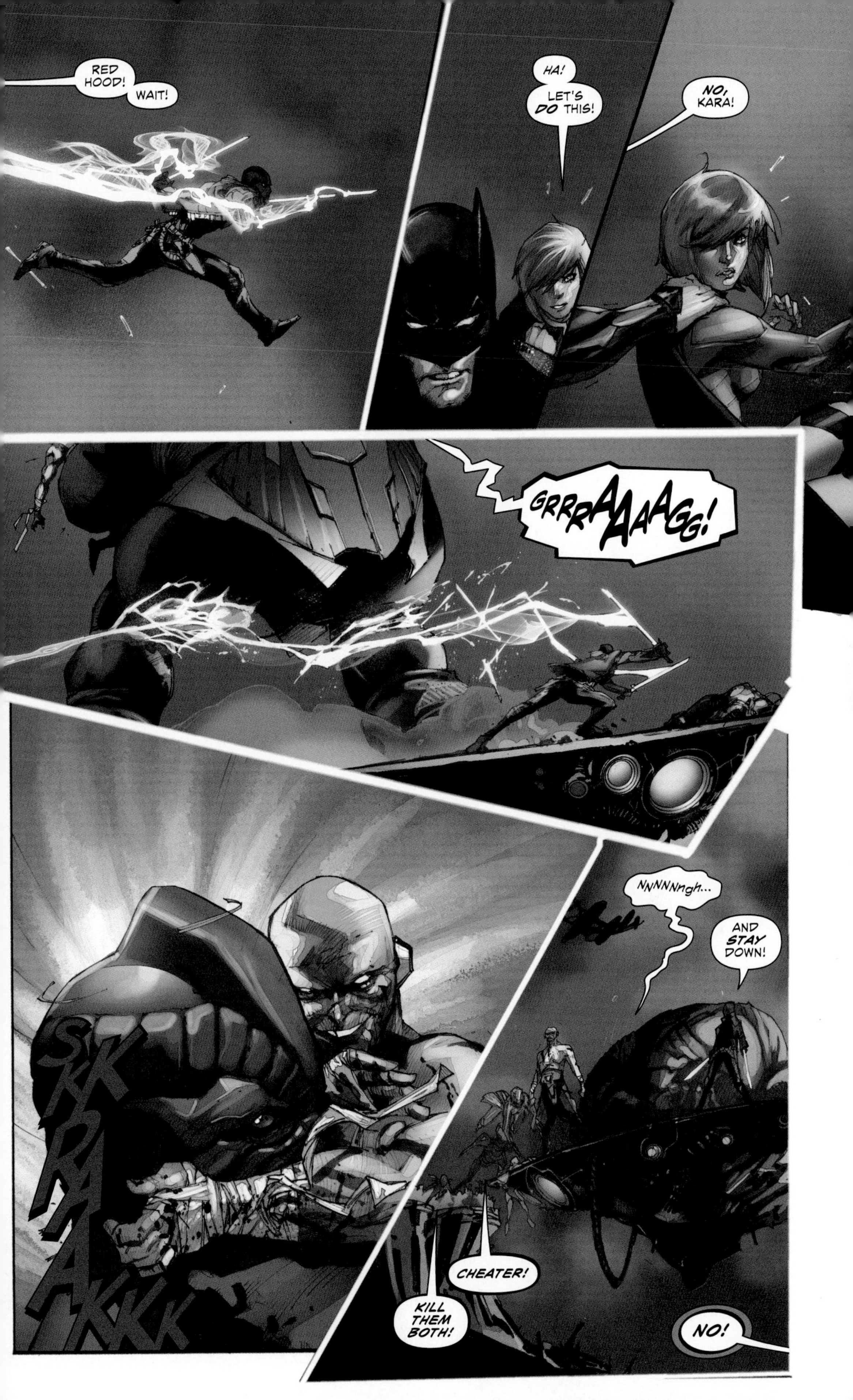
RED HOOD! WAIT!
HA! LET'S DO THIS!
NO, KARA!
GRRRAAAAGG!
SKRAKKK
NNNNNngh...
AND STAY DOWN!
CHEATER!
KILL THEM BOTH!
NO!

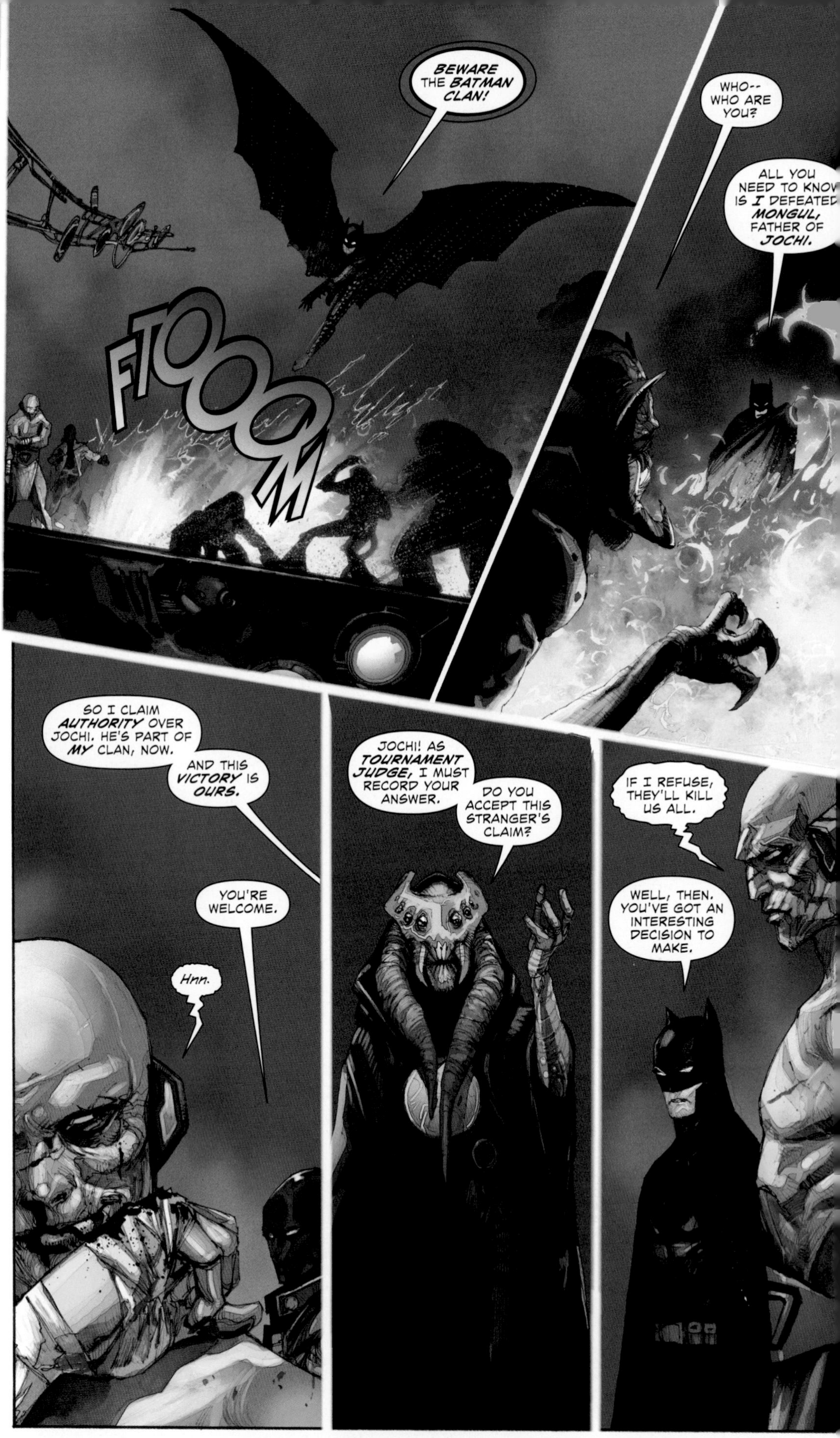
BEWARE THE BATMAN CLAN!
FTOOOM
WHO-- WHO ARE YOU?
ALL YOU NEED TO KNOW IS I DEFEATED MONGUL, FATHER OF JOCHI.
SO I CLAIM AUTHORITY OVER JOCHI. HE'S PART OF MY CLAN, NOW.
AND THIS VICTORY IS OURS.
YOU'RE WELCOME.
Hnn.
JOCHI! AS TOURNAMENT JUDGE, I MUST RECORD YOUR ANSWER.
DO YOU ACCEPT THIS STRANGER'S CLAIM?
IF I REFUSE, THEY'LL KILL US ALL.
WELL, THEN. YOU'VE GOT AN INTERESTING DECISION TO MAKE.

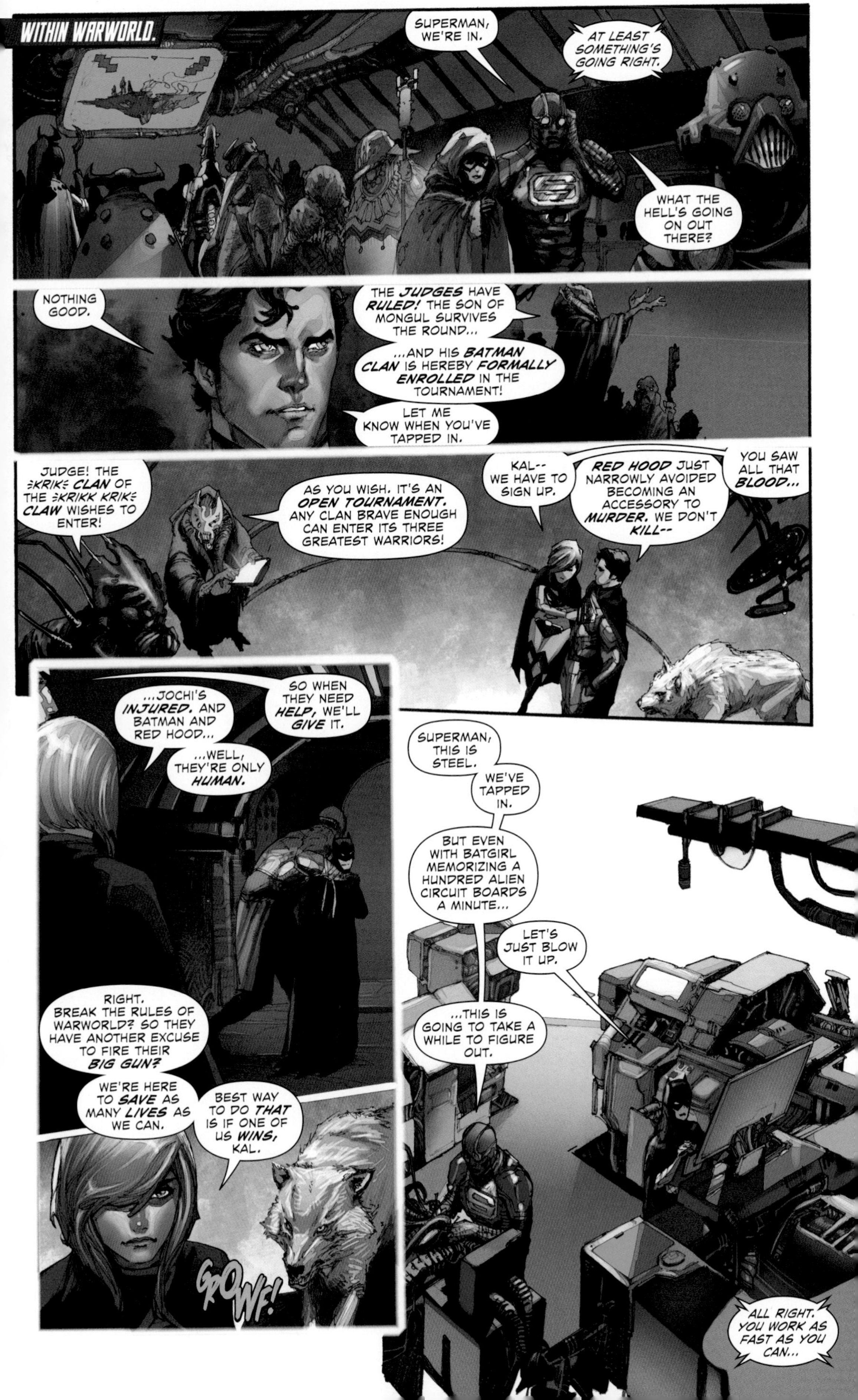
WITHIN WARWORLD.
SUPERMAN, WE'RE IN.
AT LEAST SOMETHING'S GOING RIGHT.
WHAT THE HELL'S GOING ON OUT THERE?
NOTHING GOOD.
THE JUDGES HAVE RULED! THE SON OF MONGUL SURVIVES THE ROUND...
...AND HIS BATMAN CLAN IS HEREBY FORMALLY ENROLLED IN THE TOURNAMENT!
LET ME KNOW WHEN YOU'VE TAPPED IN.
JUDGE! THE ≷KRIK≷ CLAN OF THE ≷KRIKK KRIK≷ CLAW WISHES TO ENTER!
AS YOU WISH. IT'S AN OPEN TOURNAMENT. ANY CLAN BRAVE ENOUGH CAN ENTER ITS THREE GREATEST WARRIORS!
KAL-- WE HAVE TO SIGN UP.
RED HOOD JUST NARROWLY AVOIDED BECOMING AN ACCESSORY TO MURDER. WE DON'T KILL--
YOU SAW ALL THAT BLOOD...
...JOCHI'S INJURED. AND BATMAN AND RED HOOD...
...WELL, THEY'RE ONLY HUMAN.
SO WHEN THEY NEED HELP, WE'LL GIVE IT.
RIGHT. BREAK THE RULES OF WARWORLD? SO THEY HAVE ANOTHER EXCUSE TO FIRE THEIR BIG GUN?
WE'RE HERE TO SAVE AS MANY LIVES AS WE CAN.
BEST WAY TO DO THAT IS IF ONE OF US WINS, KAL.
GROWF!
SUPERMAN, THIS IS STEEL.
WE'VE TAPPED IN.
BUT EVEN WITH BATGIRL MEMORIZING A HUNDRED ALIEN CIRCUIT BOARDS A MINUTE...
LET'S JUST BLOW IT UP.
...THIS IS GOING TO TAKE A WHILE TO FIGURE OUT.
ALL RIGHT. YOU WORK AS FAST AS YOU CAN...

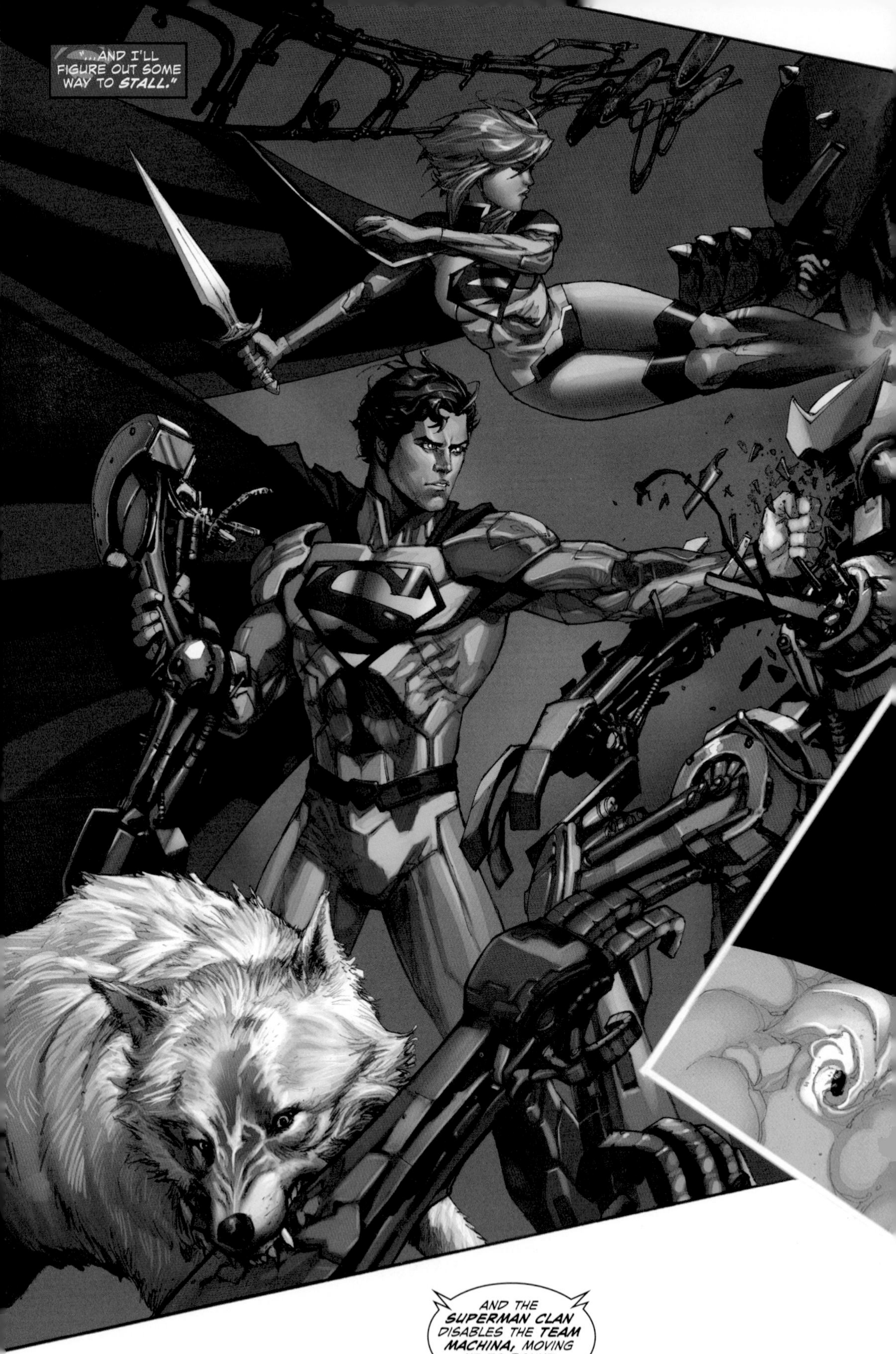
"...AND I'LL FIGURE OUT SOME WAY TO STALL."
AND THE SUPERMAN CLAN DISABLES THE TEAM MACHINA, MOVING UP TO ROUND SEVEN!

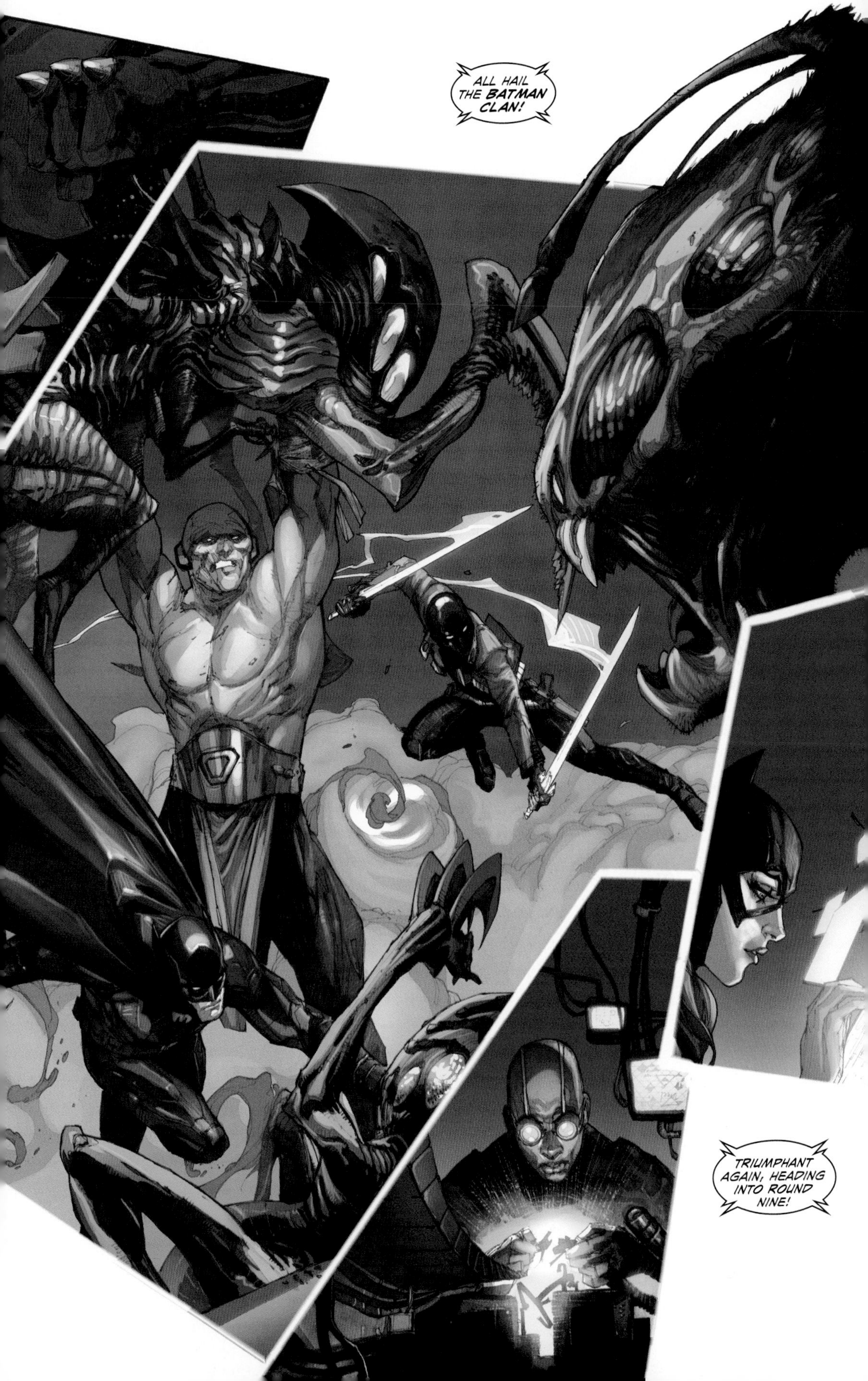
ALL HAIL THE BATMAN CLAN!
TRIUMPHANT AGAIN, HEADING INTO ROUND NINE!

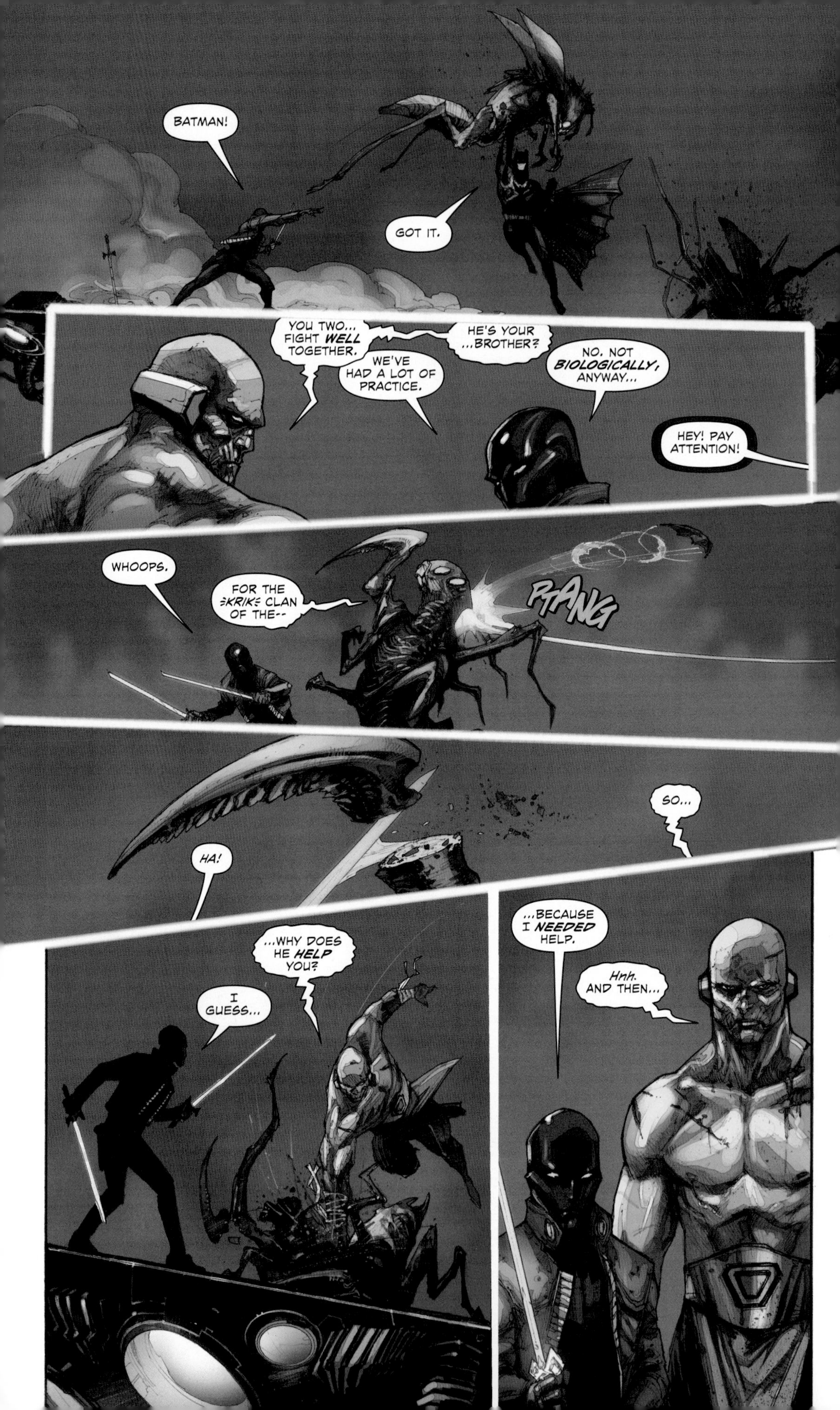
BATMAN!
GOT IT.
YOU TWO... FIGHT **WELL** TOGETHER.
WE'VE HAD A LOT OF PRACTICE.
HE'S YOUR ...BROTHER?
NO. NOT **BIOLOGICALLY,** ANYWAY...
HEY! PAY ATTENTION!
WHOOPS.
FOR THE =KRIK= CLAN OF THE--
PTANG
HA!
SO...
...WHY DOES HE **HELP** YOU?
I GUESS...
...BECAUSE I **NEEDED** HELP.
Hnh. AND THEN...

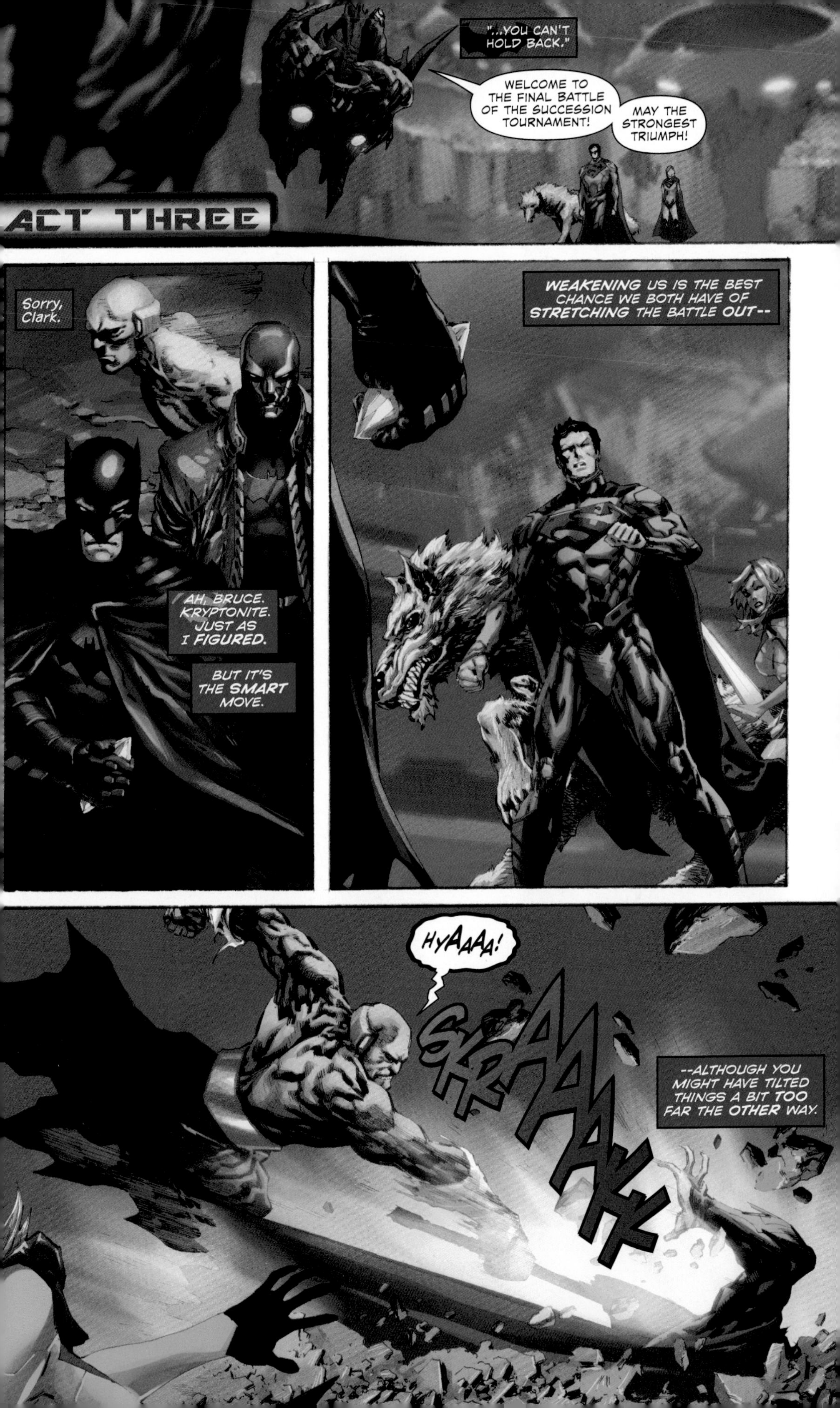
"...YOU CAN'T HOLD BACK."
WELCOME TO THE FINAL BATTLE OF THE SUCCESSION TOURNAMENT!
MAY THE STRONGEST TRIUMPH!
ACT THREE
Sorry, Clark.
AH, BRUCE. KRYPTONITE. JUST AS I FIGURED.
BUT IT'S THE SMART MOVE.
WEAKENING US IS THE BEST CHANCE WE BOTH HAVE OF STRETCHING THE BATTLE OUT--
HYAAAA!
SKRAAAKK
--ALTHOUGH YOU MIGHT HAVE TILTED THINGS A BIT TOO FAR THE OTHER WAY.

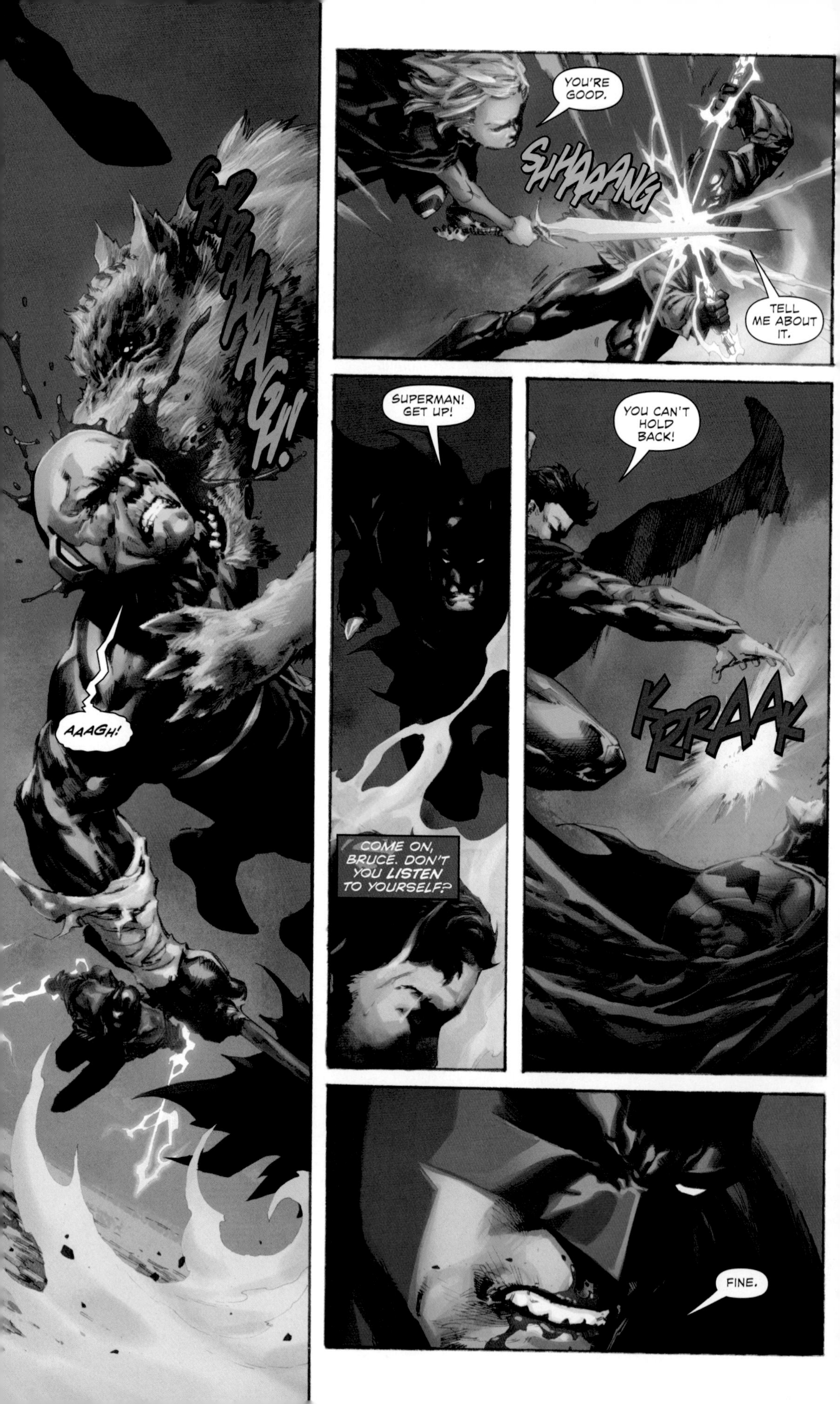
GRRAAAAAAGH!!
AAAGH!
YOU'RE GOOD.
SHHAAANG
TELL ME ABOUT IT.
SUPERMAN! GET UP!
COME ON, BRUCE. DON'T YOU LISTEN TO YOURSELF?
YOU CAN'T HOLD BACK!
KRRAAK
FINE.

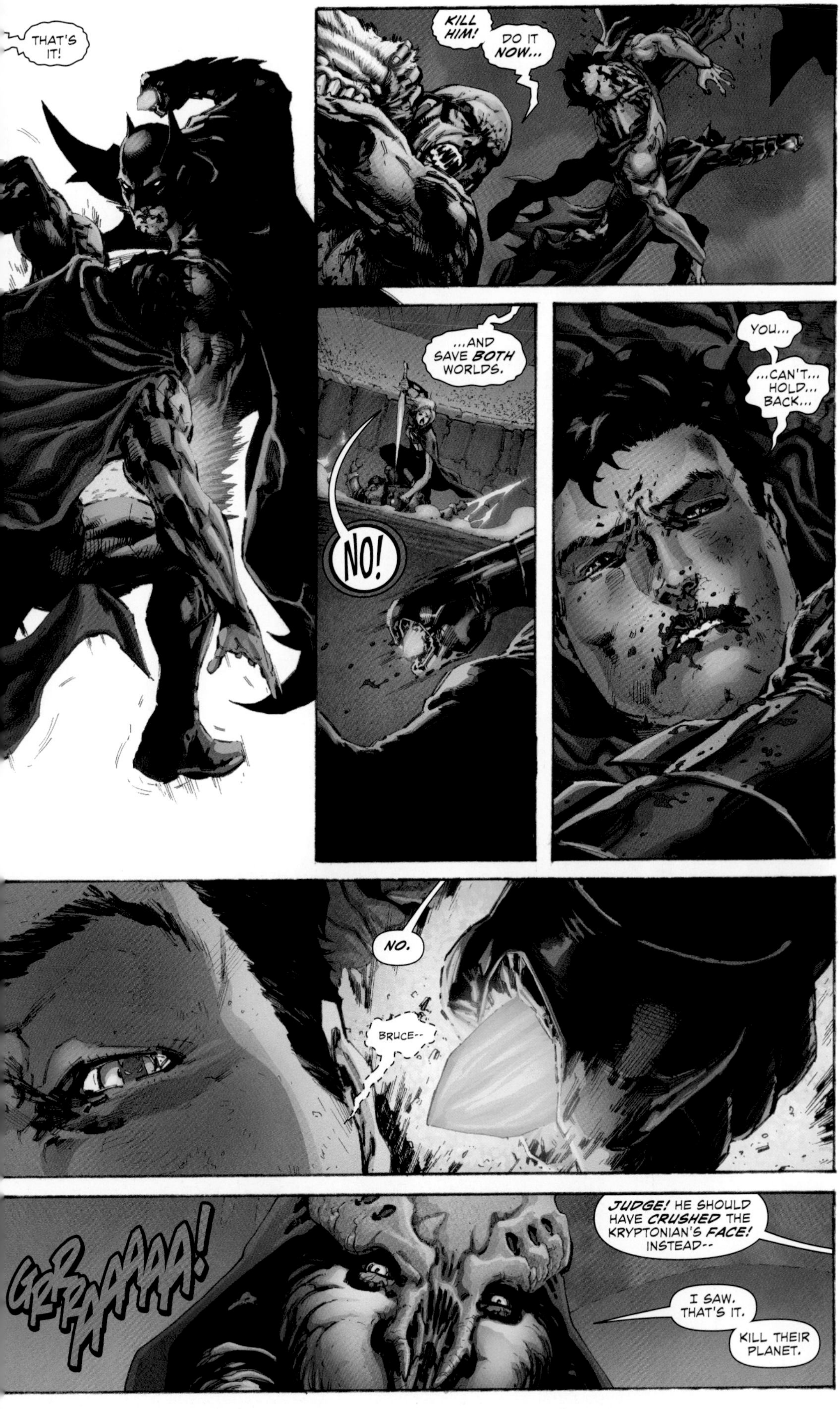
THAT'S IT!
KILL HIM!
DO IT NOW...
...AND SAVE BOTH WORLDS.
NO!
YOU...
...CAN'T...
HOLD...
BACK...
NO.
BRUCE--
GRRAAAAA!
JUDGE! HE SHOULD HAVE CRUSHED THE KRYPTONIAN'S FACE! INSTEAD--
I SAW. THAT'S IT.
KILL THEIR PLANET.

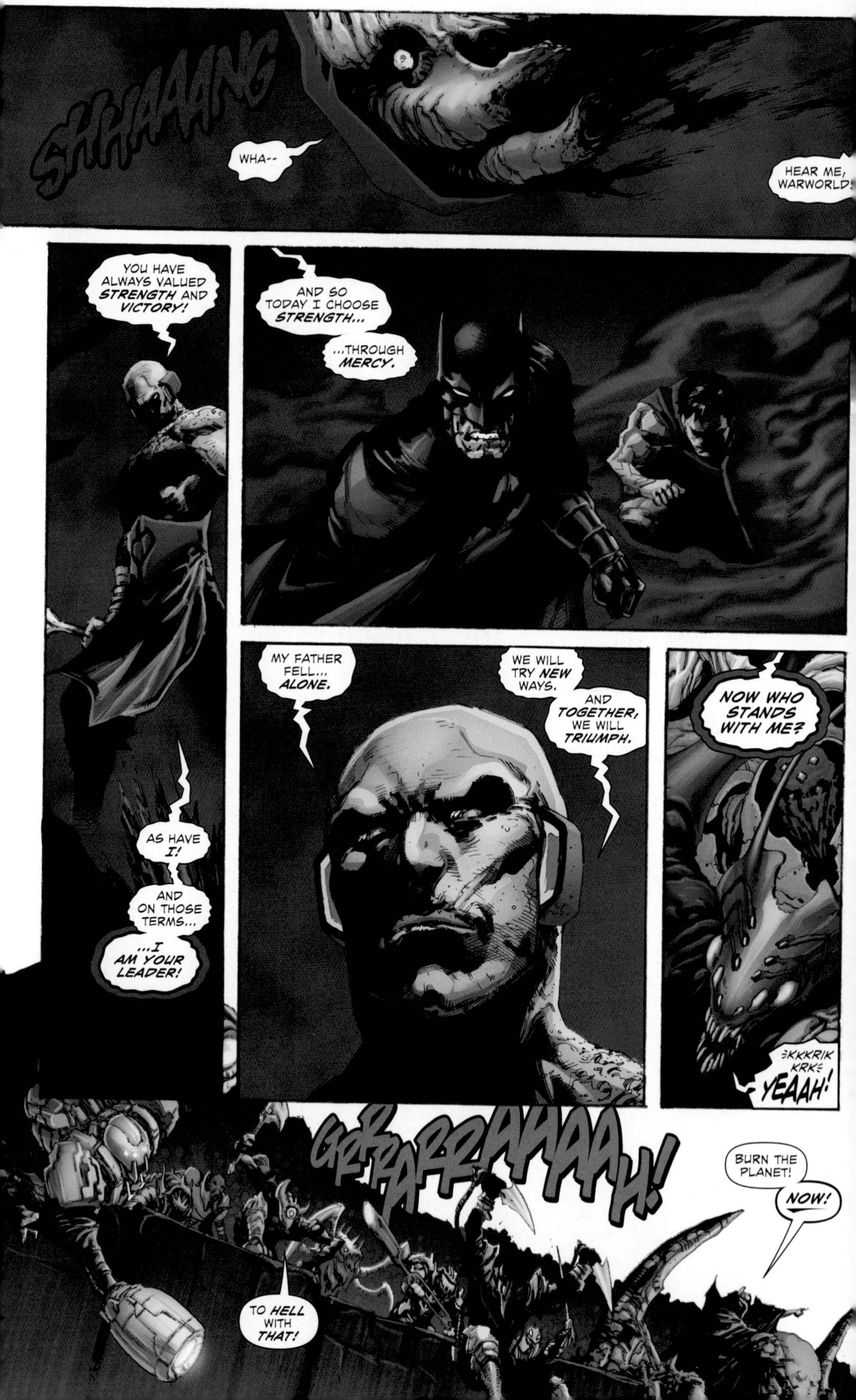
SHHAAANG
WHA--
HEAR ME, WARWORLD!
YOU HAVE ALWAYS VALUED STRENGTH AND VICTORY!
AS HAVE I!
AND ON THOSE TERMS...
...I AM YOUR LEADER!
AND SO TODAY I CHOOSE STRENGTH...
...THROUGH MERCY.
MY FATHER FELL... ALONE.
WE WILL TRY NEW WAYS.
AND TOGETHER, WE WILL TRIUMPH.
NOW WHO STANDS WITH ME?
SKKKRIK KRK-YEAAH!
GRRRARRAAAAAH!
BURN THE PLANET!
NOW!
TO HELL WITH THAT!

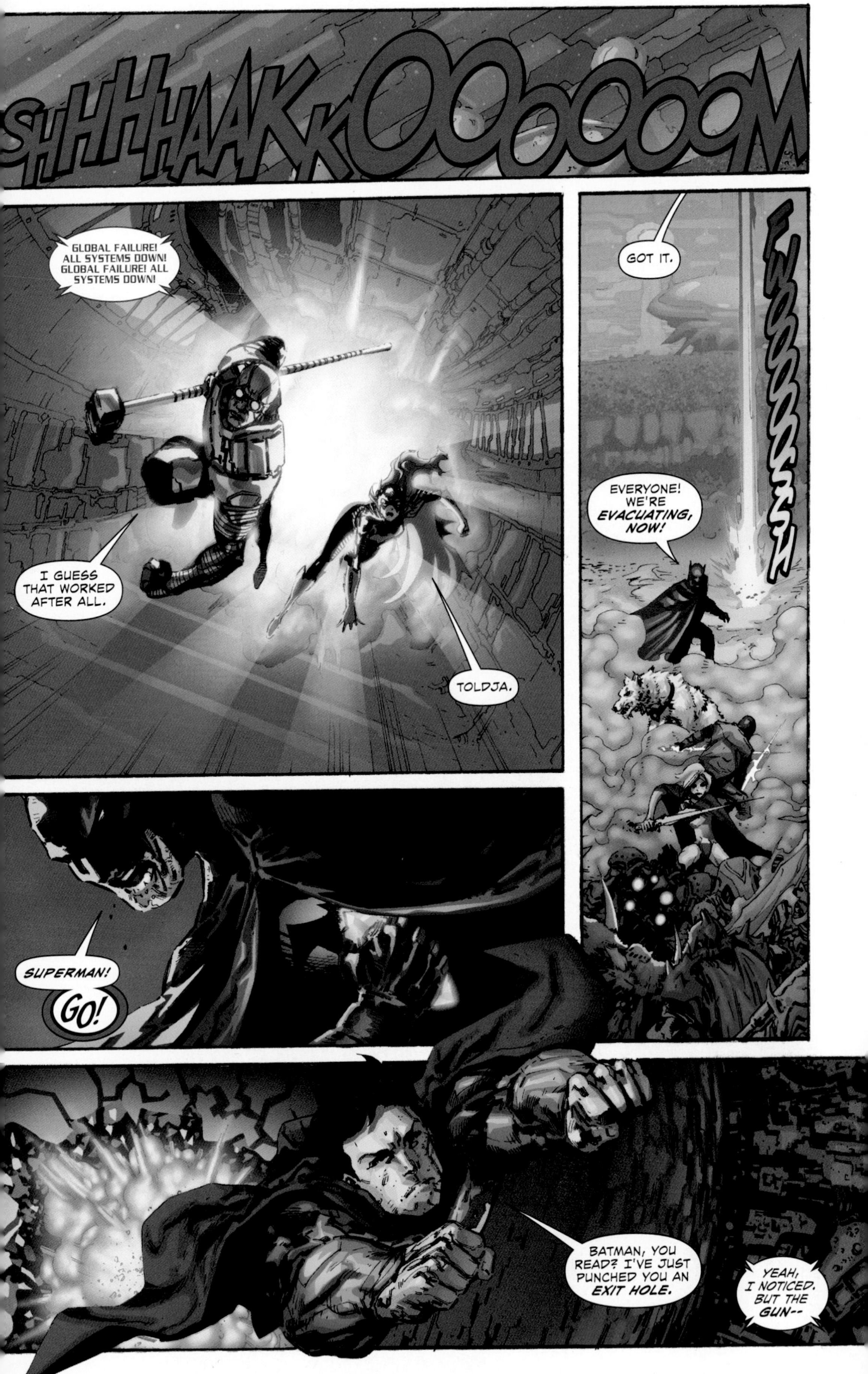
SHHHAAKKOOOOOOOM
GLOBAL FAILURE! ALL SYSTEMS DOWN! GLOBAL FAILURE! ALL SYSTEMS DOWN!
I GUESS THAT WORKED AFTER ALL.
TOLDJA.
GOT IT.
FWOOOOOSSSH
EVERYONE! WE'RE EVACUATING, NOW!
SUPERMAN!
GO!
BATMAN, YOU READ? I'VE JUST PUNCHED YOU AN EXIT HOLE.
YEAH, I NOTICED. BUT THE GUN--

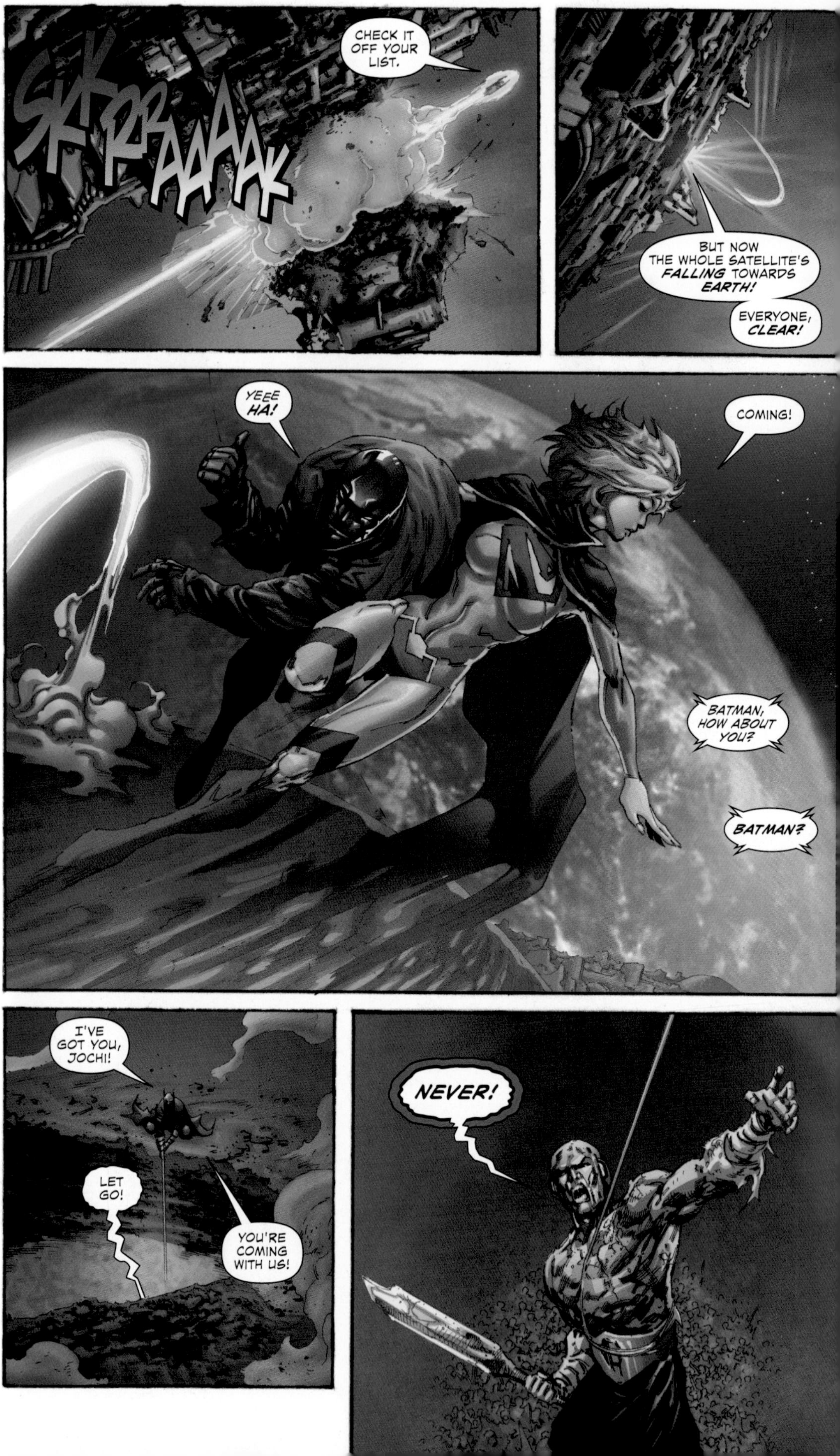
SKKRRAAAAK
CHECK IT OFF YOUR LIST.
BUT NOW THE WHOLE SATELLITE'S *FALLING* TOWARDS *EARTH!*
EVERYONE, *CLEAR!*
YEEE *HA!*
COMING!
BATMAN, HOW ABOUT YOU?
BATMAN?
I'VE GOT YOU, JOCHI!
LET GO!
YOU'RE COMING WITH US!
NEVER!

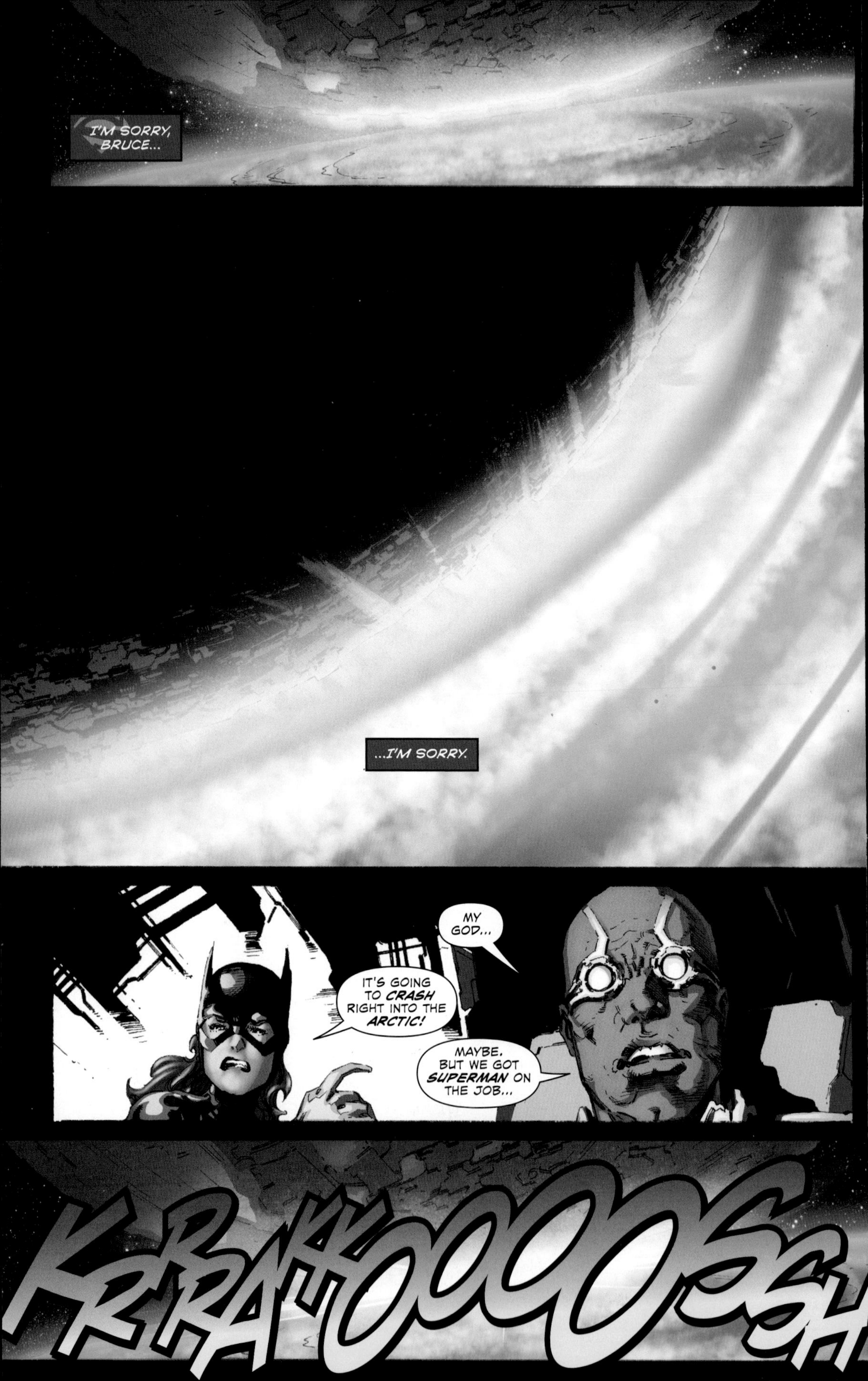
I'M SORRY, BRUCE...
...I'M SORRY.
MY GOD...
IT'S GOING TO CRASH RIGHT INTO THE ARCTIC!
MAYBE. BUT WE GOT SUPERMAN ON THE JOB...
KRRAKOOOOOSH

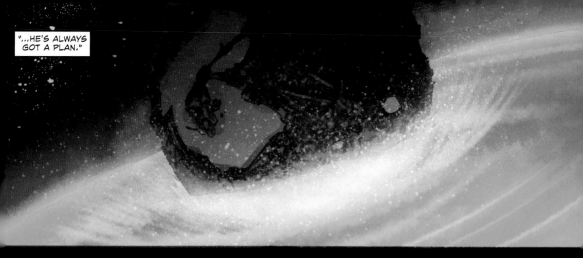

"...HE'S ALWAYS
GOT A PLAN."

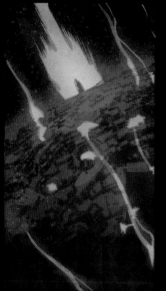

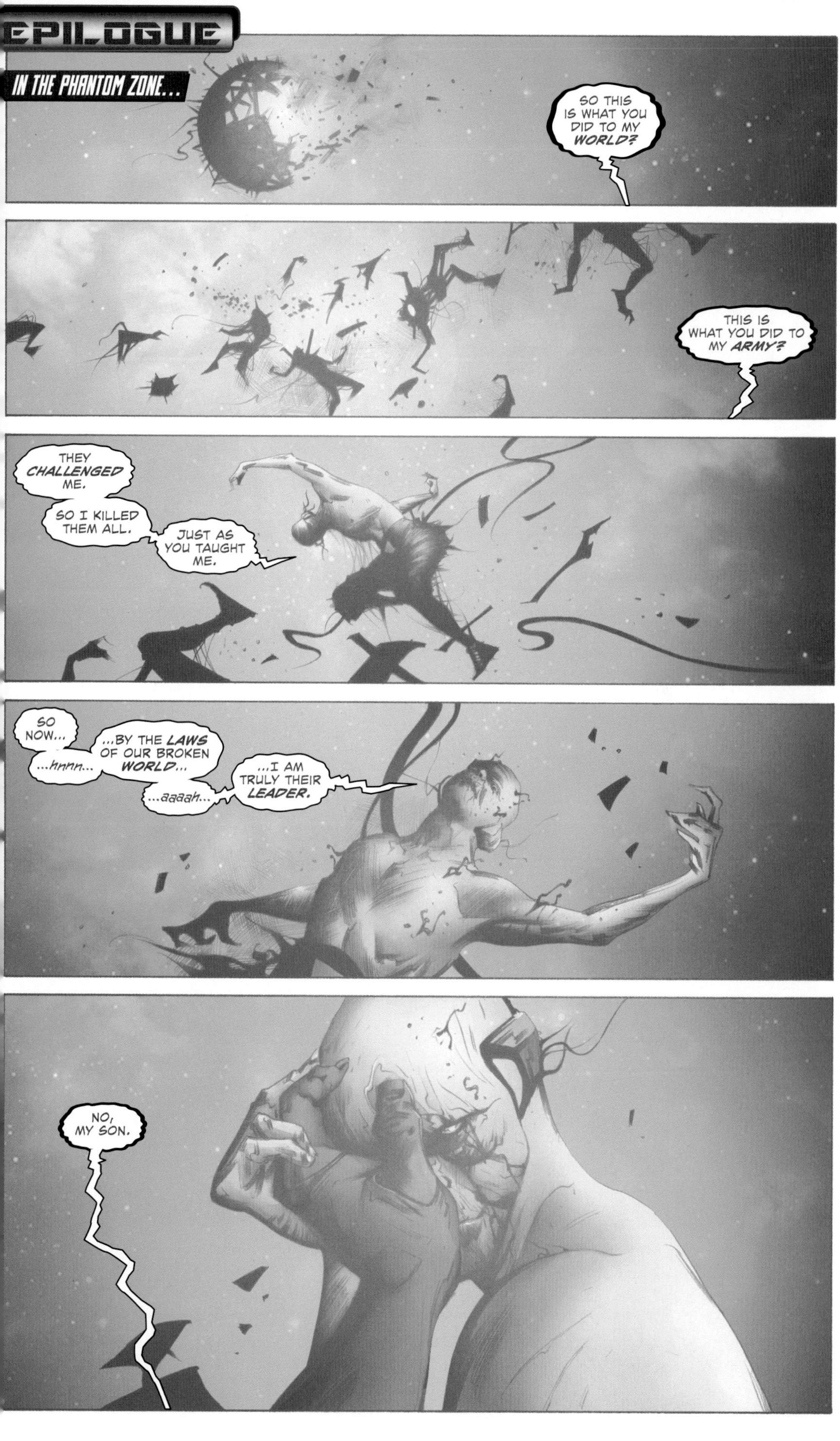
EPILOGUE
IN THE PHANTOM ZONE...
SO THIS IS WHAT YOU DID TO MY WORLD?
THIS IS WHAT YOU DID TO MY ARMY?
THEY CHALLENGED ME.
SO I KILLED THEM ALL.
JUST AS YOU TAUGHT ME.
SO NOW...
...hnnn...
...BY THE LAWS OF OUR BROKEN WORLD...
...aaaah...
...I AM TRULY THEIR LEADER.
NO, MY SON.

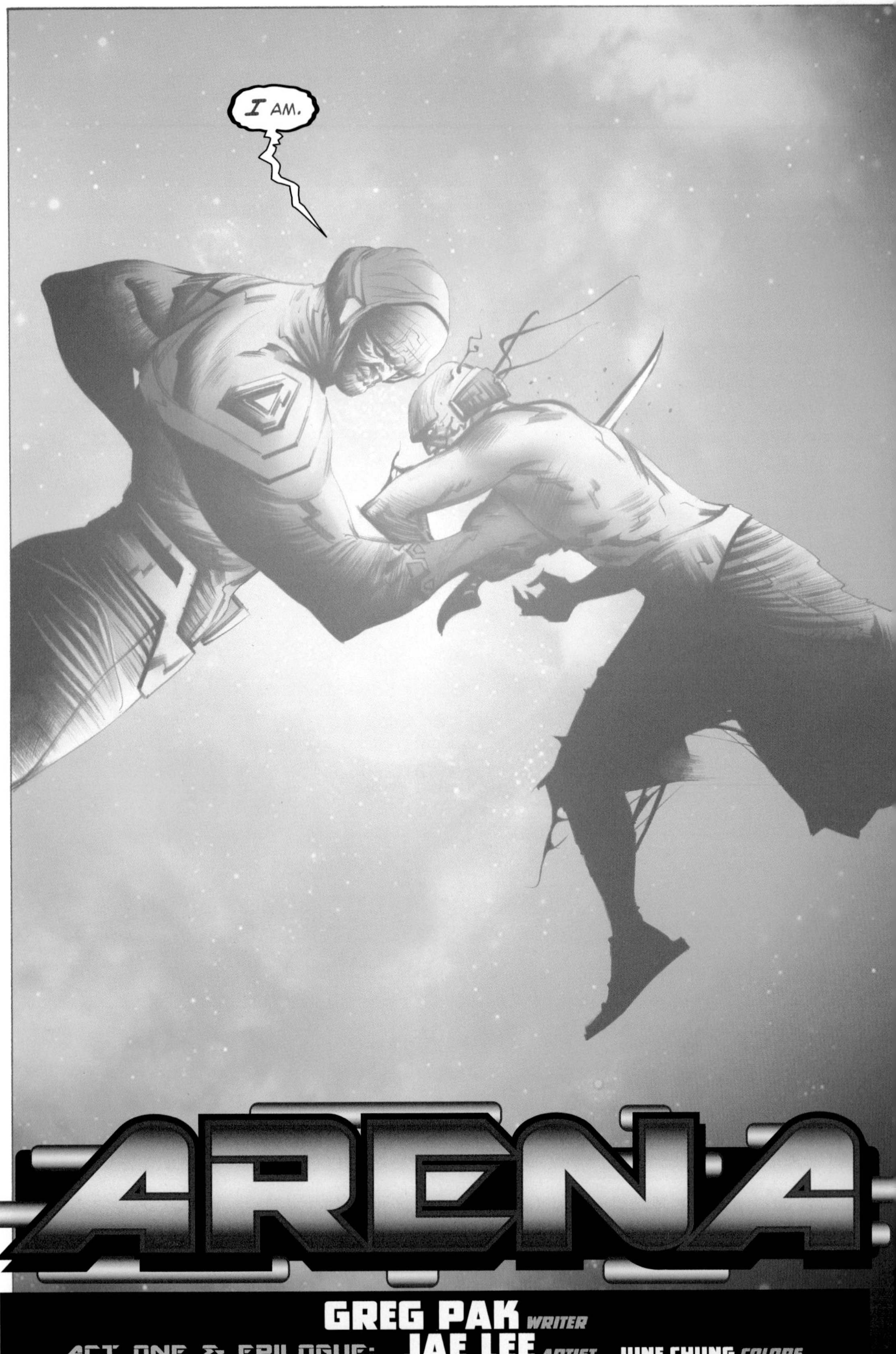

I AM.
ARENA

GREG PAK *WRITER*

ACT ONE & EPILOGUE: **JAE LEE** *ARTIST* JUNE CHUNG *COLORS*

ACT TWO: **KENNETH ROCAFORT** *ARTIST* NEI RUFFINO *COLORS*

ACT THREE: **PHILIP TAN** *ARTIST* HI-FI *COLORS*

LEE WITH CHUNG *COVER* ROB LEIGH *LETTERS*

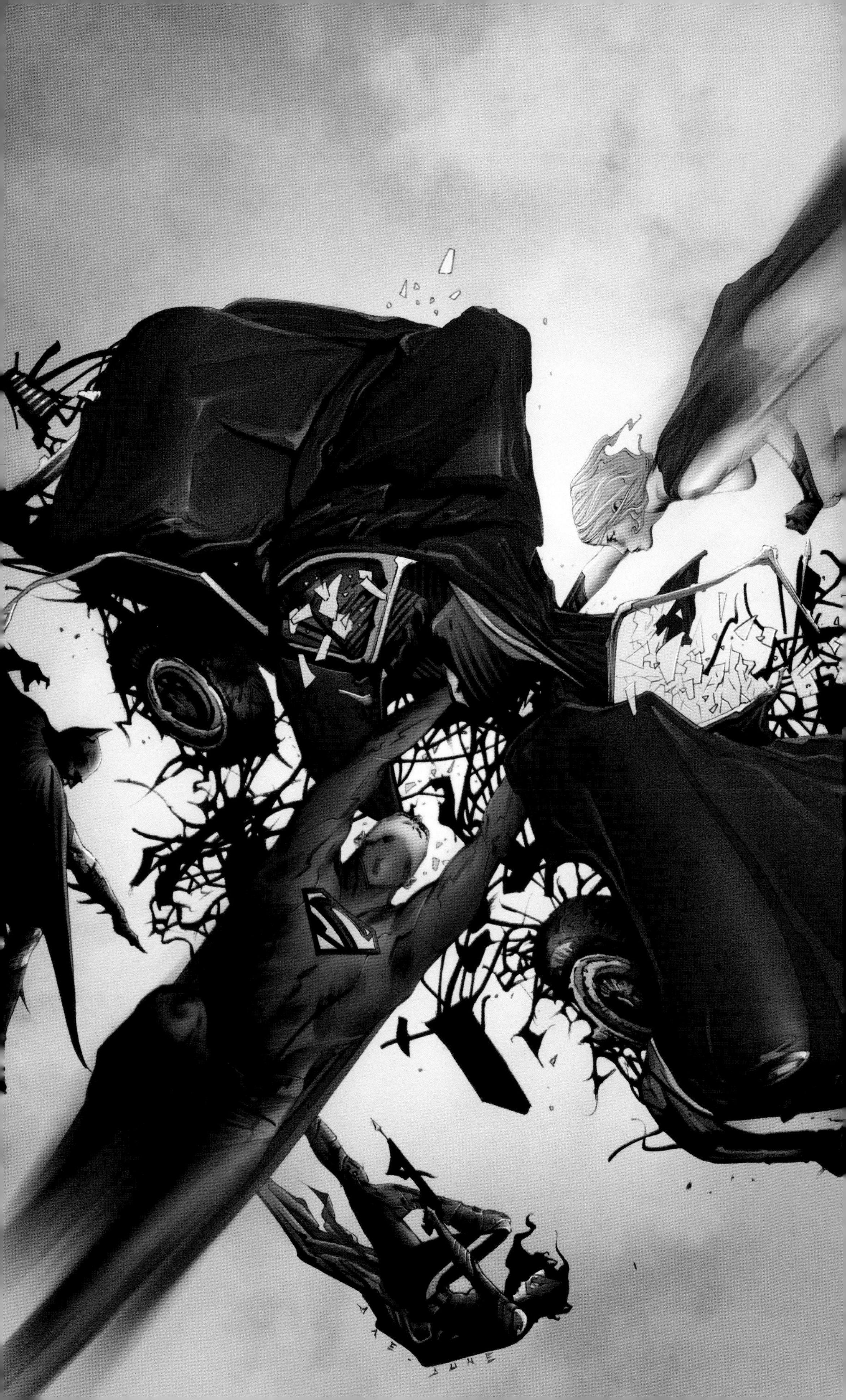

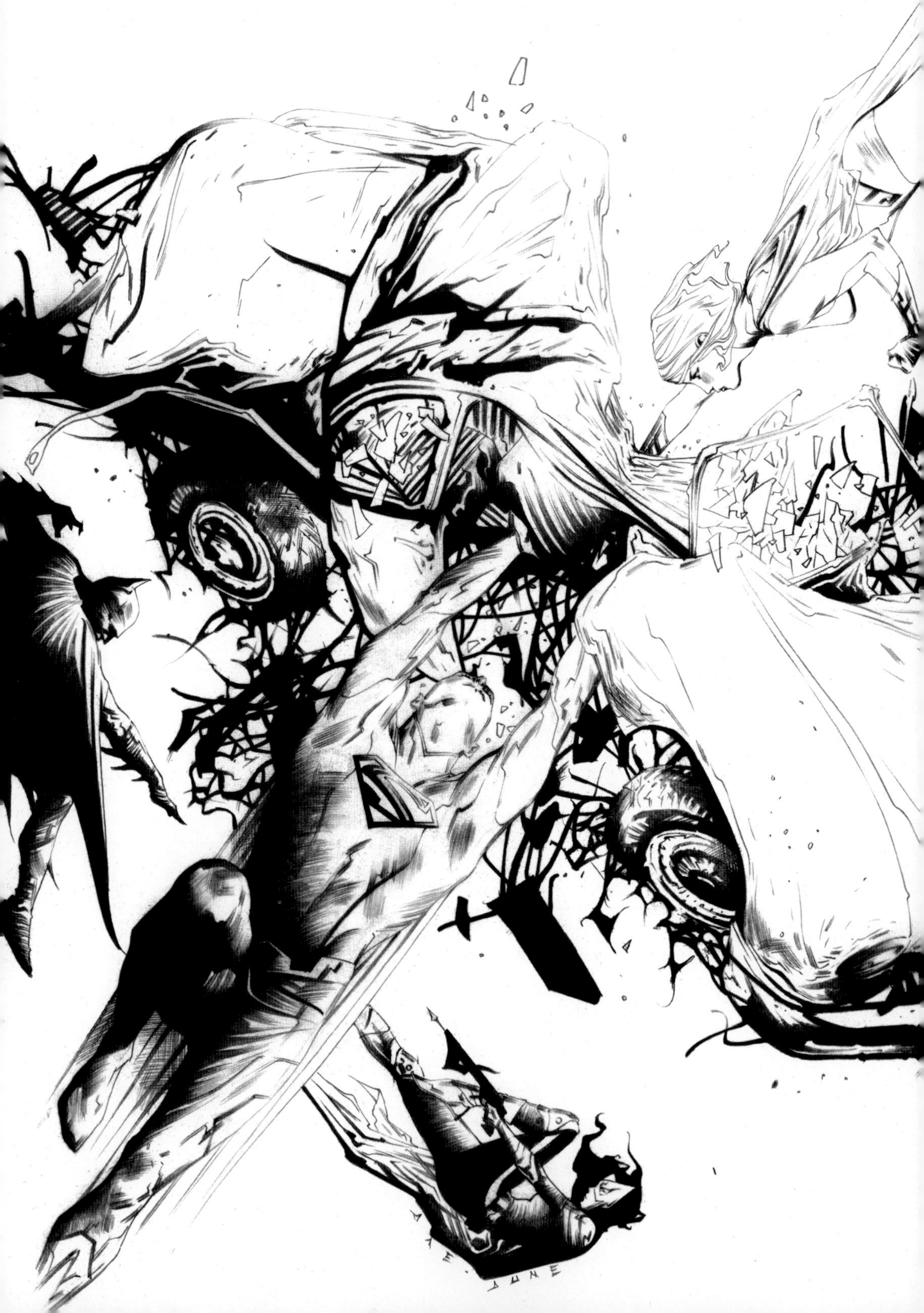

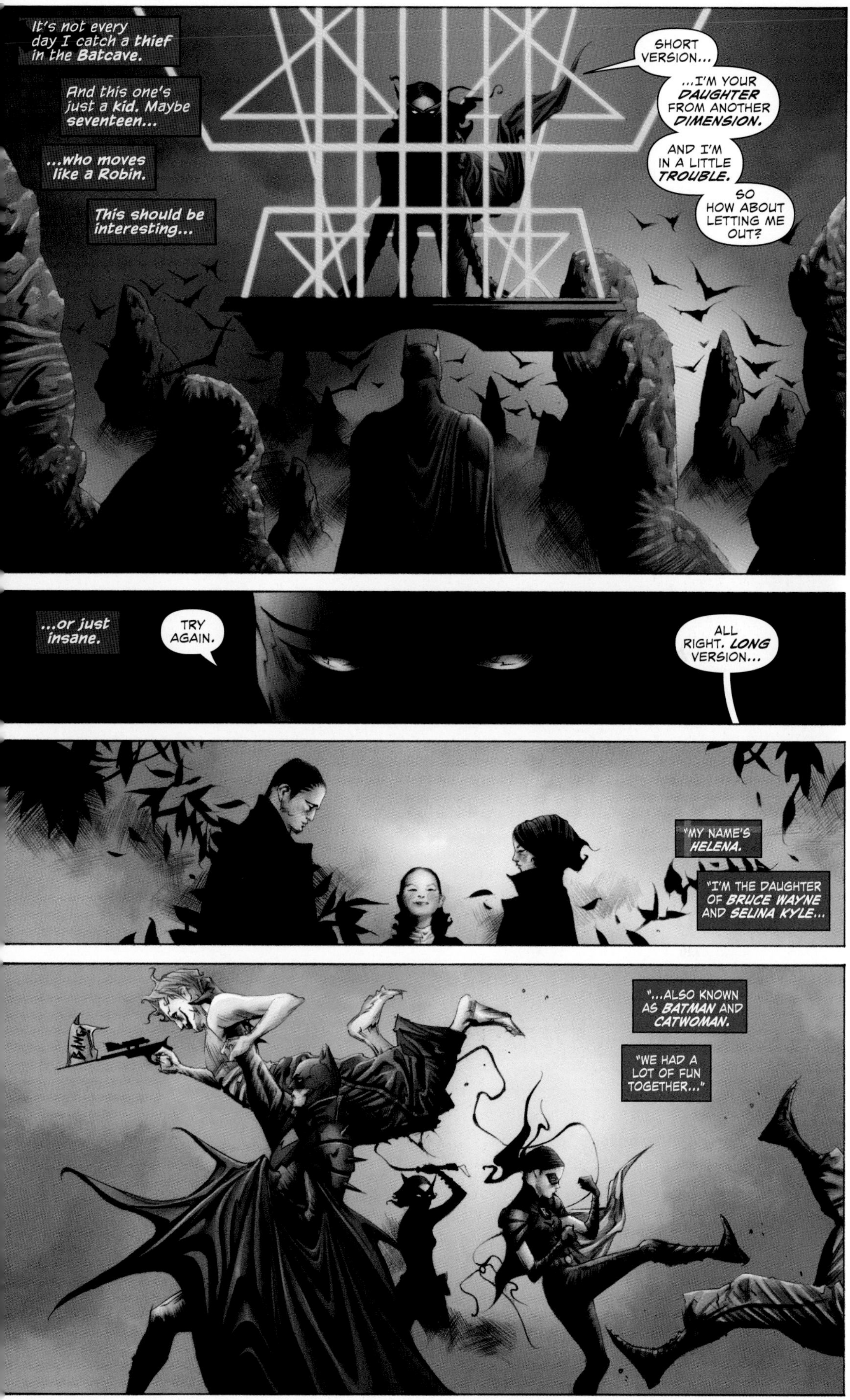

It's not every day I catch a **thief** in the **Batcave.**
And this one's just a **kid.** Maybe seventeen...
...who moves like a Robin.
This should be interesting...
SHORT VERSION...
...I'M YOUR ***DAUGHTER*** FROM ANOTHER ***DIMENSION.***
AND I'M IN A LITTLE ***TROUBLE.***
SO HOW ABOUT LETTING ME OUT?
...or just insane.
TRY AGAIN.
ALL RIGHT. ***LONG*** VERSION...
"MY NAME'S ***HELENA.***
"I'M THE DAUGHTER OF ***BRUCE WAYNE*** AND ***SELINA KYLE***...
"...ALSO KNOWN AS ***BATMAN*** AND ***CATWOMAN.***
"WE HAD A LOT OF FUN TOGETHER..."
BANG

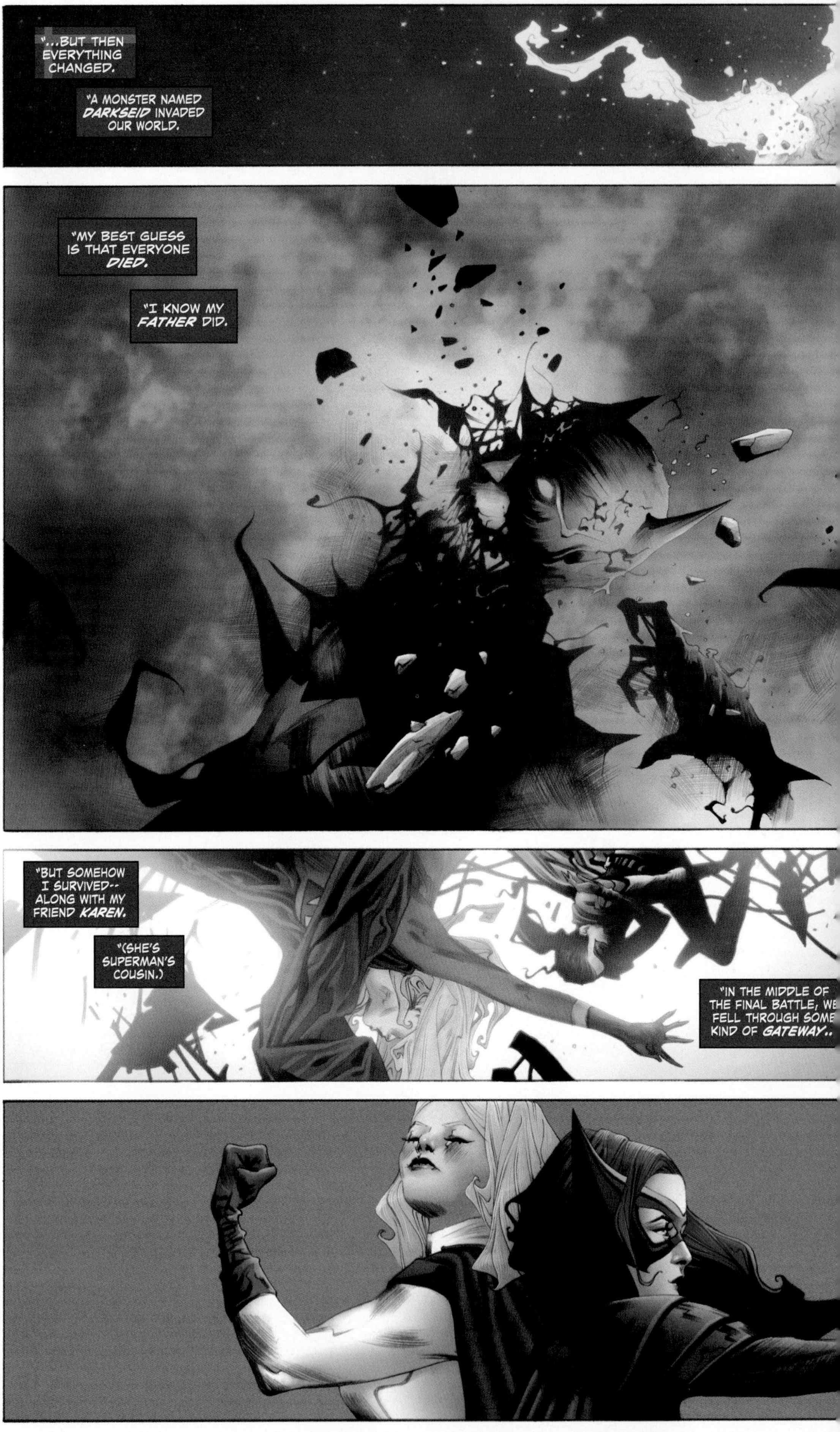
"...BUT THEN EVERYTHING CHANGED.
"A MONSTER NAMED DARKSEID INVADED OUR WORLD.
"MY BEST GUESS IS THAT EVERYONE DIED.
"I KNOW MY FATHER DID.
"BUT SOMEHOW I SURVIVED-- ALONG WITH MY FRIEND KAREN.
"(SHE'S SUPERMAN'S COUSIN.)
"IN THE MIDDLE OF THE FINAL BATTLE, WE FELL THROUGH SOME KIND OF GATEWAY..

"...AND WE ENDED UP IN *THIS* WORLD..."

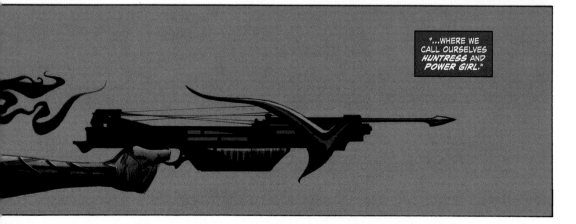

"...WHERE WE CALL OURSELVES *HUNTRESS* AND *POWER GIRL.*"

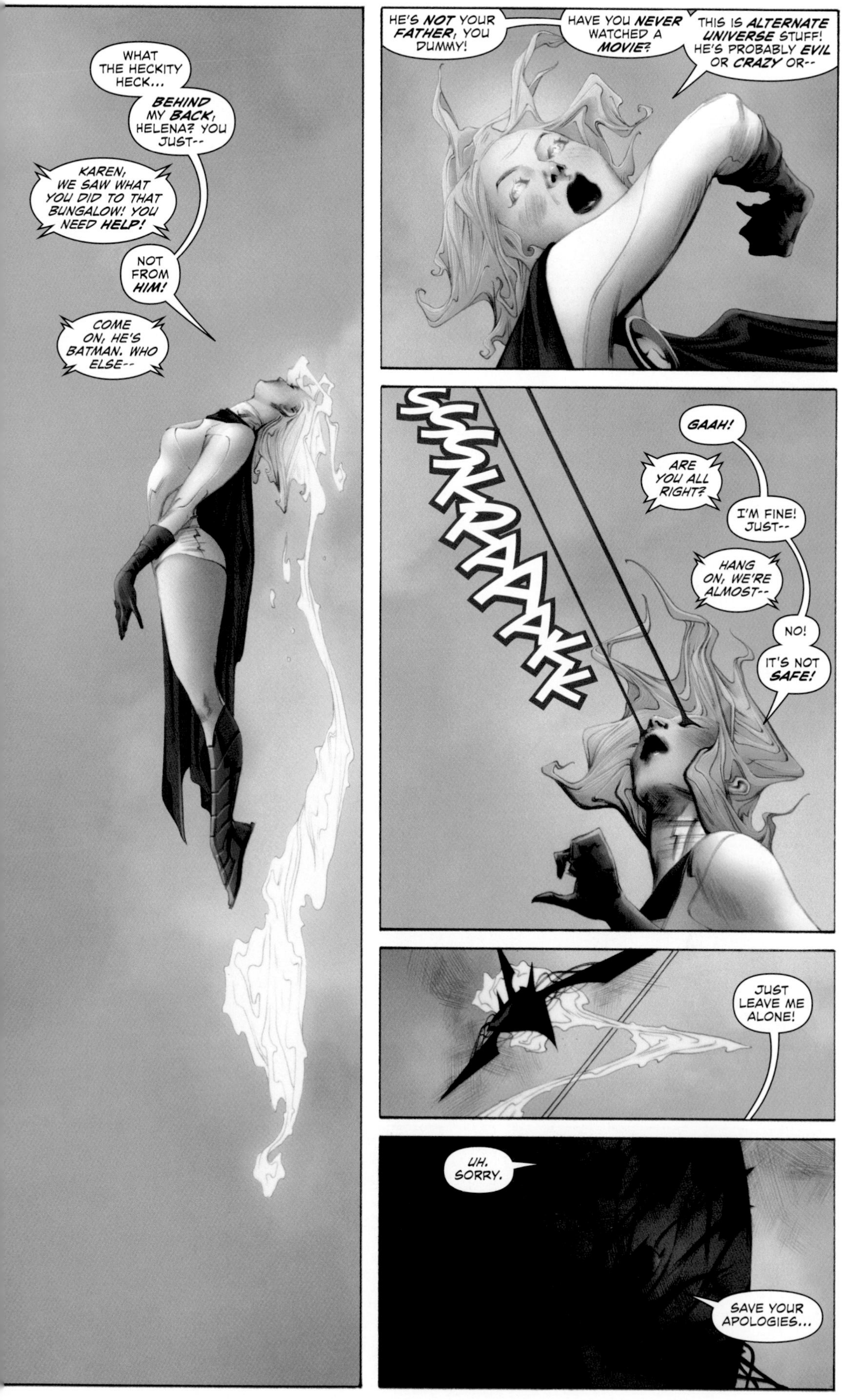

WHAT THE HECKITY HECK...
BEHIND MY BACK, HELENA? YOU JUST--
KAREN, WE SAW WHAT YOU DID TO THAT BUNGALOW! YOU NEED HELP!
NOT FROM HIM!
COME ON, HE'S BATMAN. WHO ELSE--
HE'S NOT YOUR FATHER, YOU DUMMY!
HAVE YOU NEVER WATCHED A MOVIE?
THIS IS ALTERNATE UNIVERSE STUFF! HE'S PROBABLY EVIL OR CRAZY OR--
SSSKRAAAKK
GAAH!
ARE YOU ALL RIGHT?
I'M FINE! JUST--
HANG ON, WE'RE ALMOST--
NO!
IT'S NOT SAFE!
JUST LEAVE ME ALONE!
UH. SORRY.
SAVE YOUR APOLOGIES...

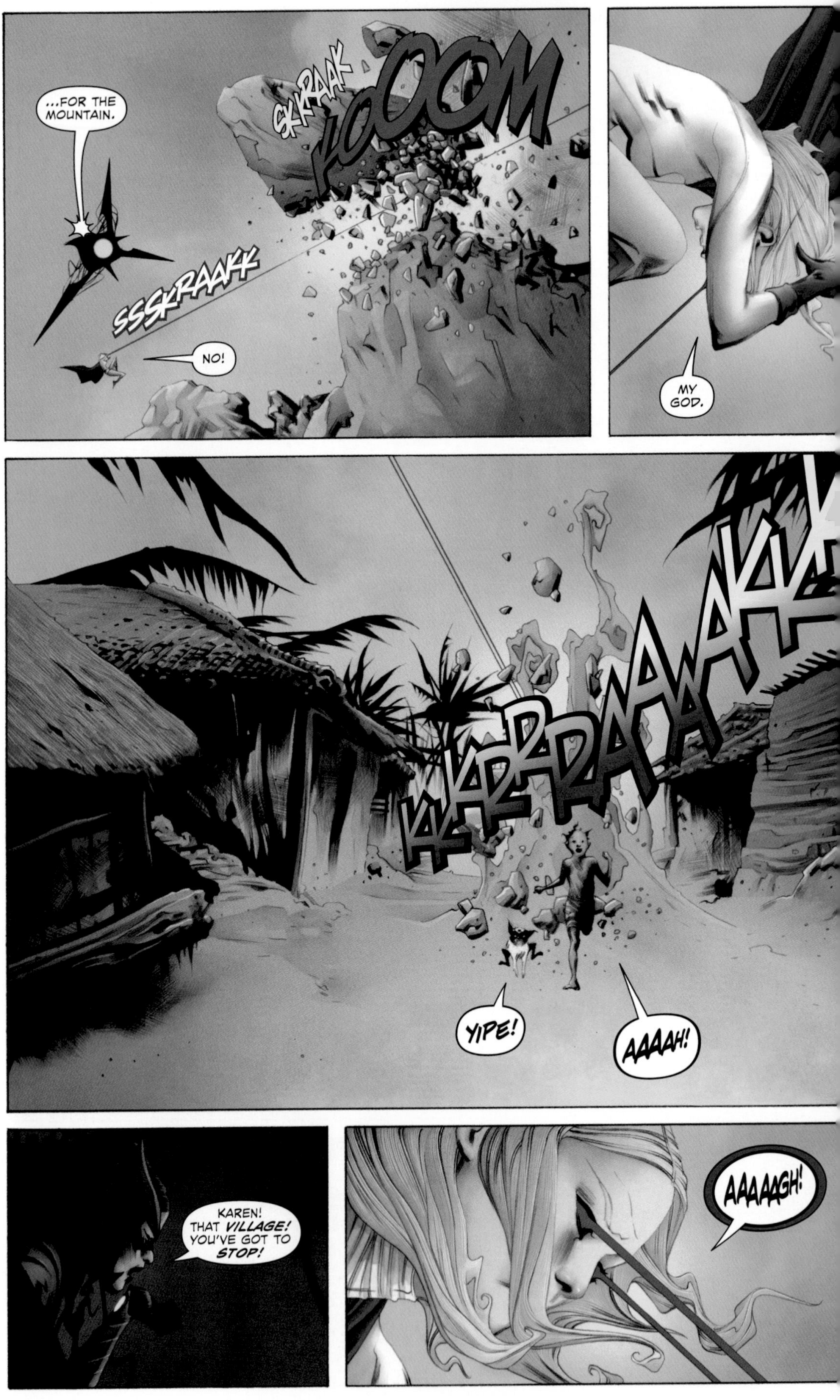
...FOR THE MOUNTAIN.
SKRAAK
KOOOOM
SSSKRAAKK
NO!
MY GOD.
KKKRRDAAAAKKK
YIPE!
AAAAH!
KAREN! THAT VILLAGE! YOU'VE GOT TO STOP!
AAAAAGH!

THAT'S *ENOUGH* OF THAT.
FIRST CONTACT
PART 1
GREG PAK WRITER JAE LEE ART
JUNE CHUNG COLORS
DEZI SIENTY & CARLOS MANGUAL LETTERS
LEE WITH CHUNG COVER

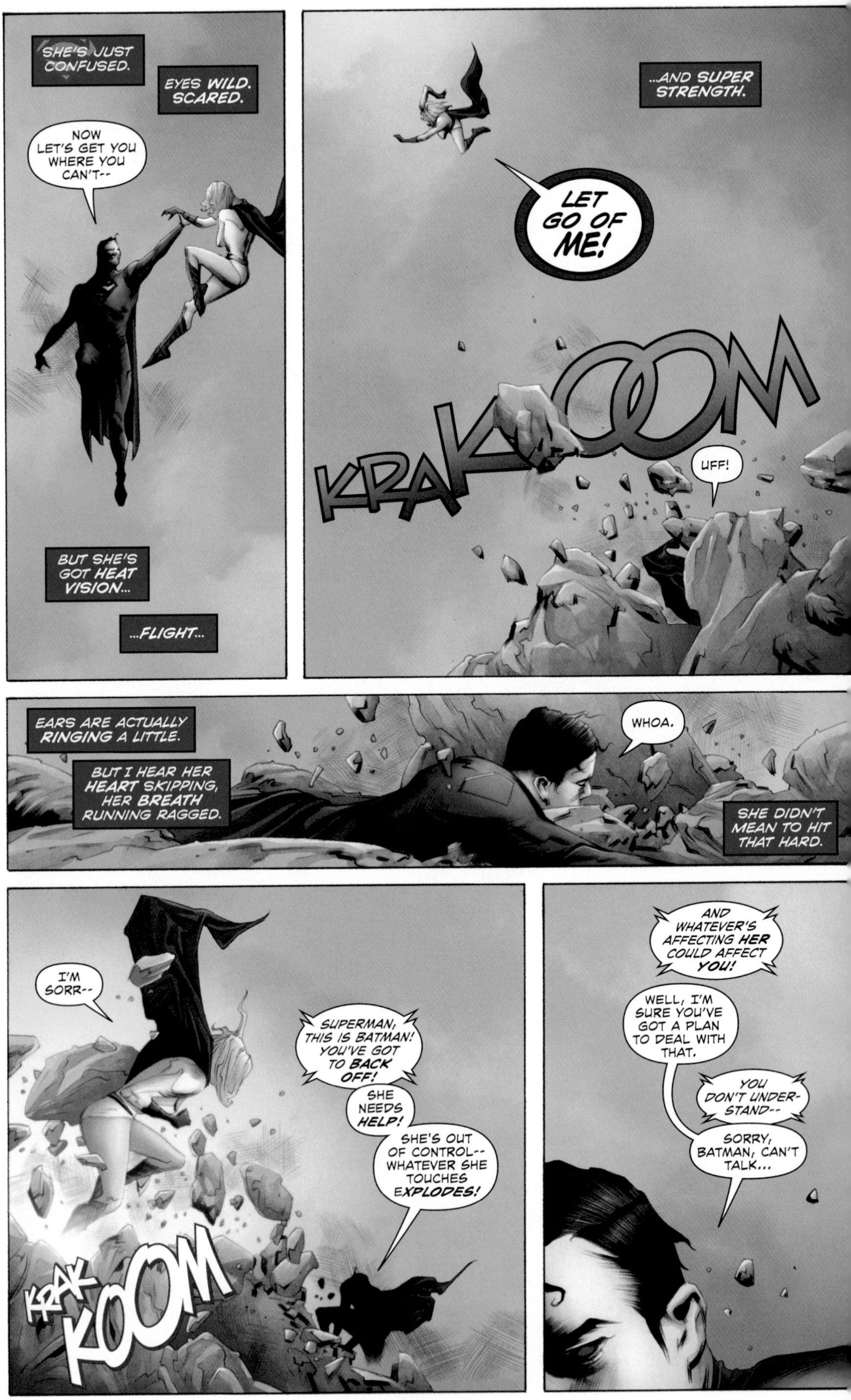
SHE'S JUST CONFUSED.
EYES WILD. SCARED.
NOW LET'S GET YOU WHERE YOU CAN'T--
BUT SHE'S GOT HEAT VISION...
...FLIGHT...
...AND SUPER STRENGTH.
LET GO OF ME!
KRAKOOM
UFF!
EARS ARE ACTUALLY RINGING A LITTLE.
BUT I HEAR HER HEART SKIPPING, HER BREATH RUNNING RAGGED.
WHOA.
SHE DIDN'T MEAN TO HIT THAT HARD.
I'M SORR--
SUPERMAN, THIS IS BATMAN! YOU'VE GOT TO BACK OFF!
SHE NEEDS HELP!
SHE'S OUT OF CONTROL-- WHATEVER SHE TOUCHES EXPLODES!
KRAK KOOM
AND WHATEVER'S AFFECTING HER COULD AFFECT YOU!
WELL, I'M SURE YOU'VE GOT A PLAN TO DEAL WITH THAT.
YOU DON'T UNDER-STAND--
SORRY, BATMAN, CAN'T TALK...

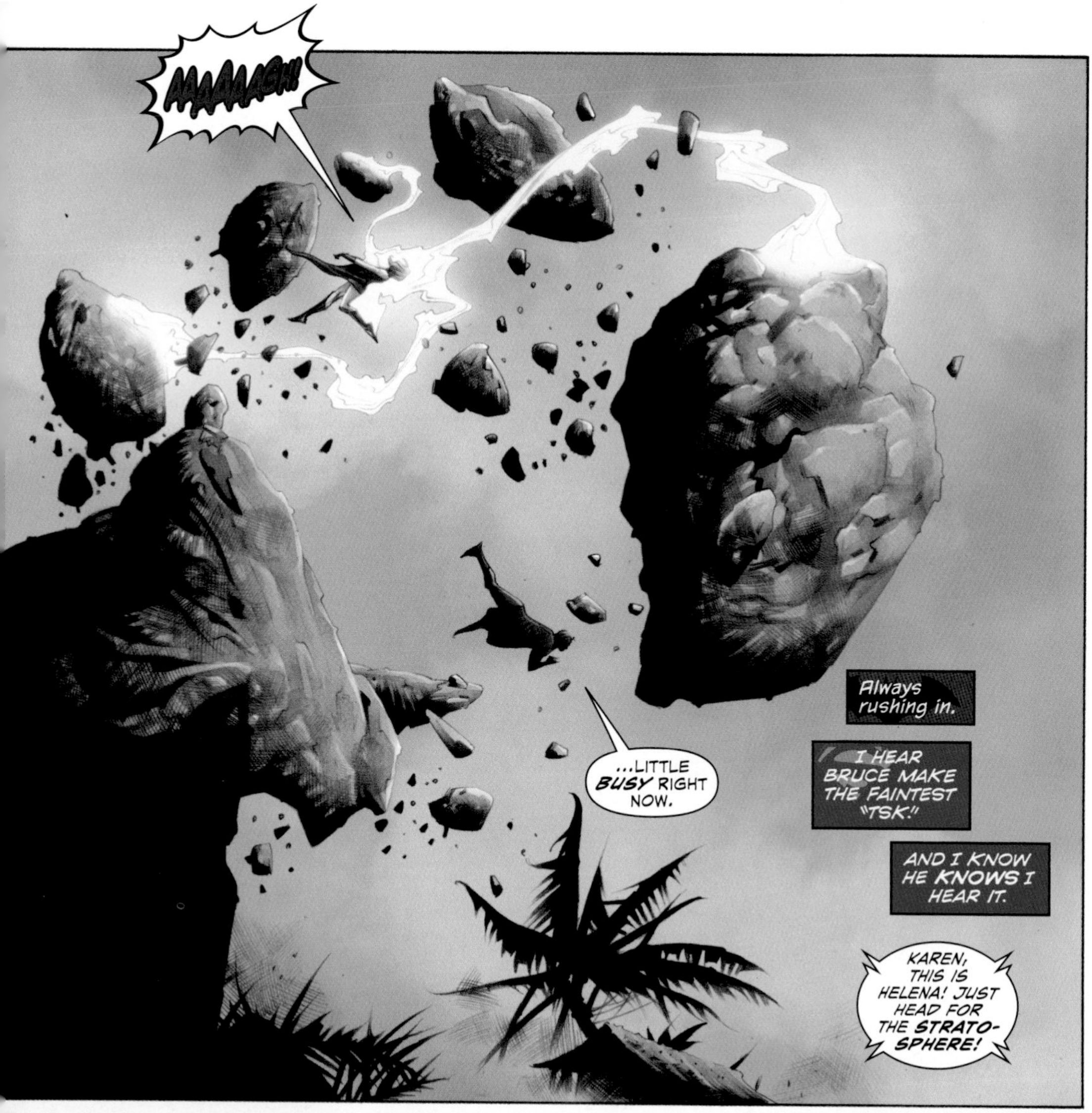
AAAAAAAGH!
...LITTLE BUSY RIGHT NOW.
Always rushing in.
I HEAR BRUCE MAKE THE FAINTEST "TSK."
AND I KNOW HE KNOWS I HEAR IT.
KAREN, THIS IS HELENA! JUST HEAD FOR THE STRATO-SPHERE!

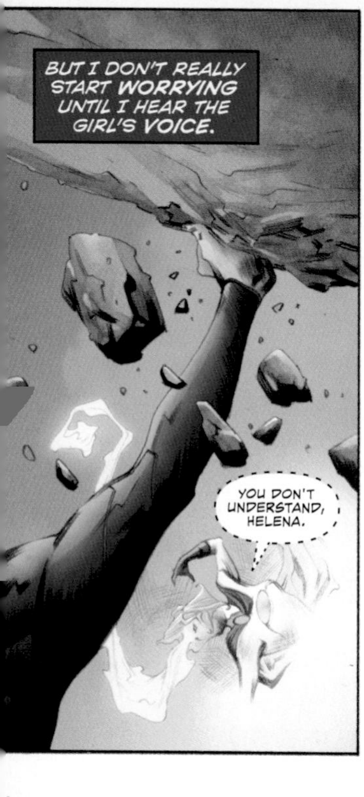
BUT I DON'T REALLY START WORRYING UNTIL I HEAR THE GIRL'S VOICE.
YOU DON'T UNDERSTAND, HELENA.

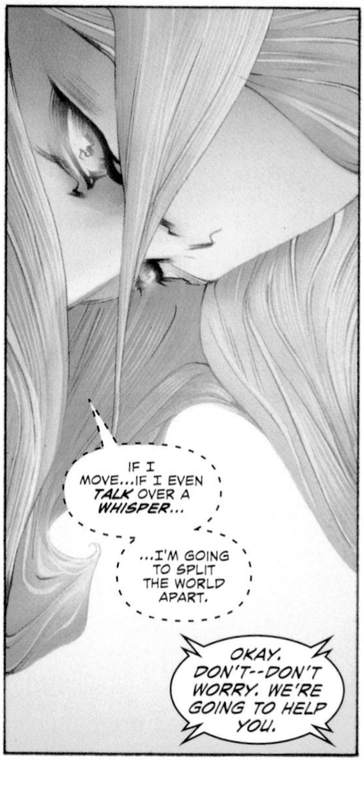
IF I MOVE...IF I EVEN TALK OVER A WHISPER...
...I'M GOING TO SPLIT THE WORLD APART.
OKAY. DON'T--DON'T WORRY. WE'RE GOING TO HELP YOU.

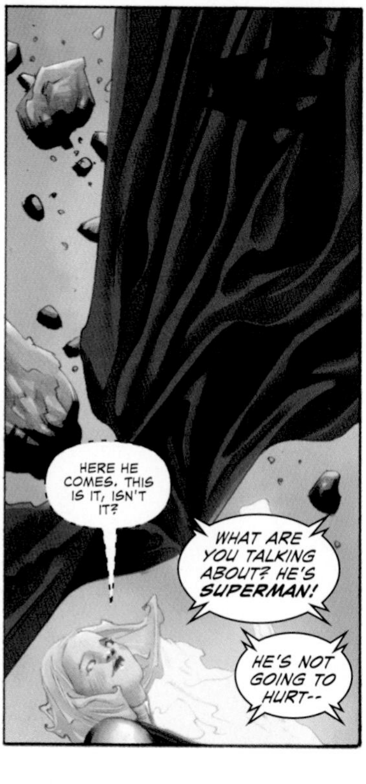
HERE HE COMES. THIS IS IT, ISN'T IT?
WHAT ARE YOU TALKING ABOUT? HE'S SUPERMAN!
HE'S NOT GOING TO HURT--

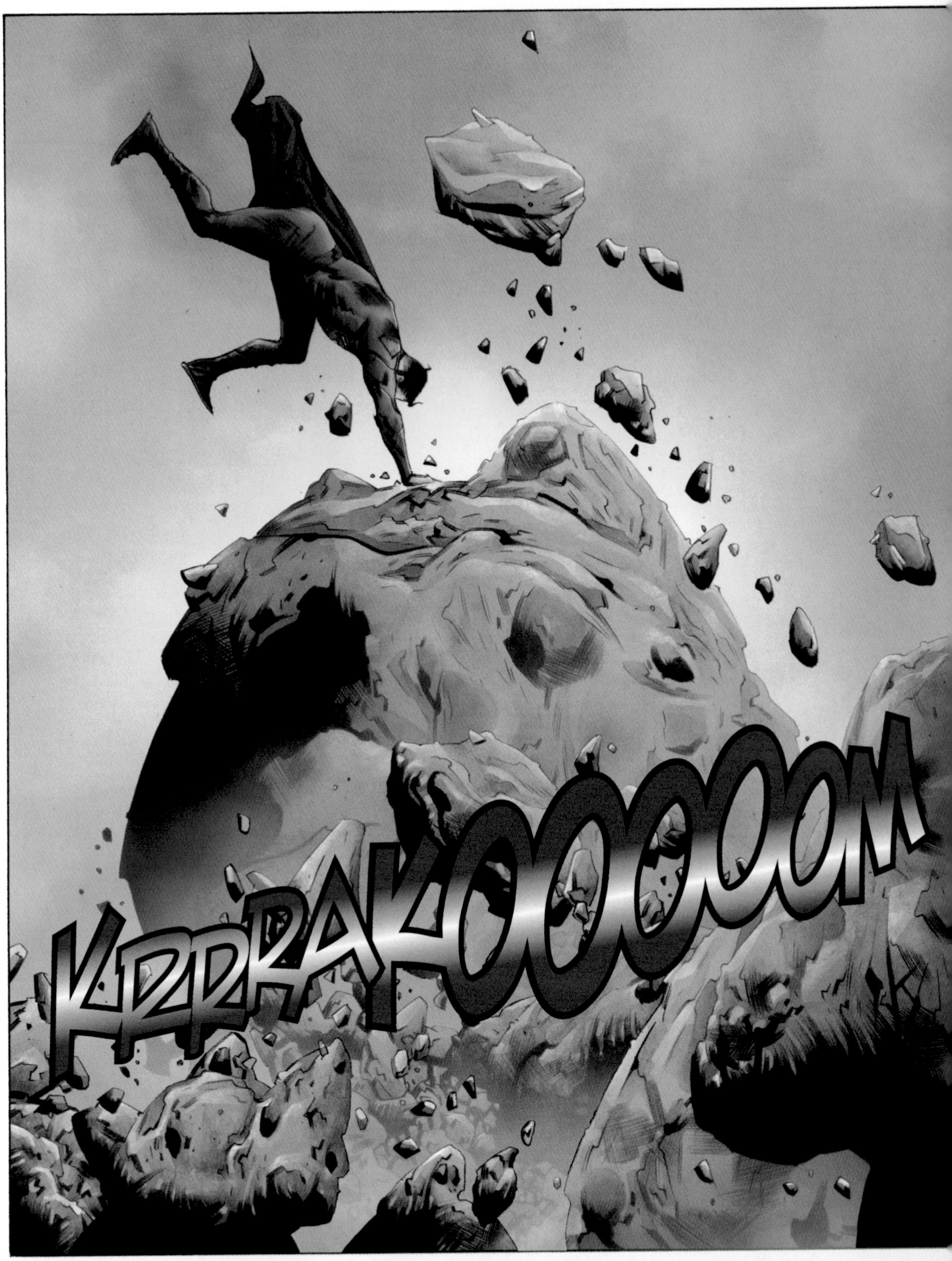
KRRRAKOOOOOOM

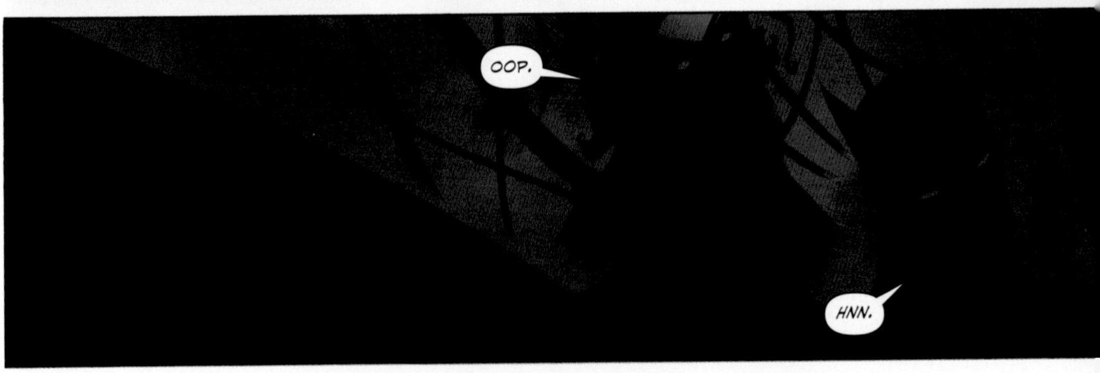
OOP.
HNN.

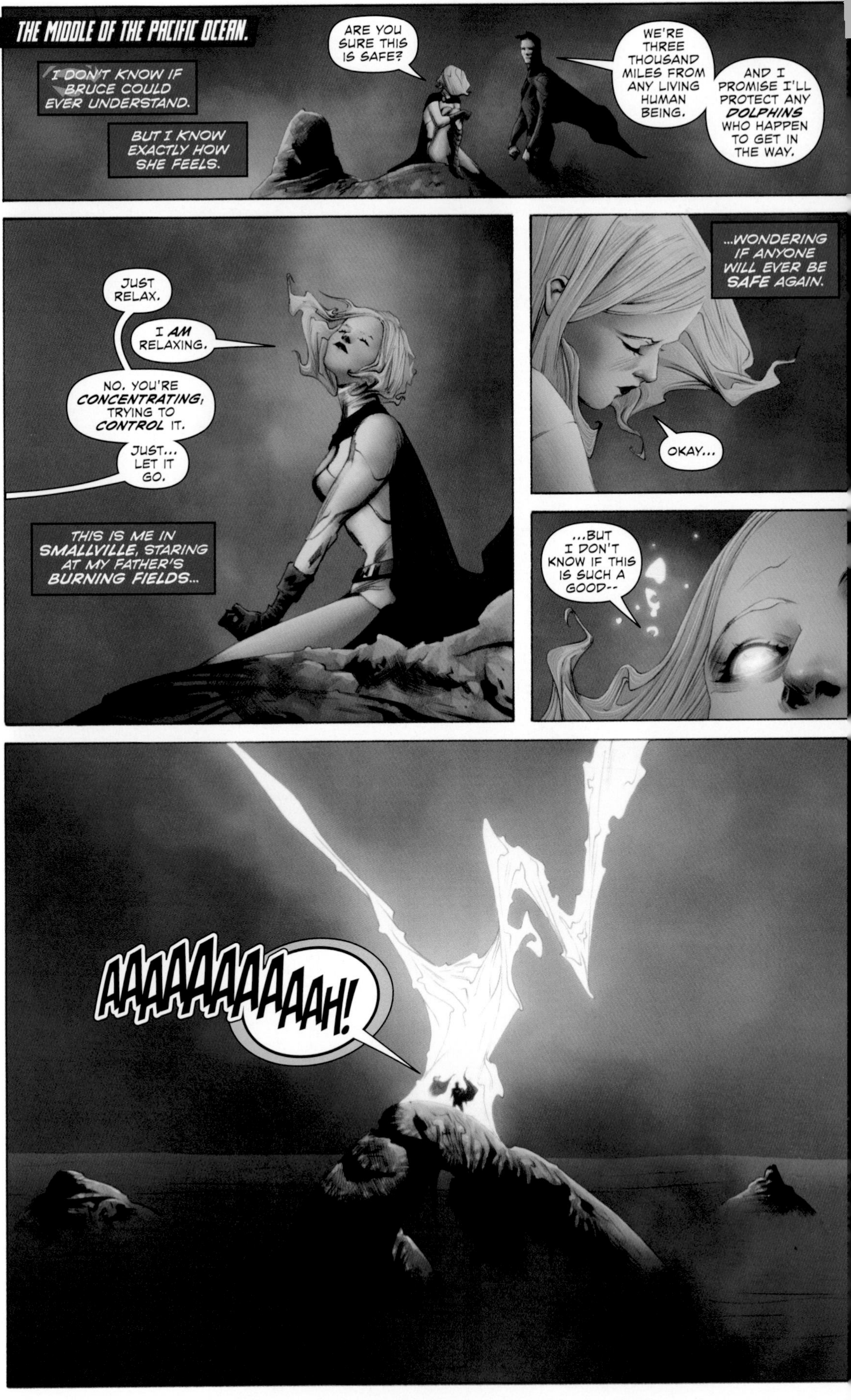
THE MIDDLE OF THE PACIFIC OCEAN.
I DON'T KNOW IF BRUCE COULD EVER UNDERSTAND.
BUT I KNOW EXACTLY HOW SHE FEELS.
ARE YOU SURE THIS IS SAFE?
WE'RE THREE THOUSAND MILES FROM ANY LIVING HUMAN BEING.
AND I PROMISE I'LL PROTECT ANY DOLPHINS WHO HAPPEN TO GET IN THE WAY.
JUST RELAX.
I AM RELAXING.
NO. YOU'RE CONCENTRATING, TRYING TO CONTROL IT.
JUST... LET IT GO.
THIS IS ME IN SMALLVILLE, STARING AT MY FATHER'S BURNING FIELDS...
...WONDERING IF ANYONE WILL EVER BE SAFE AGAIN.
OKAY...
...BUT I DON'T KNOW IF THIS IS SUCH A GOOD--
AAAAAAAAAAAAH!

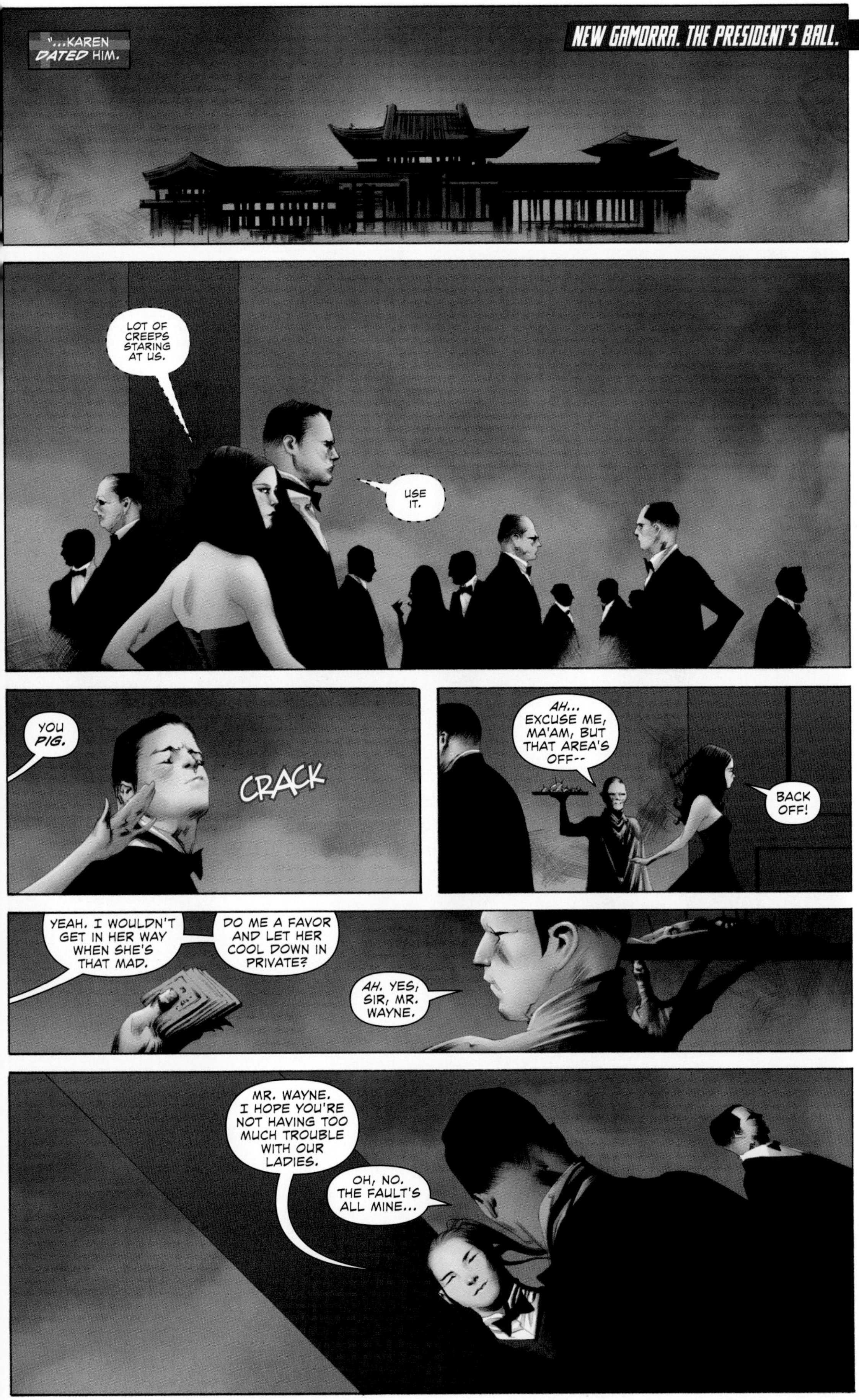
"...KAREN DATED HIM.
NEW GAMORRA. THE PRESIDENT'S BALL.
LOT OF CREEPS STARING AT US.
USE IT.
YOU PIG.
CRACK
AH... EXCUSE ME, MA'AM, BUT THAT AREA'S OFF--
BACK OFF!
YEAH. I WOULDN'T GET IN HER WAY WHEN SHE'S THAT MAD.
DO ME A FAVOR AND LET HER COOL DOWN IN PRIVATE?
AH. YES, SIR, MR. WAYNE.
MR. WAYNE. I HOPE YOU'RE NOT HAVING TOO MUCH TROUBLE WITH OUR LADIES.
OH, NO. THE FAULT'S ALL MINE...

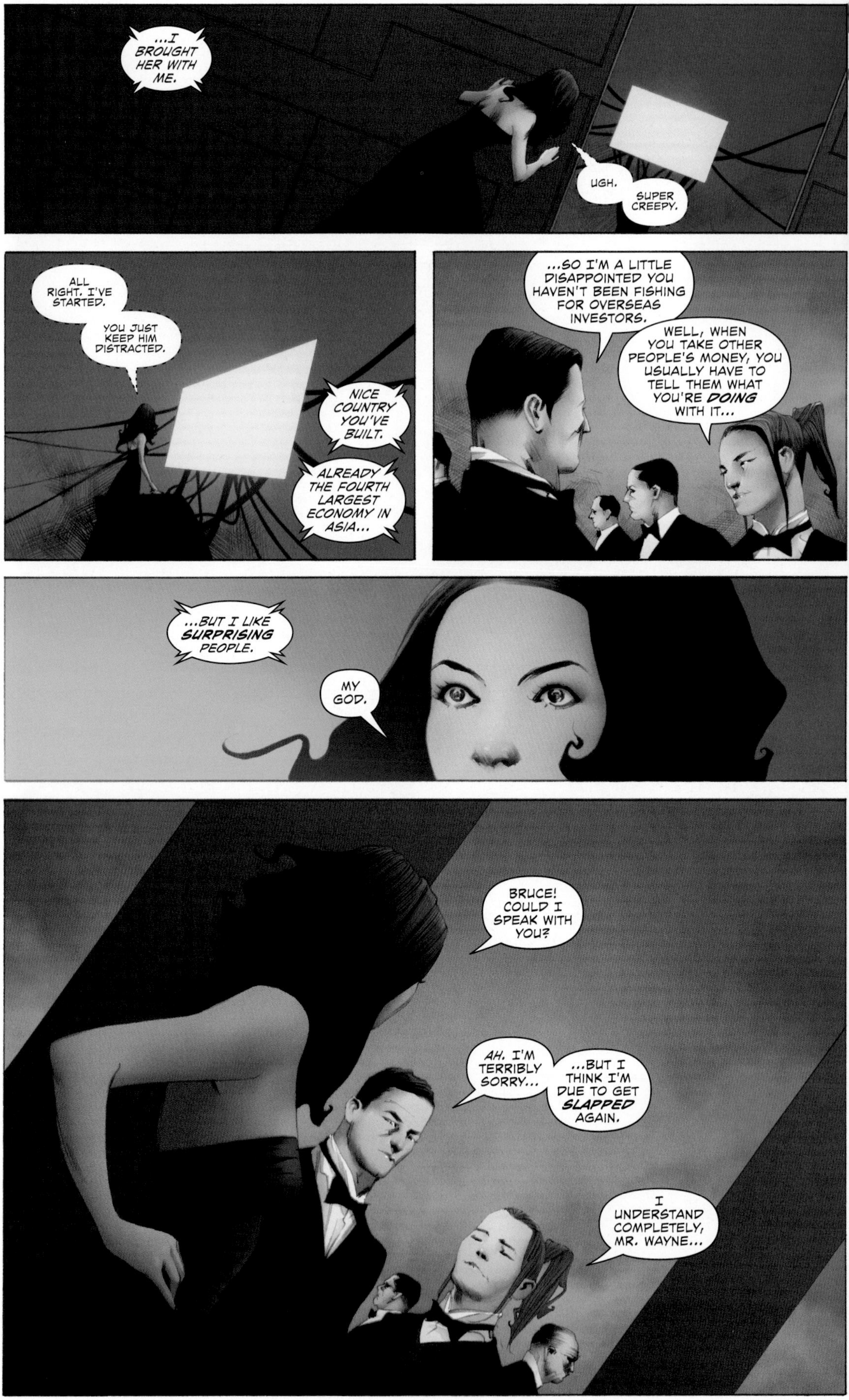
...I BROUGHT HER WITH ME.
UGH.
SUPER CREEPY.
ALL RIGHT. I'VE STARTED.
YOU JUST KEEP HIM DISTRACTED.
NICE COUNTRY YOU'VE BUILT.
ALREADY THE FOURTH LARGEST ECONOMY IN ASIA...
...SO I'M A LITTLE DISAPPOINTED YOU HAVEN'T BEEN FISHING FOR OVERSEAS INVESTORS.
WELL, WHEN YOU TAKE OTHER PEOPLE'S MONEY, YOU USUALLY HAVE TO TELL THEM WHAT YOU'RE DOING WITH IT...
...BUT I LIKE SURPRISING PEOPLE.
MY GOD.
BRUCE! COULD I SPEAK WITH YOU?
AH. I'M TERRIBLY SORRY...
...BUT I THINK I'M DUE TO GET SLAPPED AGAIN.
I UNDERSTAND COMPLETELY, MR. WAYNE...

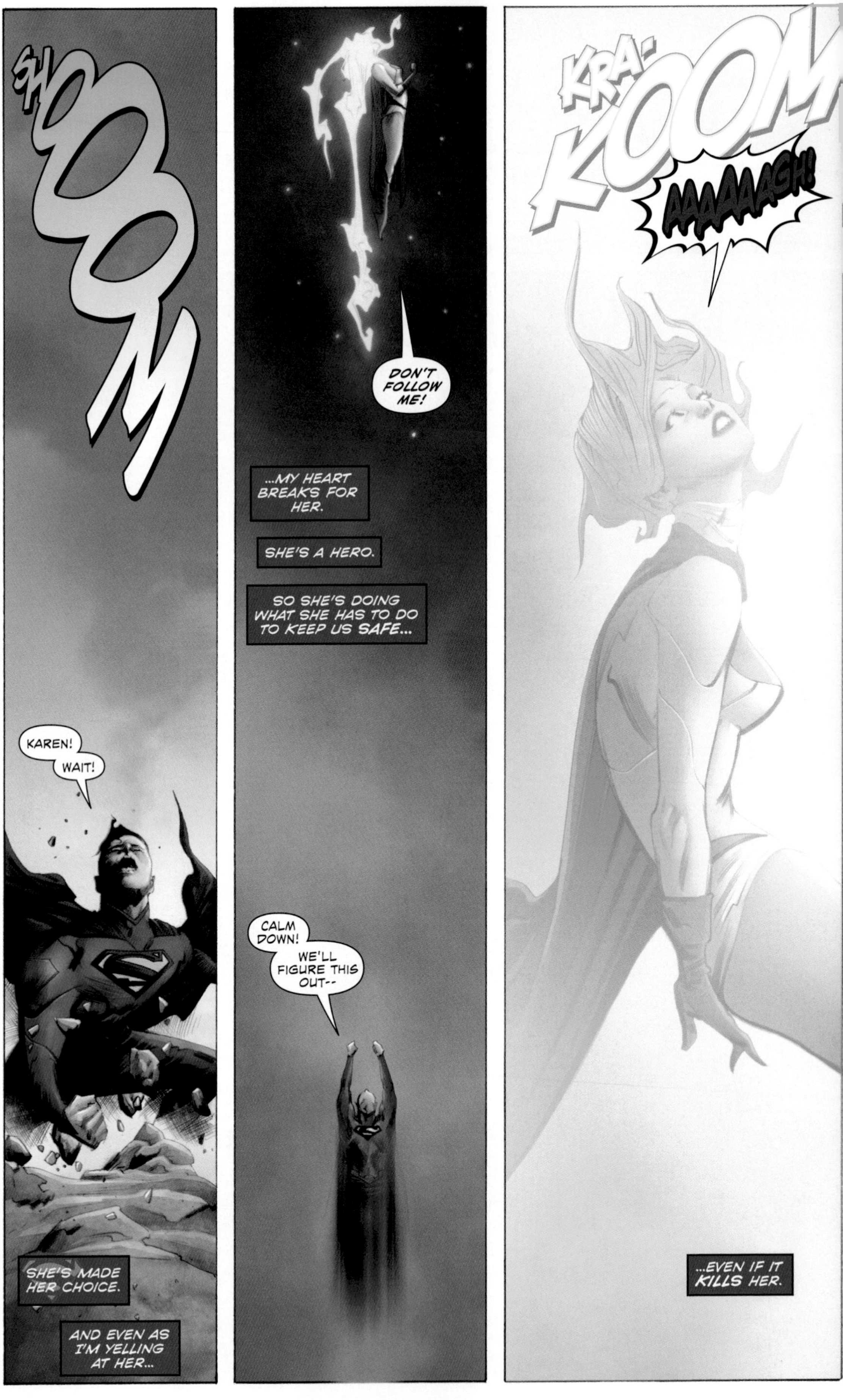
SHOOOM
KAREN!
WAIT!
SHE'S MADE HER CHOICE.
AND EVEN AS I'M YELLING AT HER...
DON'T FOLLOW ME!
...MY HEART BREAKS FOR HER.
SHE'S A HERO.
SO SHE'S DOING WHAT SHE HAS TO DO TO KEEP US SAFE...
CALM DOWN!
WE'LL FIGURE THIS OUT--
KRA-KOOOM
AAAAAACH!
...EVEN IF IT KILLS HER.

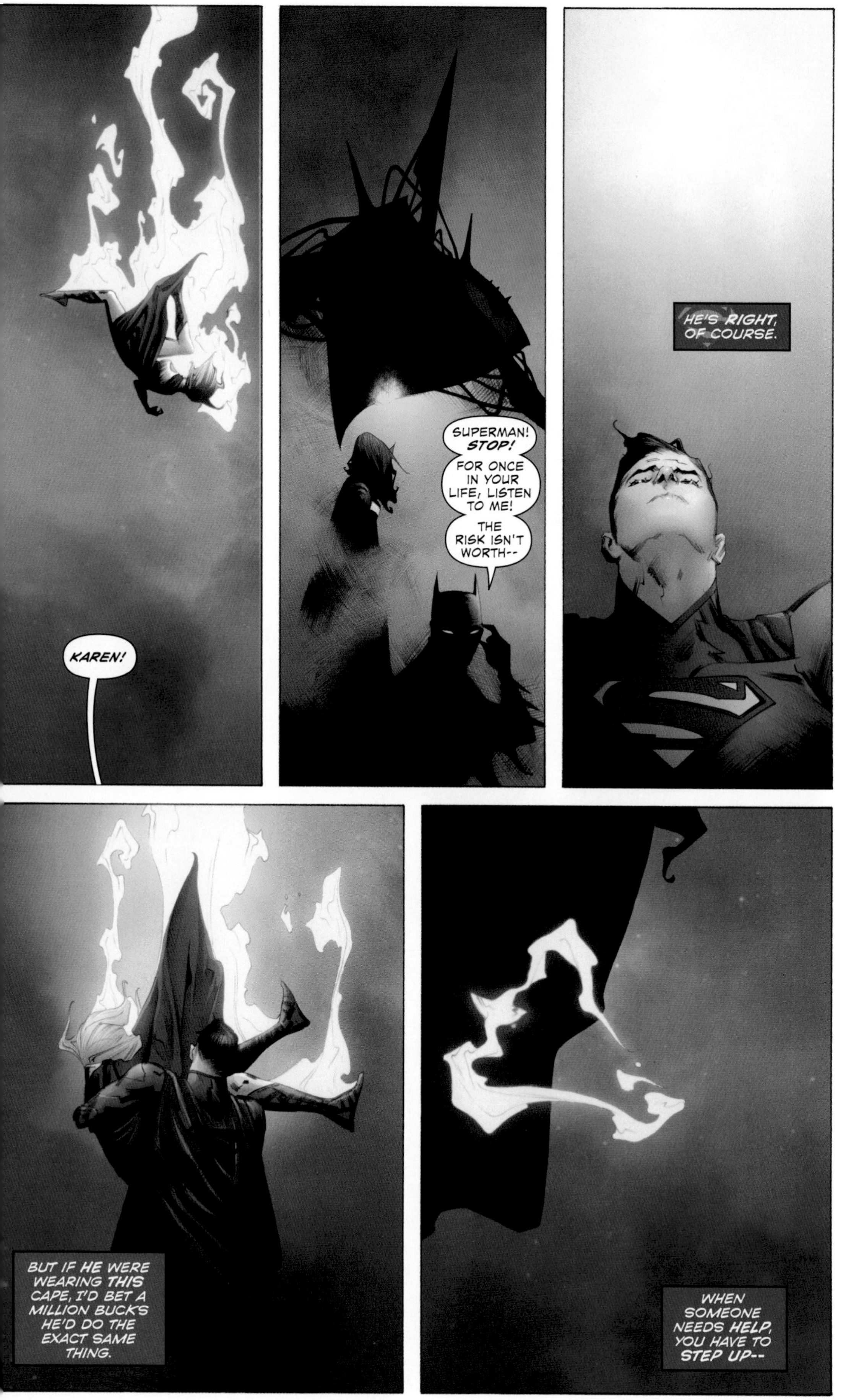

KAREN!
SUPERMAN! STOP!
FOR ONCE IN YOUR LIFE, LISTEN TO ME!
THE RISK ISN'T WORTH--
HE'S RIGHT, OF COURSE.
BUT IF HE WERE WEARING THIS CAPE, I'D BET A MILLION BUCKS HE'D DO THE EXACT SAME THING.
WHEN SOMEONE NEEDS HELP, YOU HAVE TO STEP UP--

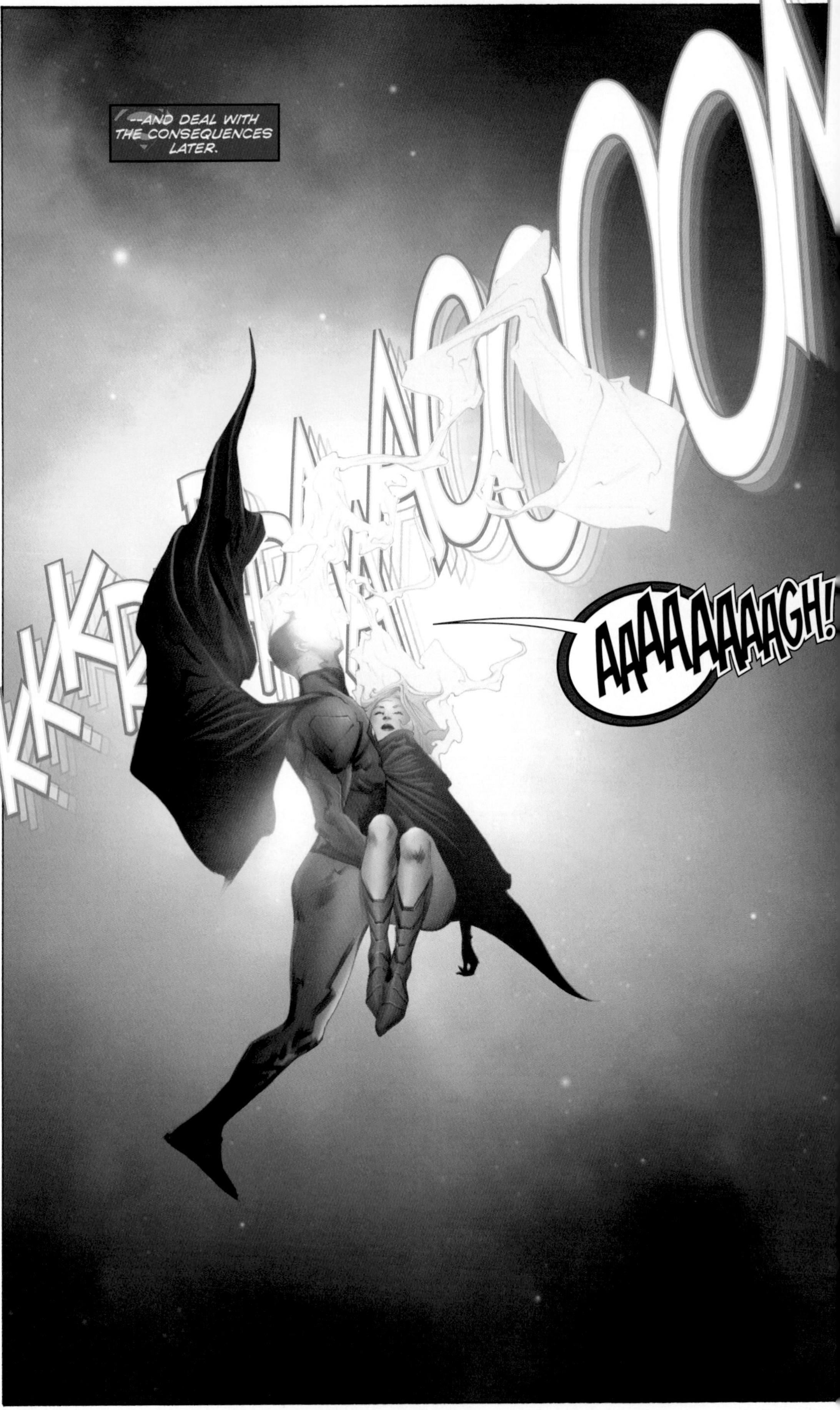
--AND DEAL WITH THE CONSEQUENCES LATER.
KKKRRRAAAOOOOOOOM
AAAAAAAAGH!

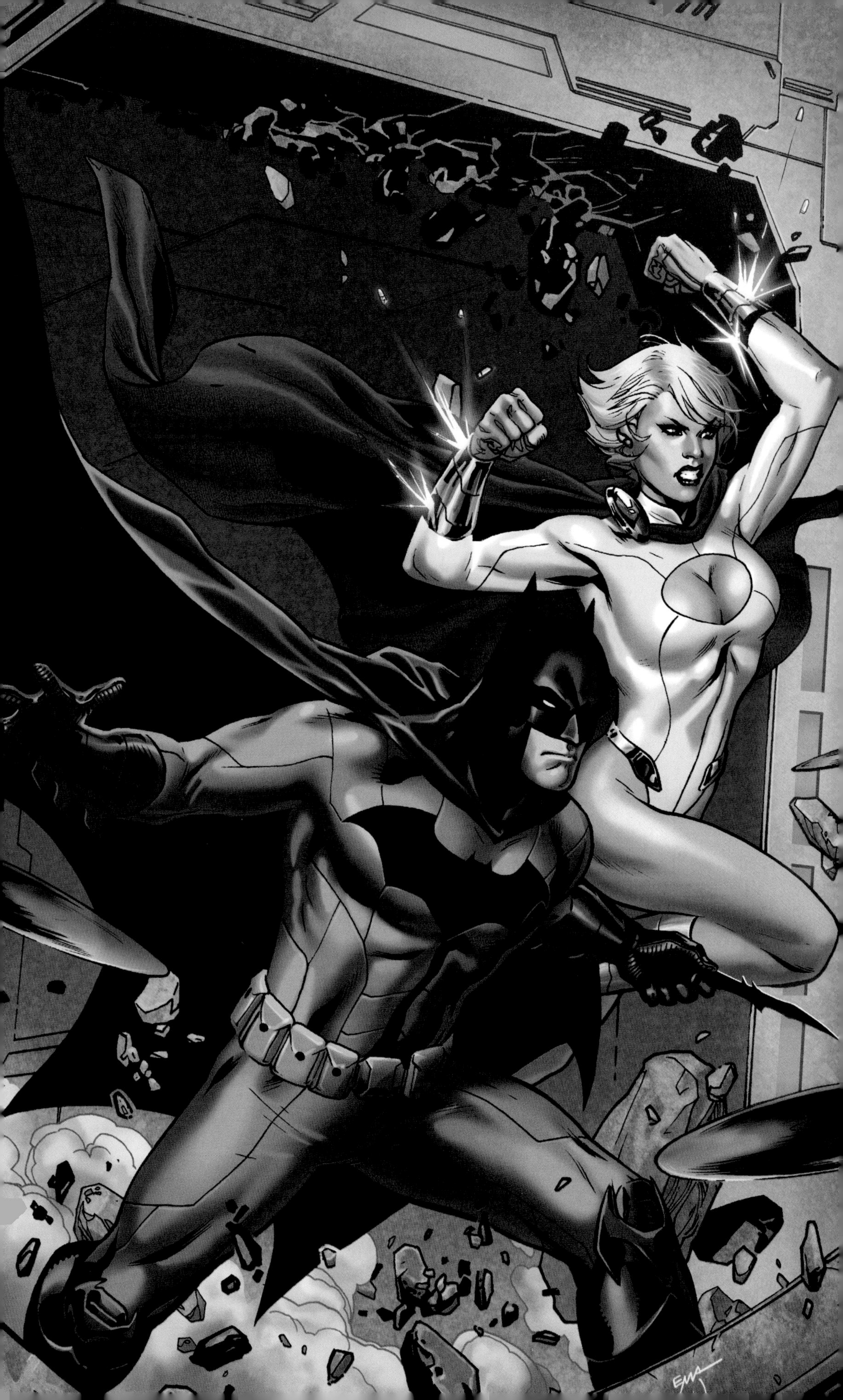

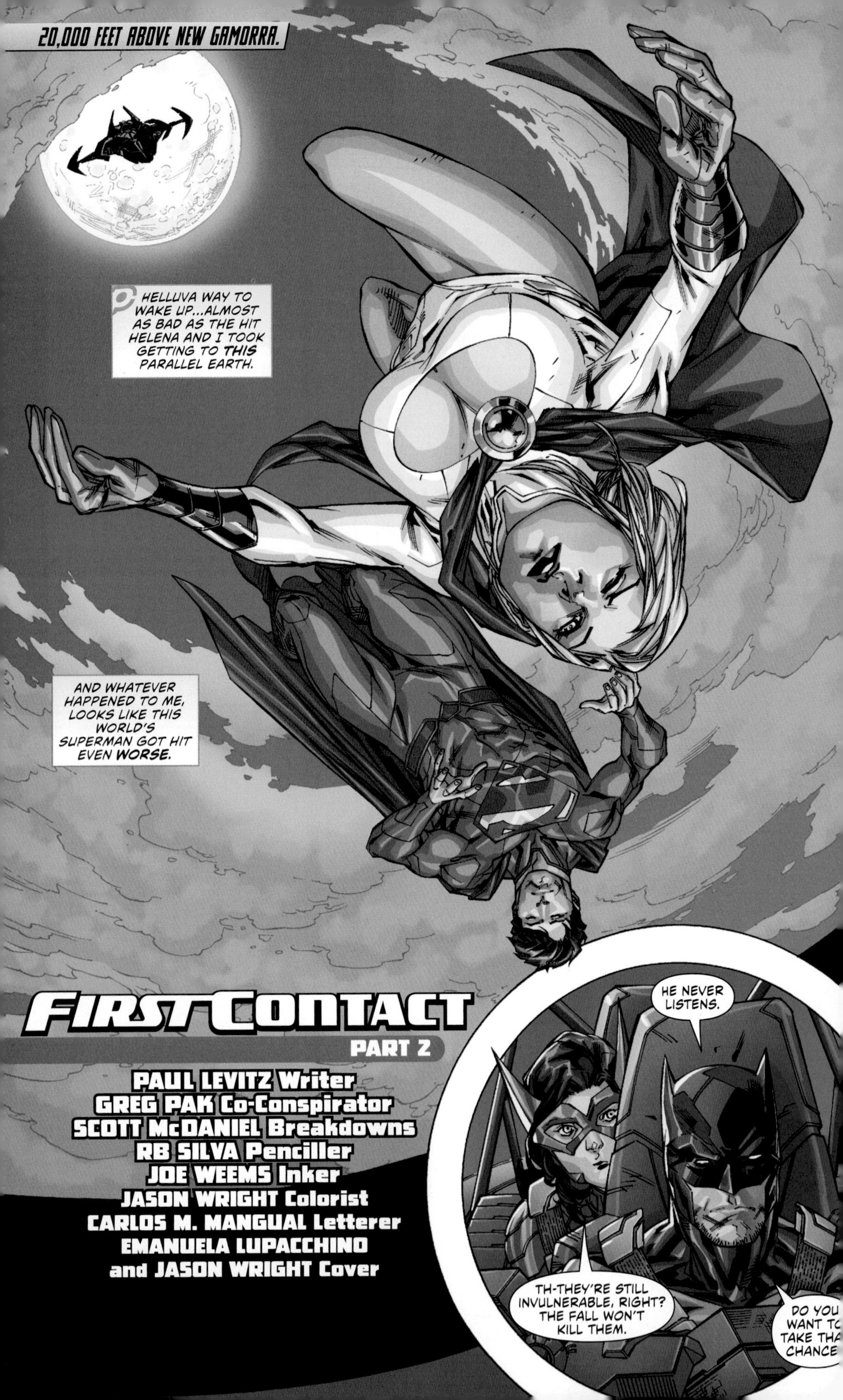
20,000 FEET ABOVE NEW GAMORRA.
HELLUVA WAY TO WAKE UP...ALMOST AS BAD AS THE HIT HELENA AND I TOOK GETTING TO THIS PARALLEL EARTH.
AND WHATEVER HAPPENED TO ME, LOOKS LIKE THIS WORLD'S SUPERMAN GOT HIT EVEN WORSE.
FIRST CONTACT
PART 2
PAUL LEVITZ Writer
GREG PAK Co-Conspirator
SCOTT McDANIEL Breakdowns
RB SILVA Penciller
JOE WEEMS Inker
JASON WRIGHT Colorist
CARLOS M. MANGUAL Letterer
EMANUELA LUPACCHINO and JASON WRIGHT Cover
HE NEVER LISTENS.
TH-THEY'RE STILL INVULNERABLE, RIGHT? THE FALL WON'T KILL THEM.
DO YOU WANT TO TAKE THA CHANCE

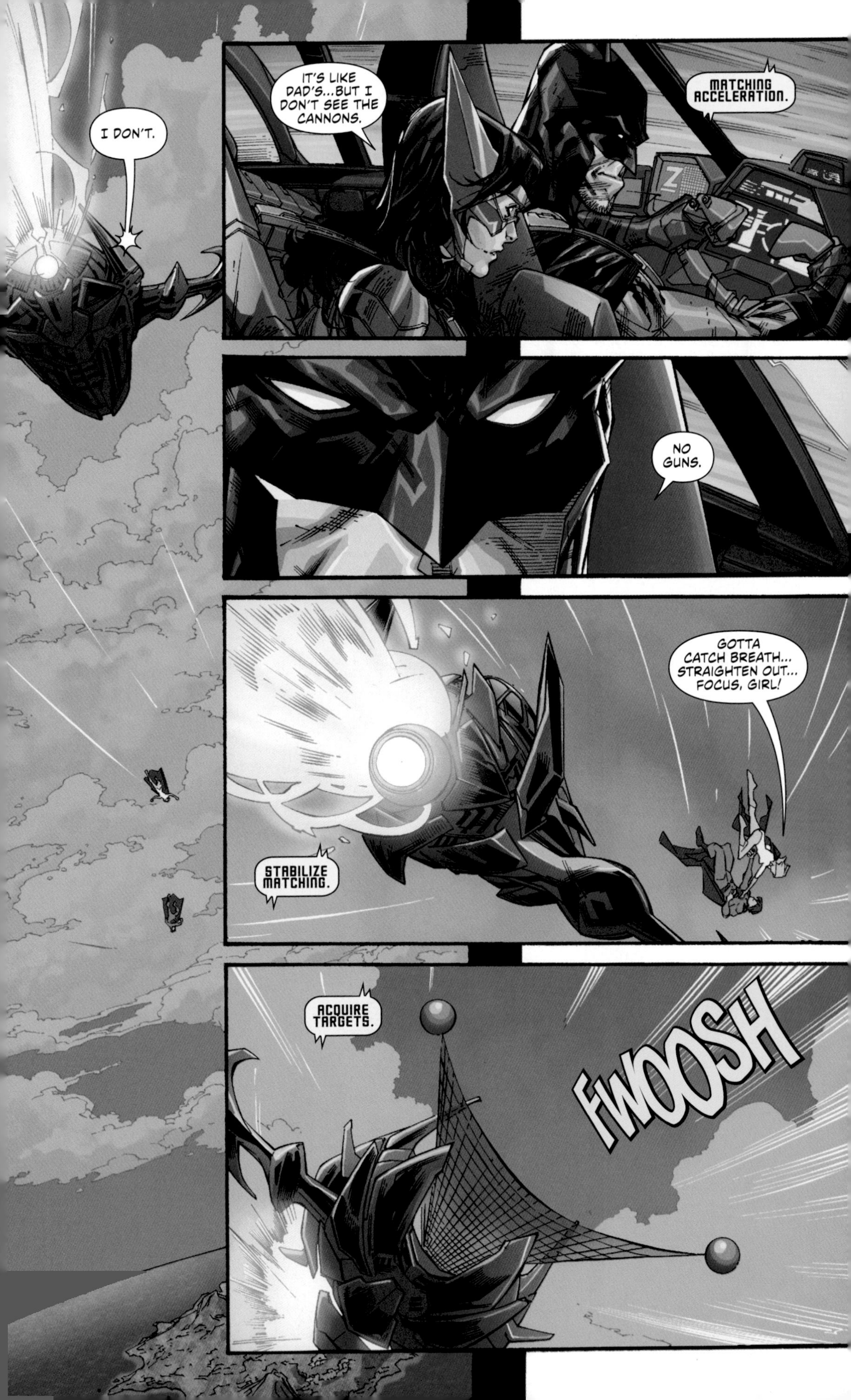
IT'S LIKE DAD'S...BUT I DON'T SEE THE CANNONS.
I DON'T.
MATCHING ACCELERATION.
NO GUNS.
GOTTA CATCH BREATH... STRAIGHTEN OUT... FOCUS, GIRL!
STABILIZE MATCHING.
ACQUIRE TARGETS.
FWOOSH

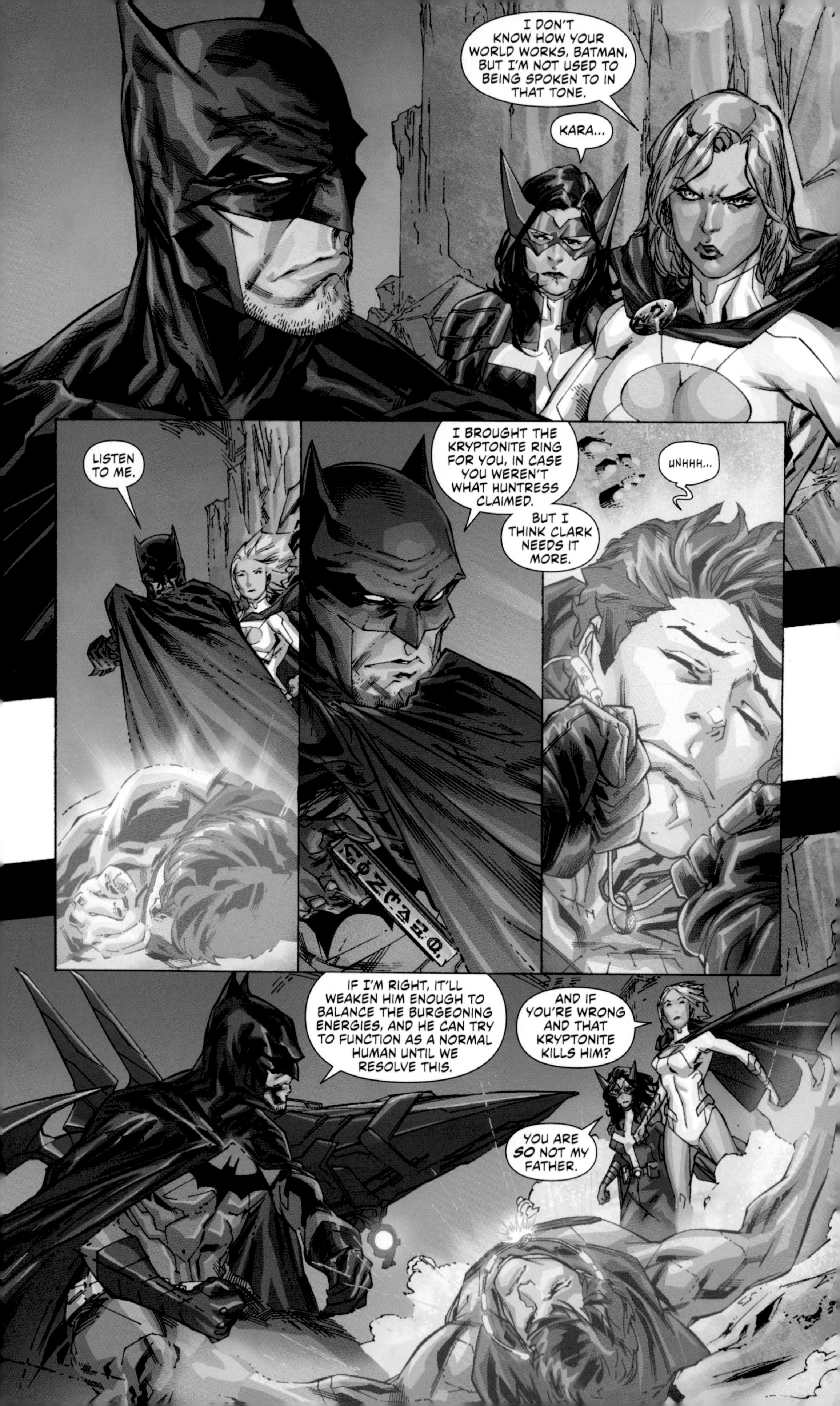
I DON'T KNOW HOW YOUR WORLD WORKS, BATMAN, BUT I'M NOT USED TO BEING SPOKEN TO IN THAT TONE.
KARA...
LISTEN TO ME.
I BROUGHT THE KRYPTONITE RING FOR YOU, IN CASE YOU WEREN'T WHAT HUNTRESS CLAIMED.
BUT I THINK CLARK NEEDS IT MORE.
UNHHH...
IF I'M RIGHT, IT'LL WEAKEN HIM ENOUGH TO BALANCE THE BURGEONING ENERGIES, AND HE CAN TRY TO FUNCTION AS A NORMAL HUMAN UNTIL WE RESOLVE THIS.
AND IF YOU'RE WRONG AND THAT KRYPTONITE KILLS HIM?
YOU ARE SO NOT MY FATHER.

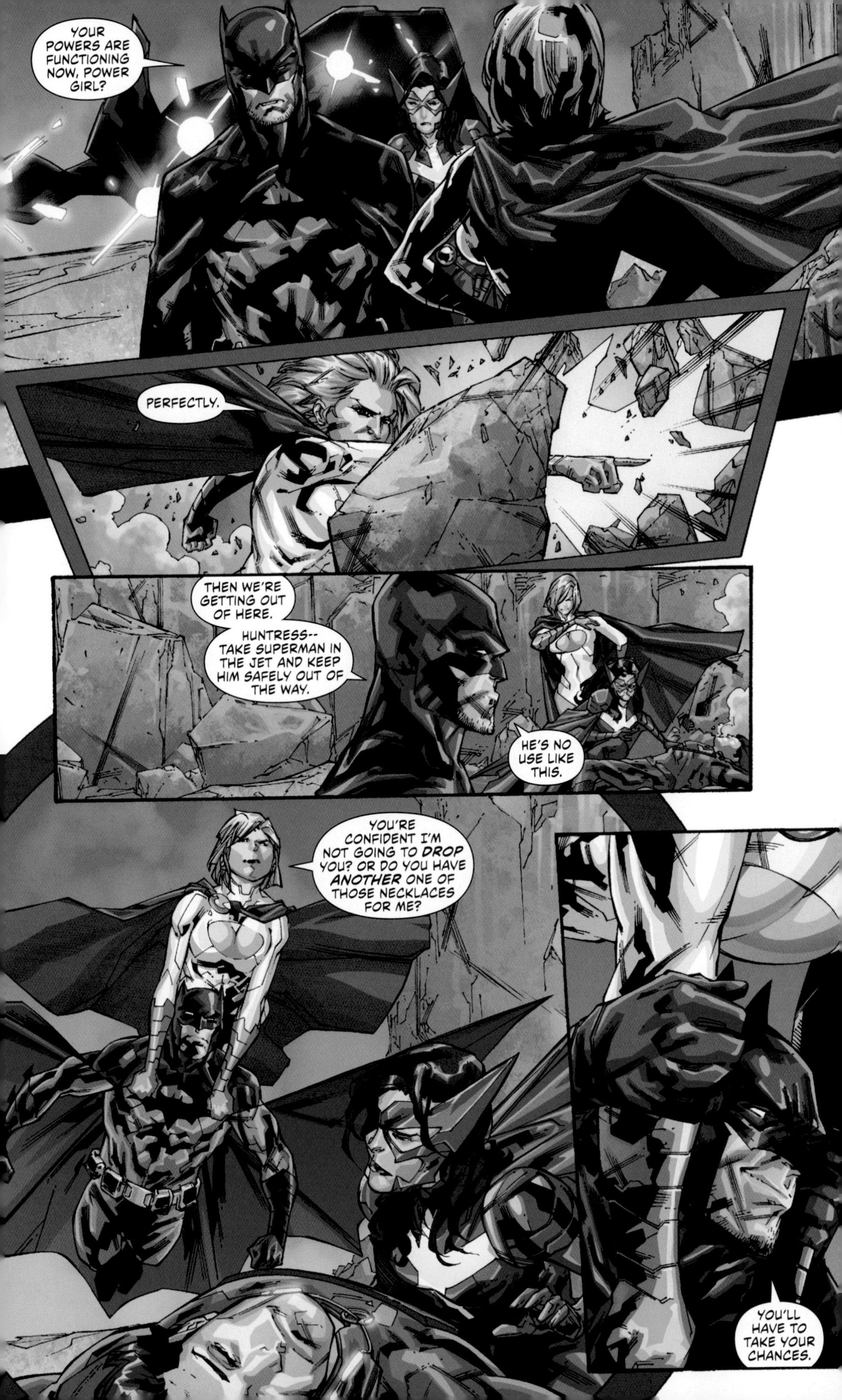
YOUR POWERS ARE FUNCTIONING NOW, POWER GIRL?
PERFECTLY.
THEN WE'RE GETTING OUT OF HERE.
HUNTRESS-- TAKE SUPERMAN IN THE JET AND KEEP HIM SAFELY OUT OF THE WAY.
HE'S NO USE LIKE THIS.
YOU'RE CONFIDENT I'M NOT GOING TO *DROP* YOU? OR DO YOU HAVE *ANOTHER* ONE OF THOSE NECKLACES FOR ME?
YOU'LL HAVE TO TAKE YOUR CHANCES.

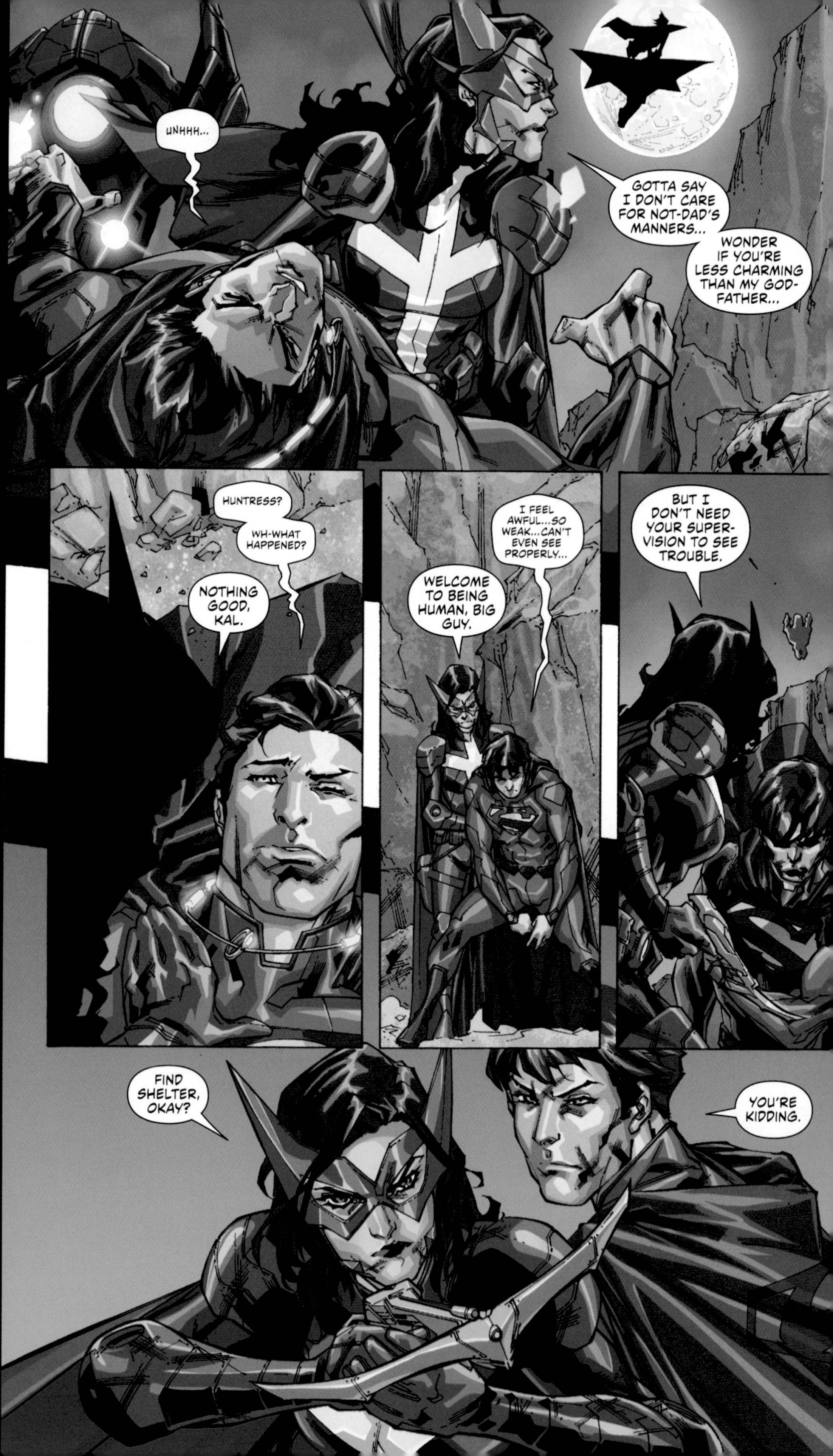
UNHHH...
GOTTA SAY I DON'T CARE FOR NOT-DAD'S MANNERS...
WONDER IF YOU'RE LESS CHARMING THAN MY GOD-FATHER...
HUNTRESS?
WH-WHAT HAPPENED?
NOTHING GOOD, KAL.
I FEEL AWFUL...SO WEAK...CAN'T EVEN SEE PROPERLY...
WELCOME TO BEING HUMAN, BIG GUY.
BUT I DON'T NEED YOUR SUPER-VISION TO SEE TROUBLE.
FIND SHELTER, OKAY?
YOU'RE KIDDING.

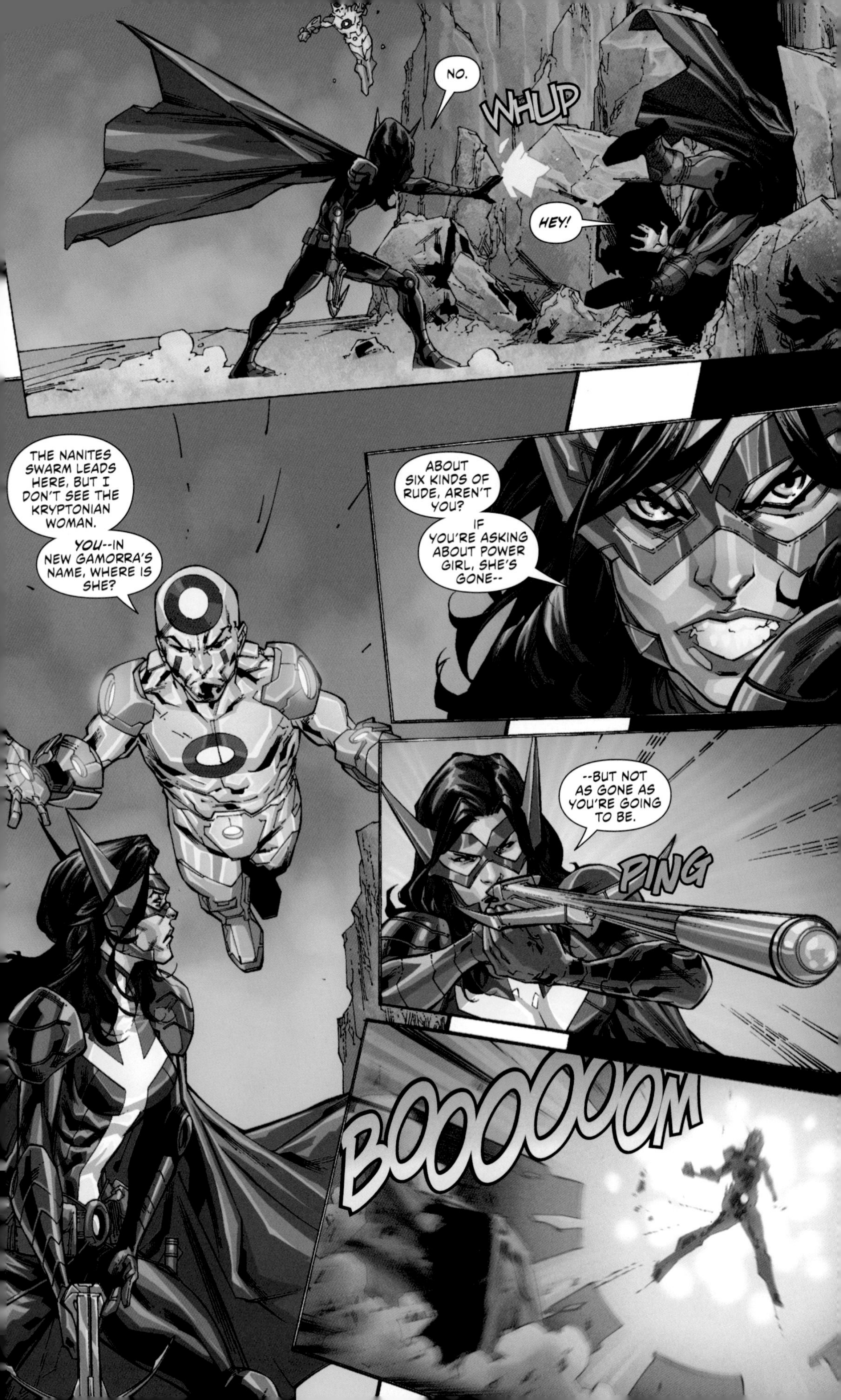
NO.
WHUP
HEY!
THE NANITES SWARM LEADS HERE, BUT I DON'T SEE THE KRYPTONIAN WOMAN.
YOU--IN NEW GAMORRA'S NAME, WHERE IS SHE?
ABOUT SIX KINDS OF RUDE, AREN'T YOU?
IF YOU'RE ASKING ABOUT POWER GIRL, SHE'S GONE--
--BUT NOT AS GONE AS YOU'RE GOING TO BE.
PING
BOOOOOOM

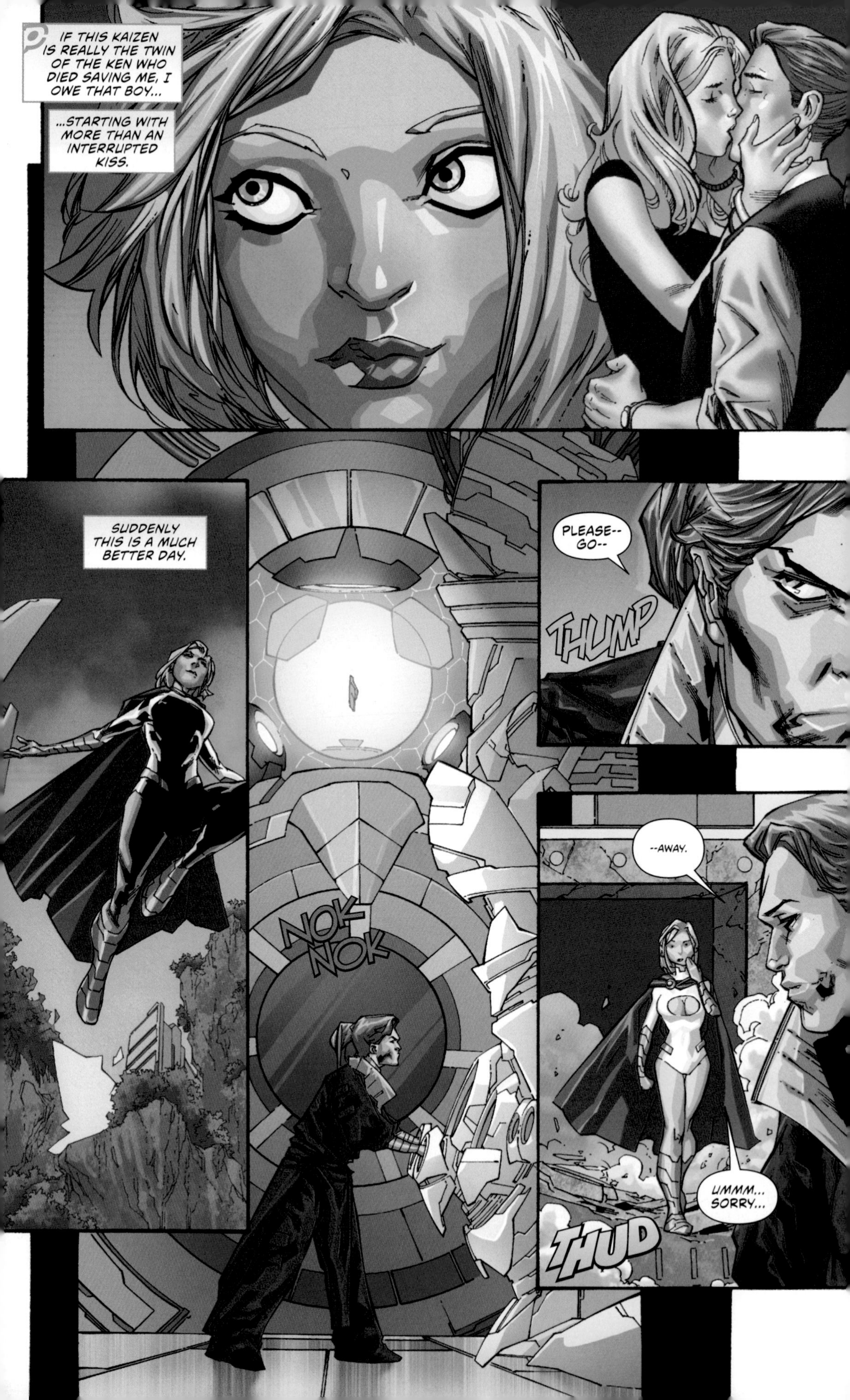
IF THIS KAIZEN IS REALLY THE TWIN OF THE KEN WHO DIED SAVING ME, I OWE THAT BOY...
...STARTING WITH MORE THAN AN INTERRUPTED KISS.
SUDDENLY THIS IS A MUCH BETTER DAY.
NOK NOK
PLEASE-- GO--
THUMP
--AWAY.
UMMM... SORRY...
THUD

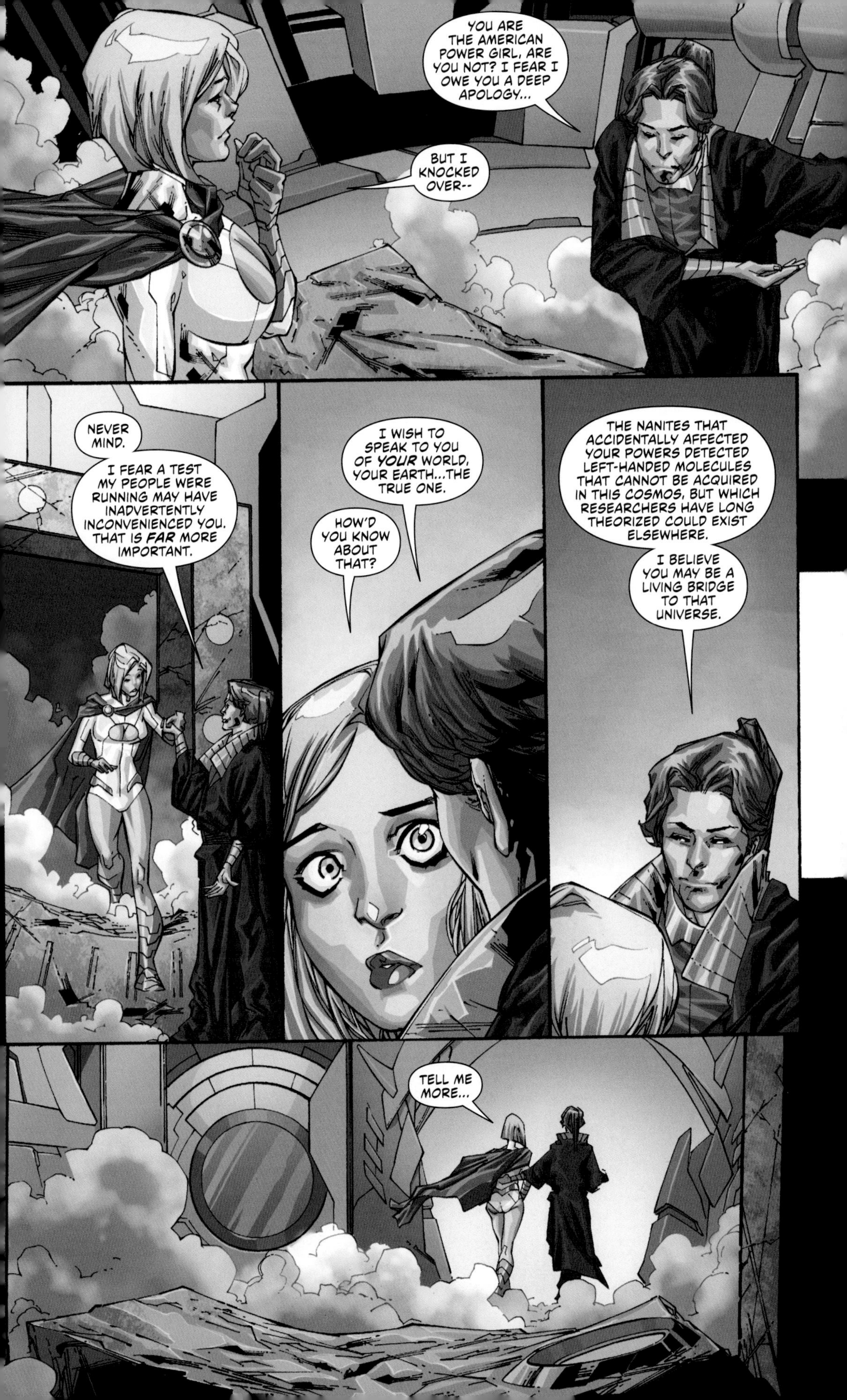
YOU ARE THE AMERICAN POWER GIRL, ARE YOU NOT? I FEAR I OWE YOU A DEEP APOLOGY...
BUT I KNOCKED OVER--
NEVER MIND.
I FEAR A TEST MY PEOPLE WERE RUNNING MAY HAVE INADVERTENTLY INCONVENIENCED YOU. THAT IS FAR MORE IMPORTANT.
I WISH TO SPEAK TO YOU OF YOUR WORLD, YOUR EARTH...THE TRUE ONE.
HOW'D YOU KNOW ABOUT THAT?
THE NANITES THAT ACCIDENTALLY AFFECTED YOUR POWERS DETECTED LEFT-HANDED MOLECULES THAT CANNOT BE ACQUIRED IN THIS COSMOS, BUT WHICH RESEARCHERS HAVE LONG THEORIZED COULD EXIST ELSEWHERE.
I BELIEVE YOU MAY BE A LIVING BRIDGE TO THAT UNIVERSE.
TELL ME MORE...

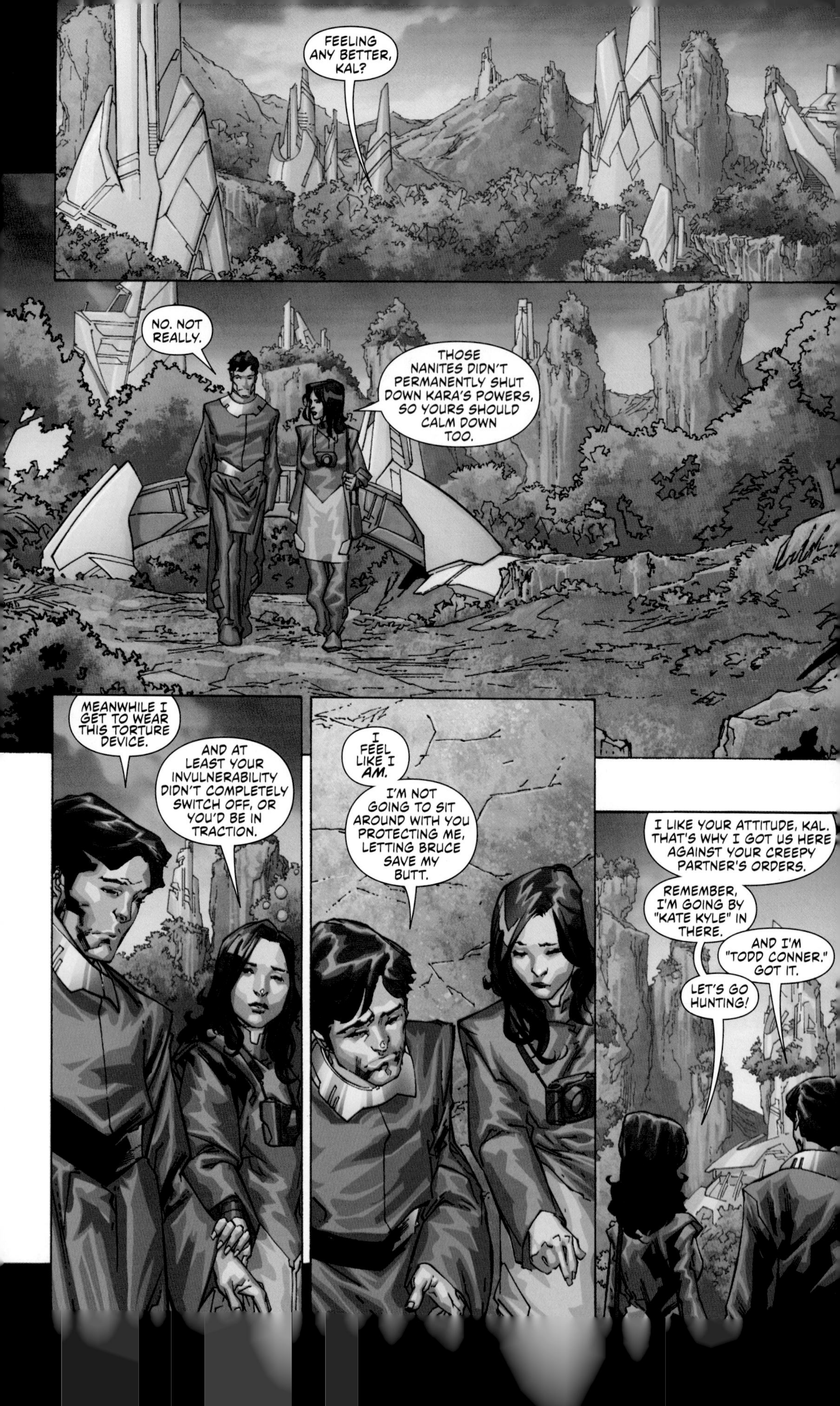
FEELING ANY BETTER, KAL?
NO. NOT REALLY.
THOSE NANITES DIDN'T PERMANENTLY SHUT DOWN KARA'S POWERS, SO YOURS SHOULD CALM DOWN TOO.
MEANWHILE I GET TO WEAR THIS TORTURE DEVICE.
AND AT LEAST YOUR INVULNERABILITY DIDN'T COMPLETELY SWITCH OFF, OR YOU'D BE IN TRACTION.
I FEEL LIKE I *AM*.
I'M NOT GOING TO SIT AROUND WITH YOU PROTECTING ME, LETTING BRUCE SAVE MY BUTT.
I LIKE YOUR ATTITUDE, KAL. THAT'S WHY I GOT US HERE AGAINST YOUR CREEPY PARTNER'S ORDERS.
REMEMBER, I'M GOING BY "KATE KYLE" IN THERE.
AND I'M "TODD CONNER." GOT IT.
LET'S GO HUNTING!

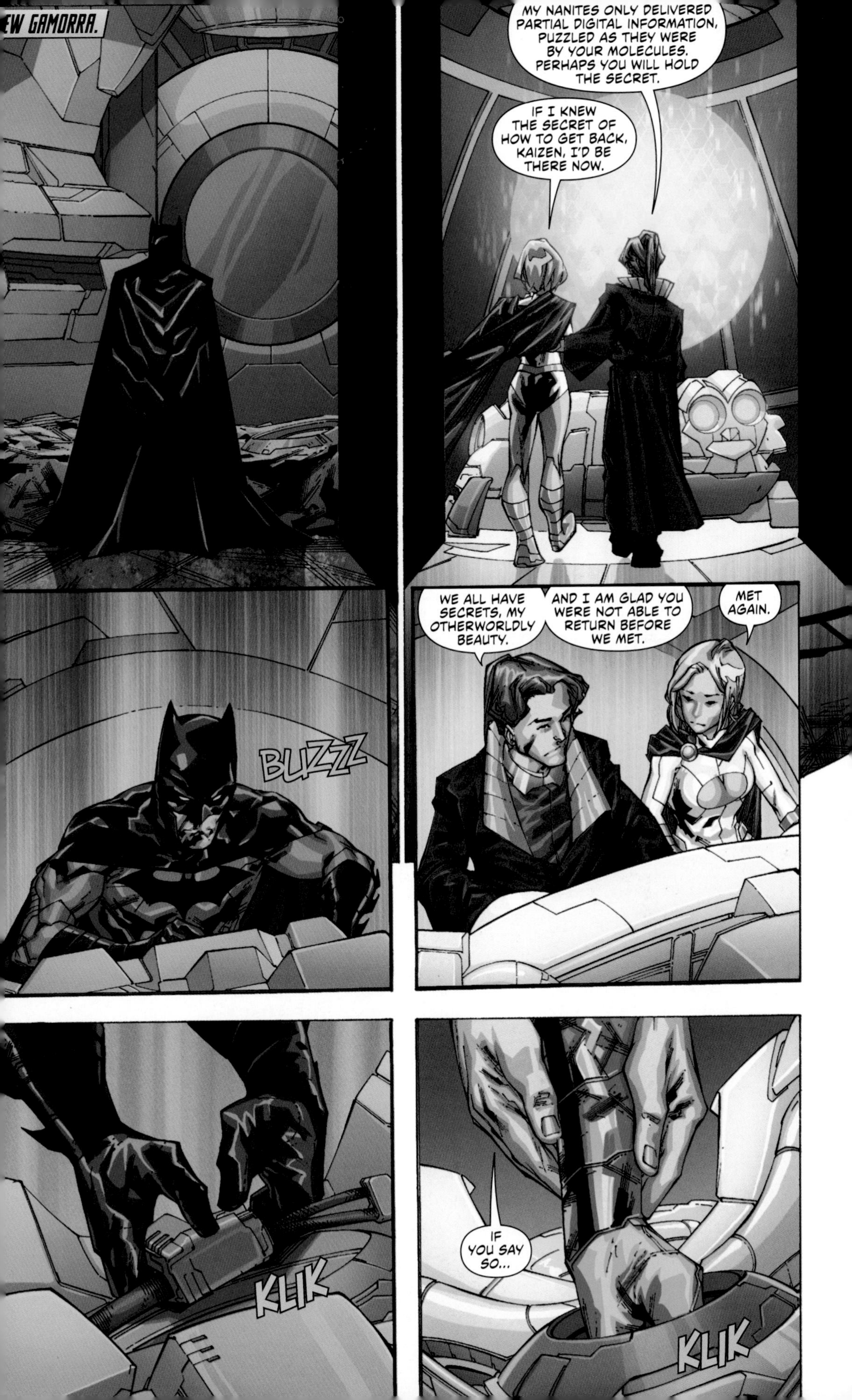
EW GAMORRA.
MY NANITES ONLY DELIVERED PARTIAL DIGITAL INFORMATION, PUZZLED AS THEY WERE BY YOUR MOLECULES. PERHAPS YOU WILL HOLD THE SECRET.
IF I KNEW THE SECRET OF HOW TO GET BACK, KAIZEN, I'D BE THERE NOW.
BUZZZ
WE ALL HAVE SECRETS, MY OTHERWORLDLY BEAUTY.
AND I AM GLAD YOU WERE NOT ABLE TO RETURN BEFORE WE MET.
MET AGAIN.
KLIK
IF YOU SAY SO...
KLIK

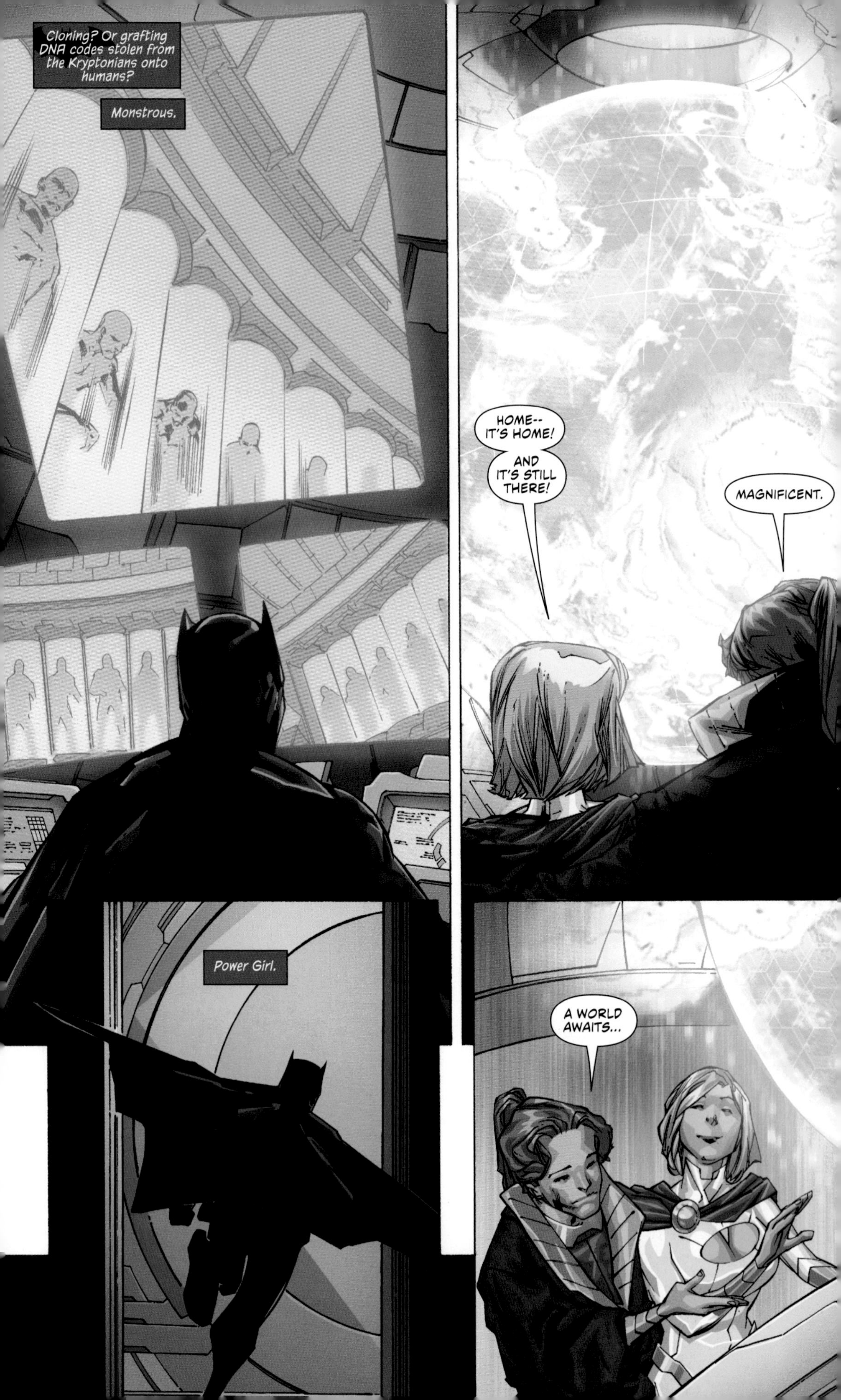
Cloning? Or grafting DNA codes stolen from the Kryptonians onto humans?
Monstrous.
HOME-- IT'S HOME!
AND IT'S STILL THERE!
MAGNIFICENT.
Power Girl.
A WORLD AWAITS...

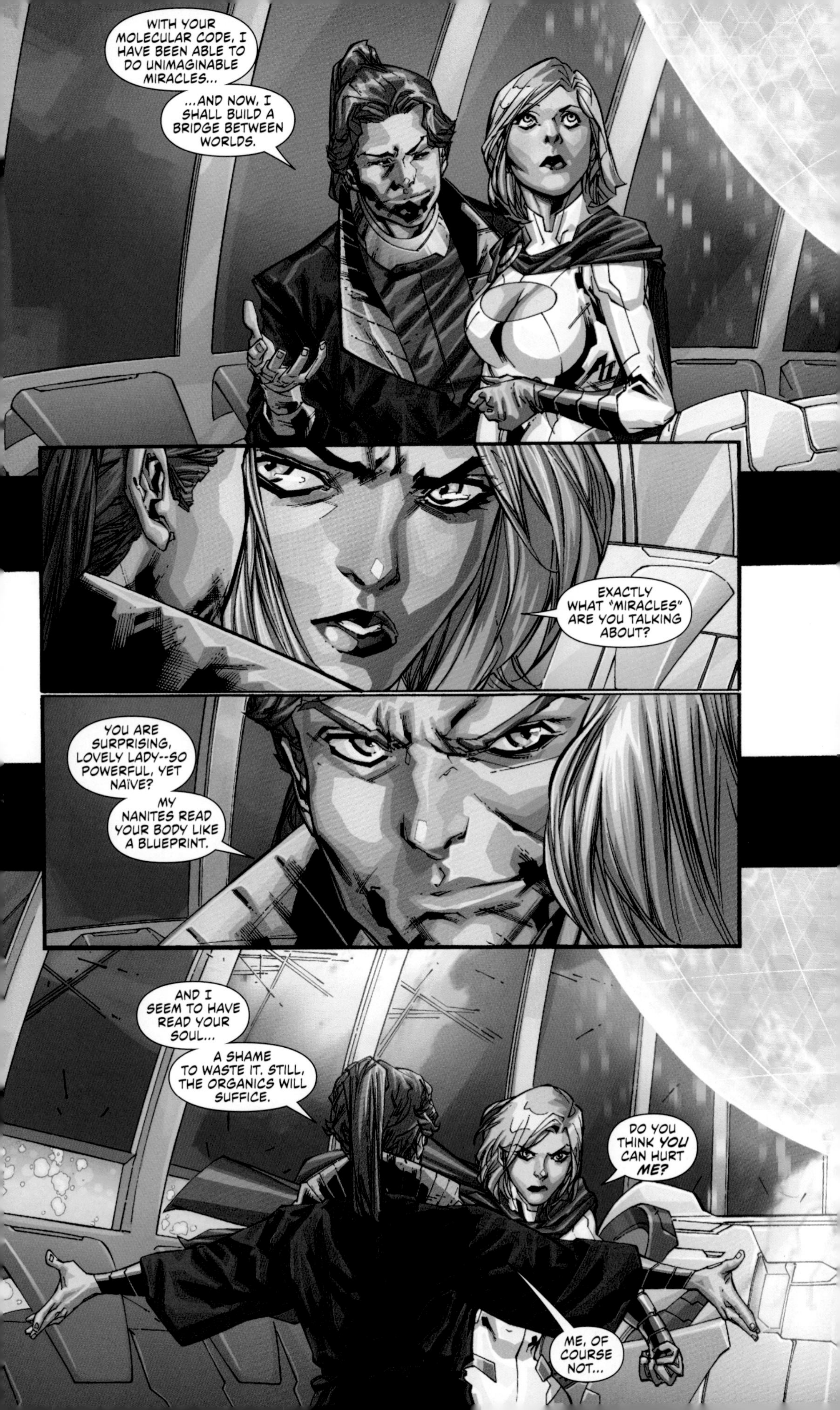
WITH YOUR MOLECULAR CODE, I HAVE BEEN ABLE TO DO UNIMAGINABLE MIRACLES...
...AND NOW, I SHALL BUILD A BRIDGE BETWEEN WORLDS.
EXACTLY WHAT "MIRACLES" ARE YOU TALKING ABOUT?
YOU ARE SURPRISING, LOVELY LADY--SO POWERFUL, YET NAÏVE?
MY NANITES READ YOUR BODY LIKE A BLUEPRINT.
AND I SEEM TO HAVE READ YOUR SOUL...
A SHAME TO WASTE IT. STILL, THE ORGANICS WILL SUFFICE.
DO YOU THINK YOU CAN HURT ME?
ME, OF COURSE NOT...

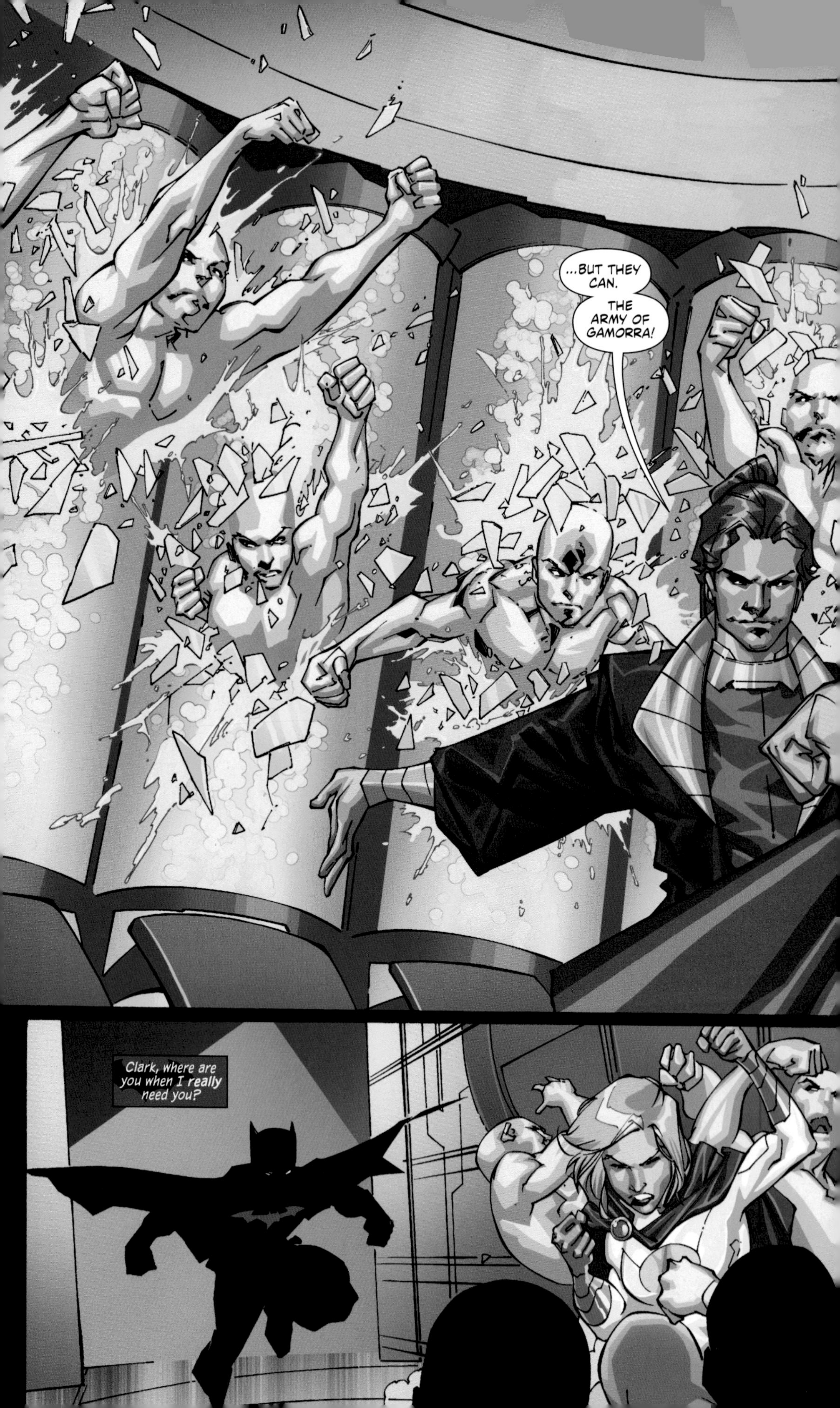
...BUT THEY CAN.
THE ARMY OF GAMORRA!
Clark, where are you when I *really* need you?

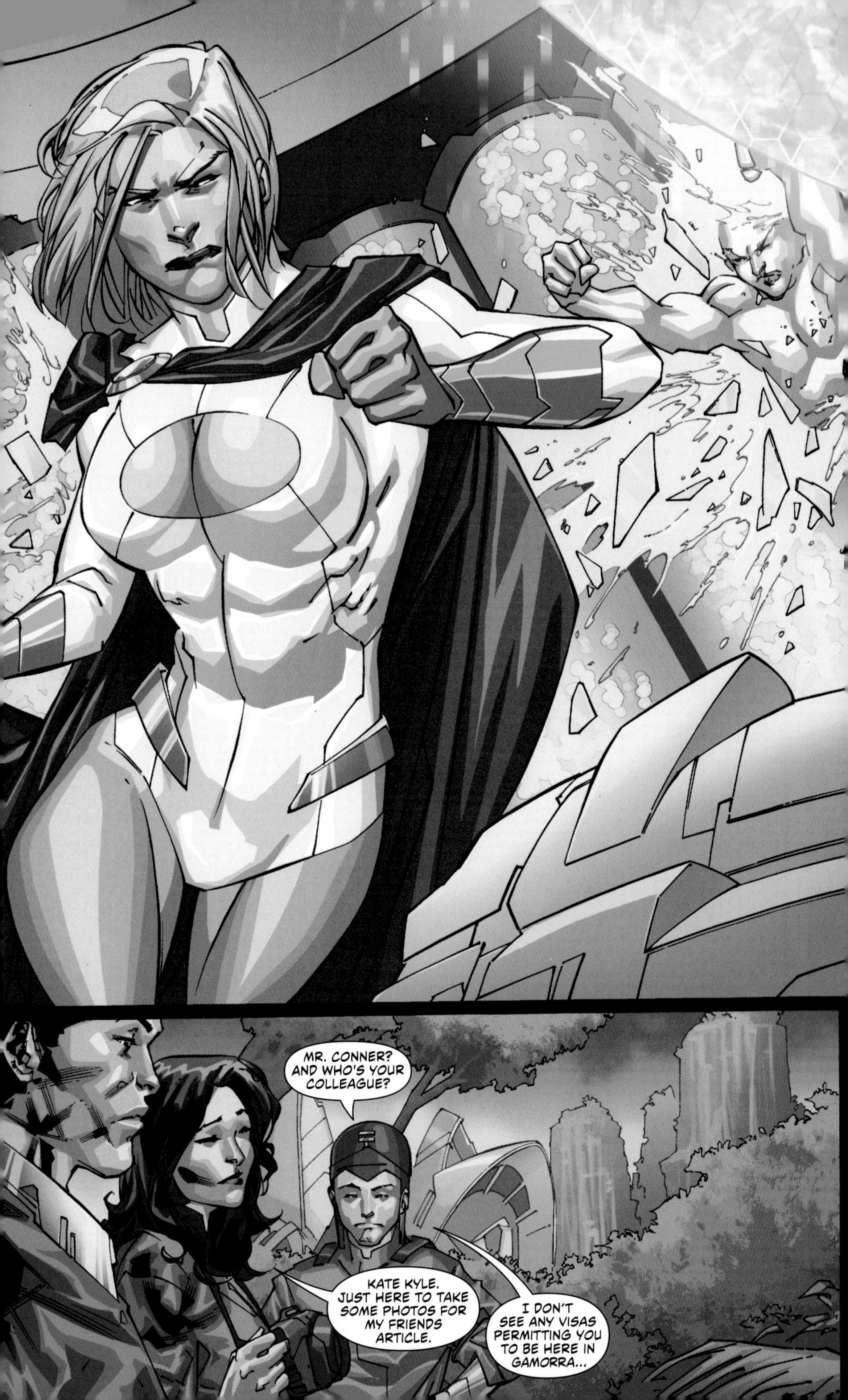
MR. CONNER? AND WHO'S YOUR COLLEAGUE?
KATE KYLE. JUST HERE TO TAKE SOME PHOTOS FOR MY FRIENDS ARTICLE.
I DON'T SEE ANY VISAS PERMITTING YOU TO BE HERE IN GAMORRA...

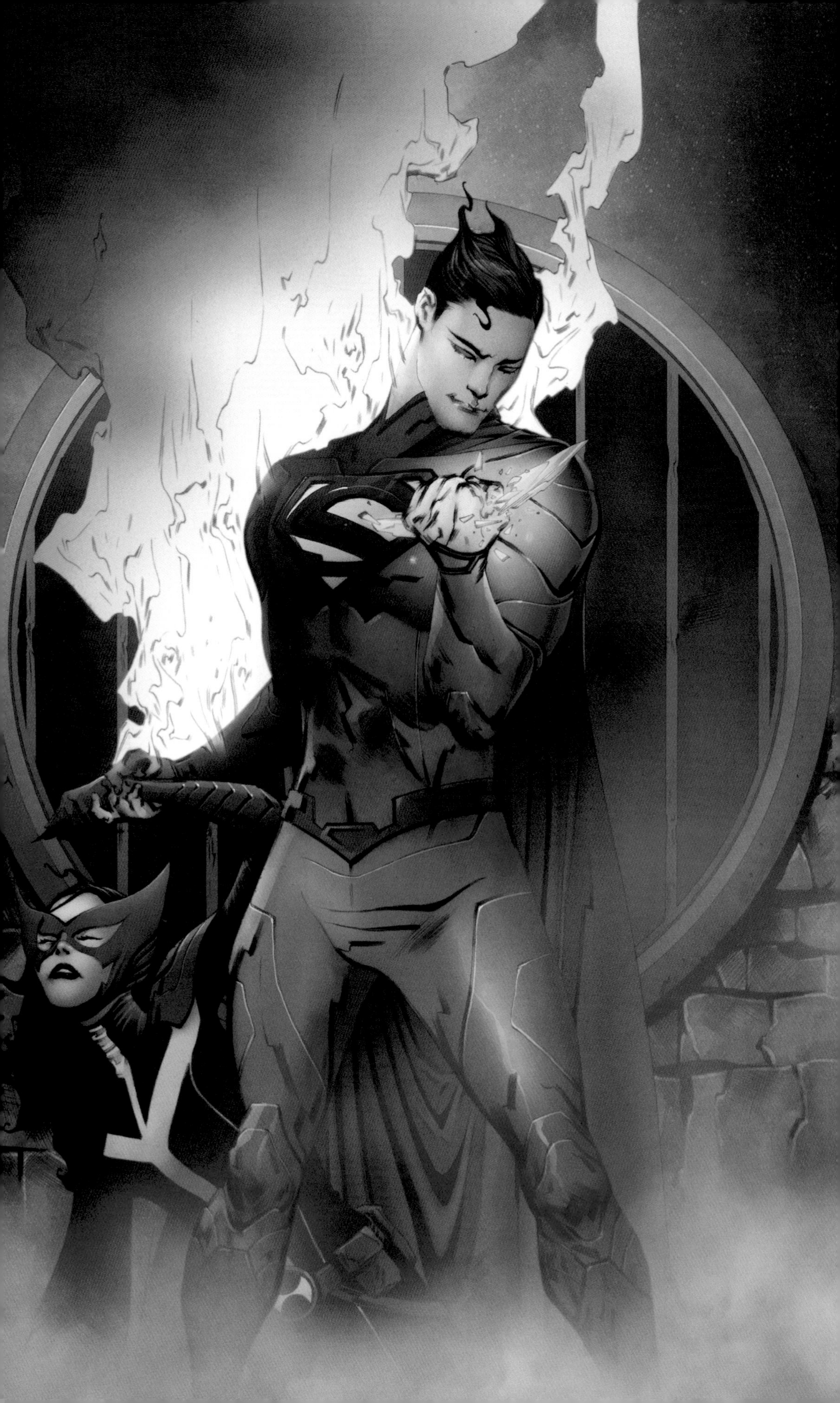

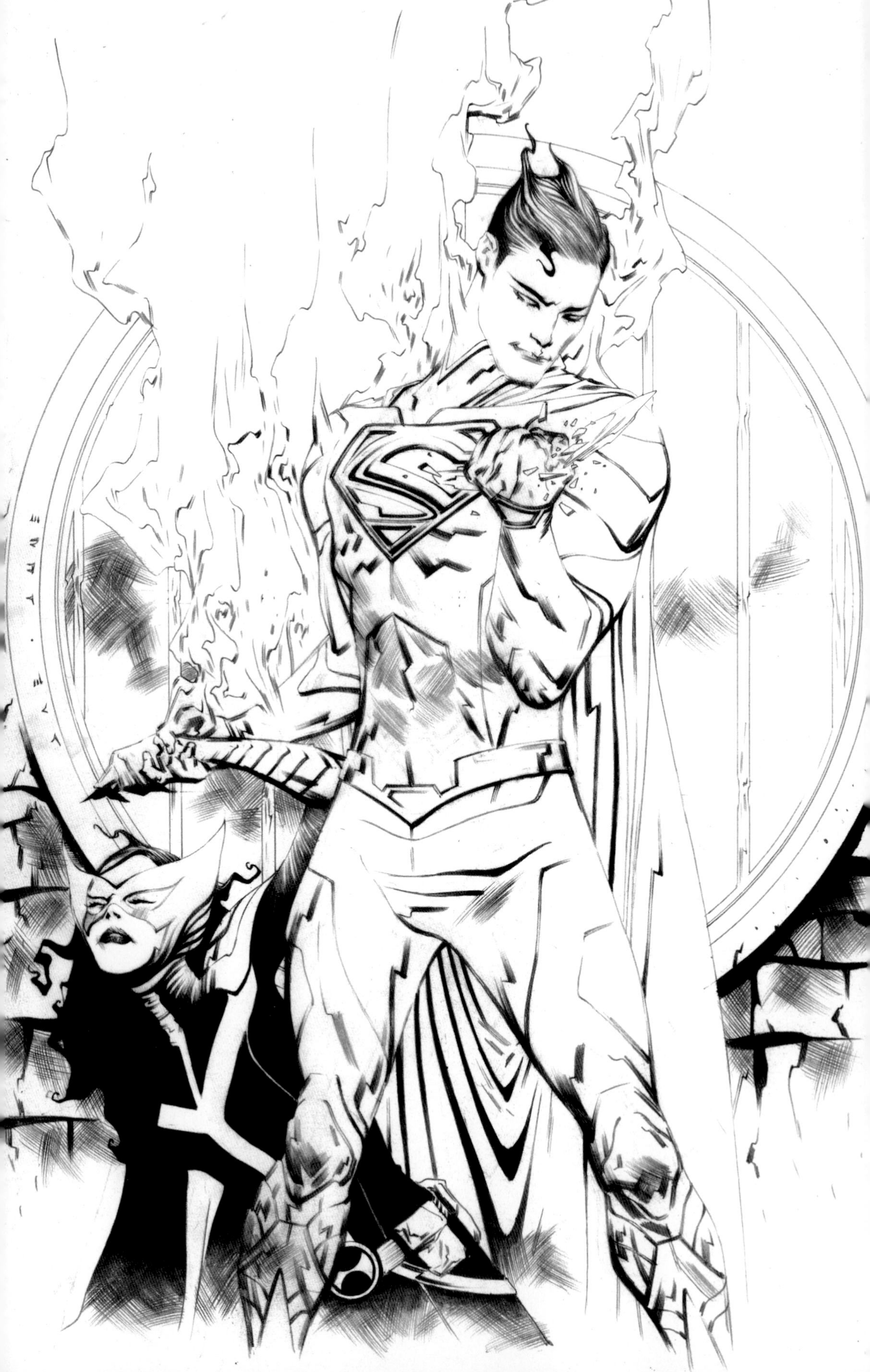

FIRST CONTACT

PART 3

GREG PAK - WRITER JAE LEE - ART
JUNE CHUNG - COLORS DC LETTERING - LETTERS
LEE WITH CHUNG - COVER

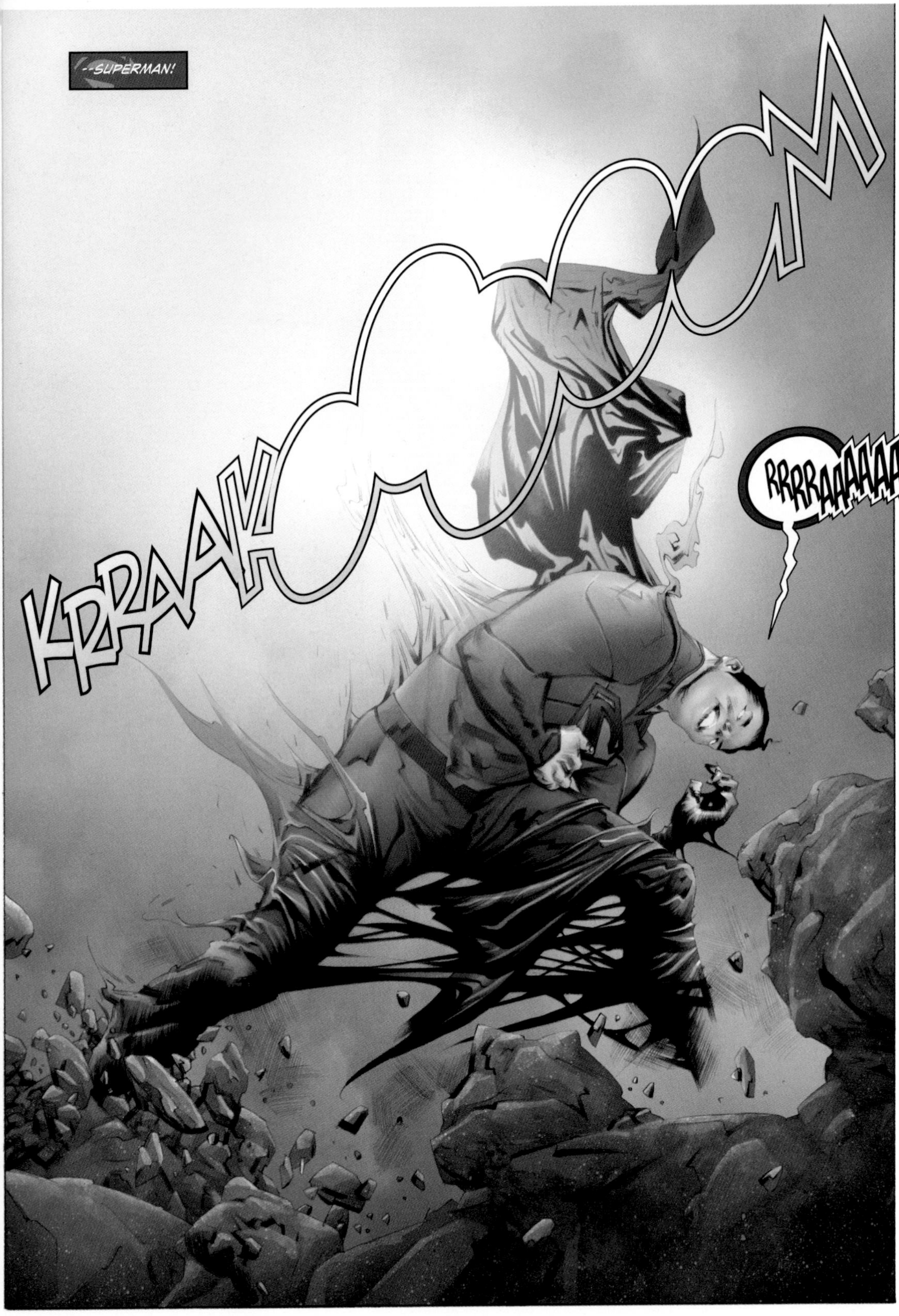
--SUPERMAN!
KRRAAKOOOOM
RRRRAAAAAA!

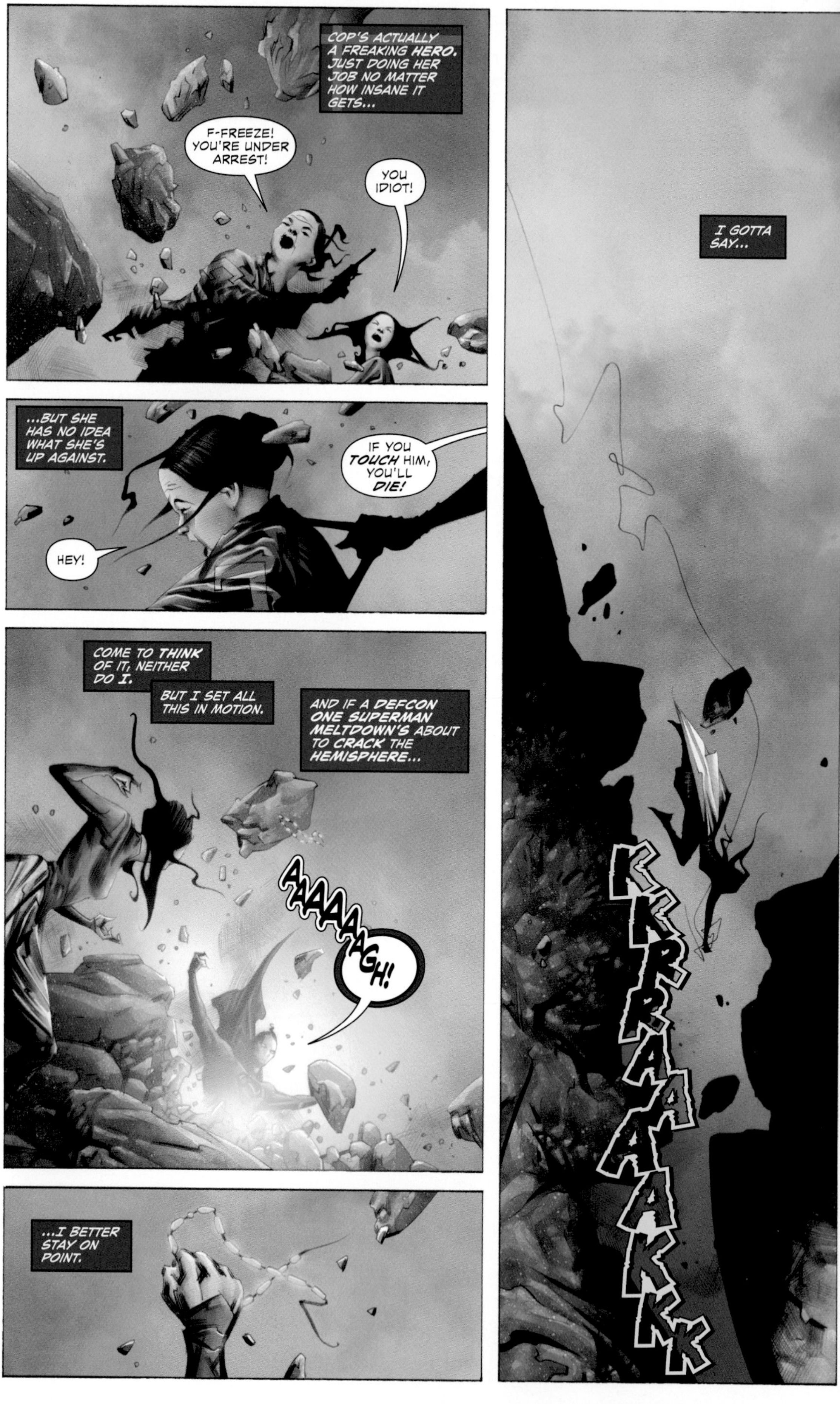
COP'S ACTUALLY A FREAKING HERO. JUST DOING HER JOB NO MATTER HOW INSANE IT GETS...
F-FREEZE! YOU'RE UNDER ARREST!
YOU IDIOT!
...BUT SHE HAS NO IDEA WHAT SHE'S UP AGAINST.
IF YOU TOUCH HIM, YOU'LL DIE!
HEY!
COME TO THINK OF IT, NEITHER DO I.
BUT I SET ALL THIS IN MOTION.
AND IF A DEFCON ONE SUPERMAN MELTDOWN'S ABOUT TO CRACK THE HEMISPHERE...
AAAAAAGH!
...I BETTER STAY ON POINT.
I GOTTA SAY...
KKRRAAAKK

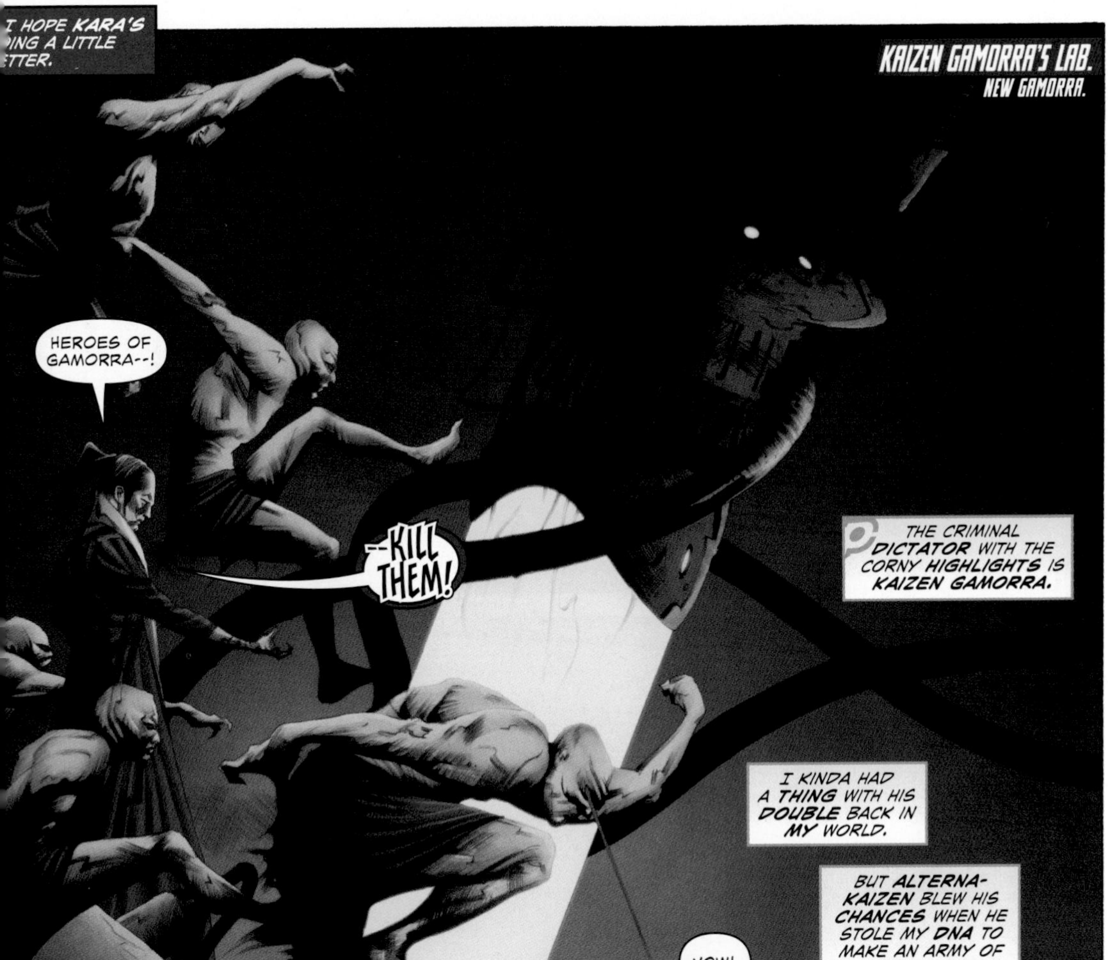
I HOPE KARA'S
ING A LITTLE
TTER.
KAIZEN GAMORRA'S LAB.
NEW GAMORRA.
HEROES OF GAMORRA--!
--KILL THEM!
THE CRIMINAL DICTATOR WITH THE CORNY HIGHLIGHTS IS KAIZEN GAMORRA.
I KINDA HAD A THING WITH HIS DOUBLE BACK IN MY WORLD.
BUT ALTERNA-KAIZEN BLEW HIS CHANCES WHEN HE STOLE MY DNA TO MAKE AN ARMY OF SUPERSOLDIERS.
YOW!

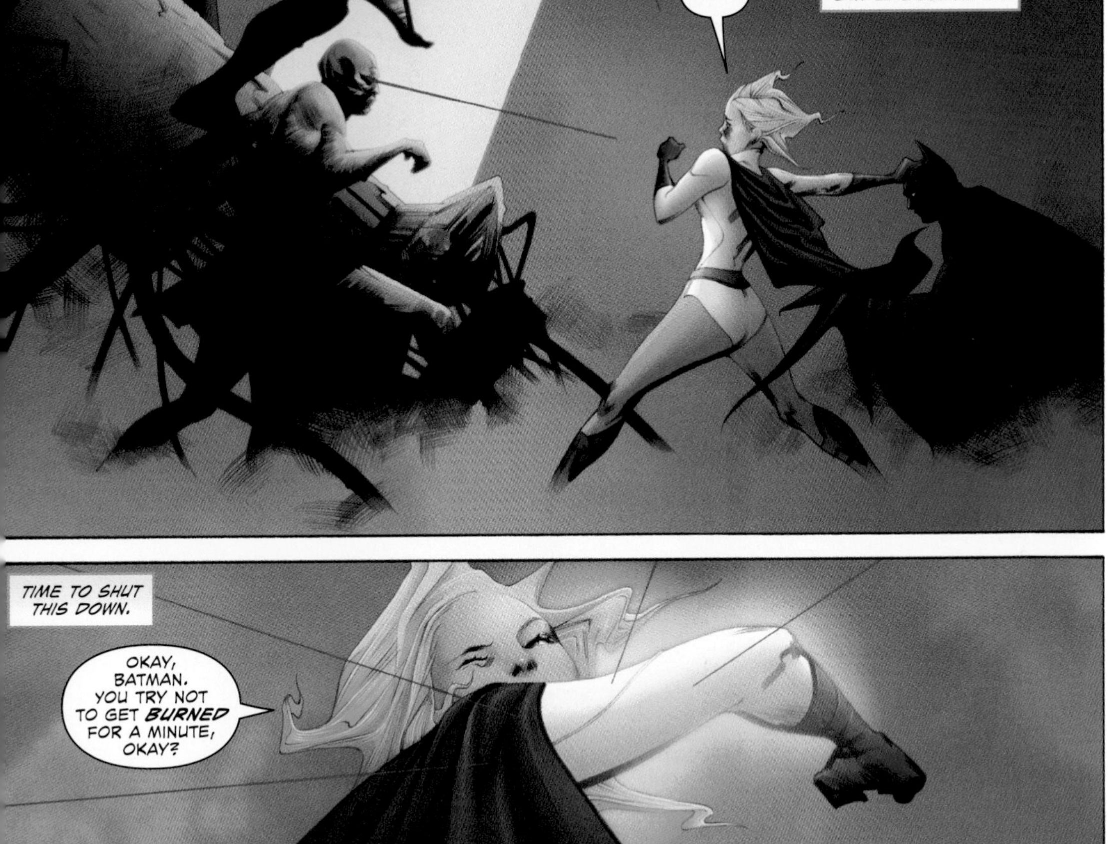
TIME TO SHUT THIS DOWN.
OKAY, BATMAN. YOU TRY NOT TO GET BURNED FOR A MINUTE, OKAY?

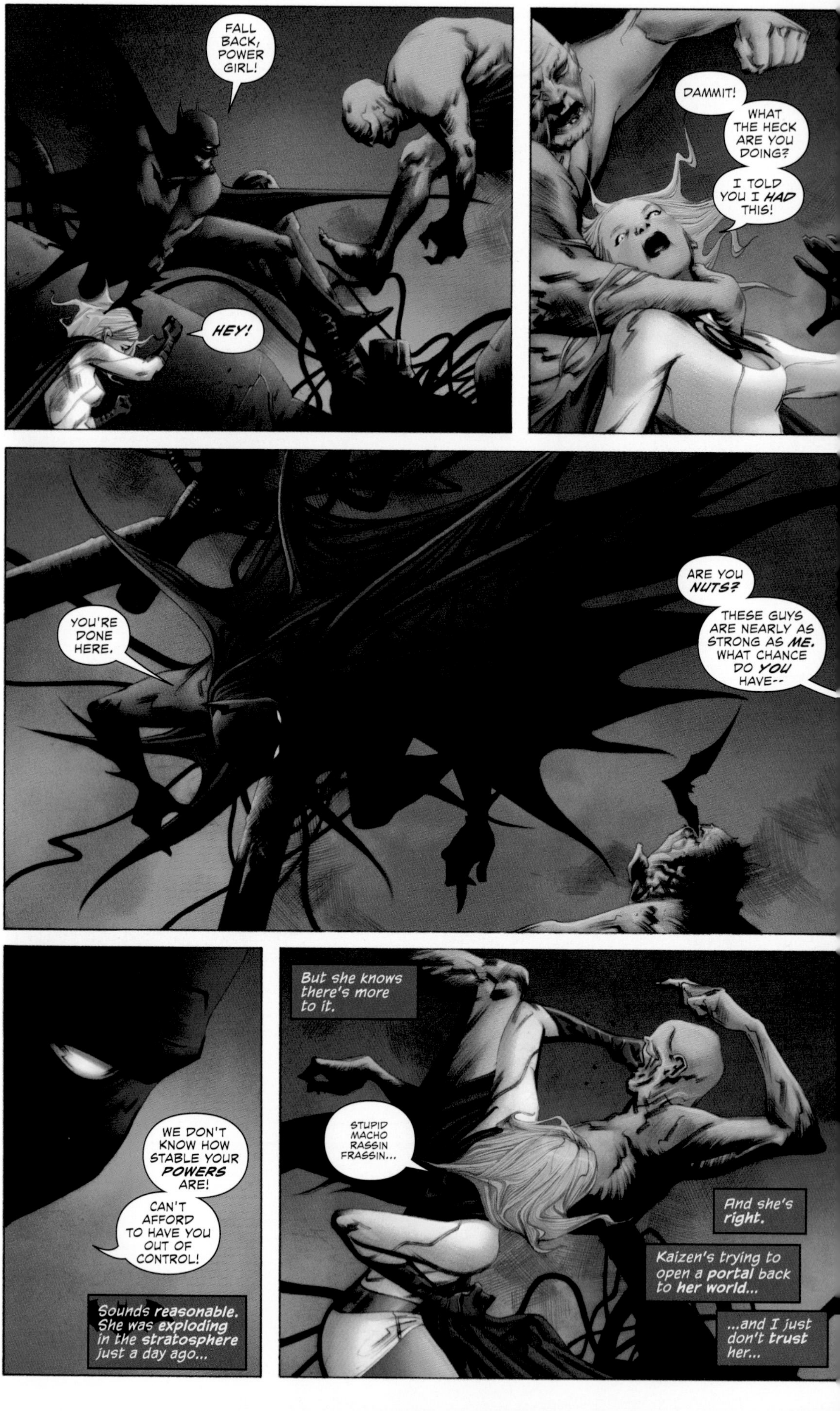

FALL BACK, POWER GIRL!
HEY!
DAMMIT!
WHAT THE HECK ARE YOU DOING?
I TOLD YOU I *HAD* THIS!
YOU'RE DONE HERE.
ARE YOU *NUTS?*
THESE GUYS ARE NEARLY AS STRONG AS *ME.* WHAT CHANCE DO *YOU* HAVE--
WE DON'T KNOW HOW STABLE YOUR *POWERS* ARE!
CAN'T AFFORD TO HAVE YOU OUT OF CONTROL!
Sounds **reasonable.** She was **exploding** in the **stratosphere** just a day ago...
But she knows there's more to it.
STUPID MACHO RASSIN FRASSIN...
And she's **right.**
Kaizen's trying to open a **portal** back to **her world...**
...and I just don't **trust** her...

...or her cousin...

...her world's Superman.

And **this** part doesn't make any sense...

...but I'm starting to **remember** this guy.

Older.

Arrogant.

Insanely powerful.

And I'm not letting her anywhere **near** a **portal** with something like **that** on the other side.

Dangerous.

I REMEMBER MEETING WITH KAREN'S COUSIN A FEW WEEKS BEFORE THE *END.*

WE WERE ALL GOING TO *DIE.* AND HE KNEW IT.

BUT HE WAS *MEASURED, CALM, COOL.*

DAD TOLD ME LATER THAT AS HE MOVED AROUND THE ROOM, HE MODULATED HIS *VOICE* TO HIT THE EXACT *FREQUENCY* NECESSARY TO *CALM DOWN* EACH SEPARATE PERSON HE MET.

BUT *THIS* GUY...

HA HA HA HA HA HA

...THIS GUY *AIN'T* MY SUPERMAN.

PUT THIS BACK ON!

GET THAT AWAY FROM ME!

YOU'VE GOT TO TAKE IT! YOU'RE NOT IN CONTROL!

NO, I'M *FINE!*

KKKRRRAAAAAKKK

UH, OH.

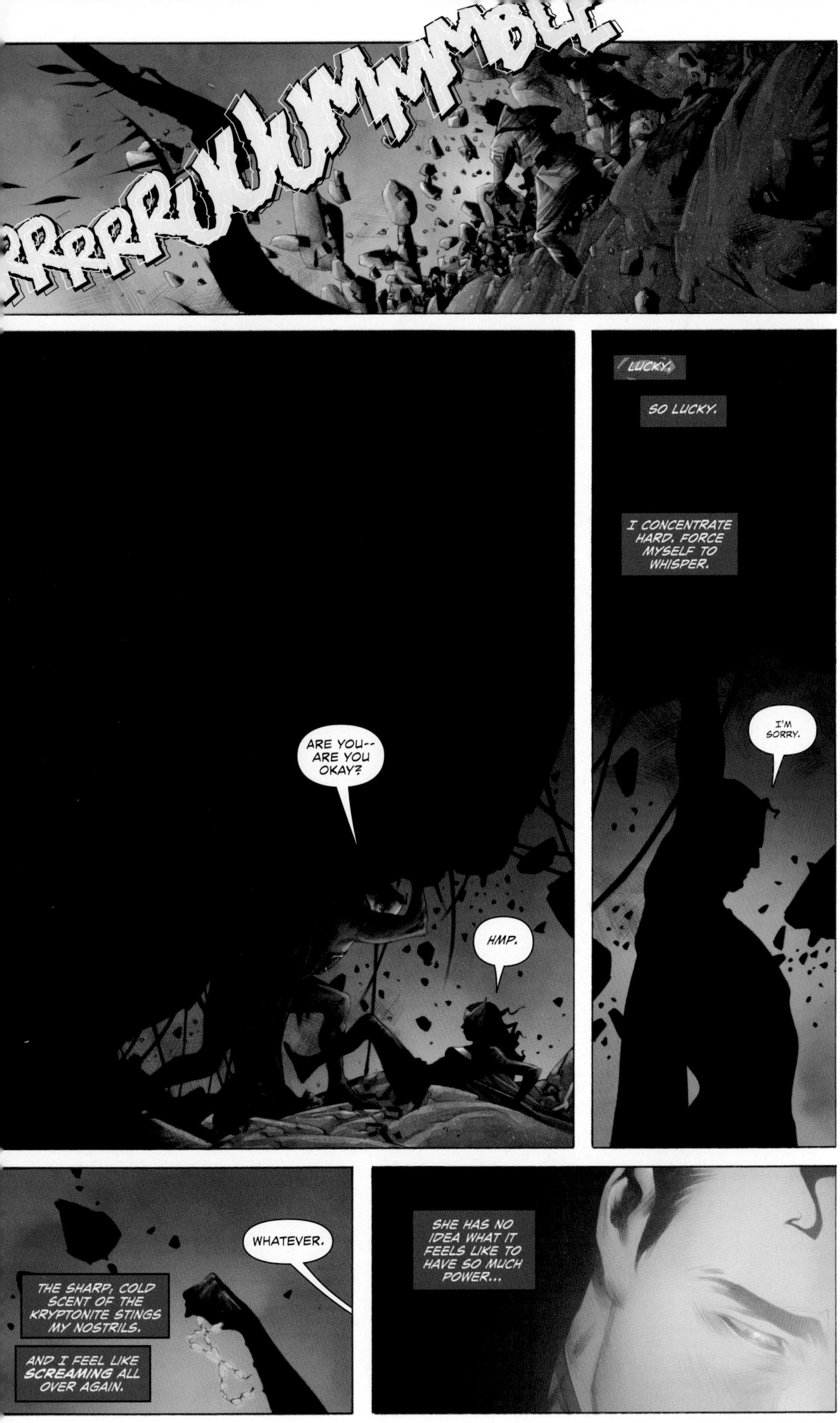
RRRRRUUUMMMBLL
LUCKY.
SO LUCKY.
I CONCENTRATE HARD. FORCE MYSELF TO WHISPER.
ARE YOU-- ARE YOU OKAY?
HMP.
I'M SORRY.
WHATEVER.
THE SHARP, COLD SCENT OF THE KRYPTONITE STINGS MY NOSTRILS.
AND I FEEL LIKE SCREAMING ALL OVER AGAIN.
SHE HAS NO IDEA WHAT IT FEELS LIKE TO HAVE SO MUCH POWER...

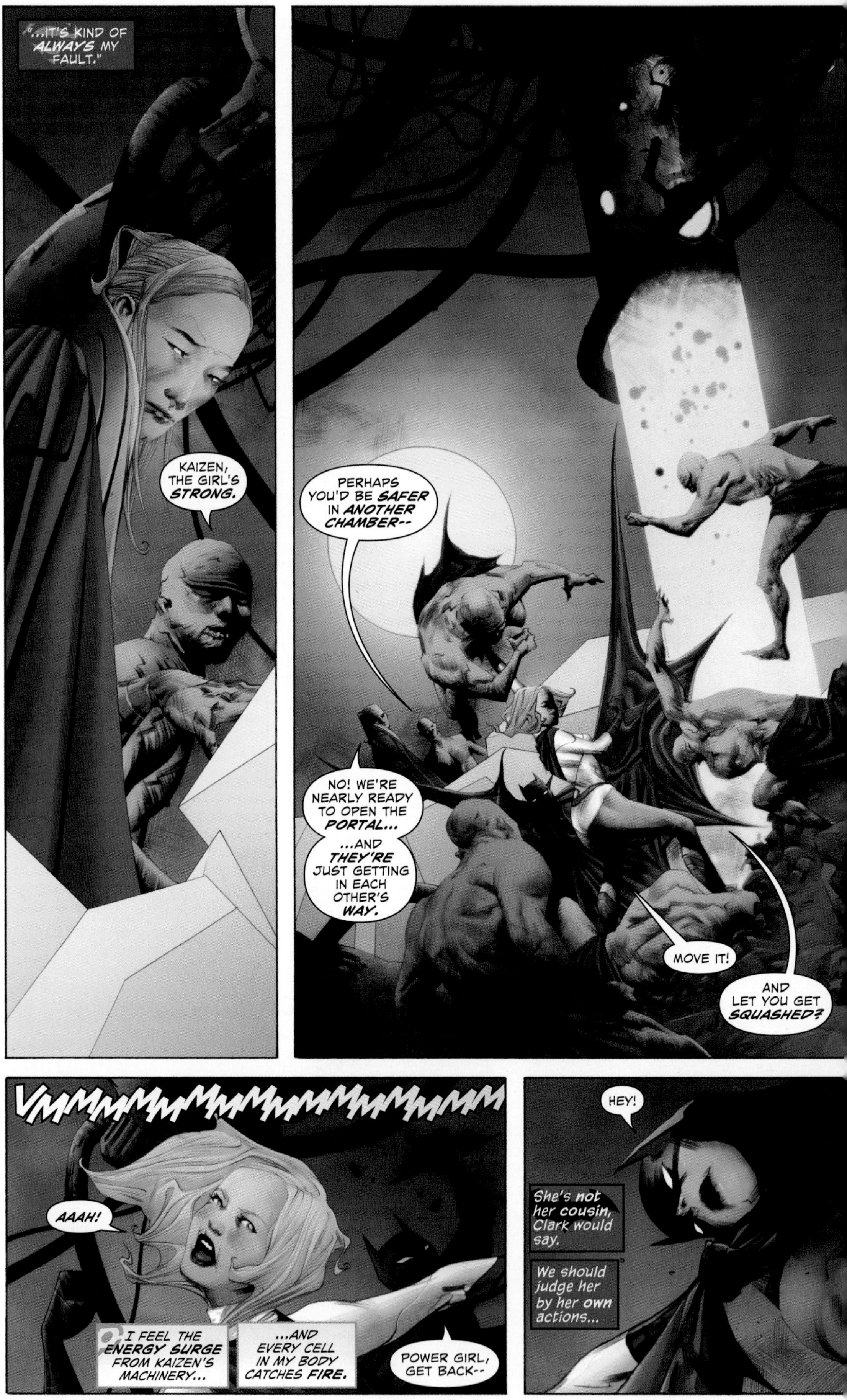
"...IT'S KIND OF ALWAYS MY FAULT."
KAIZEN, THE GIRL'S STRONG.
PERHAPS YOU'D BE SAFER IN ANOTHER CHAMBER--
NO! WE'RE NEARLY READY TO OPEN THE PORTAL...
...AND THEY'RE JUST GETTING IN EACH OTHER'S WAY.
MOVE IT!
AND LET YOU GET SQUASHED?
VMMMMMMMMMMMMMMMMMMMMM
AAAH!
I FEEL THE ENERGY SURGE FROM KAIZEN'S MACHINERY...
...AND EVERY CELL IN MY BODY CATCHES FIRE.
POWER GIRL, GET BACK--
HEY!
She's not her cousin, Clark would say.
We should judge her by her own actions...

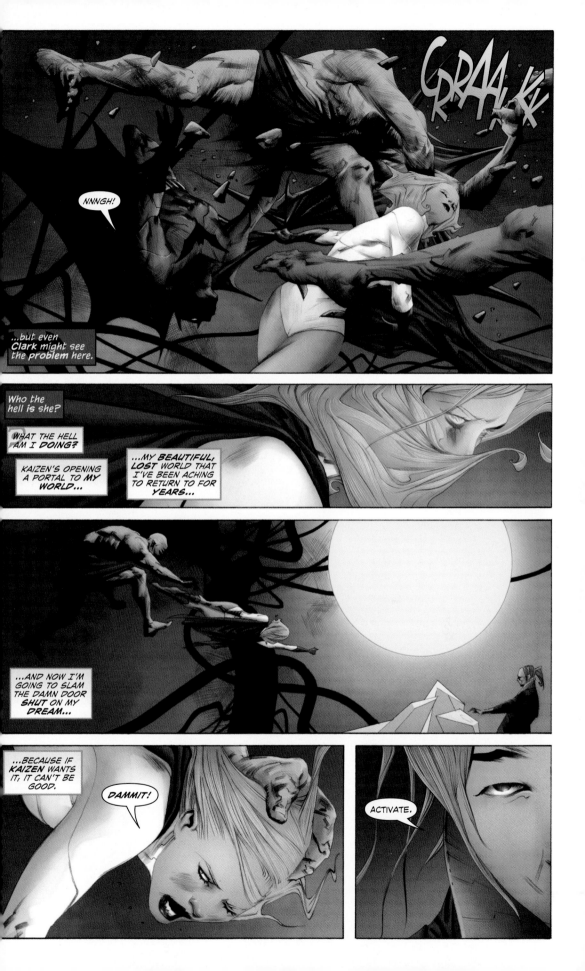

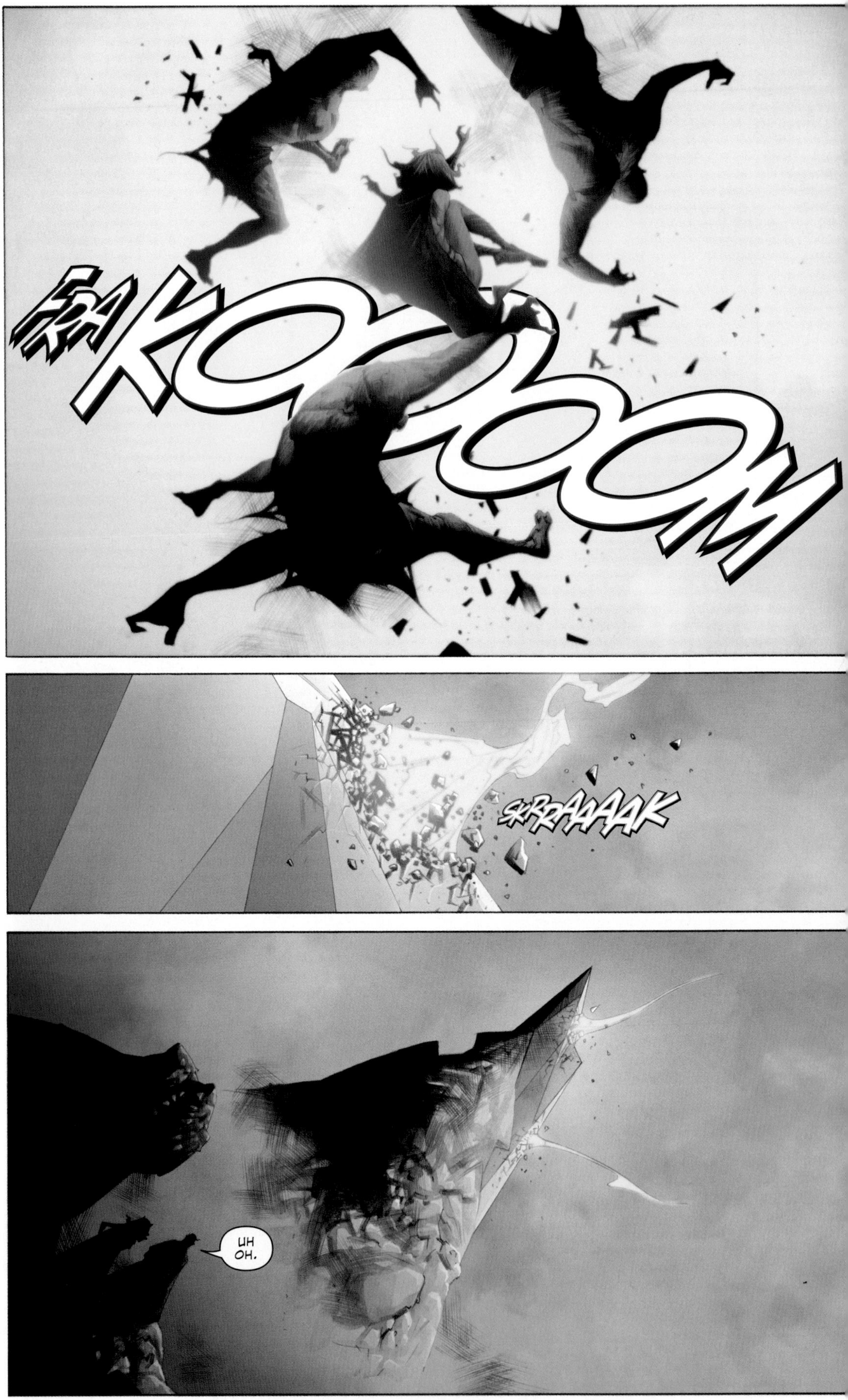
KRA KOOOOM
SKRRAAAAK
UH OH.

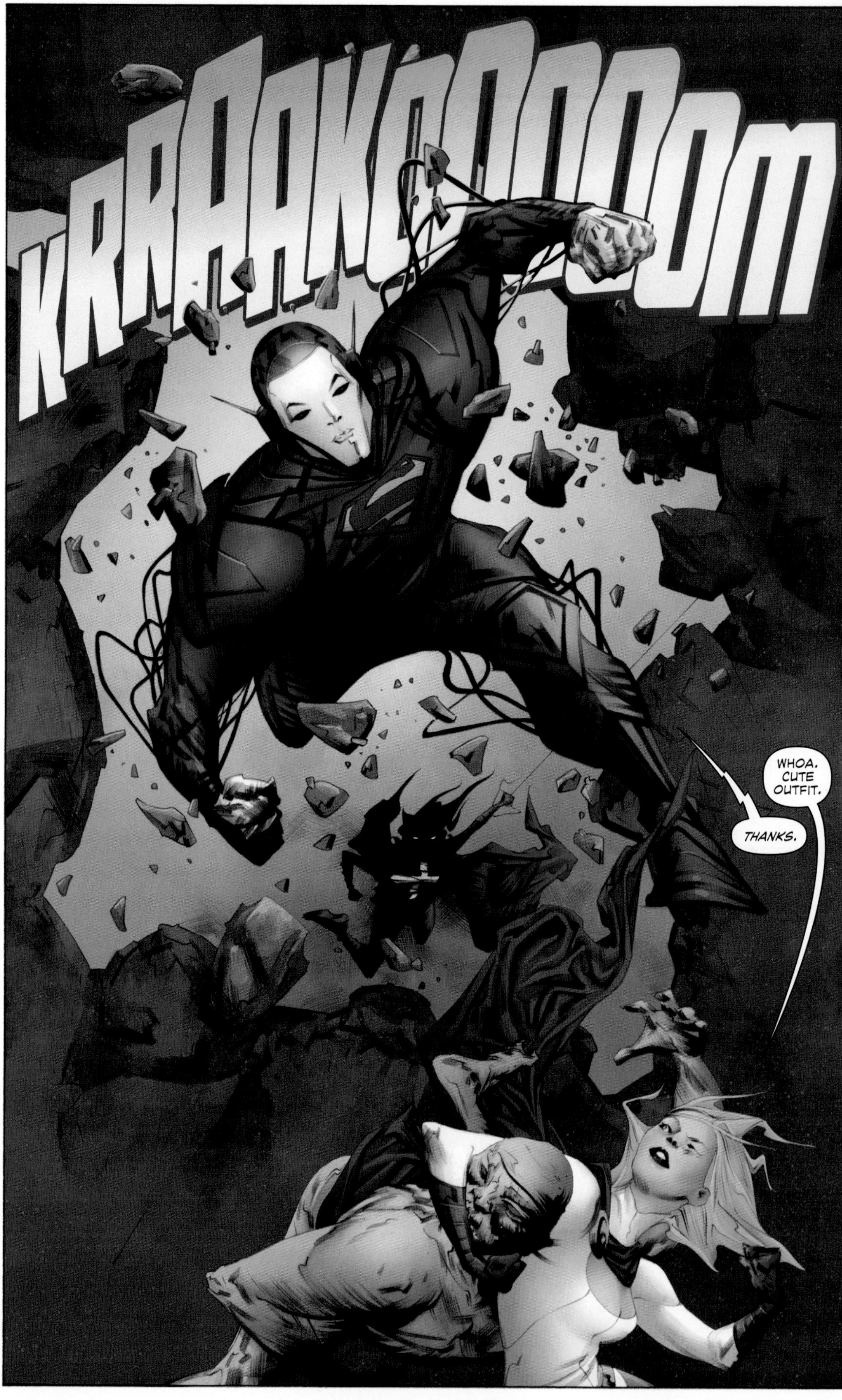
KRRAAKOOOOOOM
WHOA. CUTE OUTFIT.
THANKS.

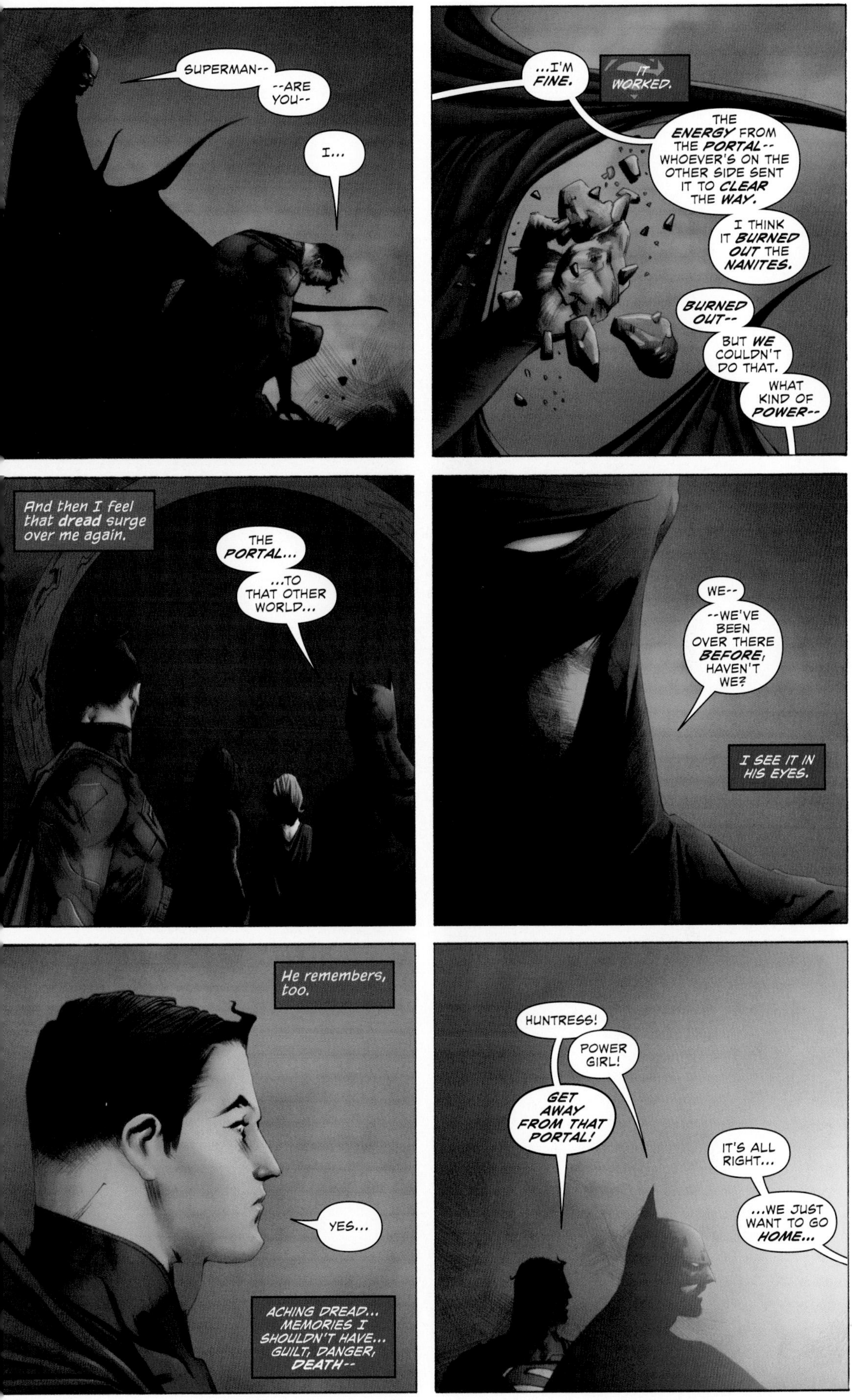
SUPERMAN--
--ARE YOU--
I...
...I'M FINE.
IT WORKED.
THE ENERGY FROM THE PORTAL--WHOEVER'S ON THE OTHER SIDE SENT IT TO CLEAR THE WAY.
I THINK IT BURNED OUT THE NANITES.
BURNED OUT--
BUT WE COULDN'T DO THAT.
WHAT KIND OF POWER--
And then I feel that dread surge over me again.
THE PORTAL...
...TO THAT OTHER WORLD...
WE--
--WE'VE BEEN OVER THERE BEFORE; HAVEN'T WE?
I SEE IT IN HIS EYES.
He remembers, too.
YES...
ACHING DREAD... MEMORIES I SHOULDN'T HAVE... GUILT, DANGER, DEATH--
HUNTRESS!
POWER GIRL!
GET AWAY FROM THAT PORTAL!
IT'S ALL RIGHT...
...WE JUST WANT TO GO HOME...

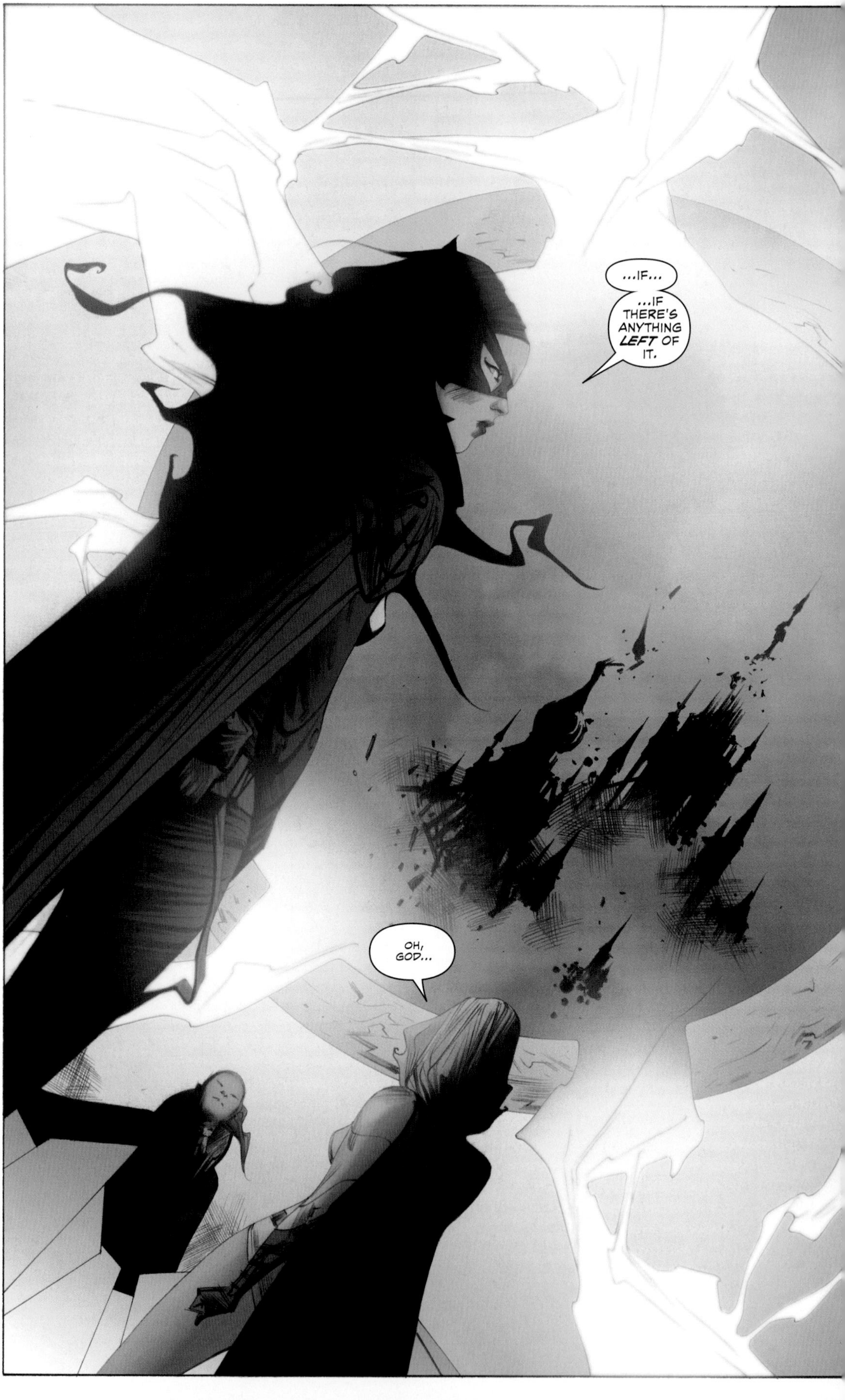

...IF...
...IF THERE'S ANYTHING LEFT OF IT.
OH, GOD...

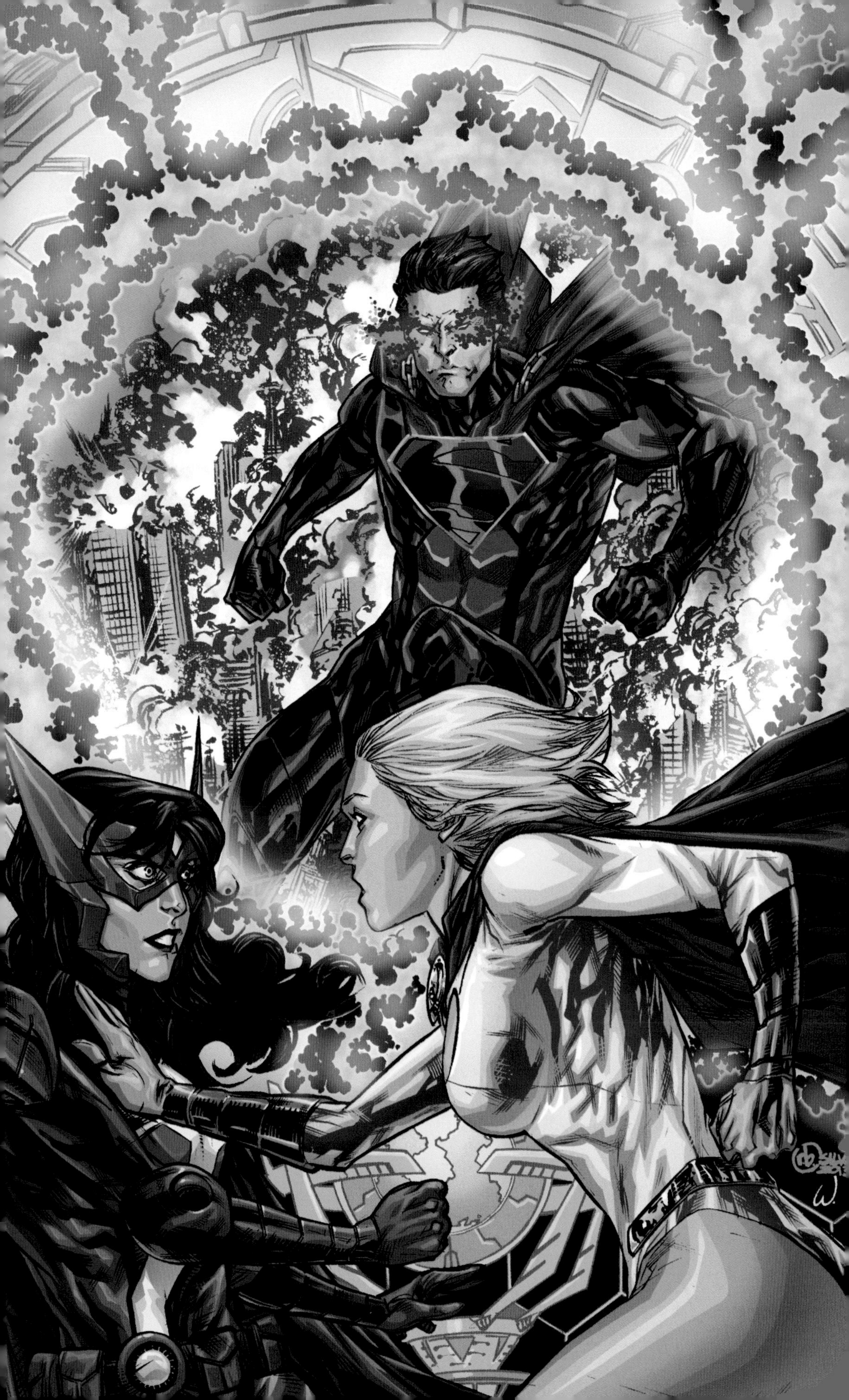

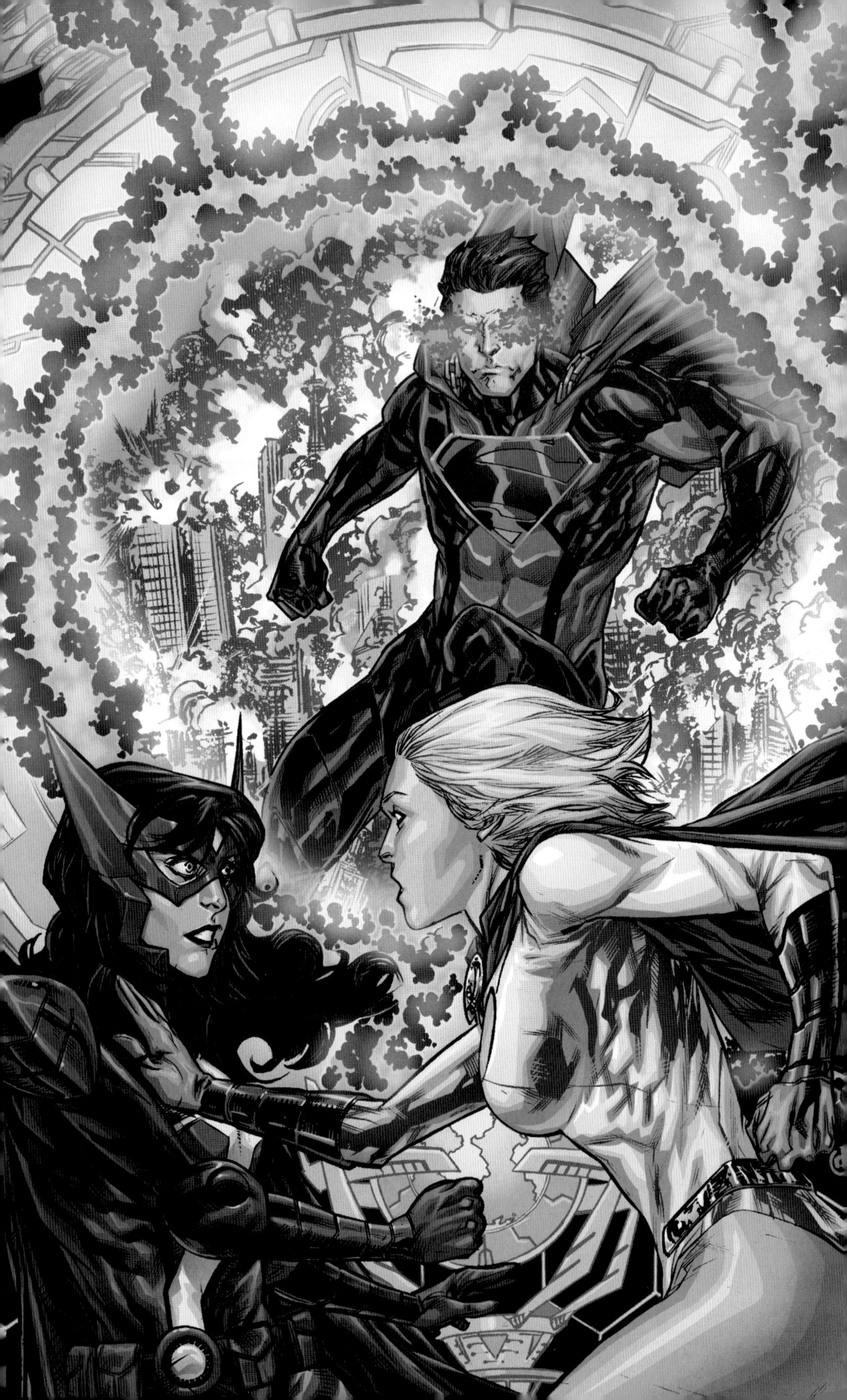

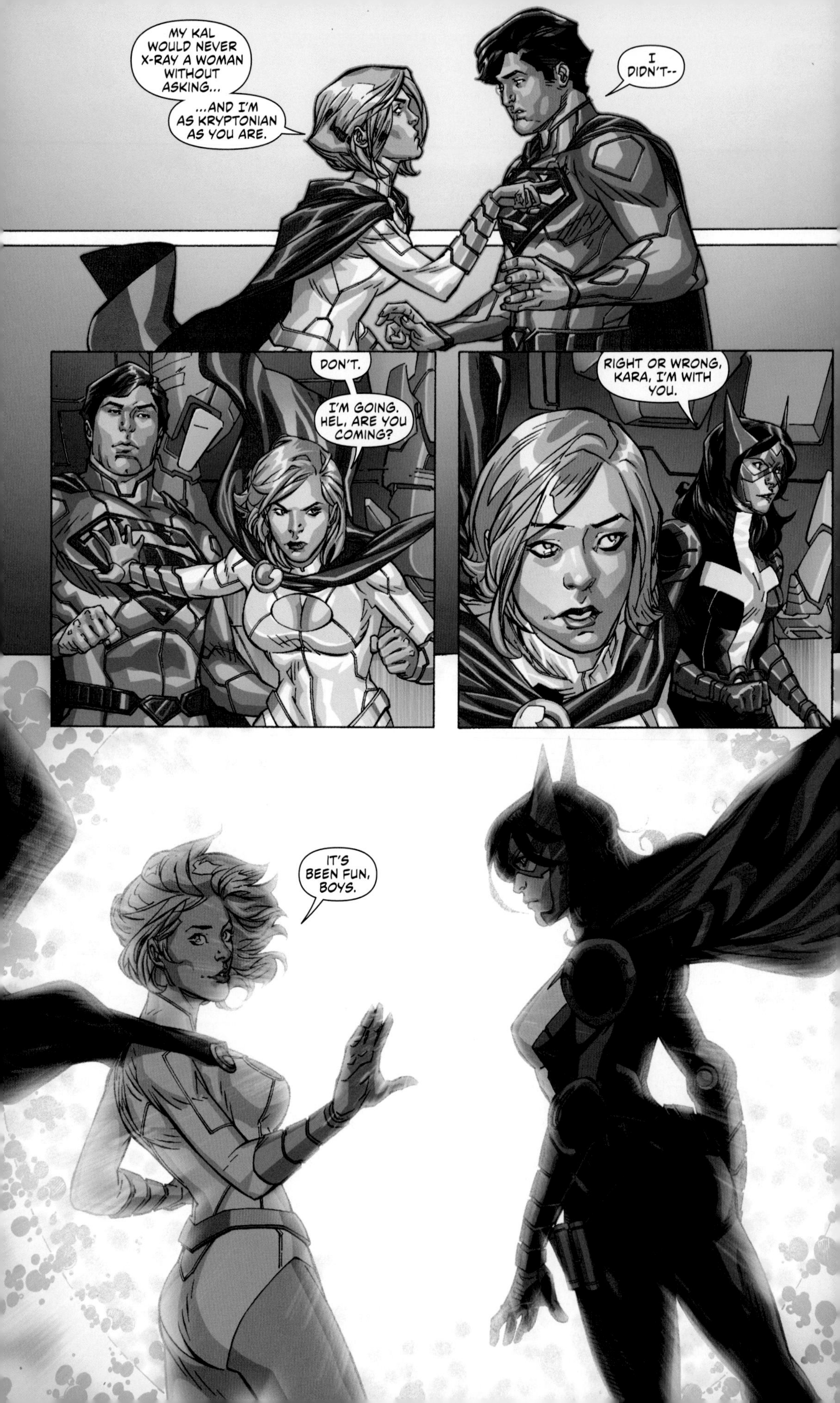
MY KAL WOULD NEVER X-RAY A WOMAN WITHOUT ASKING...
...AND I'M AS KRYPTONIAN AS YOU ARE.
I DIDN'T--
DON'T.
I'M GOING. HEL, ARE YOU COMING?
RIGHT OR WRONG, KARA, I'M WITH YOU.
IT'S BEEN FUN, BOYS.

COME HOME, KARA! COME HOME TO ME!
--HE LOVES YOU MOST OF ALL!
KAL?!
Not Darkseid, but the alternate world's Clark? Memory's so vague, but he didn't seem capable of this...
MY TWIN--BUT COULD HE BE SO CORRUPTED?

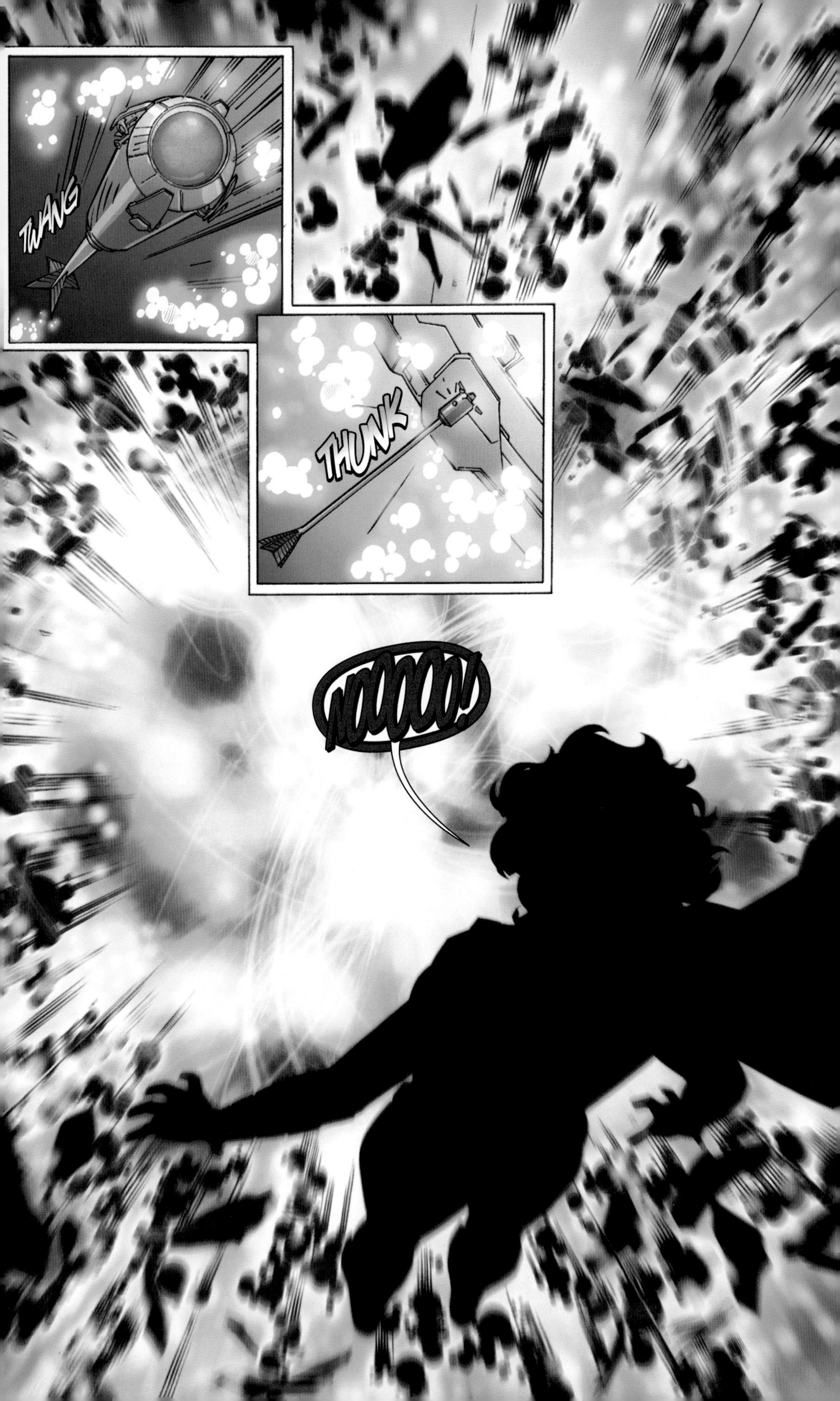
TWANG
THUNK
NOOOOO!

VARIANT COVER GALLERY

BATMAN/SUPERMAN 5
By Jon Bogdanove with Daniel Brown

BATMAN/SUPERMAN 6
By Cliff Chiang

BATMAN/SUPERMAN 7
Scribblenauts variant by Jon Katz, after Frank Miller

BATMAN/SUPERMAN 8
By Tommy Lee Edwards

BATMAN/SUPERMAN 9
Robot Chicken variant by RC Stoodios

BATMAN/SUPERMAN ANNUAL 1
By Ed Benes & Pete Pantazis

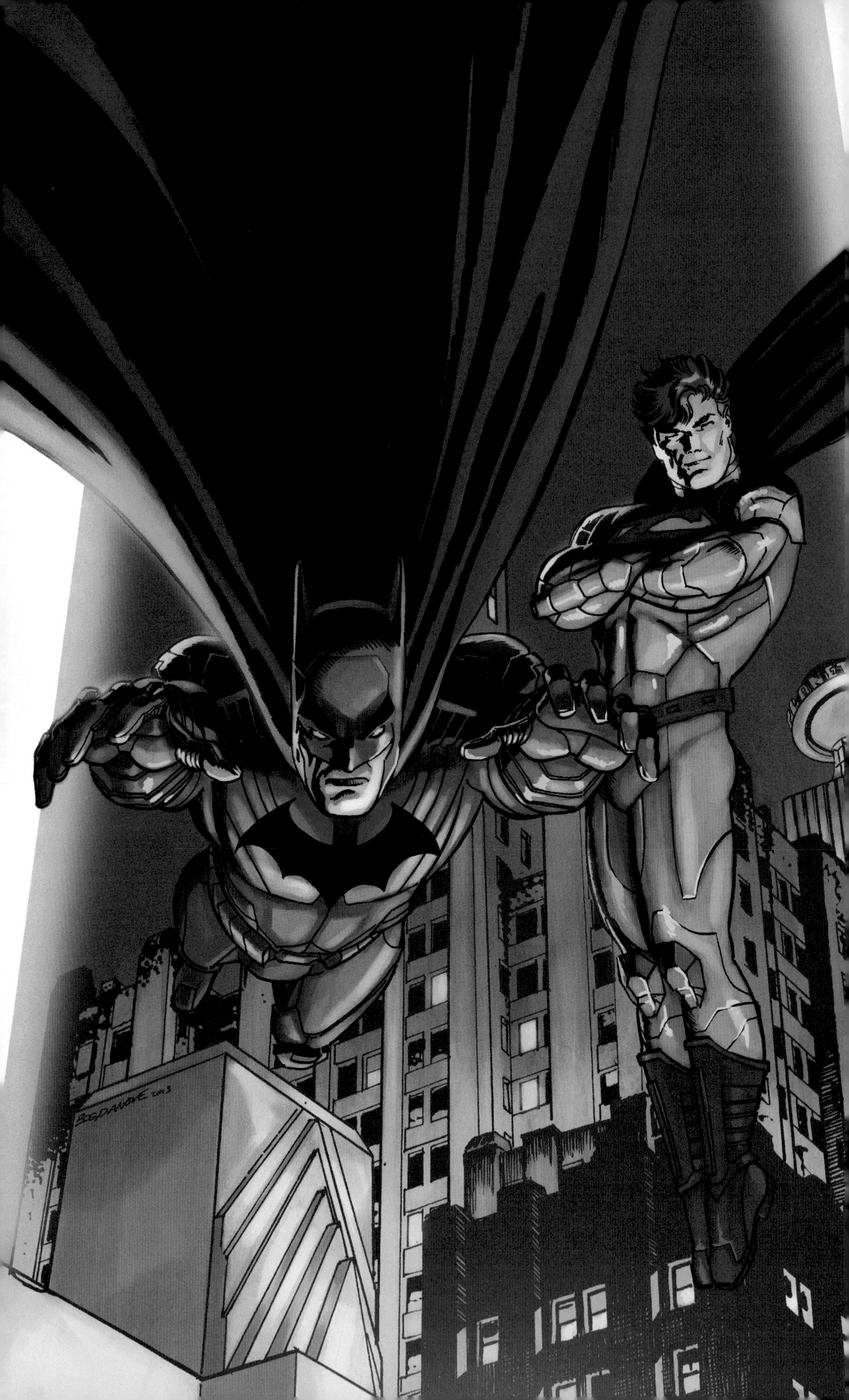

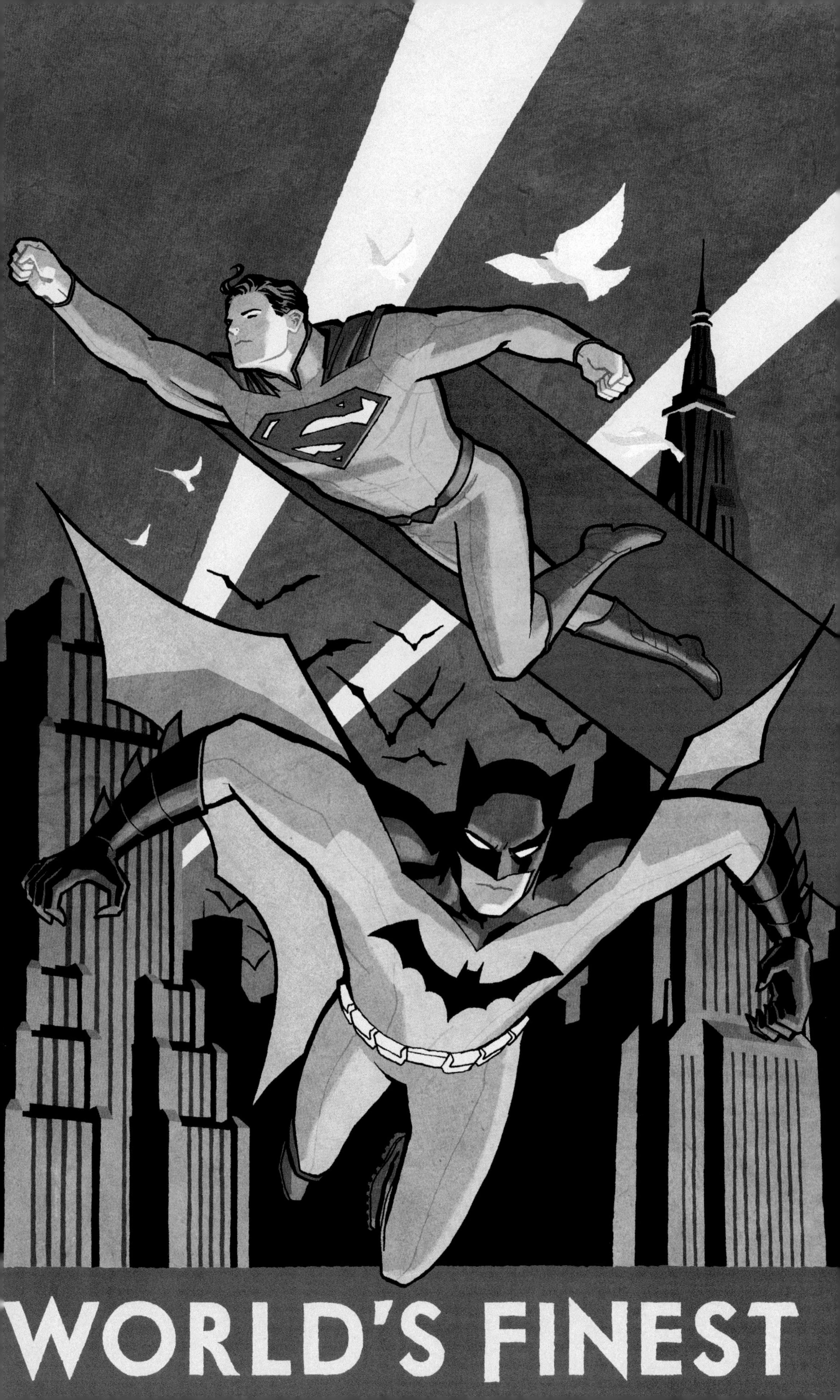
WORLD'S FINEST

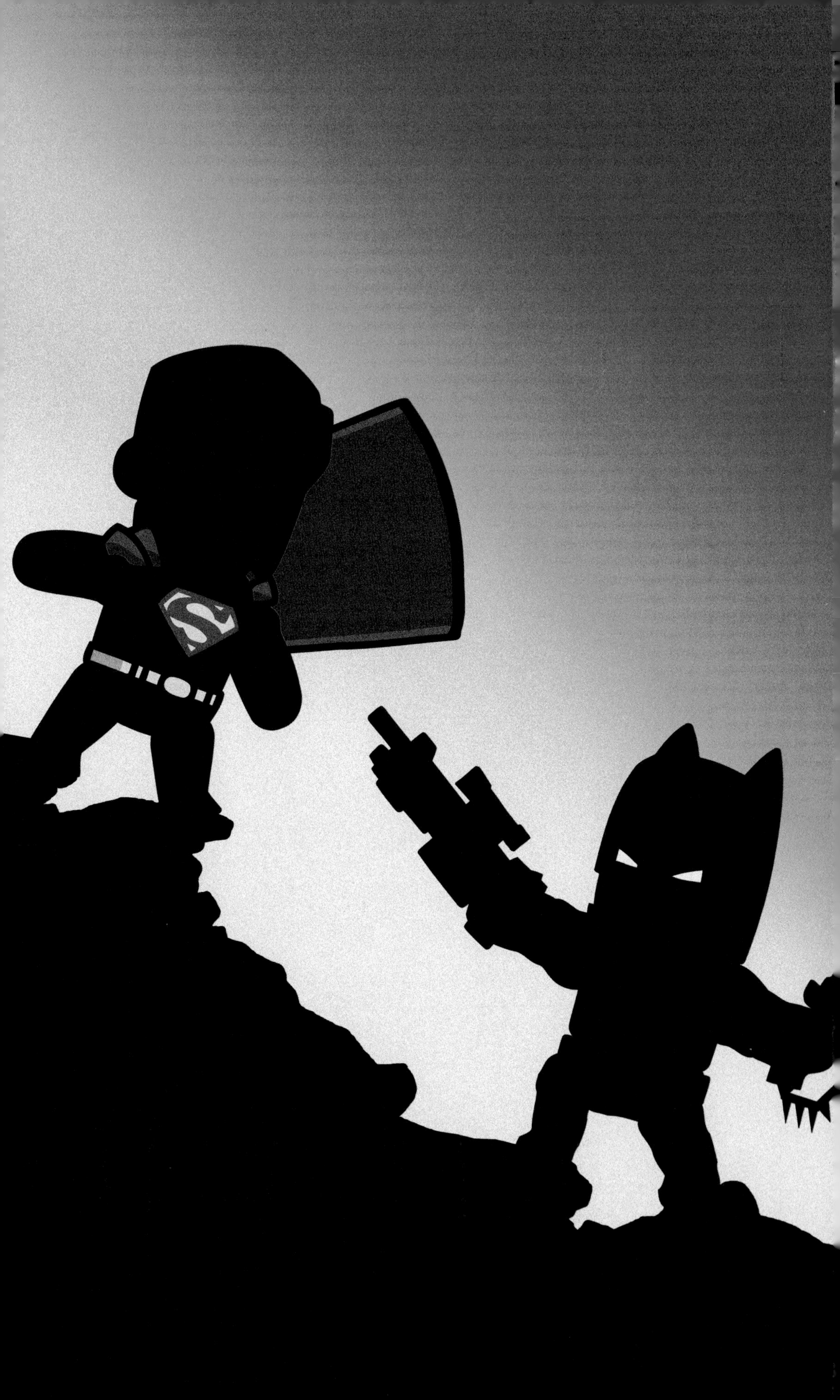

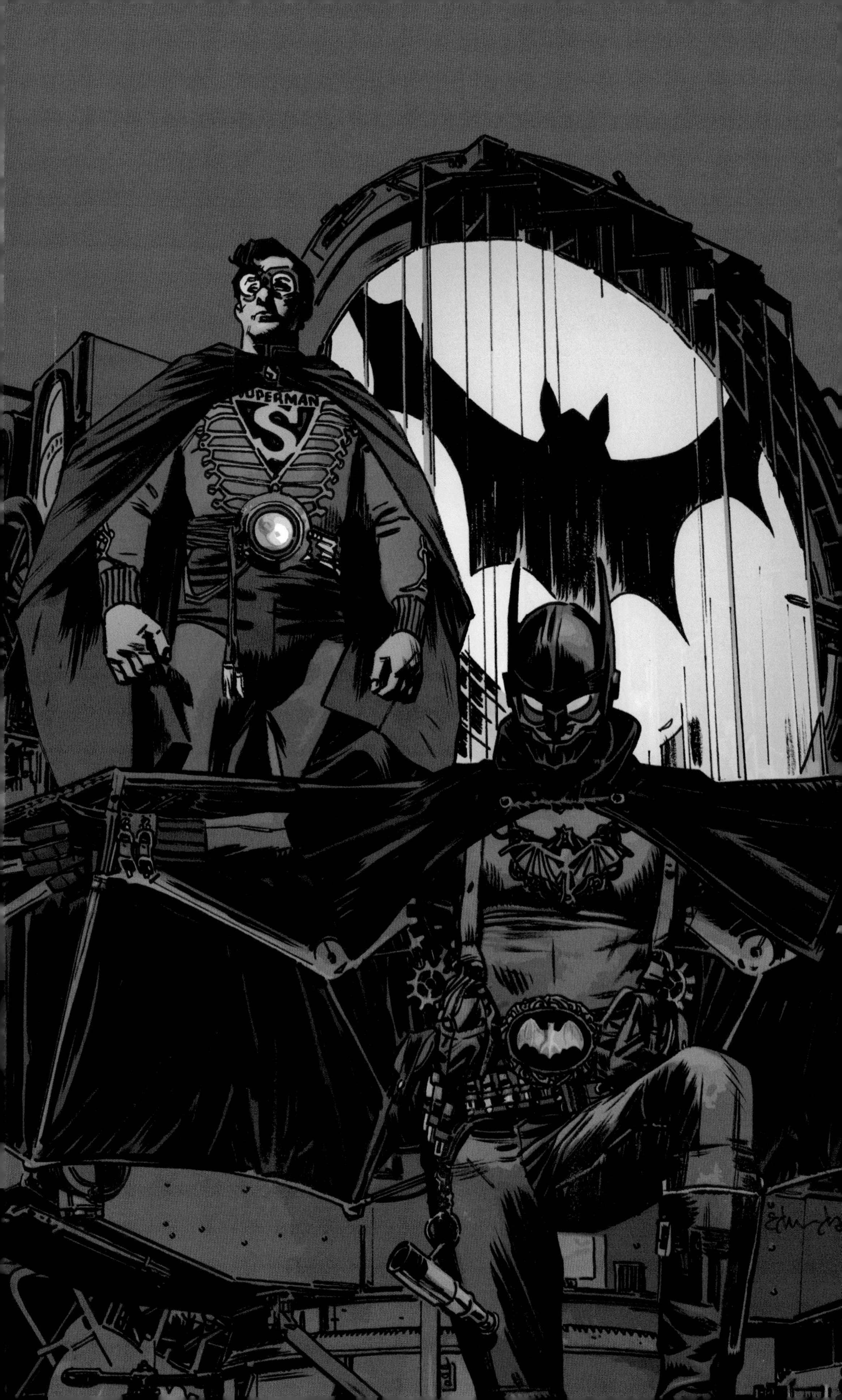
SUPERMAN

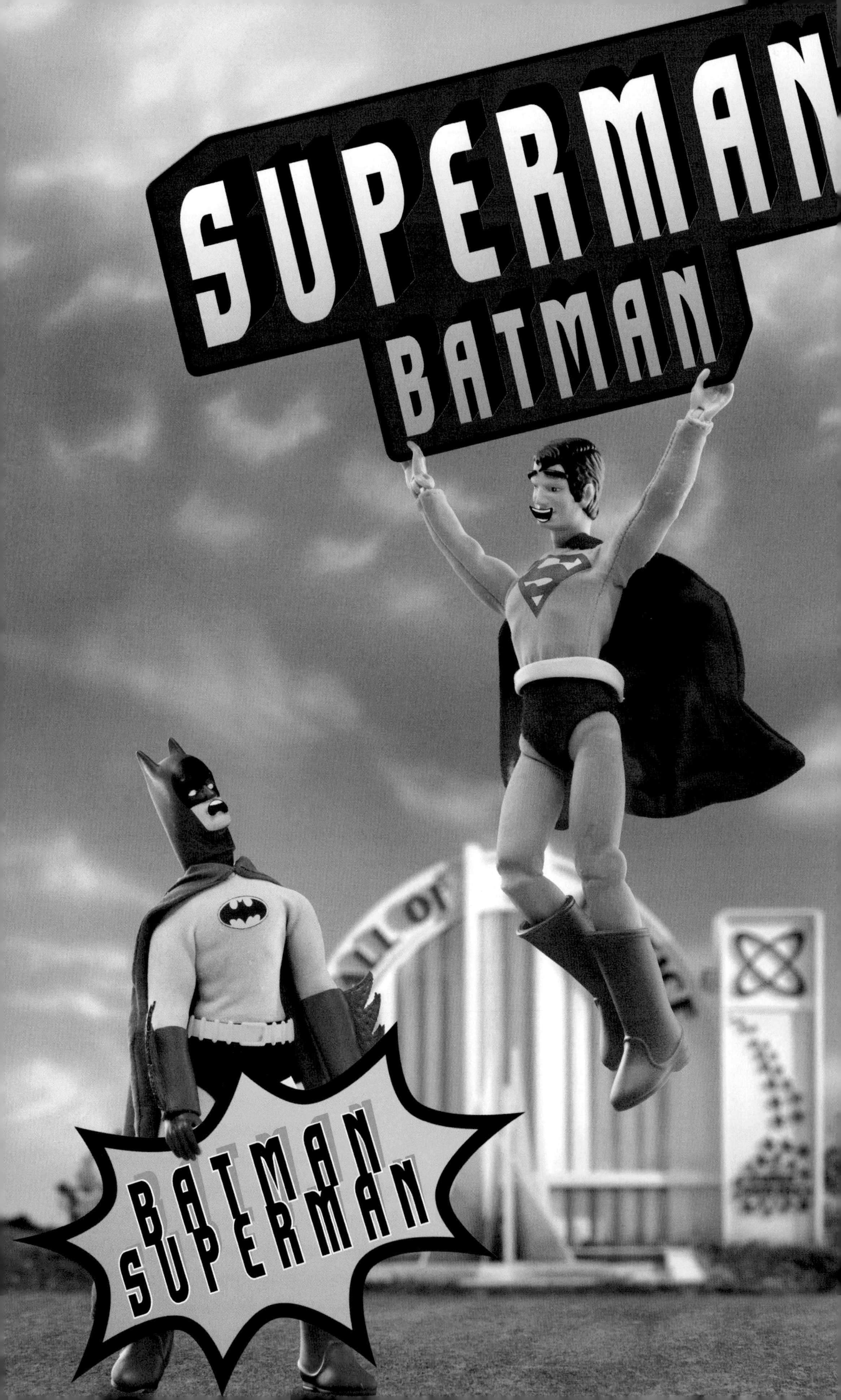
SUPERMAN
BATMAN
BATMAN
SUPERMAN

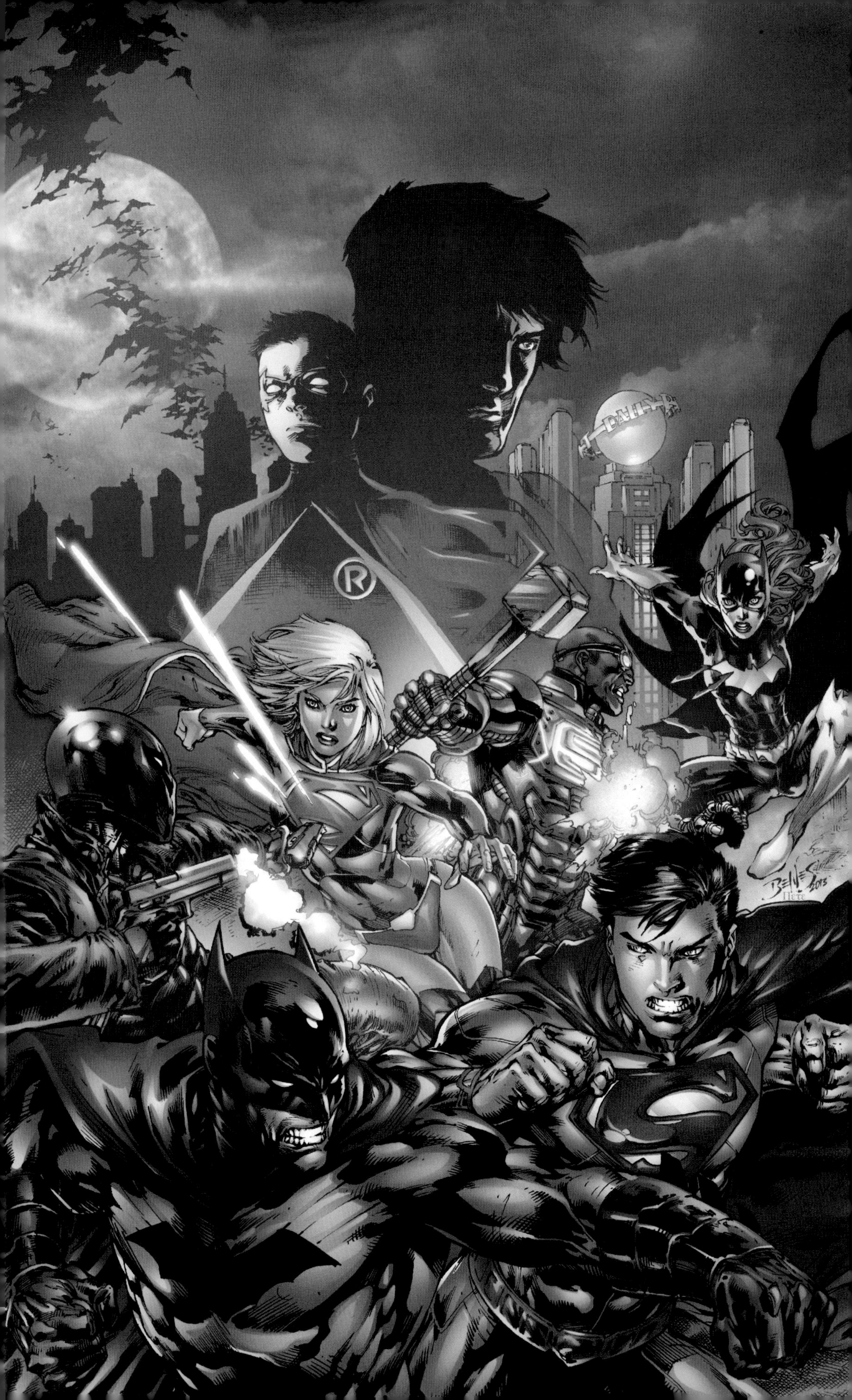

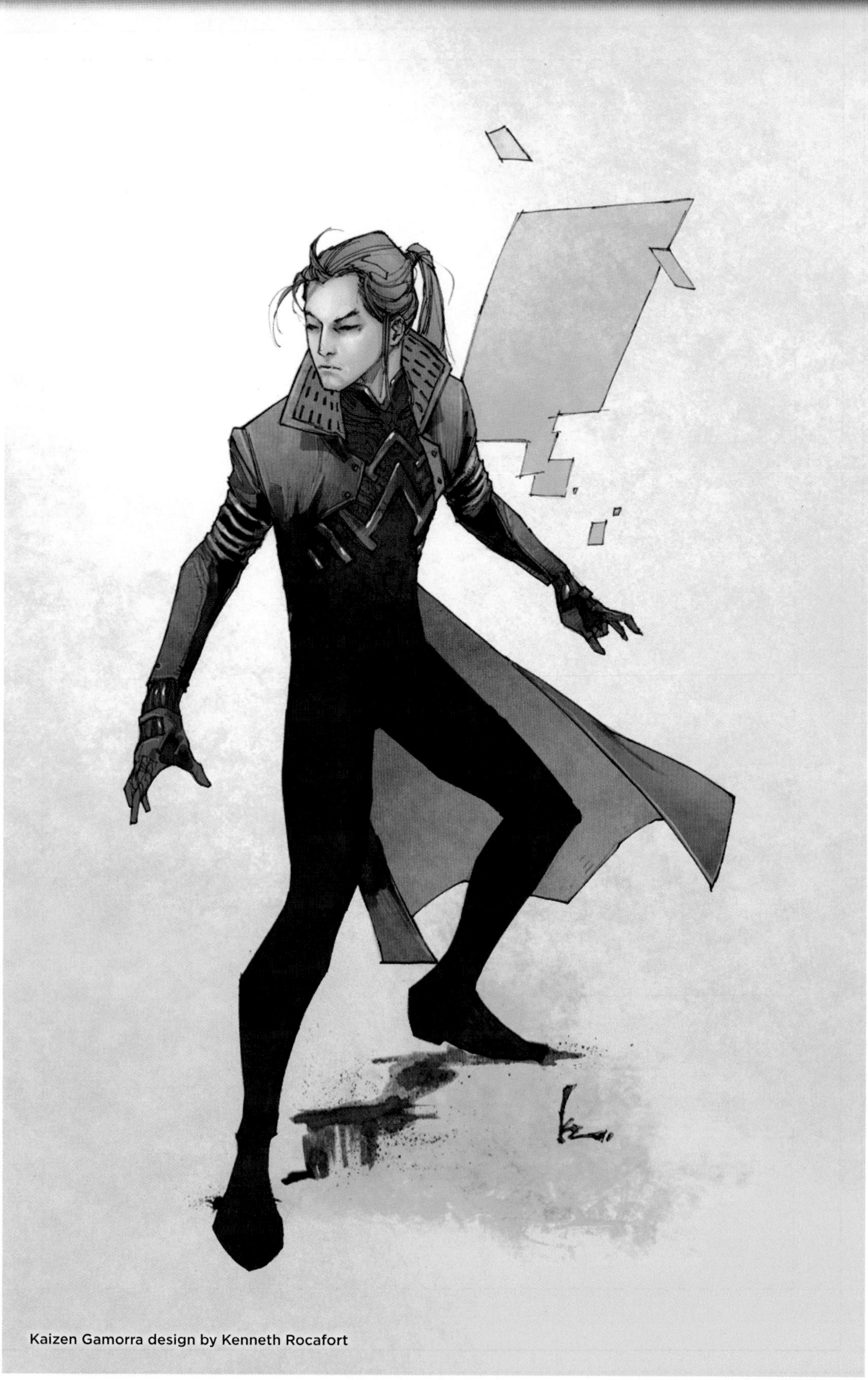

Kaizen Gamorra design by Kenneth Rocafort

Brett Booth's thumbnail layouts and pencil artwork for
BATMAN/SUPERMAN #5 cover

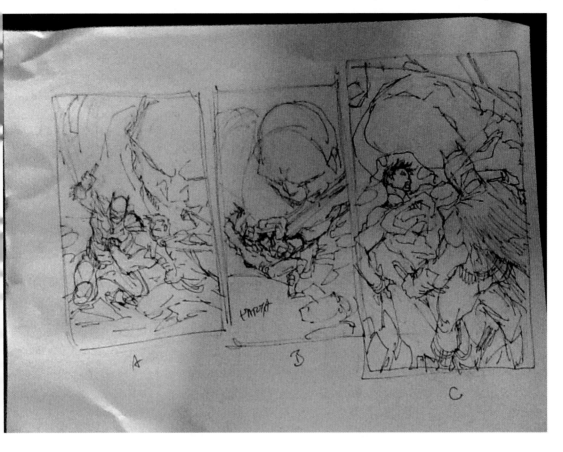

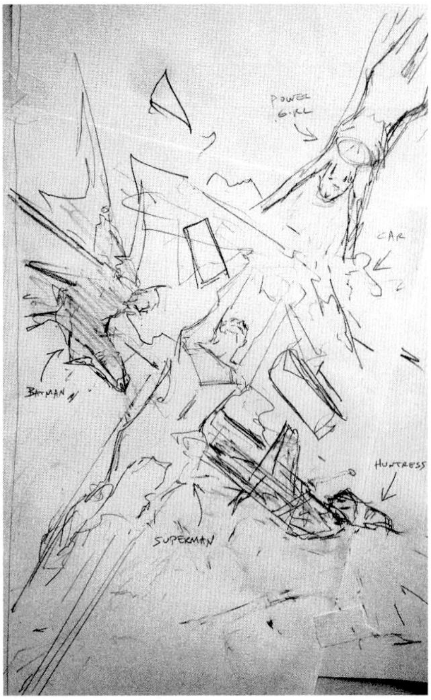
POWER GIRL
CAR
BATMAN
HUNTRESS
SUPERMAN

Sketches and pencils for
BATMAN/SUPERMAN #8 and #9 covers by Jae Lee

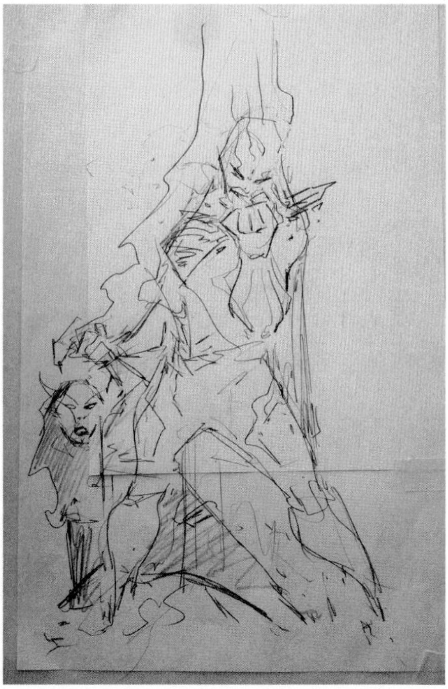

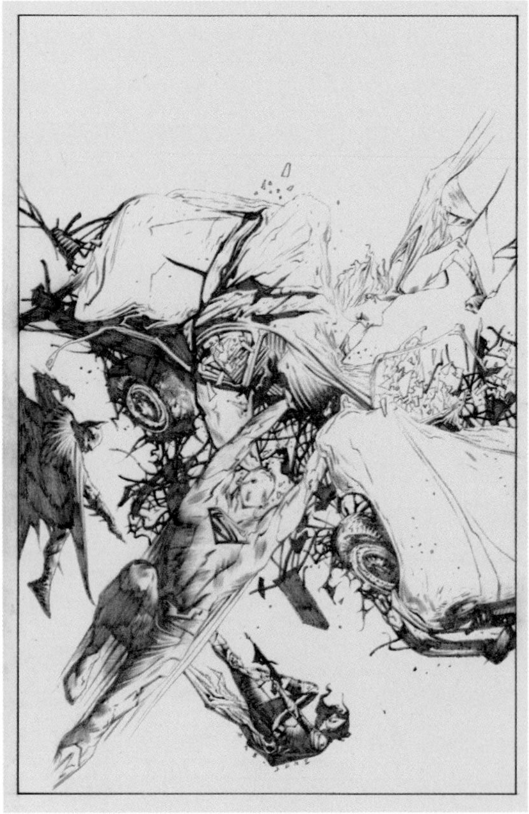

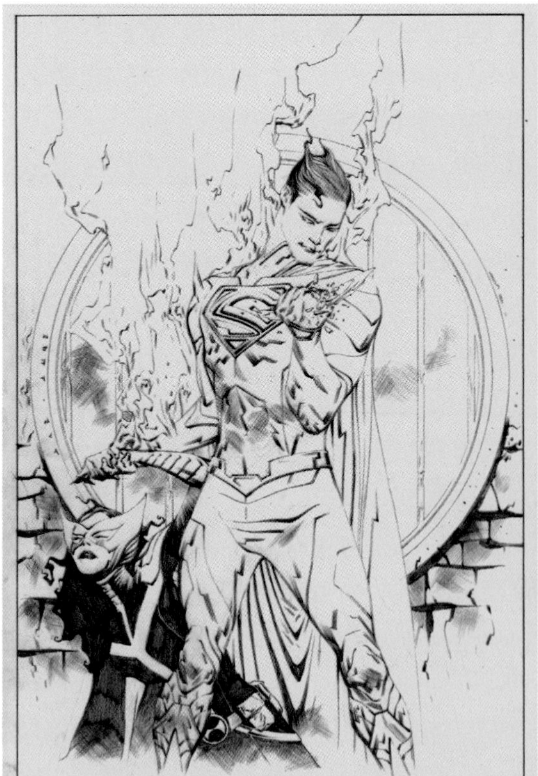

Jae Lee's rough sketch and pencils for
BATMAN/SUPERMAN ANNUAL #1

Pencils for BATMAN/SUPERMAN #5
variant cover by Jon Bogdanove

Pencils for BATMAN/SUPERMAN ANNUAL
variant cover by Ed Be

Sketch by Cliff Chiang for
BATMAN/SUPERMAN #6 variant cover

START AT THE BEGINNING!

BATMAN VOLUME 1: THE COURT OF OWLS

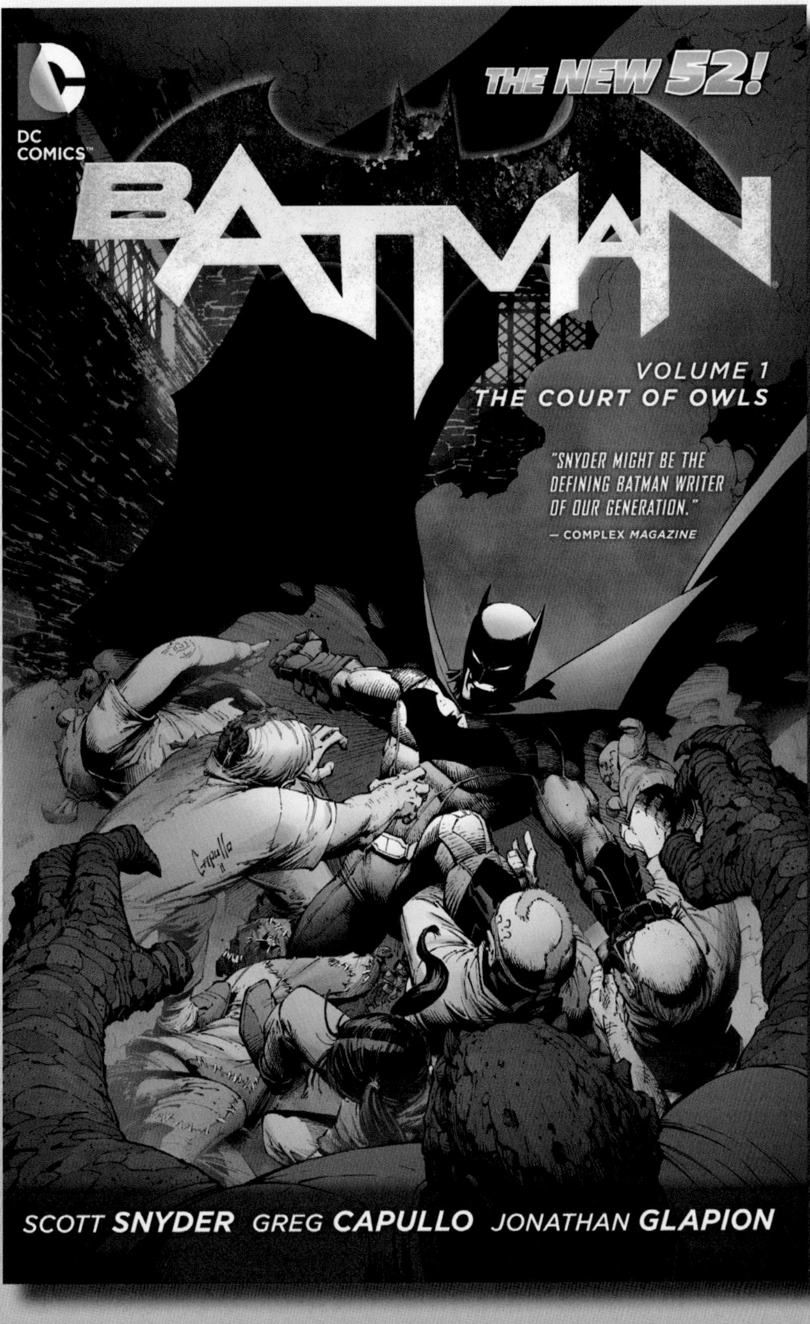

BATMAN & ROBIN VOLUME 1: BORN TO KILL

Peter J. Tomasi · Patrick Gleason · Mick Gray

BATMAN: DETECTIVE COMICS VOLUME 1: FACES OF DEATH

Tony S. Daniel

BATMAN: THE DARK KNIGHT VOLUME 1: KNIGHT TERRORS

David Finch · Paul Jenkins · Richard Friend

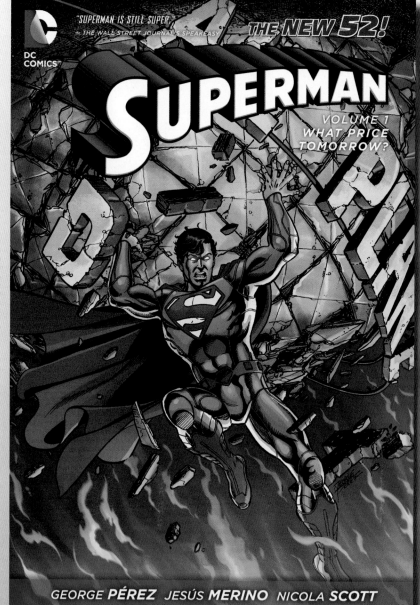